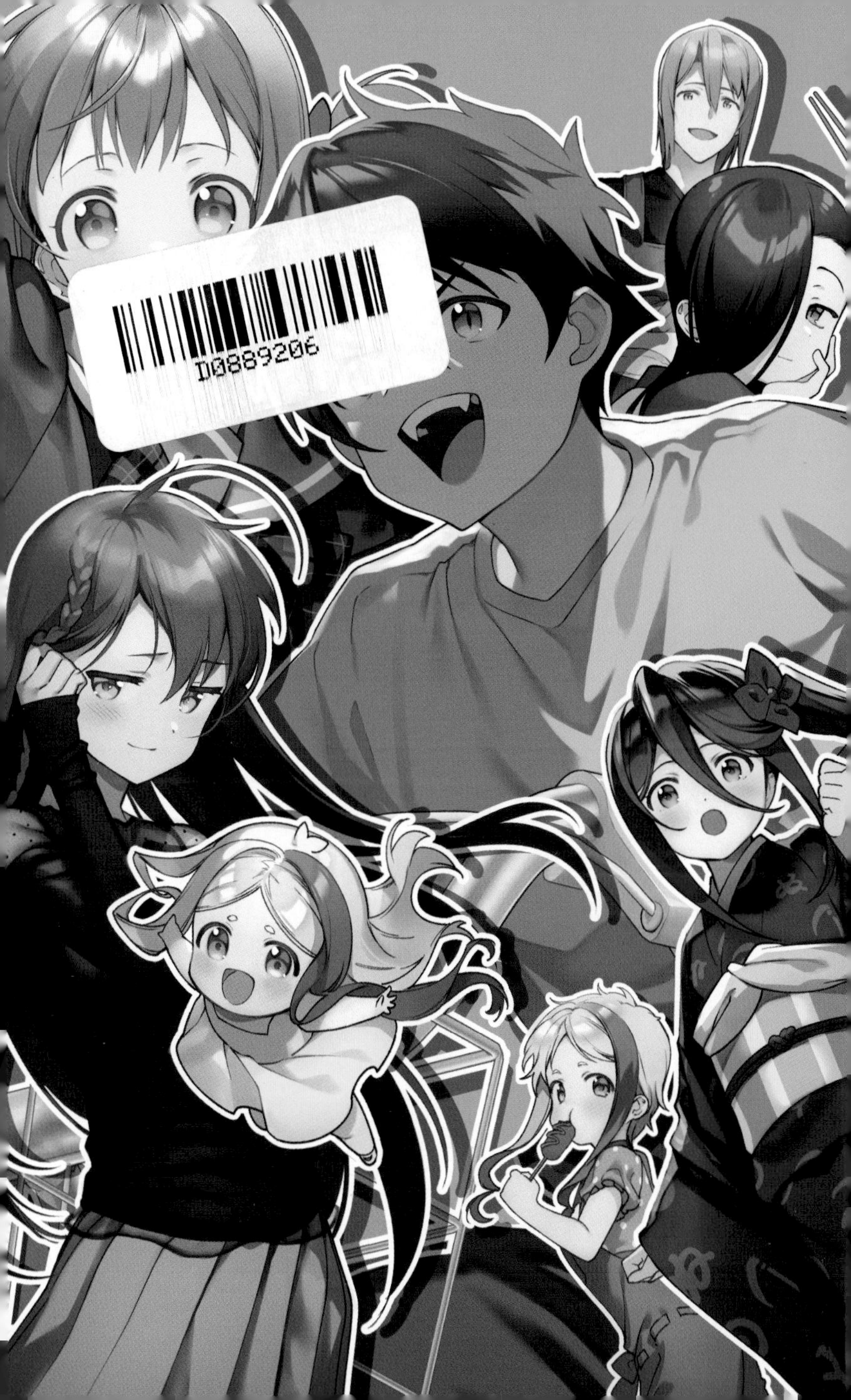

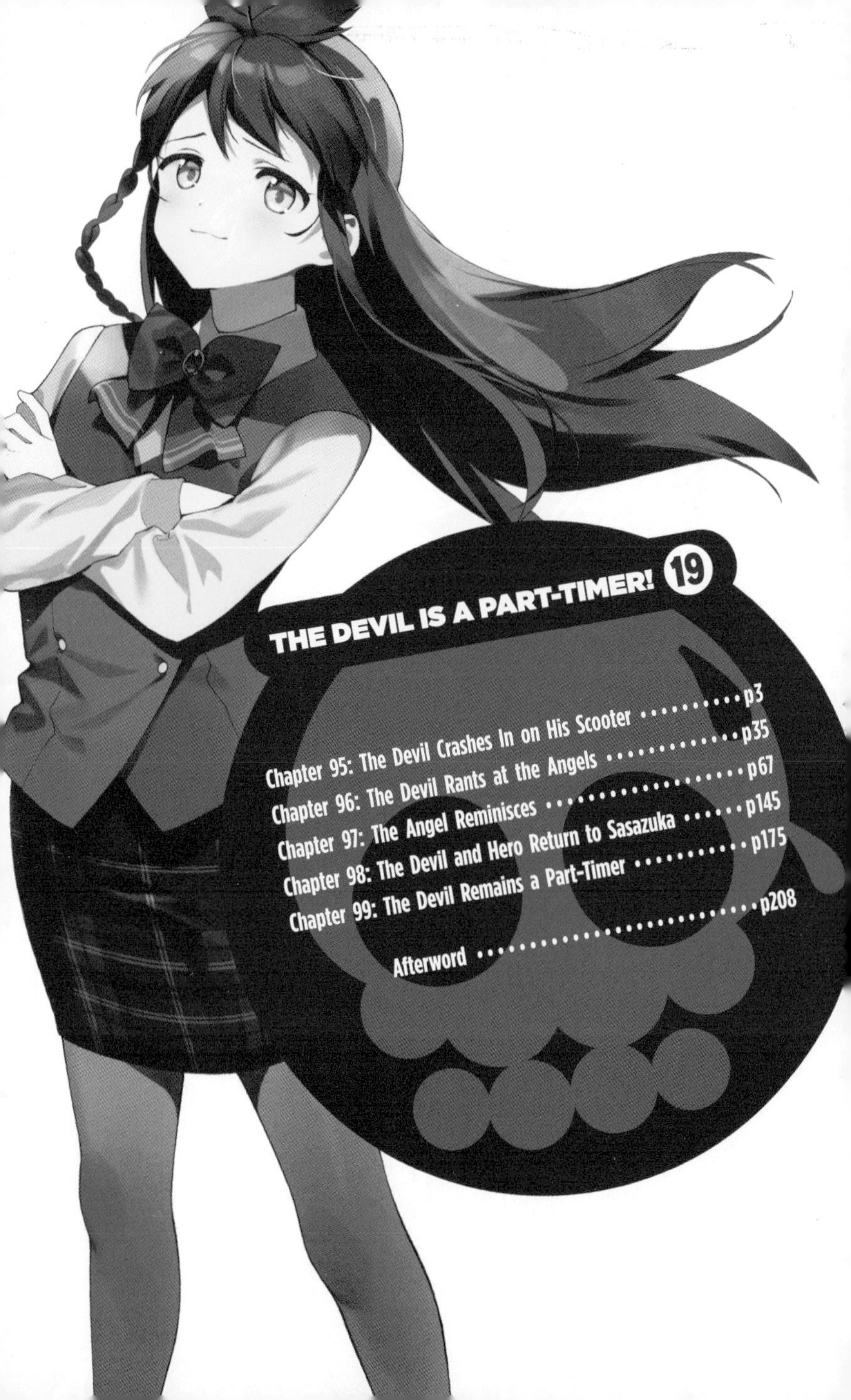

THE DEVIL IS A PART-TIMER! 19

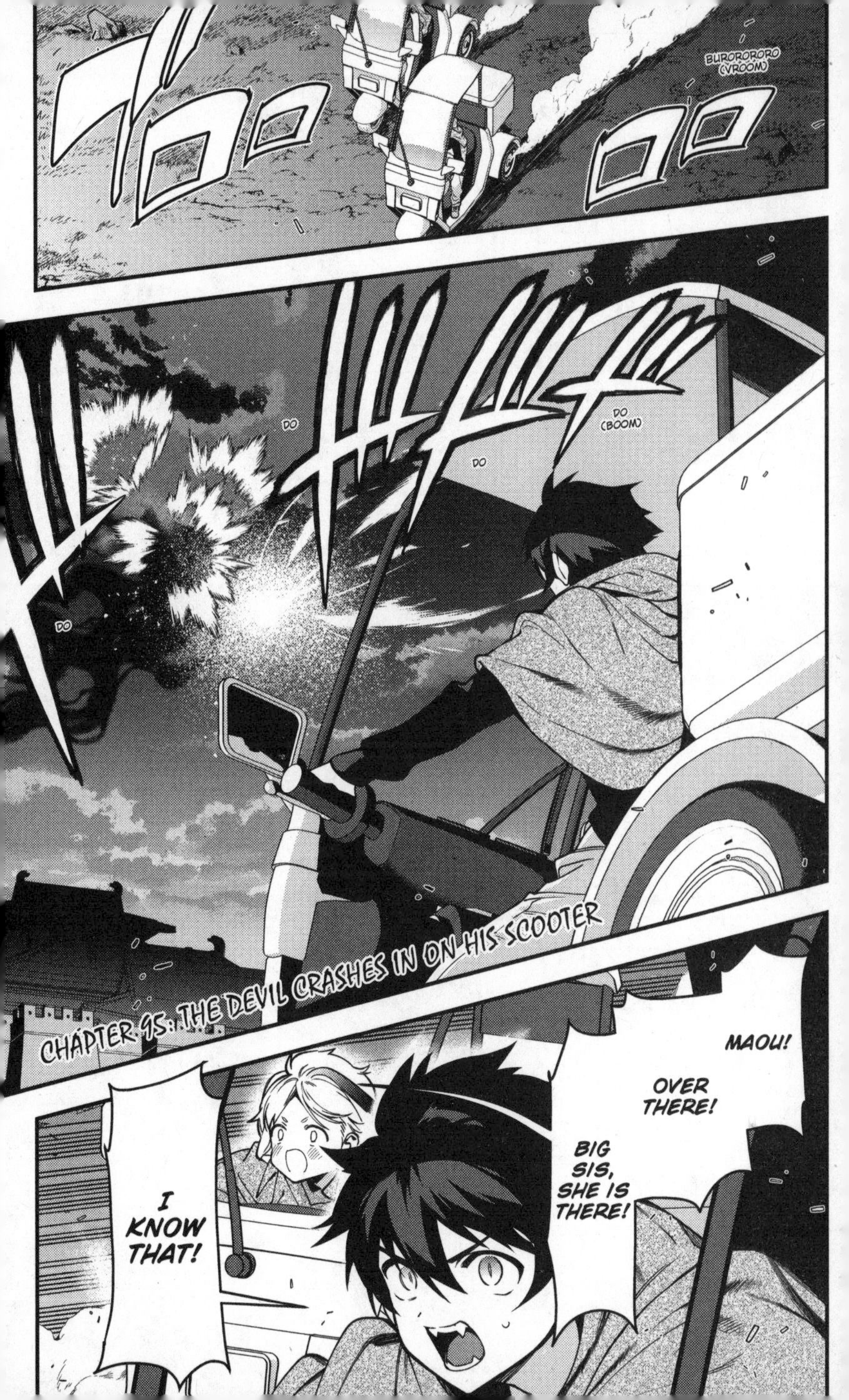
BURORORORO (VROOM)
DO (BOOM)
DO
DO
DO
CHAPTER 95: THE DEVIL CRASHES IN ON HIS SCOOTER
MAOU! OVER THERE!
BIG SIS, SHE IS THERE!
I KNOW THAT!

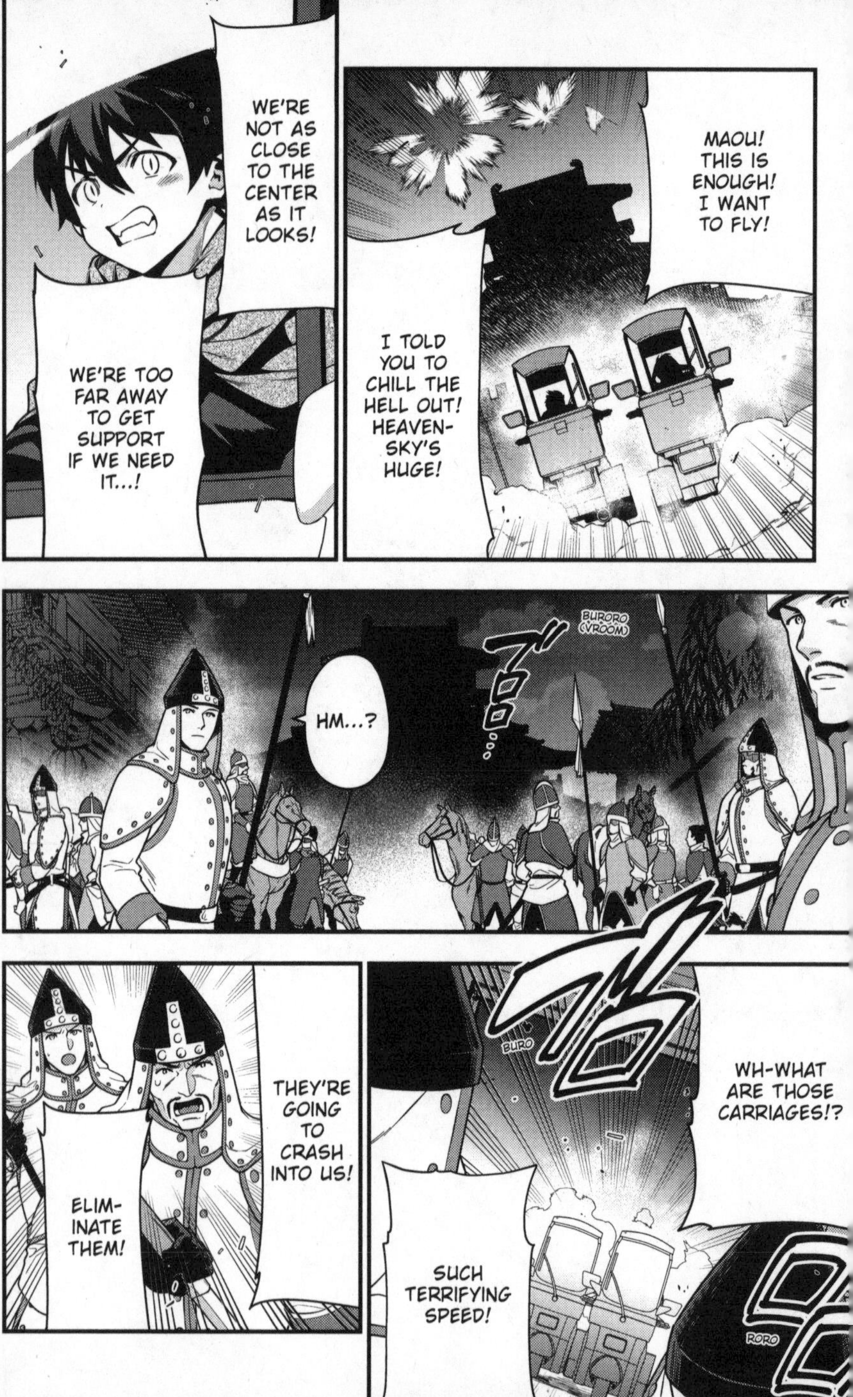
MAOU! THIS IS ENOUGH! I WANT TO FLY!
I TOLD YOU TO CHILL THE HELL OUT! HEAVEN-SKY'S HUGE!
WE'RE NOT AS CLOSE TO THE CENTER AS IT LOOKS!
WE'RE TOO FAR AWAY TO GET SUPPORT IF WE NEED IT...!
BURORO (VROOM)
HM...?
WH-WHAT ARE THOSE CARRIAGES!?
BURO
SUCH TERRIFYING SPEED!
RORO
THEY'RE GOING TO CRASH INTO US!
ELIM-INATE THEM!

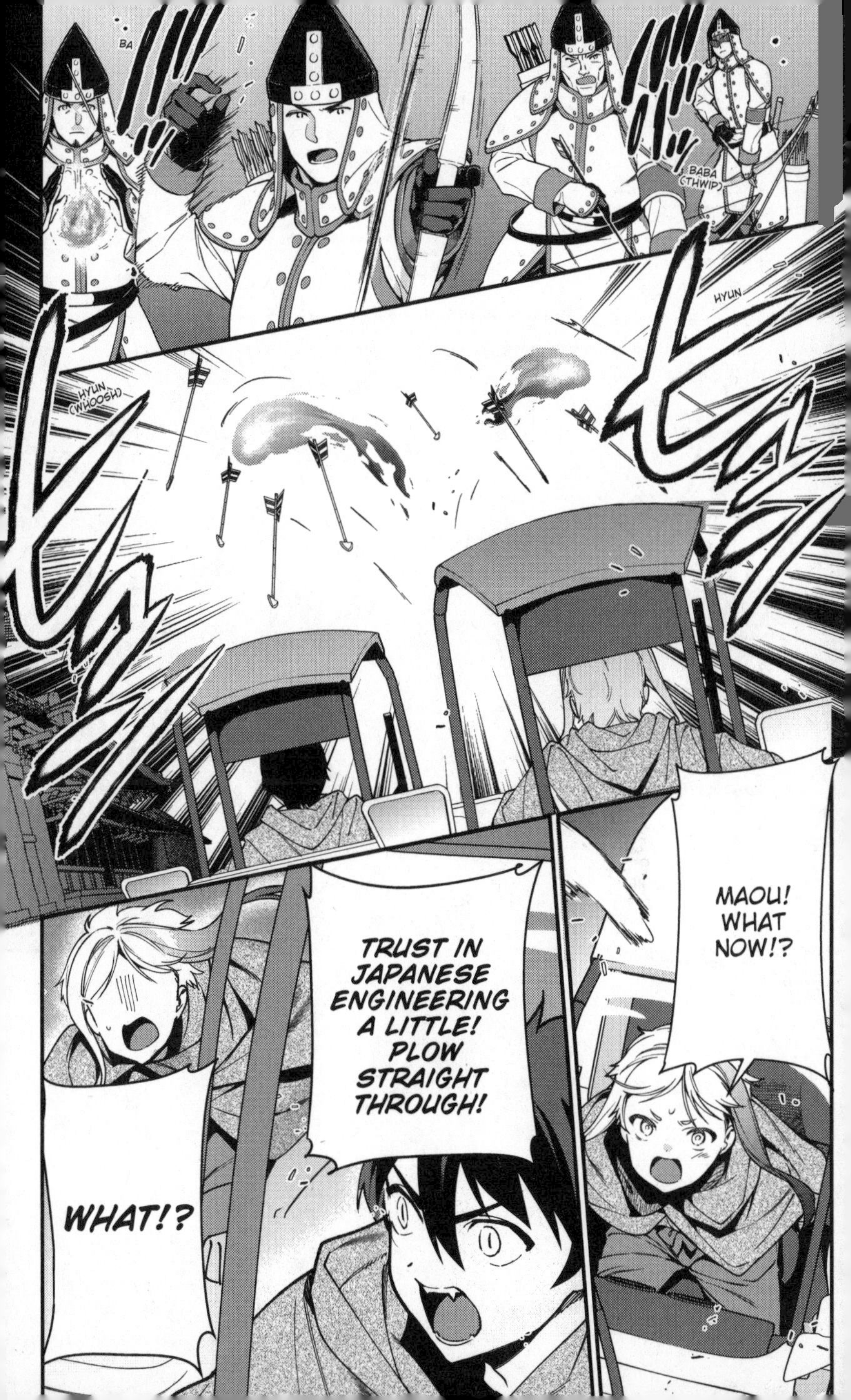

BABA (THWIP)
BA
HYUN
HYUN (WHOOSH)
MAOU! WHAT NOW!?
TRUST IN JAPANESE ENGINEERING A LITTLE! PLOW STRAIGHT THROUGH!
WHAT!?

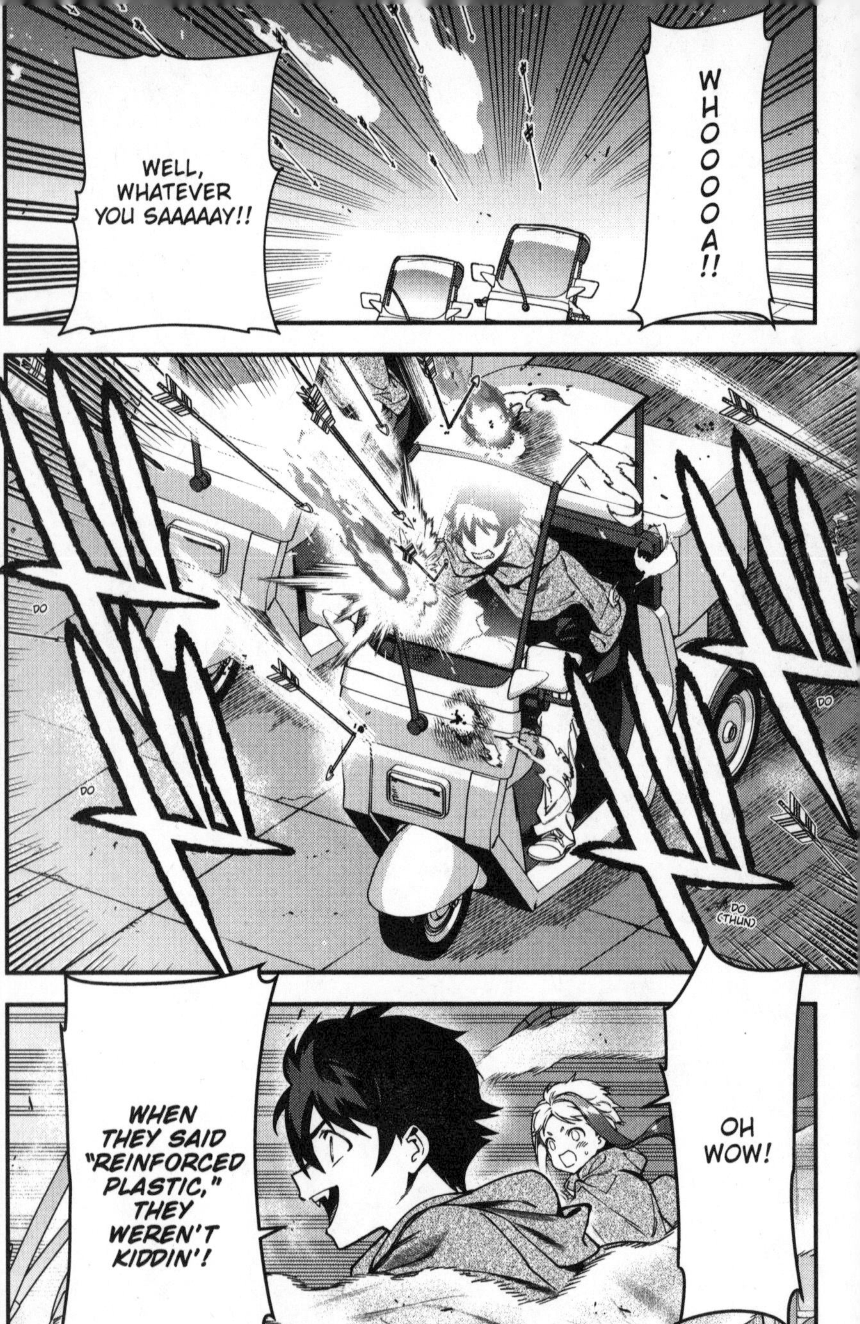
WHOOOOOA!!
WELL, WHATEVER YOU SAAAAAY!!
DO
DO
DO
DO
(THUND)
OH WOW!
WHEN THEY SAID "REINFORCED PLASTIC," THEY WEREN'T KIDDIN'!

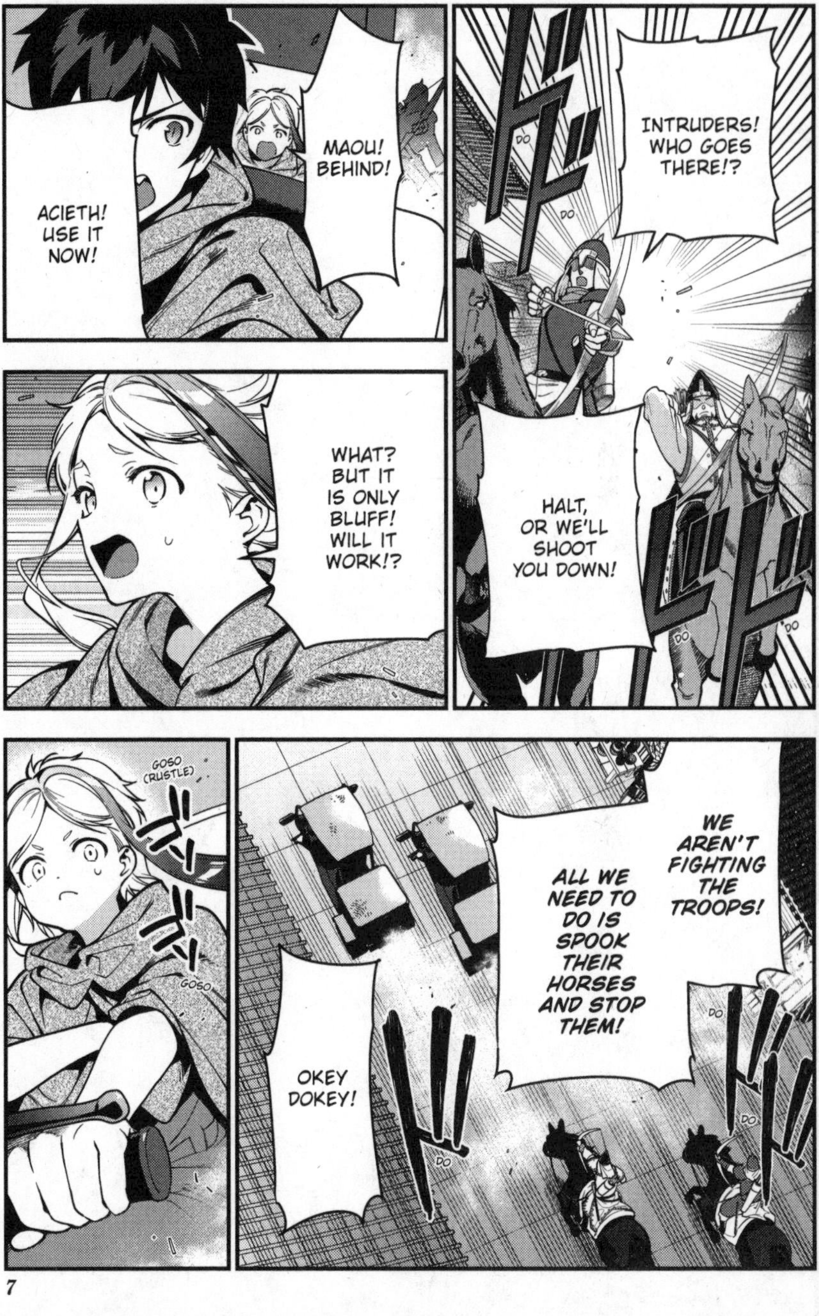
INTRUDERS! WHO GOES THERE!?
DO
DO
HALT, OR WE'LL SHOOT YOU DOWN!
DO
DO
MAOU! BEHIND!
ACIETH! USE IT NOW!
WHAT? BUT IT IS ONLY BLUFF! WILL IT WORK!?
WE AREN'T FIGHTING THE TROOPS!
ALL WE NEED TO DO IS SPOOK THEIR HORSES AND STOP THEM!
DO
DO
OKEY DOKEY!
DO
GOSO (RUSTLE)
GOSO

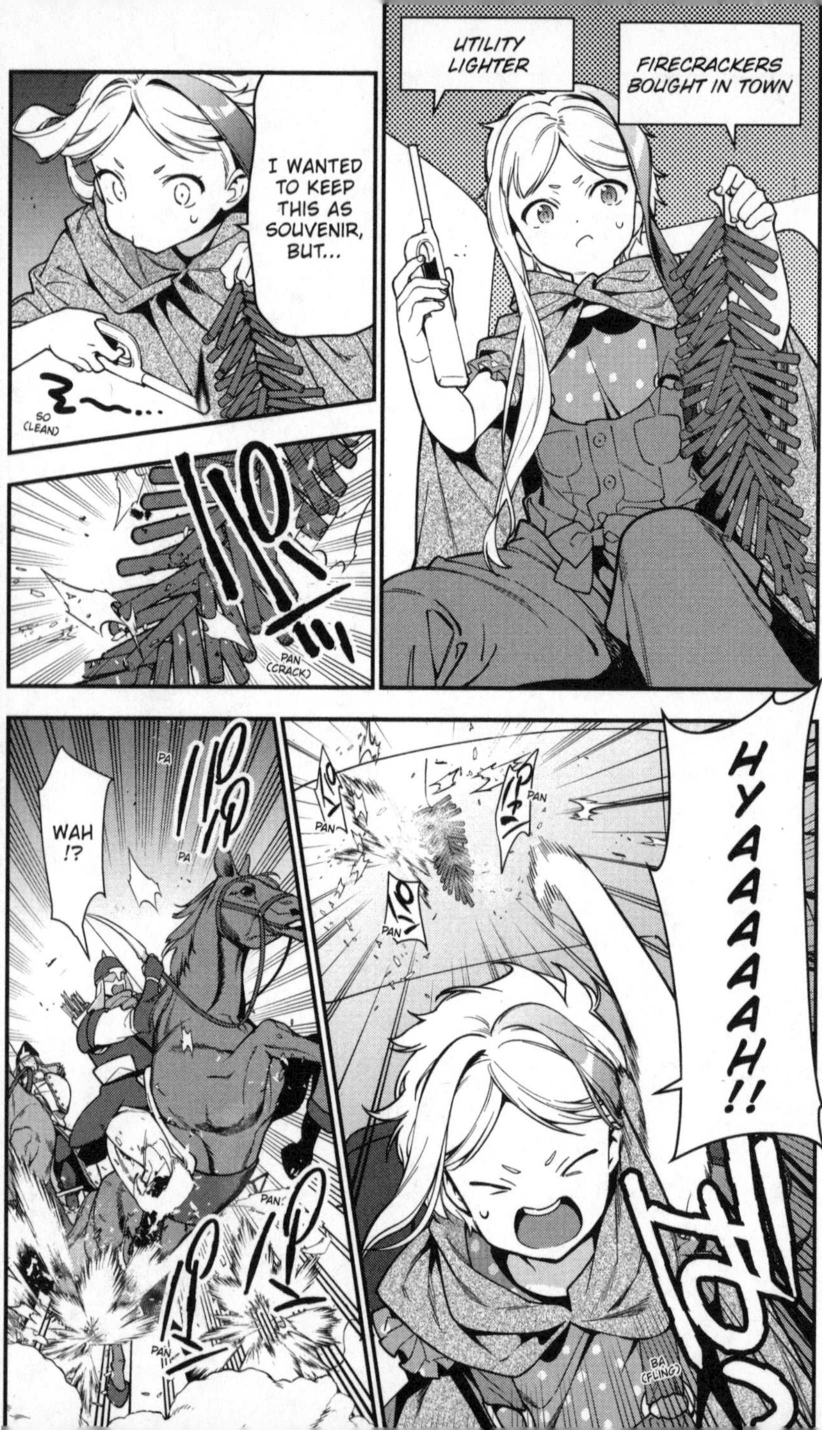
UTILITY LIGHTER
FIRECRACKERS BOUGHT IN TOWN
I WANTED TO KEEP THIS AS SOUVENIR, BUT...
SO (LEAN)
PAN (CRACK)
HYAAAAAAAH!!
PAN
PAN
PAN
BA (FLING)
WAH !?
PA
PA
PAN
PAN

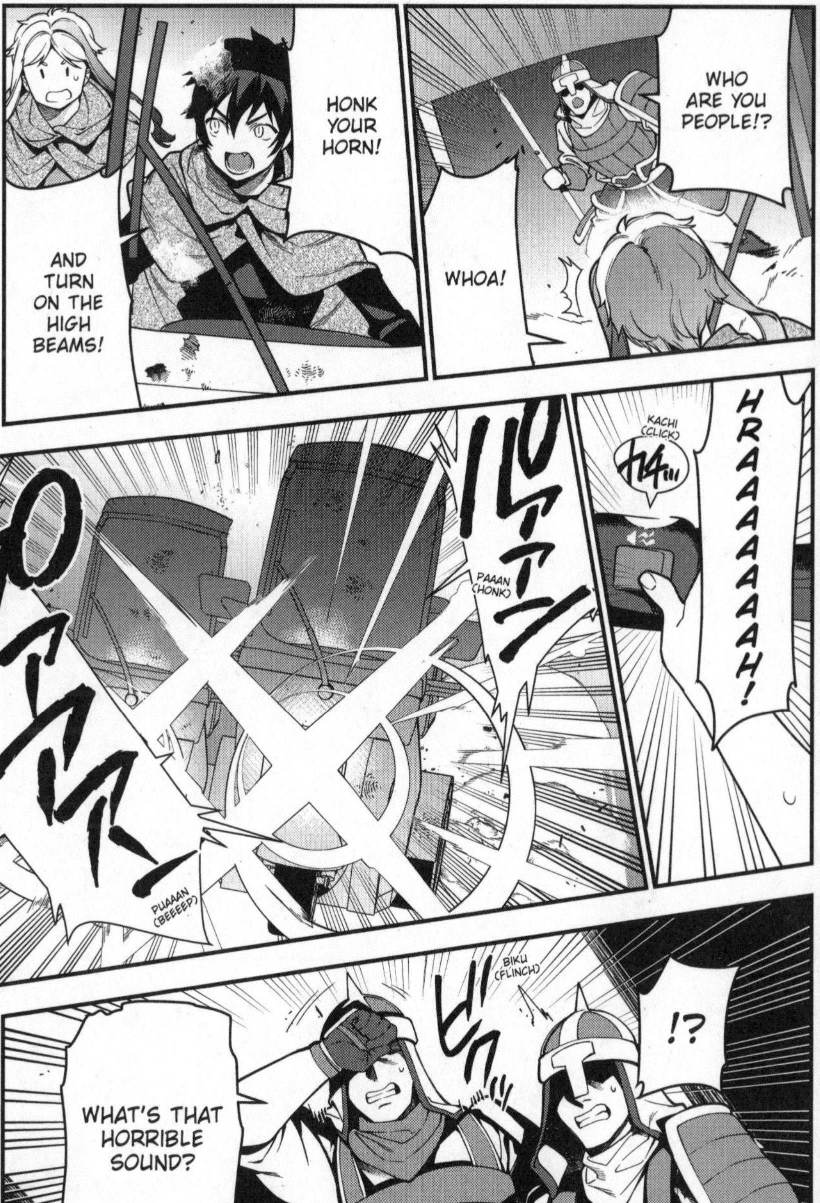
WHO ARE YOU PEOPLE!?
WHOA!
HONK YOUR HORN!
AND TURN ON THE HIGH BEAMS!
KACHI (CLICK)
HRAAAAAAAH!
PAAAN (HONK)
PUAAAN (BEEEEP)
BIKU (FLINCH)
!?
WHAT'S THAT HORRIBLE SOUND?

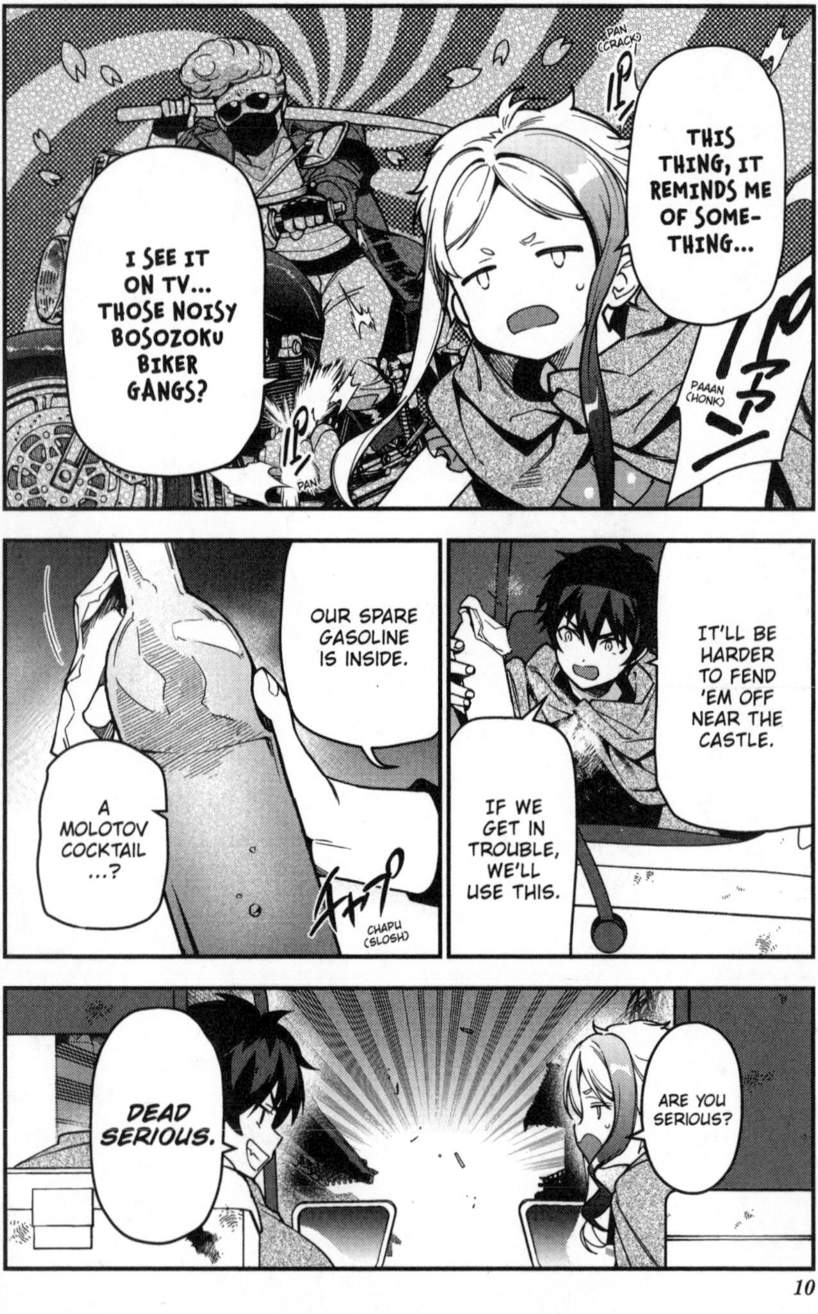
PAN (CRACK)
THIS THING, IT REMINDS ME OF SOME-THING...
PAAAN (HONK)
I SEE IT ON TV... THOSE NOISY BOSOZOKU BIKER GANGS?
PAN
IT'LL BE HARDER TO FEND 'EM OFF NEAR THE CASTLE.
IF WE GET IN TROUBLE, WE'LL USE THIS.
OUR SPARE GASOLINE IS INSIDE.
A MOLOTOV COCKTAIL ...?
CHAPU (SLOSH)
ARE YOU SERIOUS?
DEAD SERIOUS.

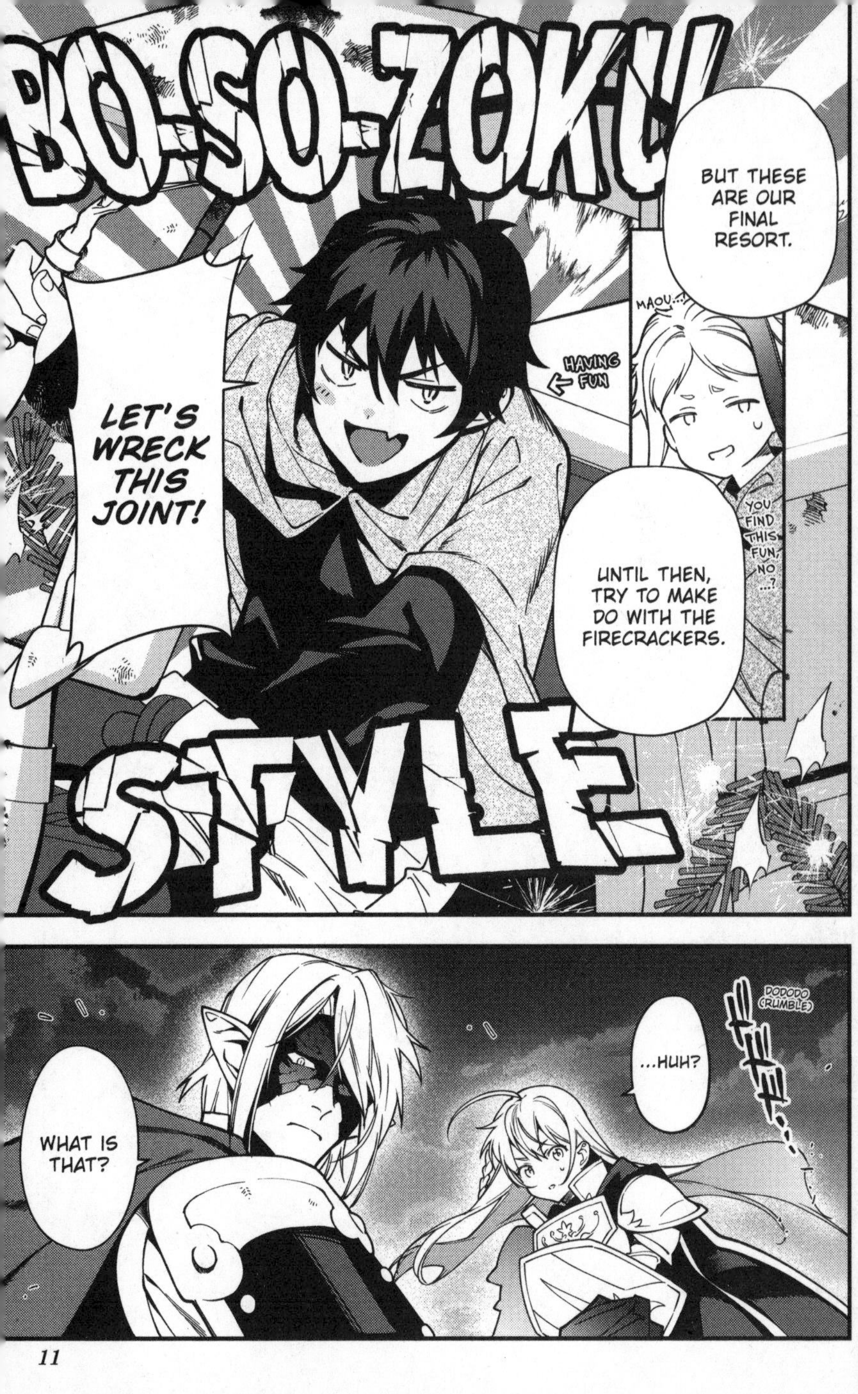
BUT THESE ARE OUR FINAL RESORT.
MAOU...
UNTIL THEN, TRY TO MAKE DO WITH THE FIRECRACKERS.
YOU FIND THIS FUN, NO...?
BO-SO-ZOKU!
HAVING FUN
LET'S WRECK THIS JOINT!
STYLE.
DODODO (RUMBLE)
...HUH?
WHAT IS THAT?

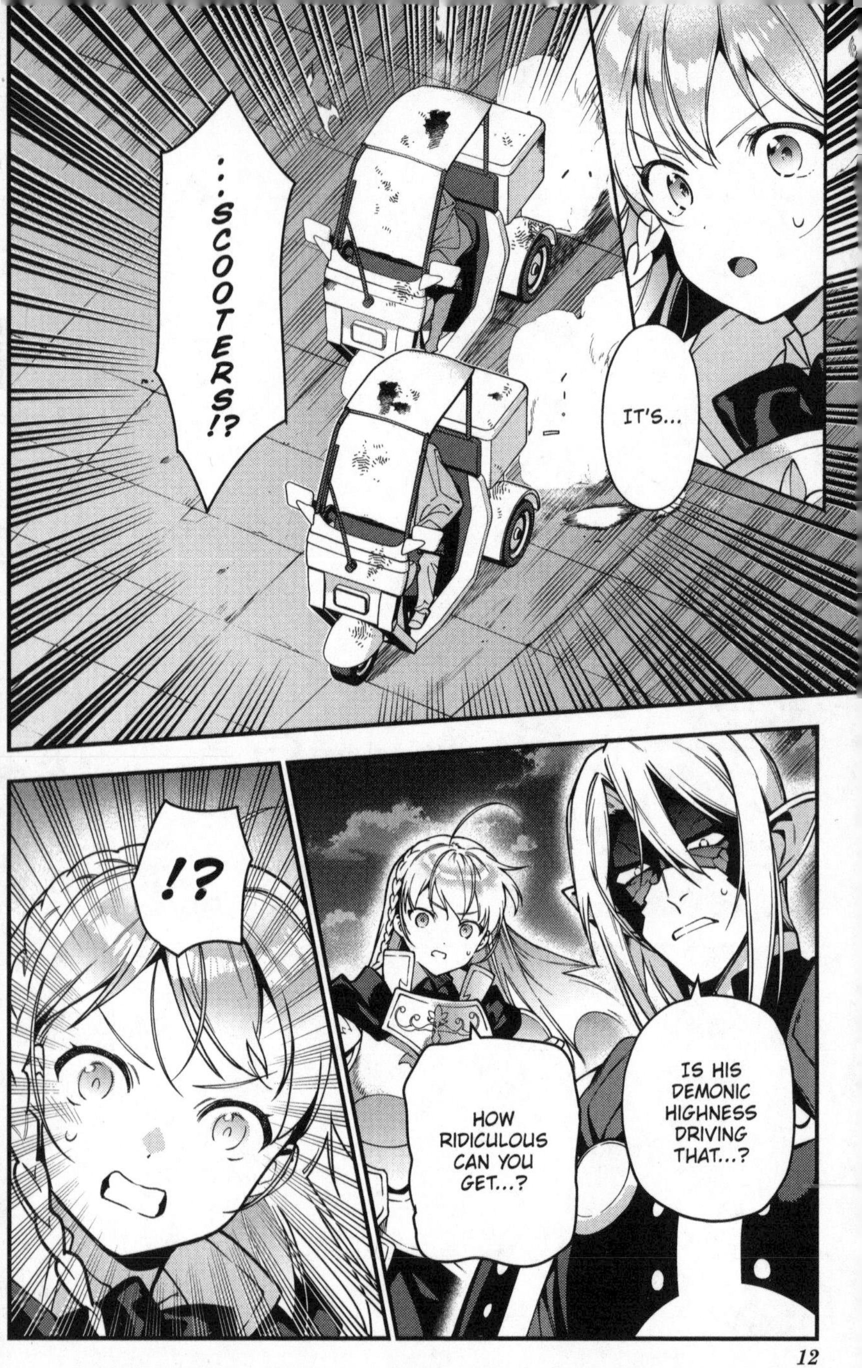
IT'S...
...SCOOTERS!?
IS HIS DEMONIC HIGHNESS DRIVING THAT...?
HOW RIDICULOUS CAN YOU GET...?
!?

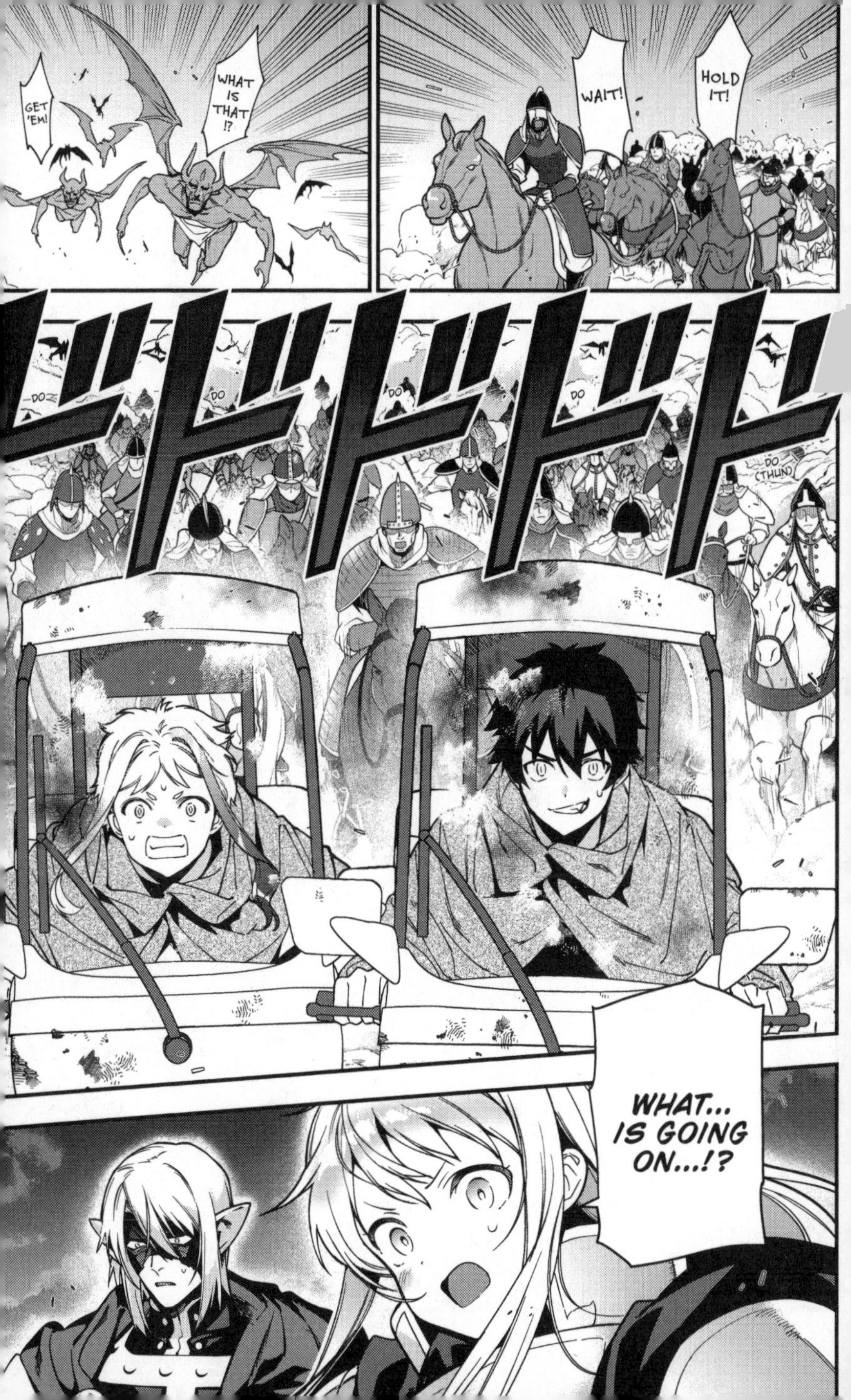
HOLD IT!
WAIT!
WHAT IS THAT!?
GET 'EM!
ドドドドド
DO
DO
DO
DO
DO (THUND)
WHAT... IS GOING ON...!?

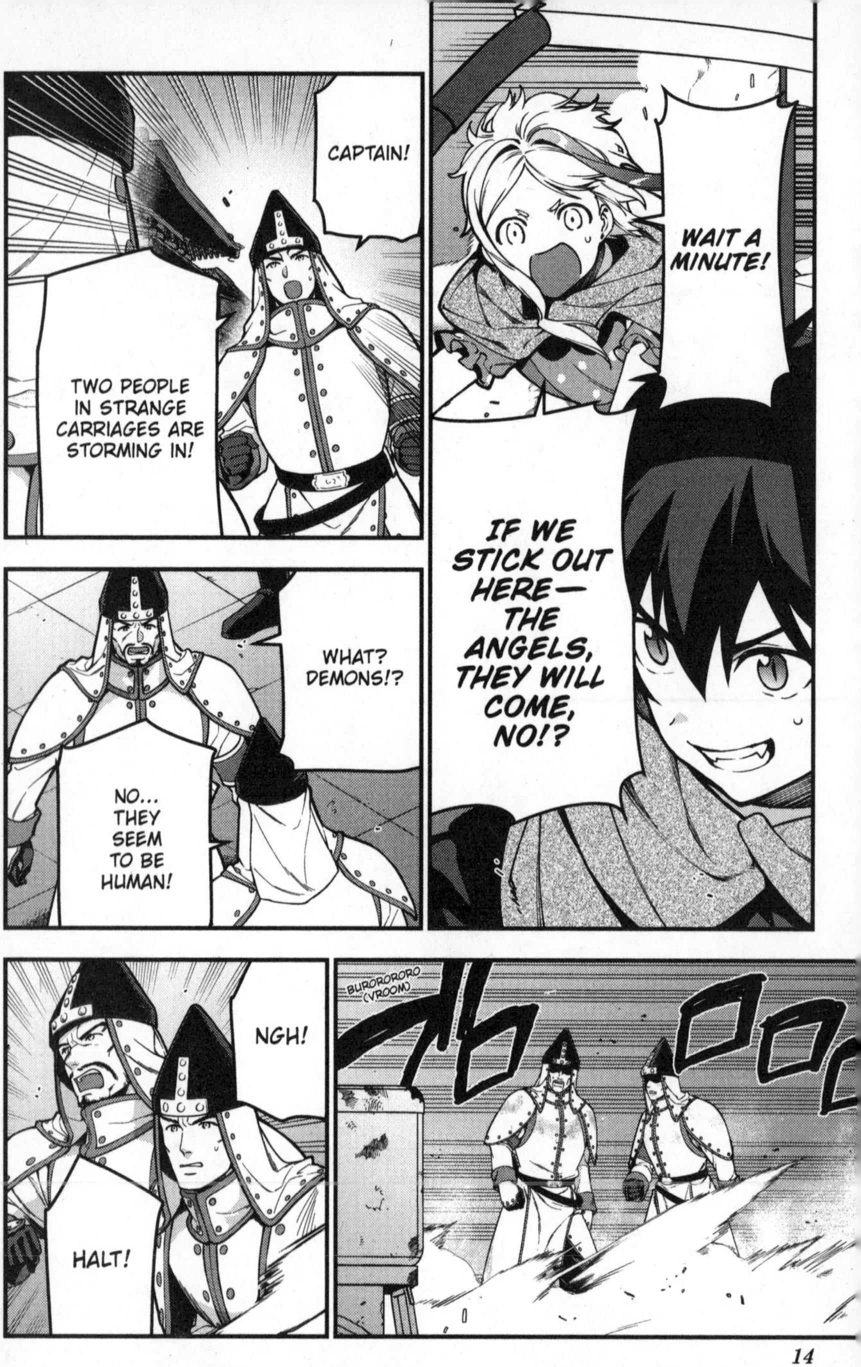
WAIT A MINUTE!
IF WE STICK OUT HERE— THE ANGELS, THEY WILL COME, NO!?
CAPTAIN!
TWO PEOPLE IN STRANGE CARRIAGES ARE STORMING IN!
WHAT? DEMONS!?
NO... THEY SEEM TO BE HUMAN!
BURORORORO (VROOM)
NGH!
HALT!

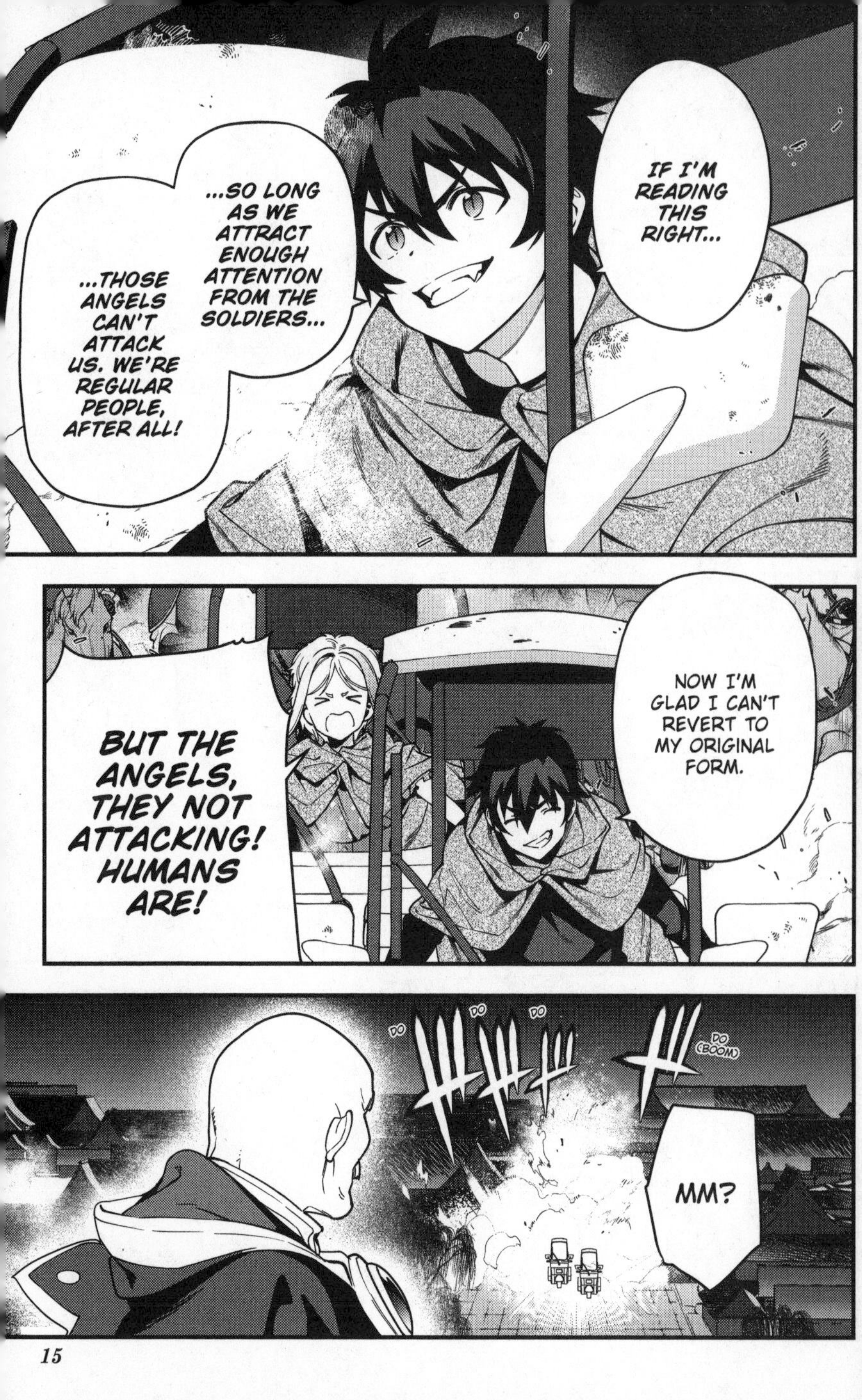
IF I'M READING THIS RIGHT...
...SO LONG AS WE ATTRACT ENOUGH ATTENTION FROM THE SOLDIERS...
...THOSE ANGELS CAN'T ATTACK US. WE'RE REGULAR PEOPLE, AFTER ALL!
NOW I'M GLAD I CAN'T REVERT TO MY ORIGINAL FORM.
BUT THE ANGELS, THEY NOT ATTACKING! HUMANS ARE!
DO (BOOM)
DO
DO
DO
MM?

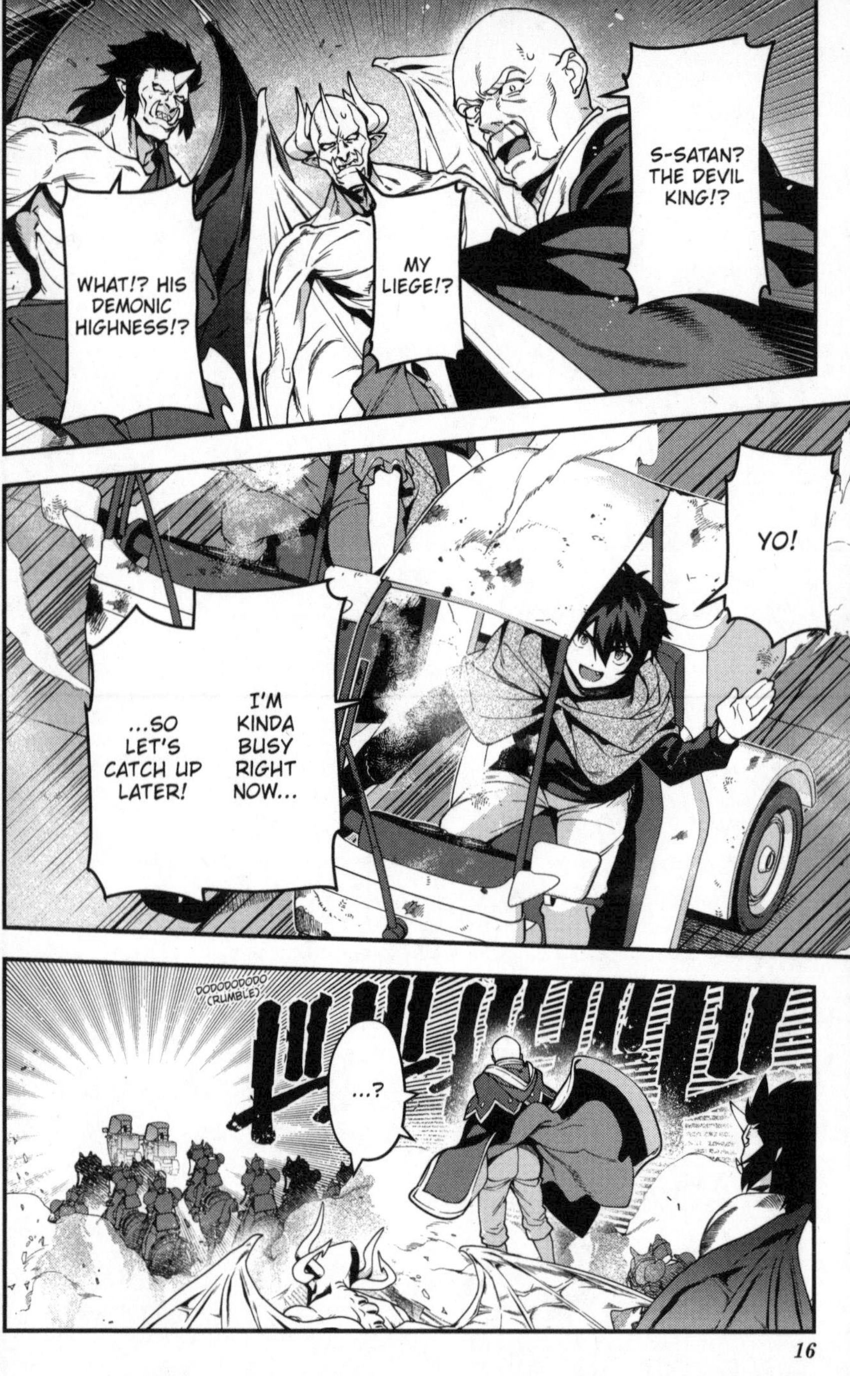
S-SATAN? THE DEVIL KING!?
MY LIEGE!?
WHAT!? HIS DEMONIC HIGHNESS!?
YO!
I'M KINDA BUSY RIGHT NOW...
...SO LET'S CATCH UP LATER!
DODODODODO (RUMBLE)
...?

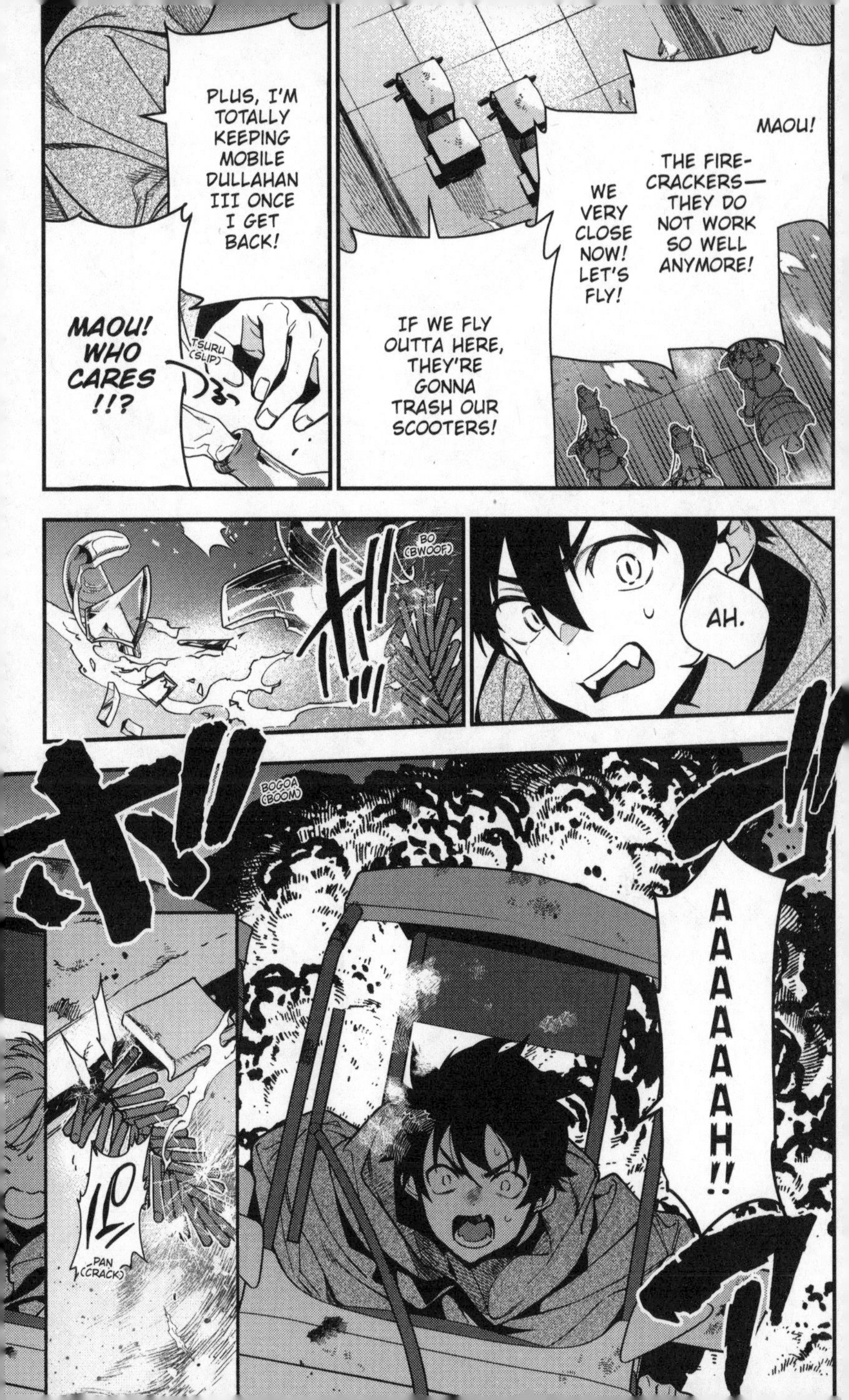
MAOU!
THE FIRE-CRACKERS—THEY DO NOT WORK SO WELL ANYMORE!
WE VERY CLOSE NOW! LET'S FLY!
IF WE FLY OUTTA HERE, THEY'RE GONNA TRASH OUR SCOOTERS!
PLUS, I'M TOTALLY KEEPING MOBILE DULLAHAN III ONCE I GET BACK!
TSURU (SLIP)
MAOU! WHO CARES!!?
AH.
BO (BWOOF)
BOGOA (BOOM)
AAAAAAAH!!
PAN (CRACK)

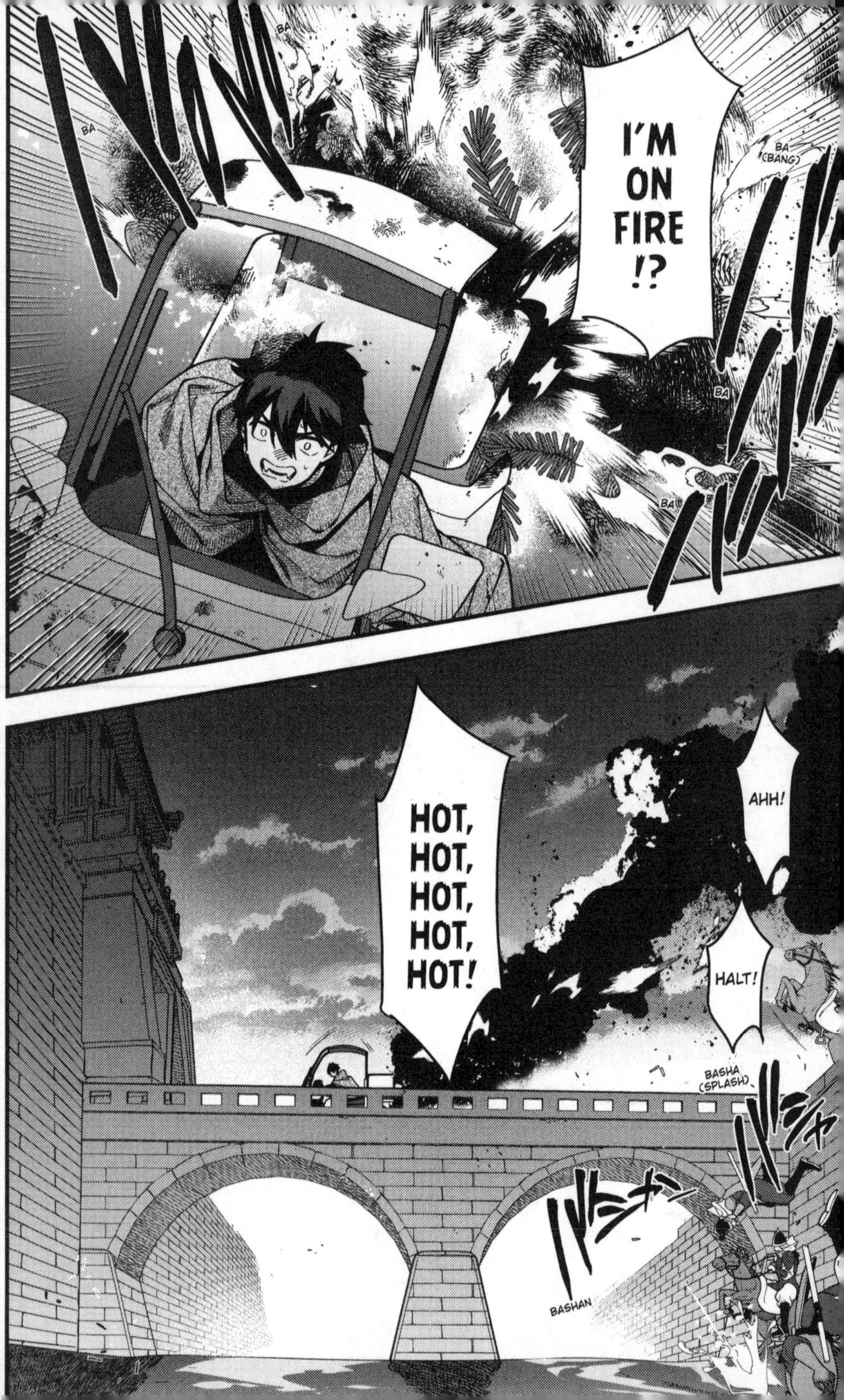
BA (BANG)
BA
BA
I'M ON FIRE!?
BA
BA
AHH!
HALT!
HOT, HOT, HOT, HOT, HOT!
BASHA (SPLASH)
BASHAN

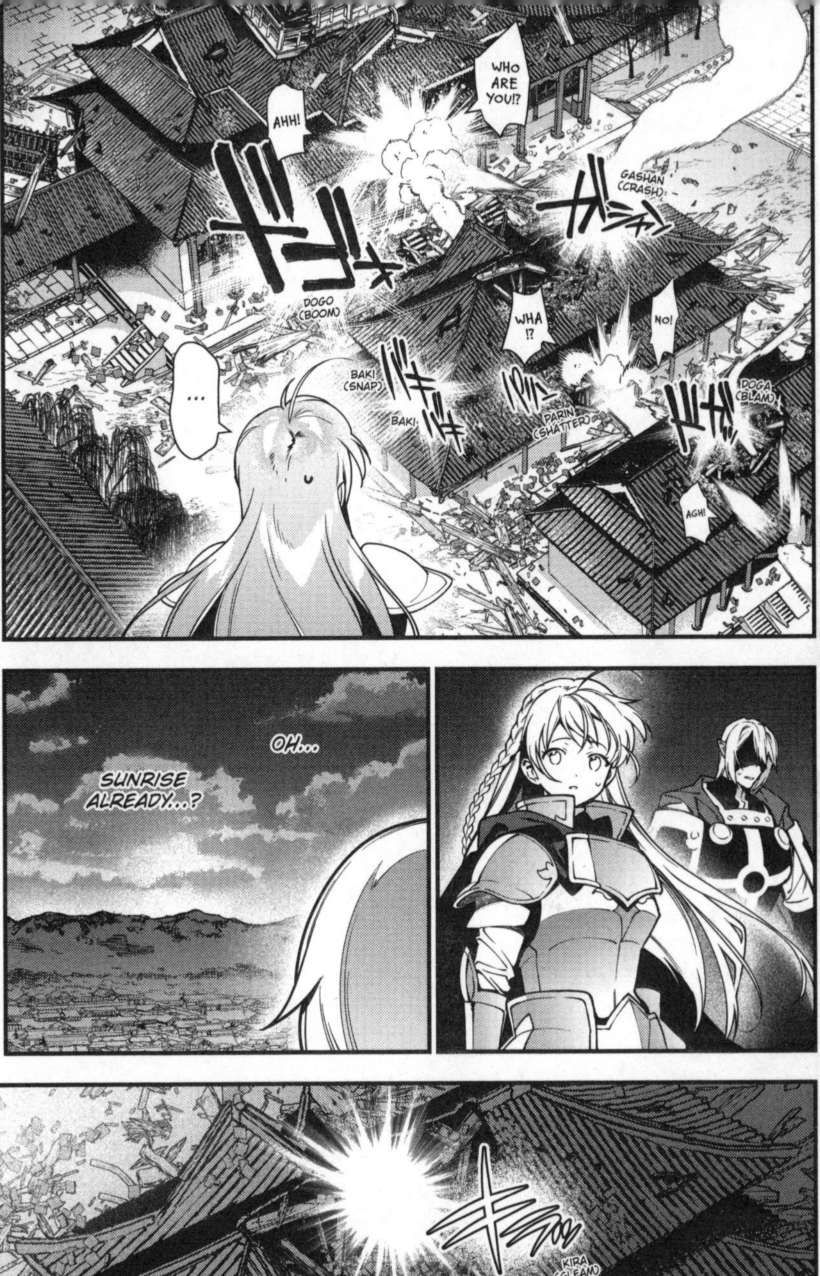
WHO ARE YOU!?
AHH!
GASHAN (CRASH)
DOGO (BOOM)
NO!
WHA !?
DOGA (BLAM)
AGH!
PARIN (SHATTER)
BAKI (SNAP)
BAKI
...
OH...
SUNRISE ALREADY...?
KIRA (GLEAM)

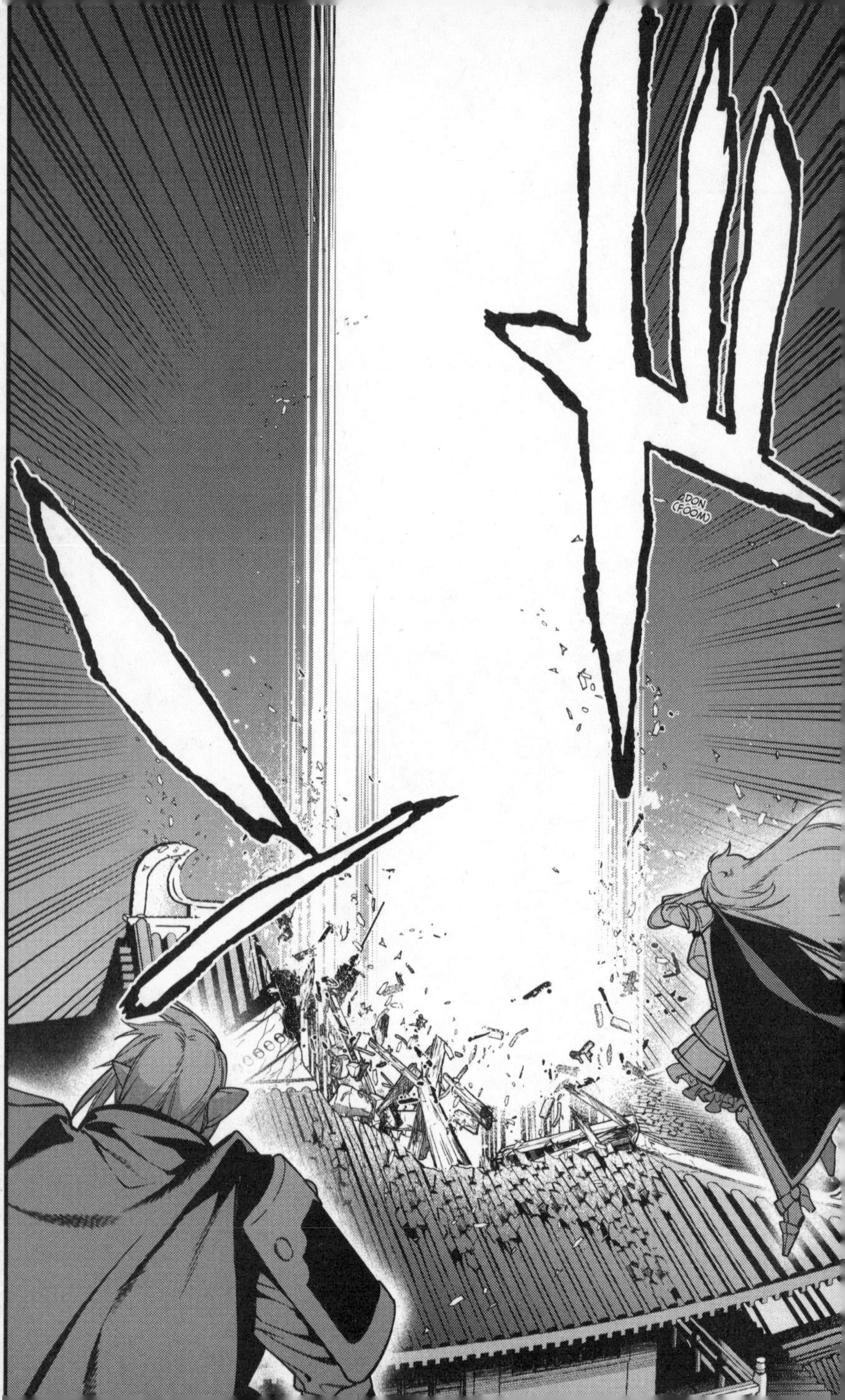
DON
(FOOM)

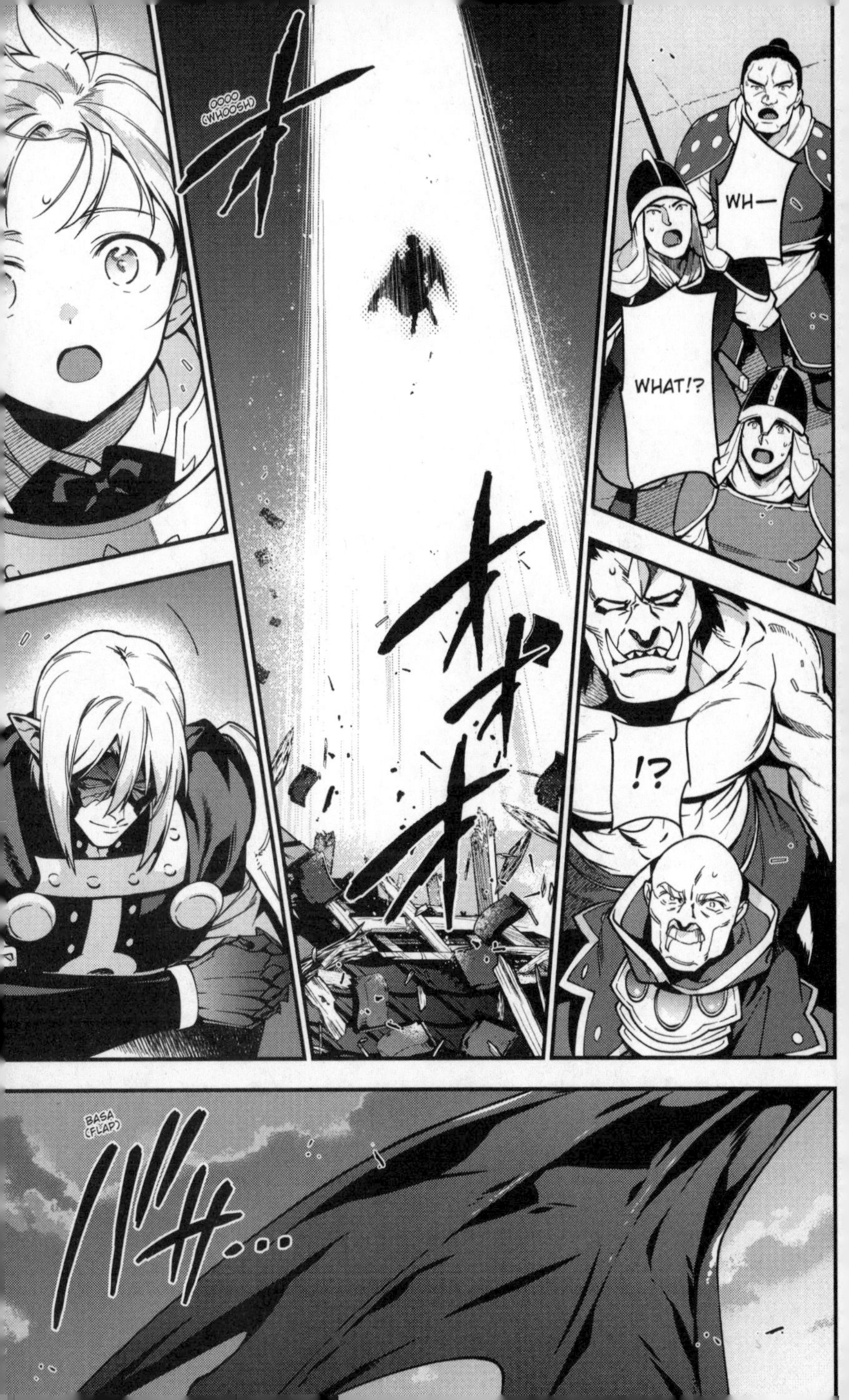
WH—
WHAT!?
!?
OOOO (WHOOSH)
BASA (FLAP)

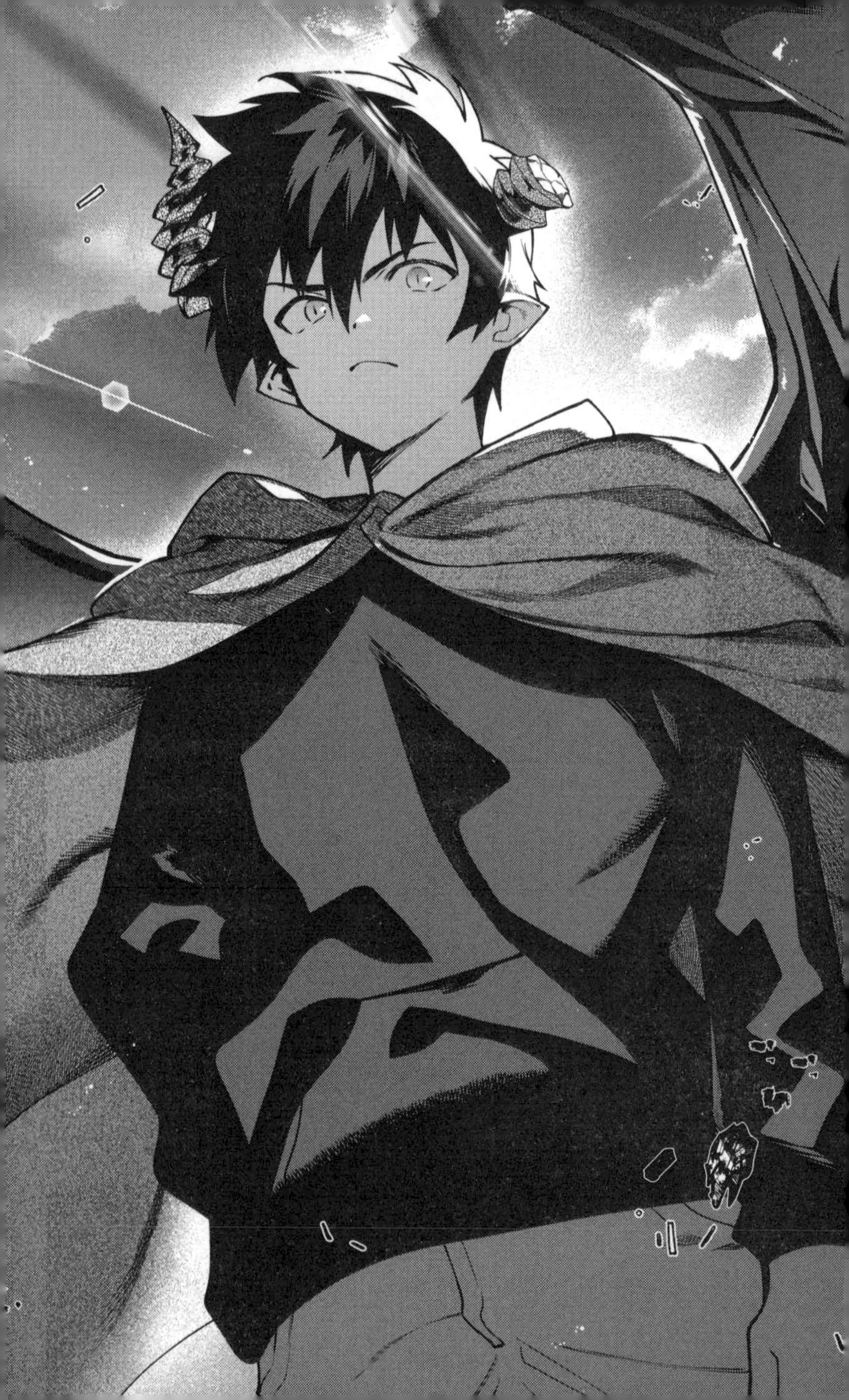

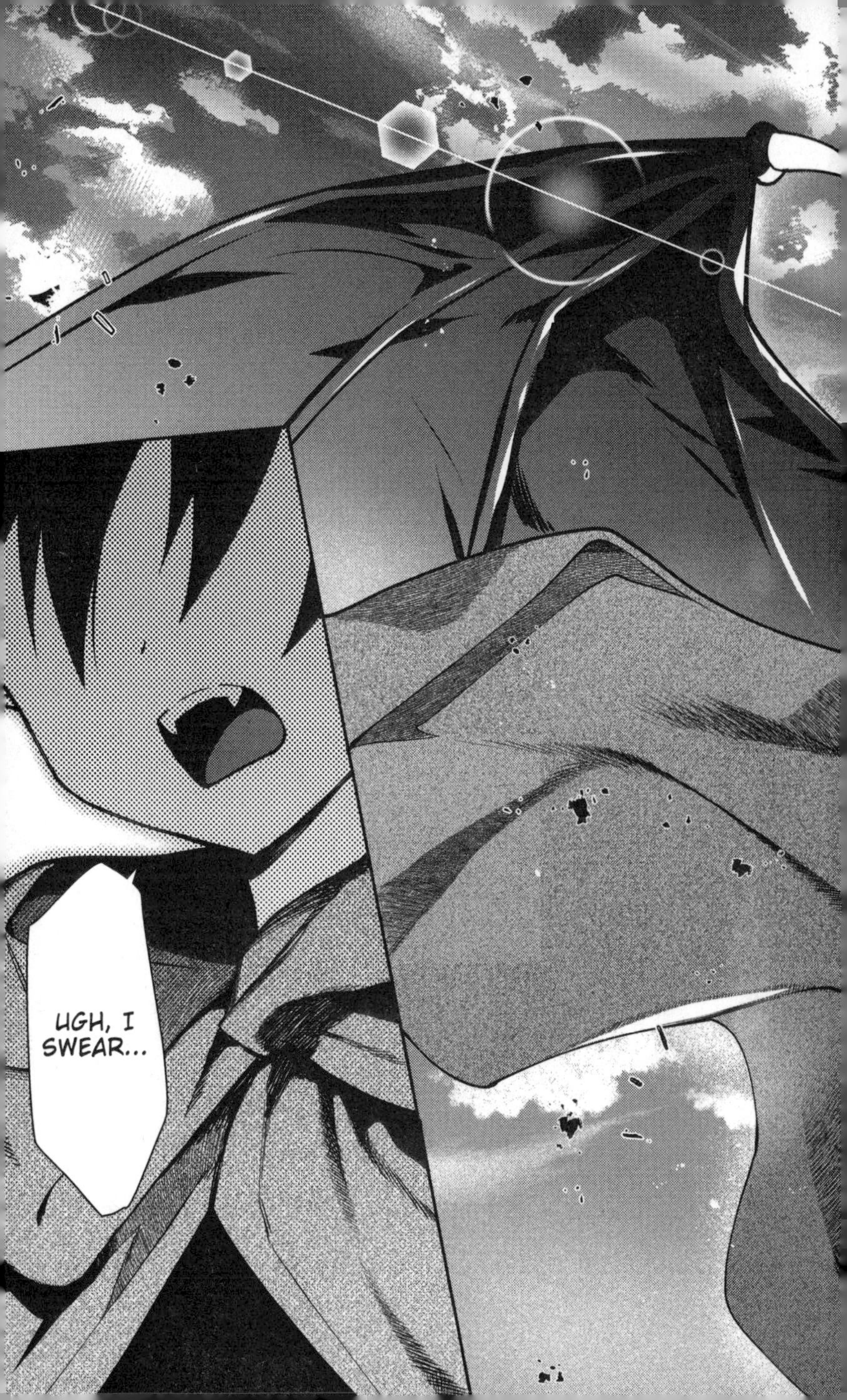
UGH, I SWEAR...

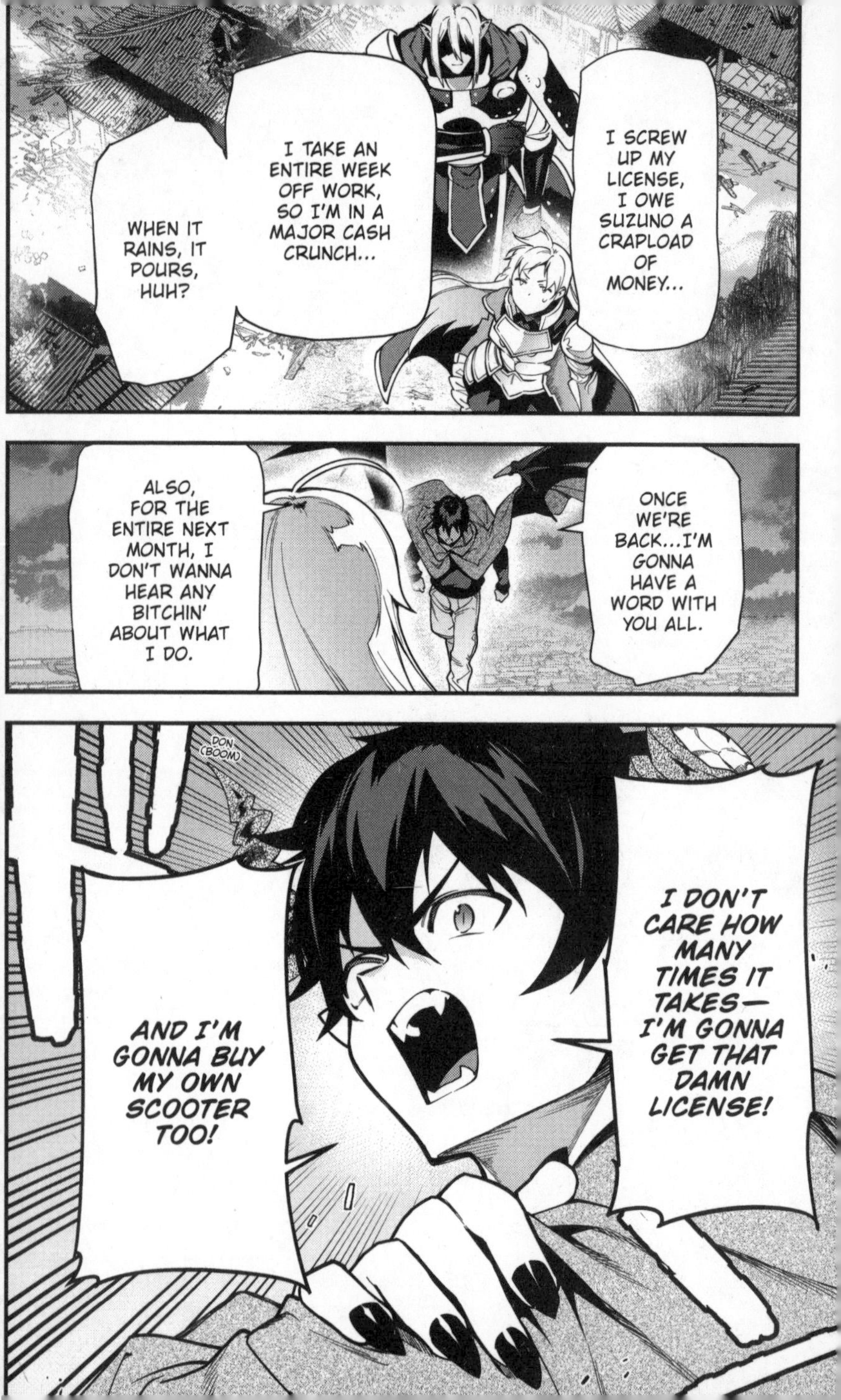
I SCREW UP MY LICENSE, I OWE SUZUNO A CRAPLOAD OF MONEY...
I TAKE AN ENTIRE WEEK OFF WORK, SO I'M IN A MAJOR CASH CRUNCH...
WHEN IT RAINS, IT POURS, HUH?
ONCE WE'RE BACK...I'M GONNA HAVE A WORD WITH YOU ALL.
ALSO, FOR THE ENTIRE NEXT MONTH, I DON'T WANNA HEAR ANY BITCHIN' ABOUT WHAT I DO.
I DON'T CARE HOW MANY TIMES IT TAKES— I'M GONNA GET THAT DAMN LICENSE!
DON (BOOM)
AND I'M GONNA BUY MY OWN SCOOTER TOO!

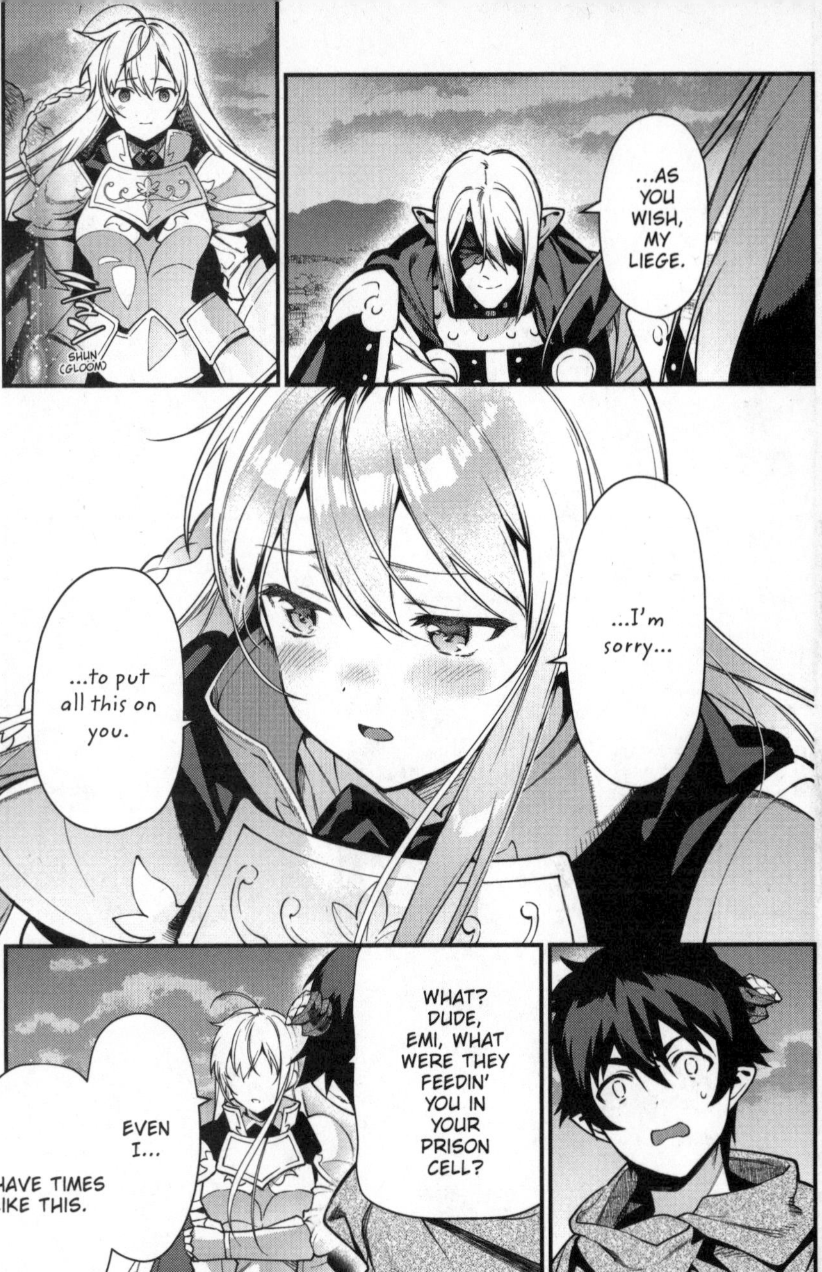
...AS YOU WISH, MY LIEGE.
SHUN (GLOOM)
...I'm sorry...
...to put all this on you.
WHAT? DUDE, EMI, WHAT WERE THEY FEEDIN' YOU IN YOUR PRISON CELL?
EVEN I...
...HAVE TIMES LIKE THIS.

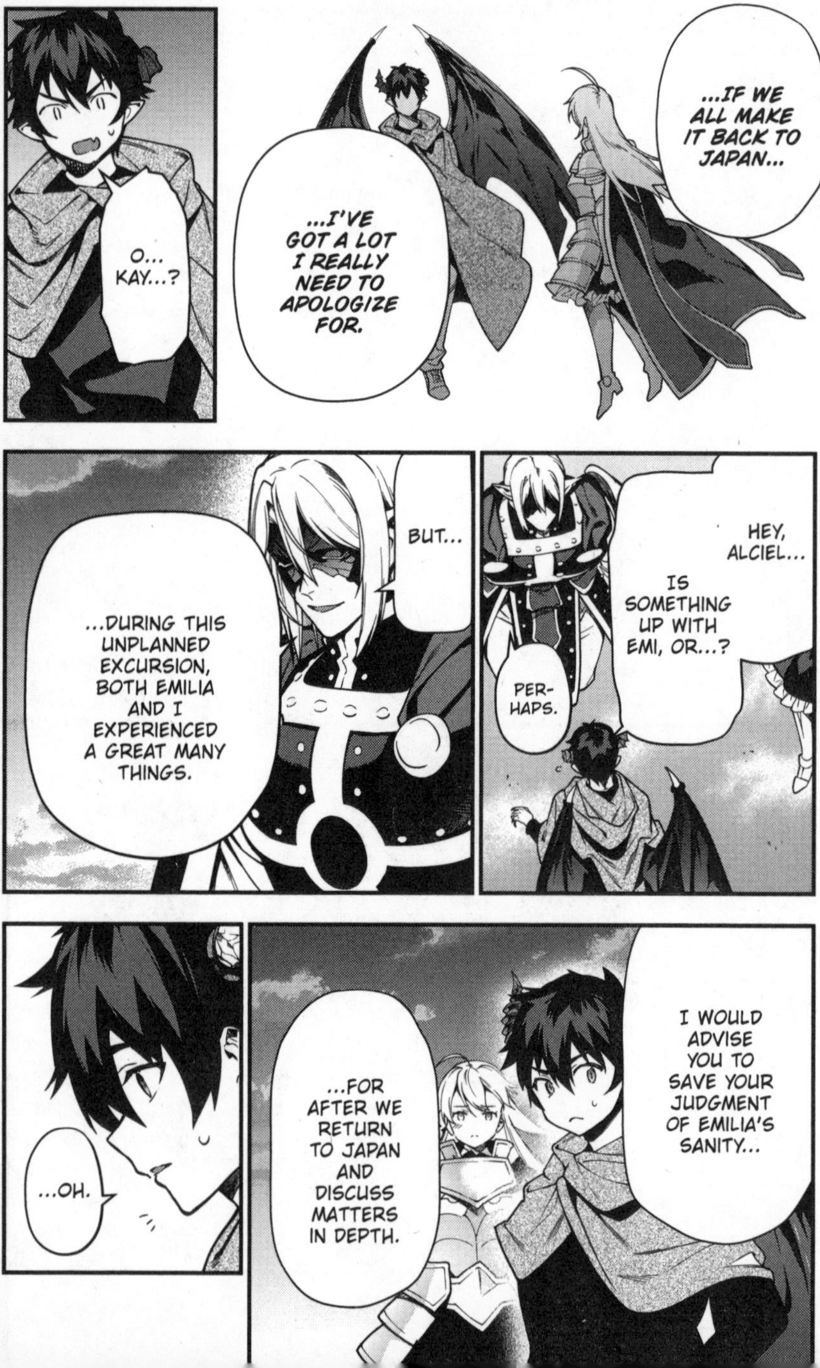
...IF WE ALL MAKE IT BACK TO JAPAN...
...I'VE GOT A LOT I REALLY NEED TO APOLOGIZE FOR.
O... KAY...?
HEY, ALCIEL...
IS SOMETHING UP WITH EMI, OR...?
PER-HAPS.
BUT...
...DURING THIS UNPLANNED EXCURSION, BOTH EMILIA AND I EXPERIENCED A GREAT MANY THINGS.
I WOULD ADVISE YOU TO SAVE YOUR JUDGMENT OF EMILIA'S SANITY...
...FOR AFTER WE RETURN TO JAPAN AND DISCUSS MATTERS IN DEPTH.
...OH.

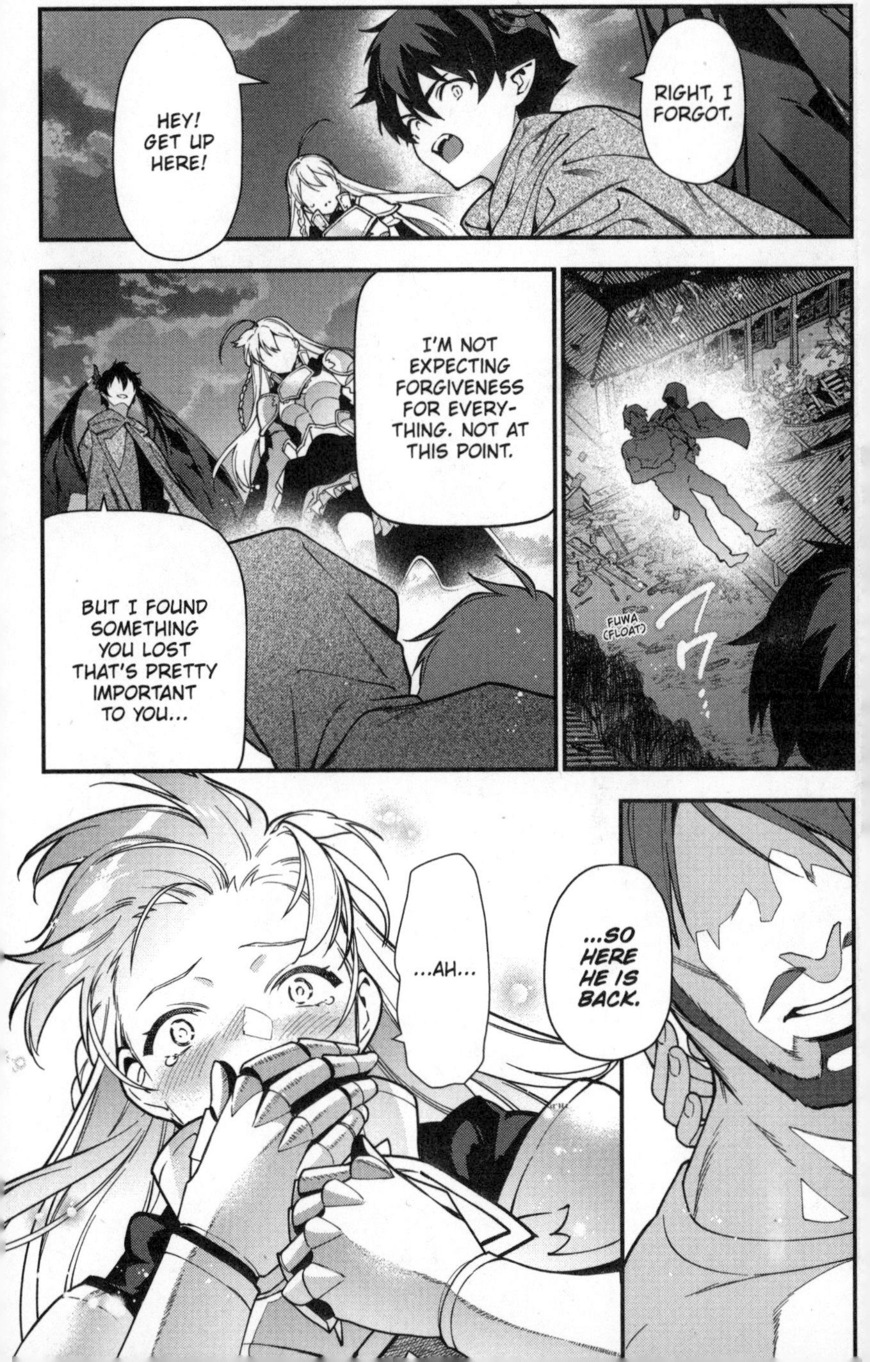
RIGHT, I FORGOT.
HEY! GET UP HERE!
FUWA (FLOAT)
I'M NOT EXPECTING FORGIVENESS FOR EVERY-THING. NOT AT THIS POINT.
BUT I FOUND SOMETHING YOU LOST THAT'S PRETTY IMPORTANT TO YOU...
...SO HERE HE IS BACK.
...AH...

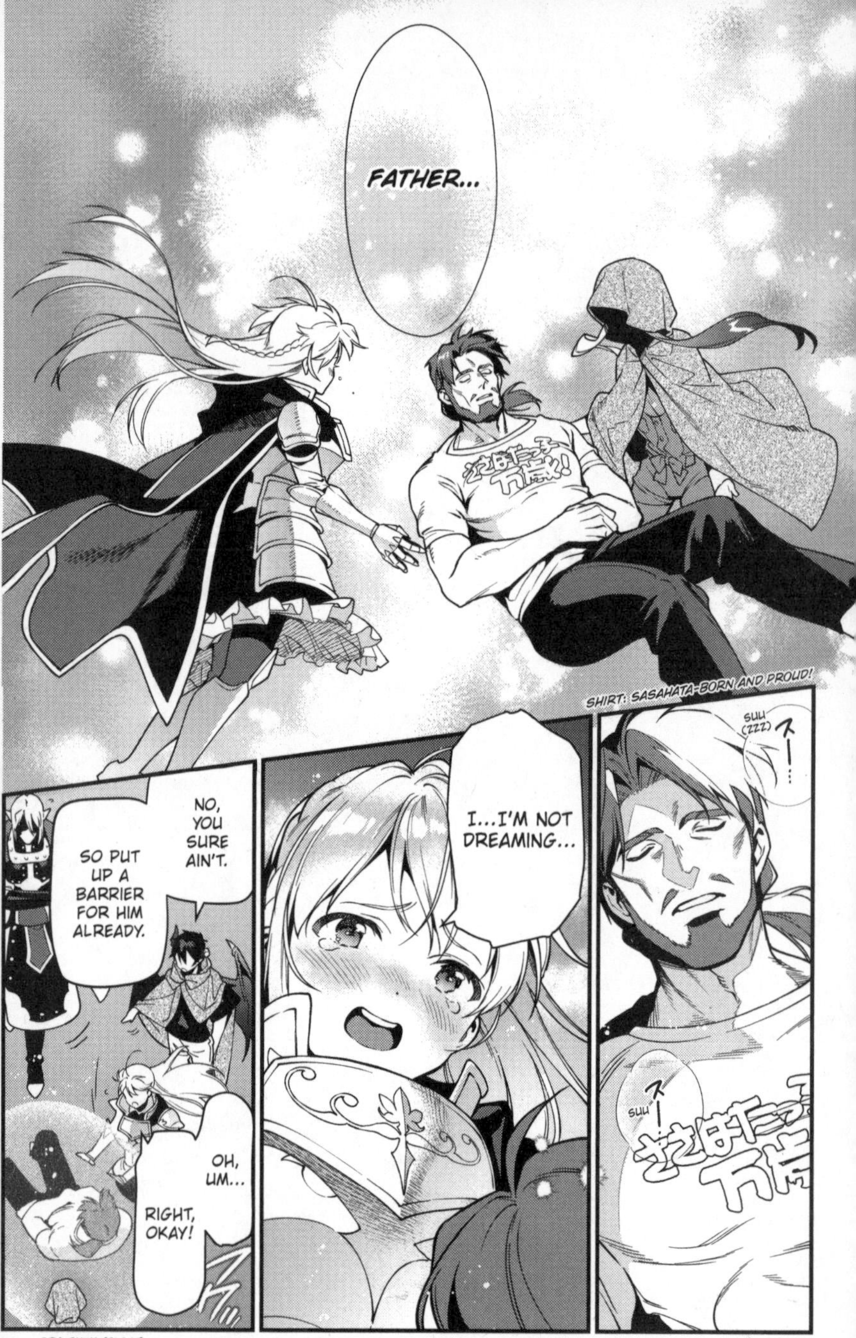
FATHER...
SHIRT: SASAHATA-BORN AND PROUD!
SUU (ZZZ) スー…
SUU スー
I...I'M NOT DREAMING...
NO, YOU SURE AIN'T.
SO PUT UP A BARRIER FOR HIM ALREADY.
OH, UM...
RIGHT, OKAY!

SFX: FUWA (FLOAT)

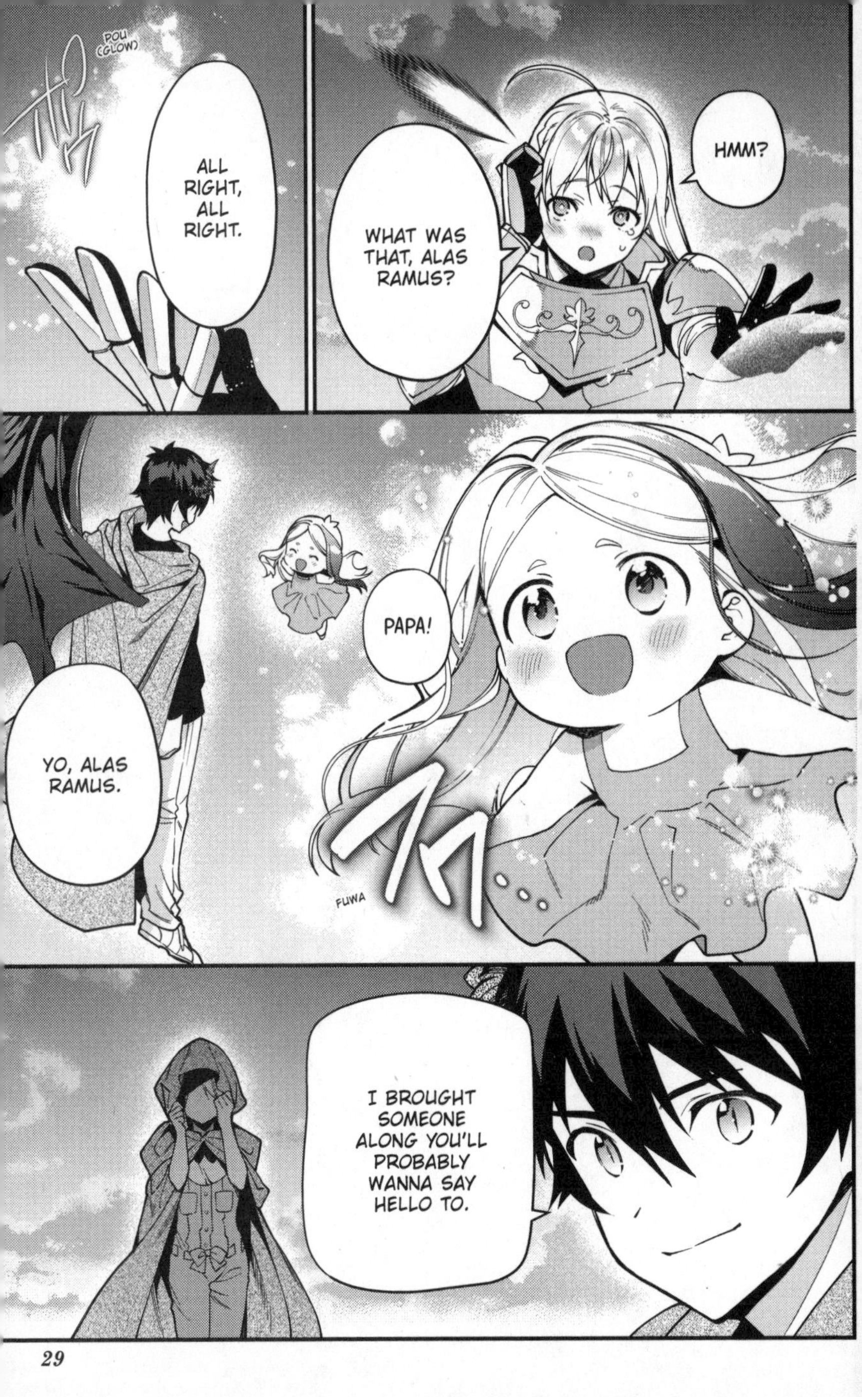
HMM?
WHAT WAS THAT, ALAS RAMUS?
POU (GLOW)
ALL RIGHT, ALL RIGHT.
PAPA!
FUWA
YO, ALAS RAMUS.
I BROUGHT SOMEONE ALONG YOU'LL PROBABLY WANNA SAY HELLO TO.

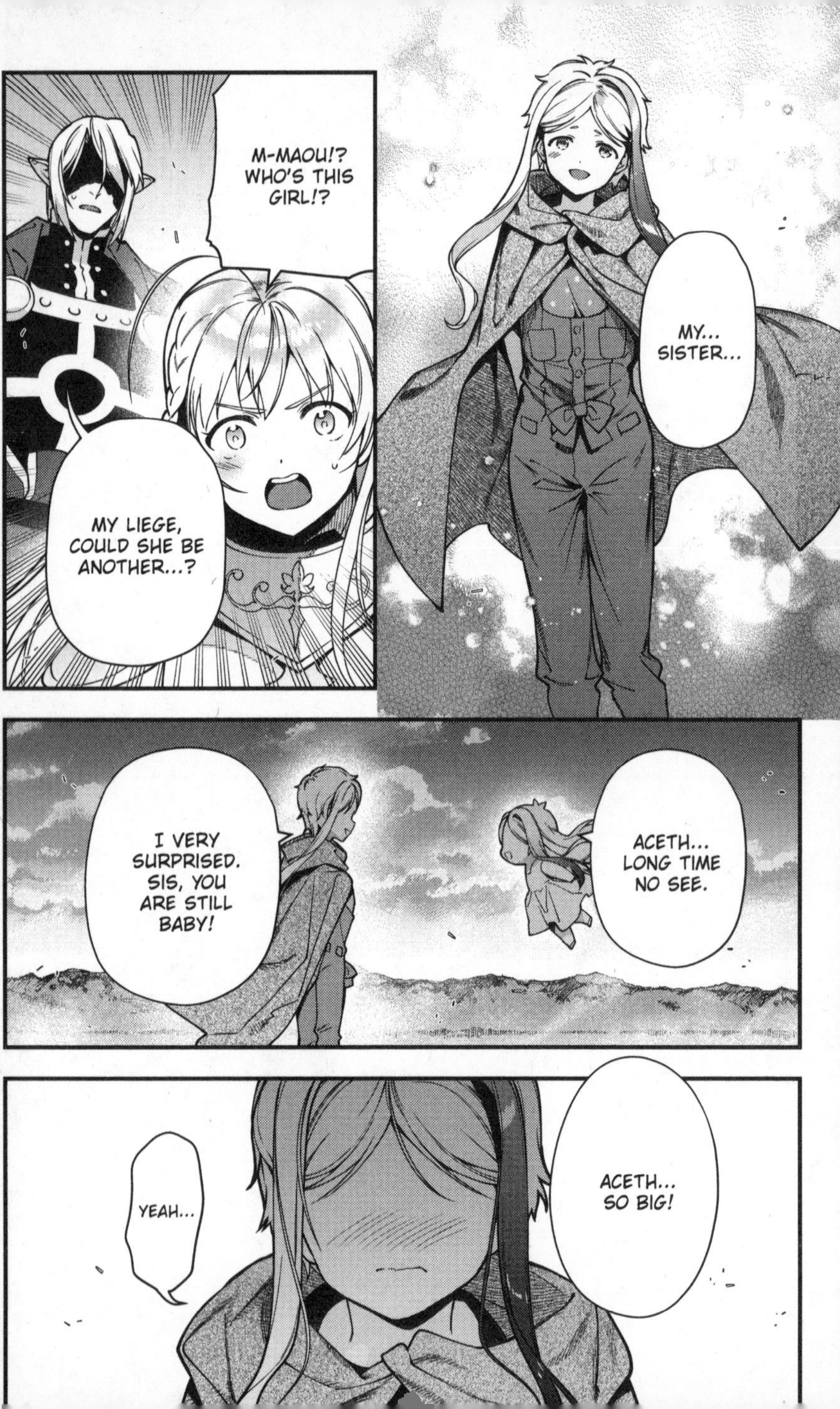
MY... SISTER...
M-MAOU!? WHO'S THIS GIRL!?
MY LIEGE, COULD SHE BE ANOTHER...?
ACETH... LONG TIME NO SEE.
I VERY SURPRISED. SIS, YOU ARE STILL BABY!
ACETH... SO BIG!
YEAH...

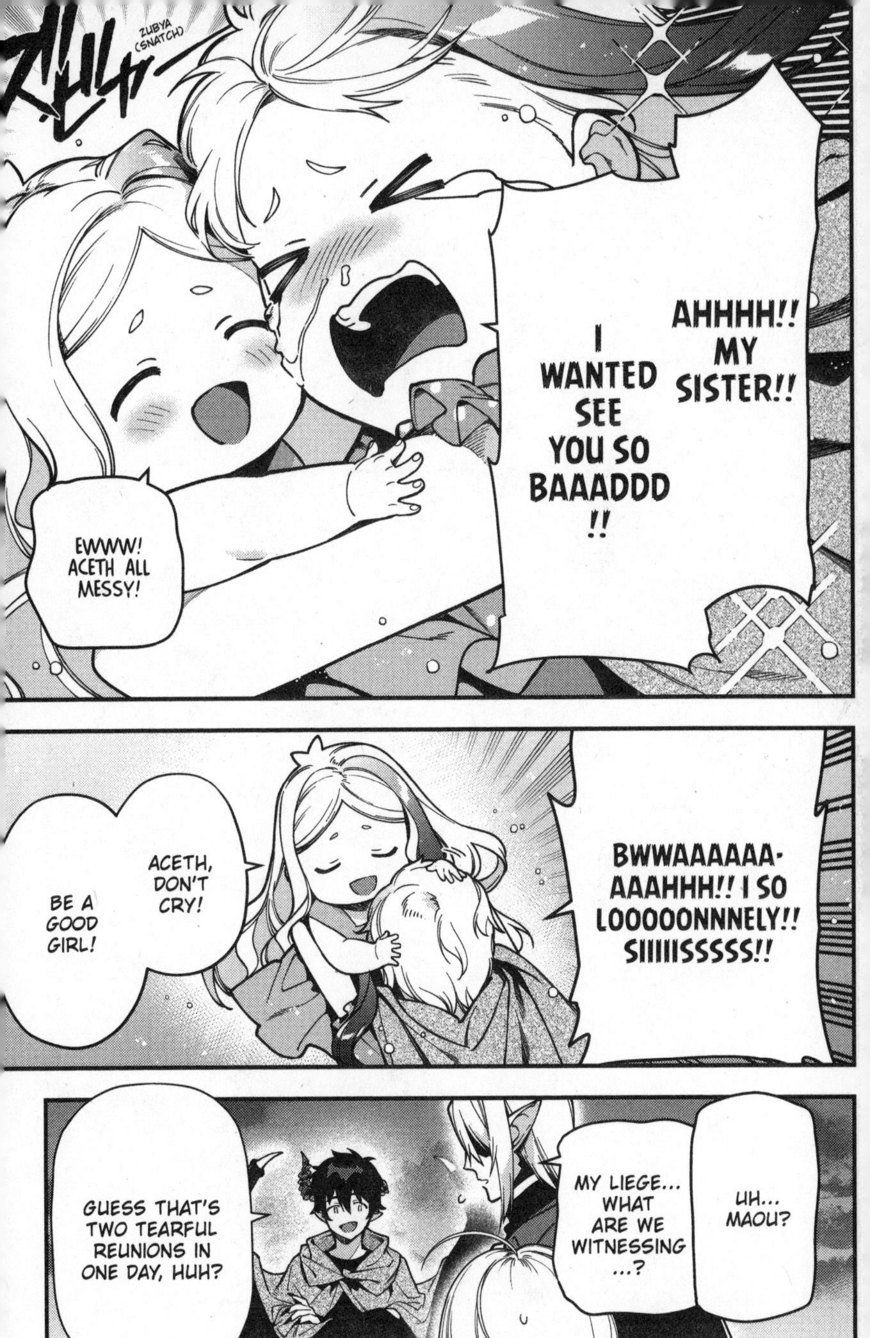
AHHHH!! MY SISTER!!
I WANTED SEE YOU SO BAAADDD!!
ZUBYA (SNATCH)
EWWW! ACETH ALL MESSY!
BWWAAAAAA-AAAHHH!! I SO LOOOOONNNELY!! SIIIIISSSSS!!
ACETH, DON'T CRY!
BE A GOOD GIRL!
UH... MAOU?
MY LIEGE... WHAT ARE WE WITNESSING...?
GUESS THAT'S TWO TEARFUL REUNIONS IN ONE DAY, HUH?

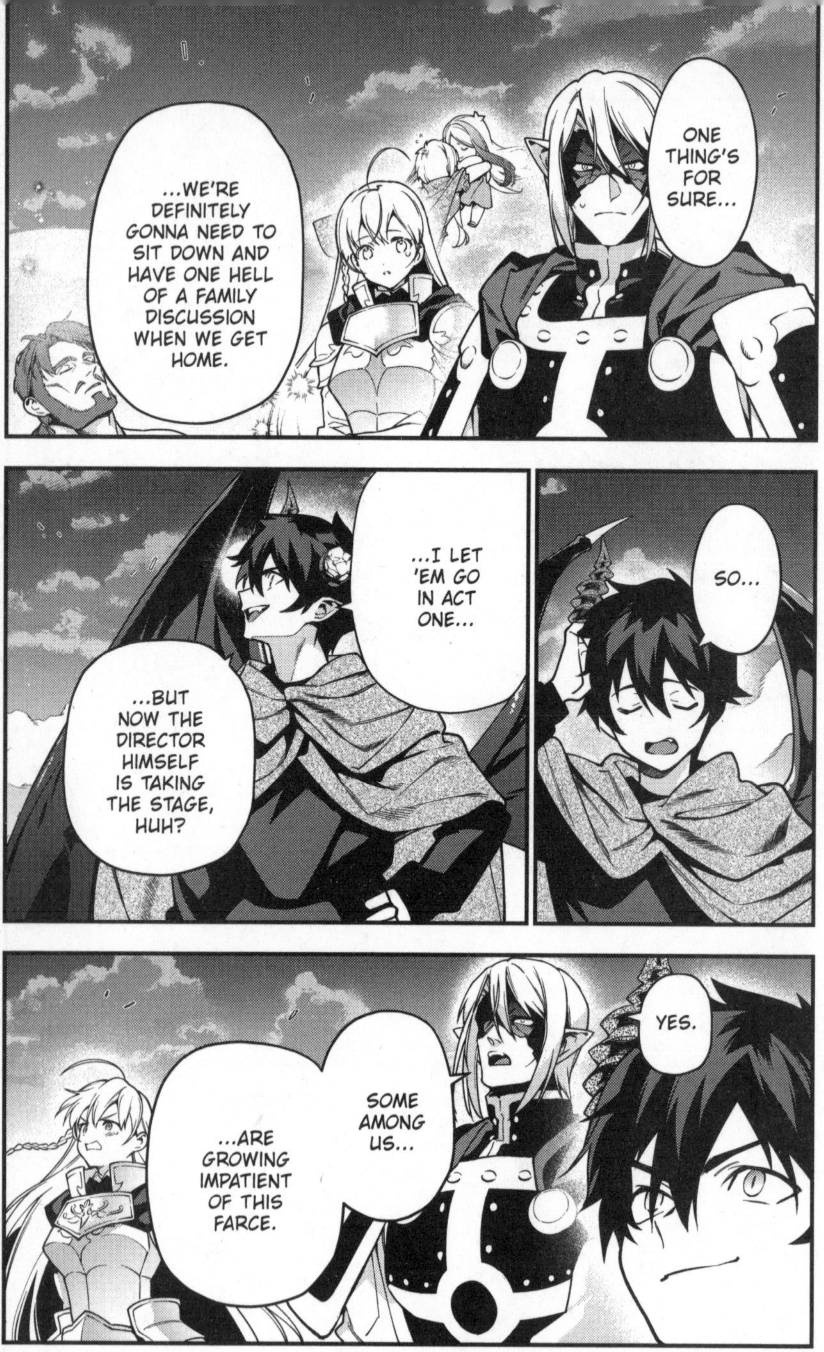
ONE THING'S FOR SURE...
...WE'RE DEFINITELY GONNA NEED TO SIT DOWN AND HAVE ONE HELL OF A FAMILY DISCUSSION WHEN WE GET HOME.
SO...
...I LET 'EM GO IN ACT ONE...
...BUT NOW THE DIRECTOR HIMSELF IS TAKING THE STAGE, HUH?
YES.
SOME AMONG US...
...ARE GROWING IMPATIENT OF THIS FARCE.

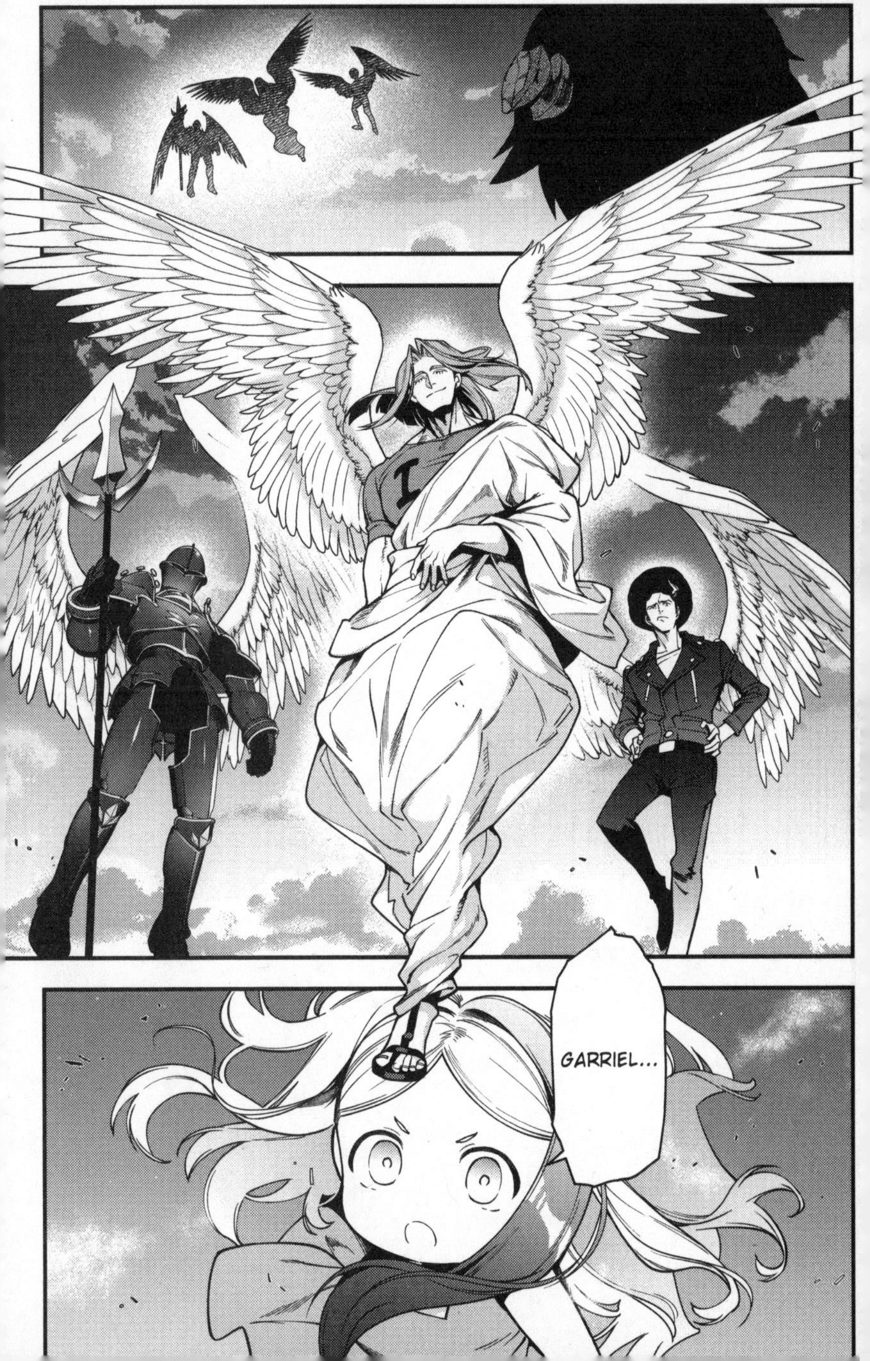
GARRIEL...

THE DEVIL IS A PART-TIMER!

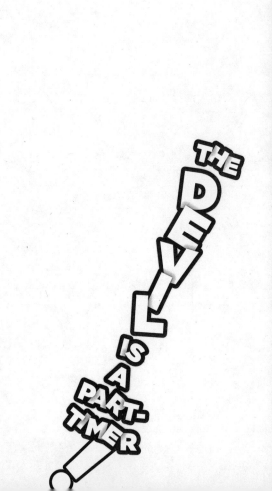

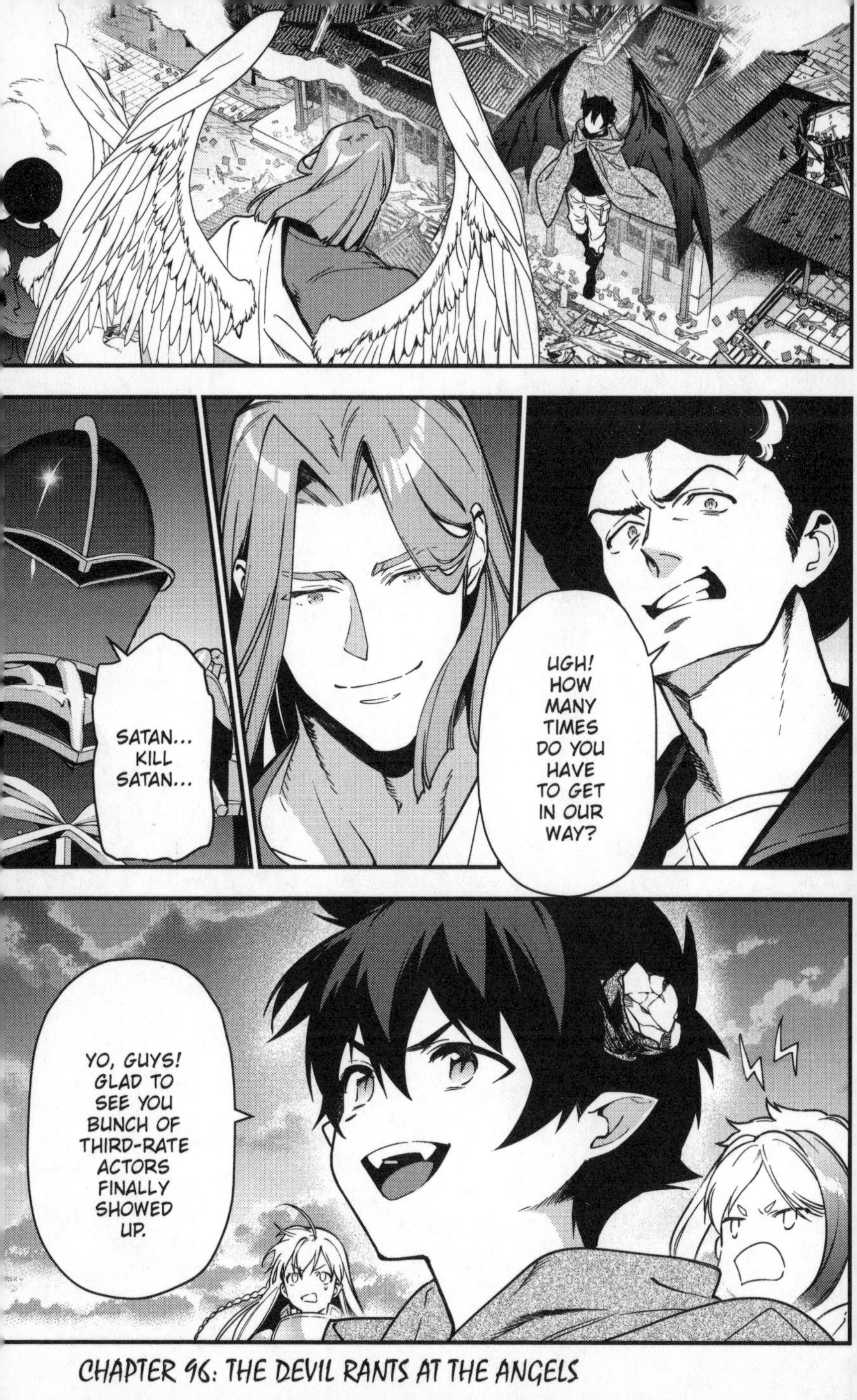
UGH! HOW MANY TIMES DO YOU HAVE TO GET IN OUR WAY?
SATAN... KILL SATAN...
YO, GUYS! GLAD TO SEE YOU BUNCH OF THIRD-RATE ACTORS FINALLY SHOWED UP.

CHAPTER 96: THE DEVIL RANTS AT THE ANGELS

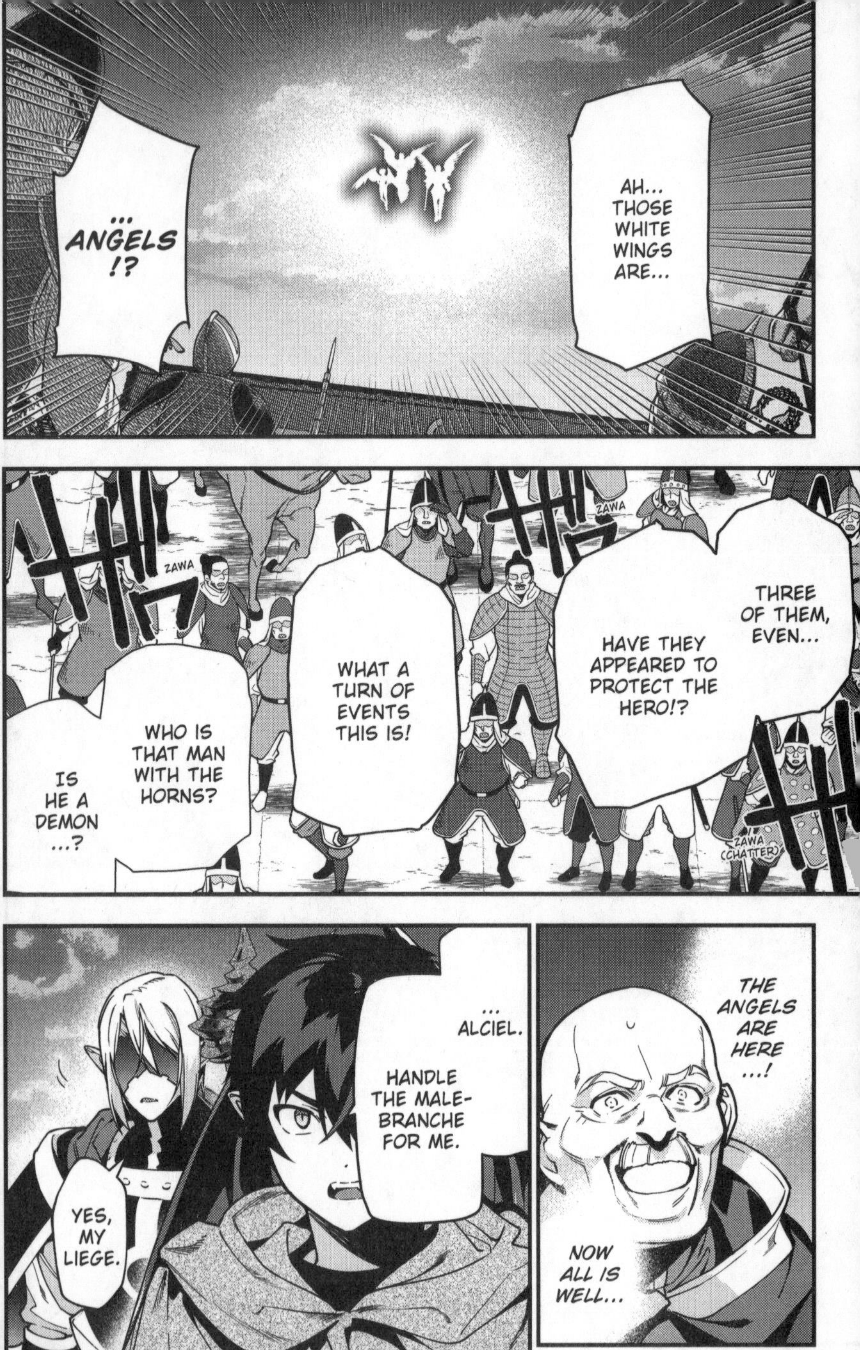
AH... THOSE WHITE WINGS ARE...
...ANGELS!?
ZAWA
THREE OF THEM, EVEN...
HAVE THEY APPEARED TO PROTECT THE HERO!?
ZAWA (CHATTER)
WHAT A TURN OF EVENTS THIS IS!
ZAWA
WHO IS THAT MAN WITH THE HORNS?
IS HE A DEMON...?
THE ANGELS ARE HERE...!
NOW ALL IS WELL...
...ALCIEL.
HANDLE THE MALE-BRANCHE FOR ME.
YES, MY LIEGE.

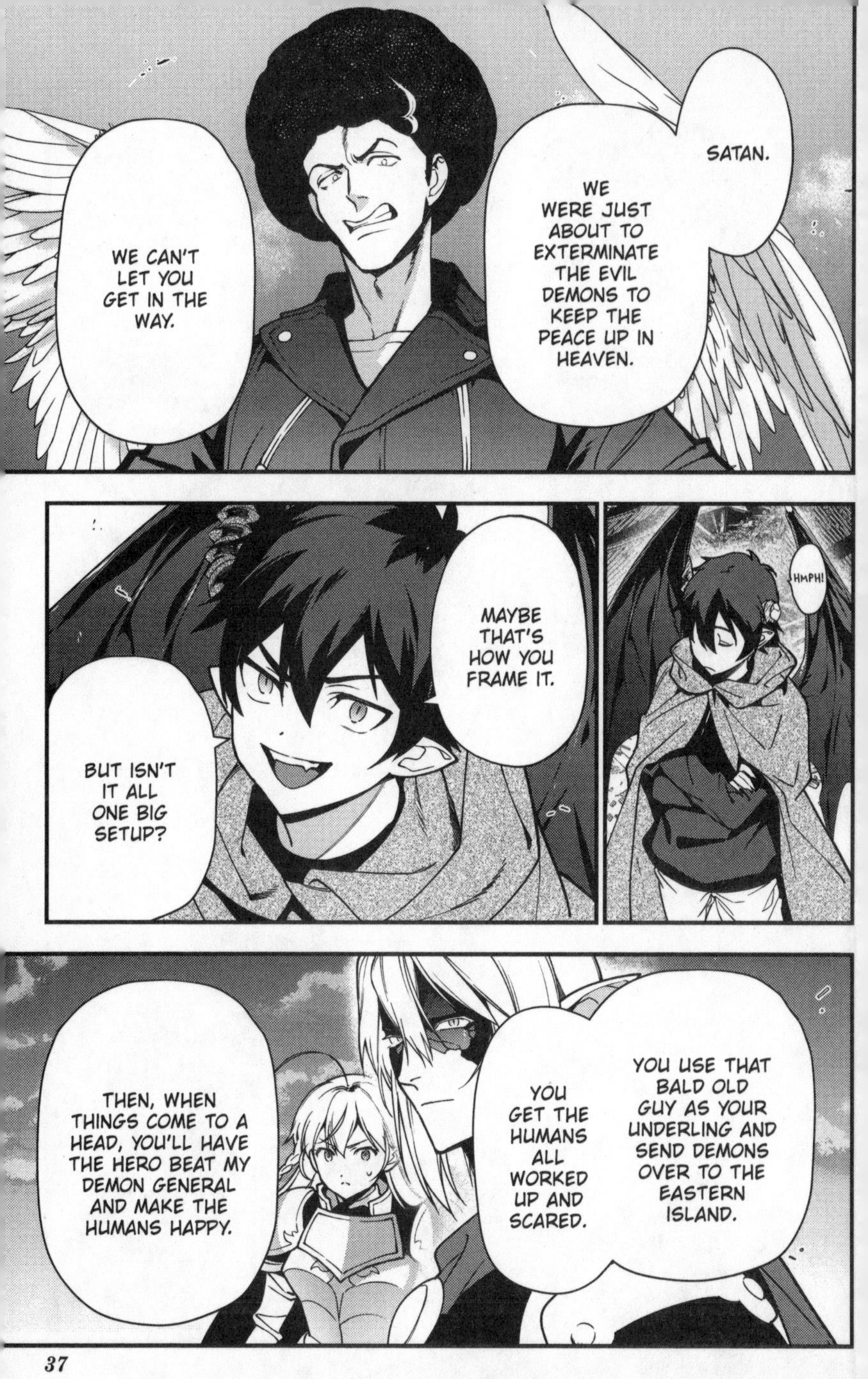
SATAN.
WE WERE JUST ABOUT TO EXTERMINATE THE EVIL DEMONS TO KEEP THE PEACE UP IN HEAVEN.
WE CAN'T LET YOU GET IN THE WAY.
HMPH!
MAYBE THAT'S HOW YOU FRAME IT.
BUT ISN'T IT ALL ONE BIG SETUP?
YOU USE THAT BALD OLD GUY AS YOUR UNDERLING AND SEND DEMONS OVER TO THE EASTERN ISLAND.
YOU GET THE HUMANS ALL WORKED UP AND SCARED.
THEN, WHEN THINGS COME TO A HEAD, YOU'LL HAVE THE HERO BEAT MY DEMON GENERAL AND MAKE THE HUMANS HAPPY.

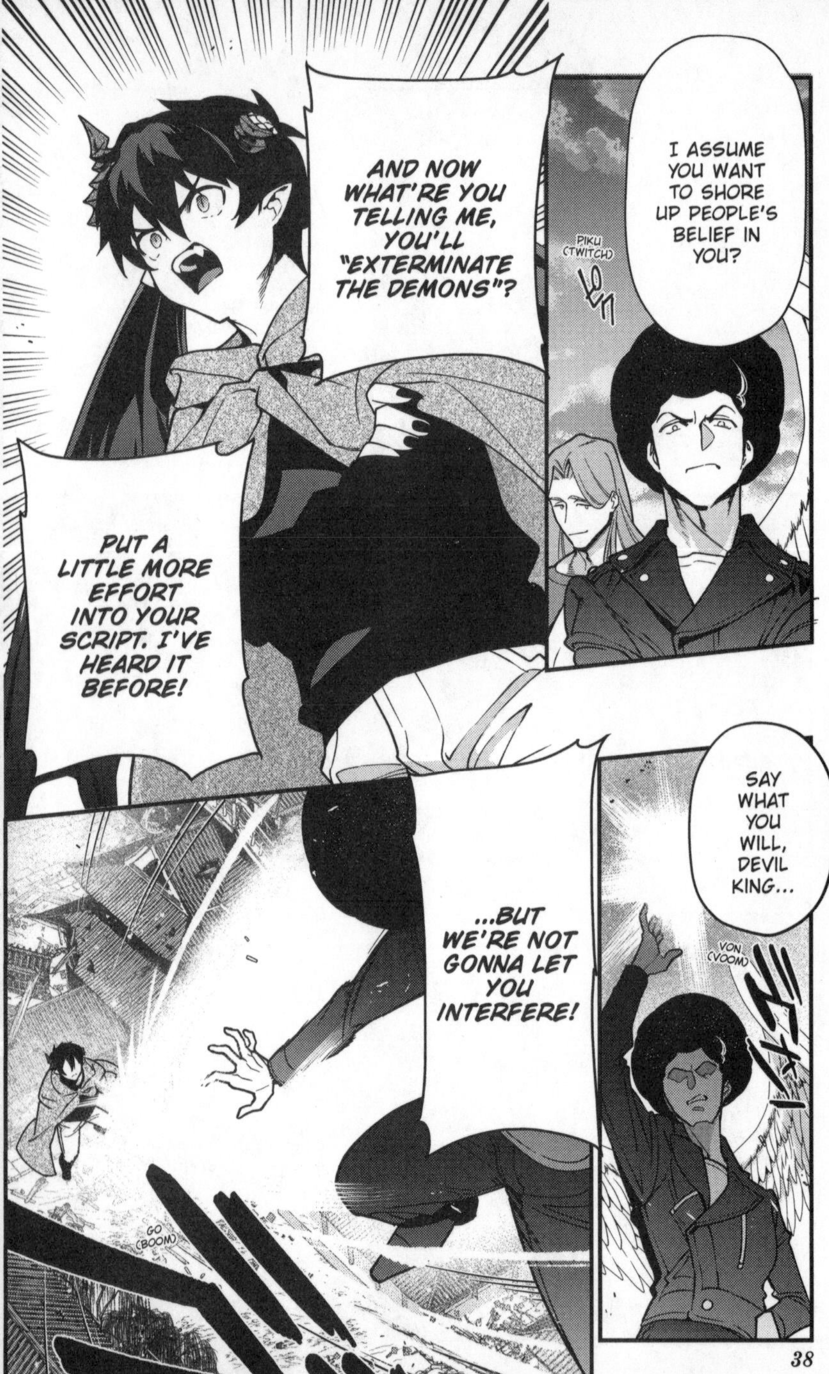
I ASSUME YOU WANT TO SHORE UP PEOPLE'S BELIEF IN YOU?
PIKU (TWITCH)
AND NOW WHAT'RE YOU TELLING ME, YOU'LL "EXTERMINATE THE DEMONS"?
PUT A LITTLE MORE EFFORT INTO YOUR SCRIPT. I'VE HEARD IT BEFORE!
SAY WHAT YOU WILL, DEVIL KING...
VON (VOOM)
...BUT WE'RE NOT GONNA LET YOU INTERFERE!
GO (BOOM)

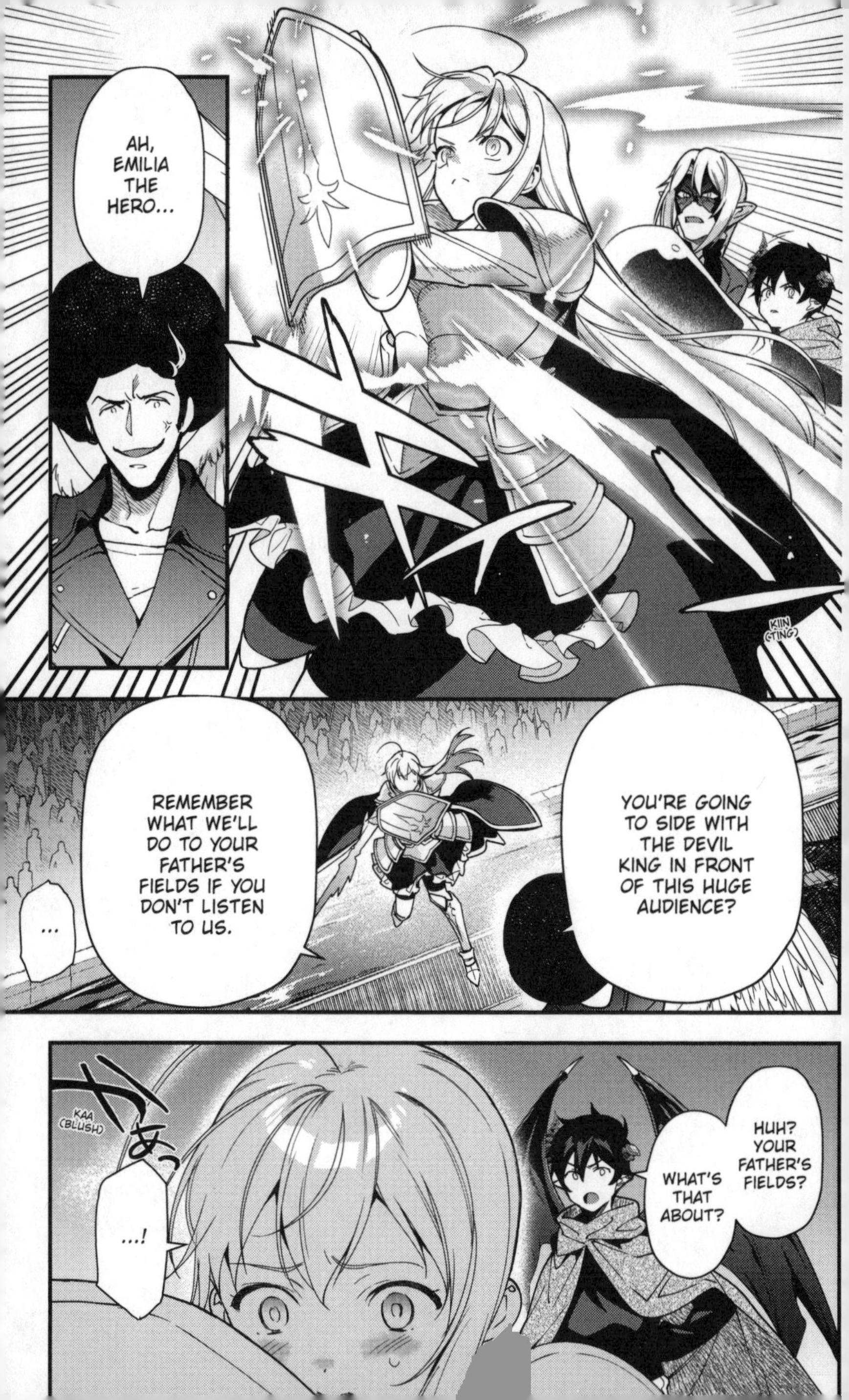
KIIN (TING)
AH, EMILIA THE HERO...
YOU'RE GOING TO SIDE WITH THE DEVIL KING IN FRONT OF THIS HUGE AUDIENCE?
REMEMBER WHAT WE'LL DO TO YOUR FATHER'S FIELDS IF YOU DON'T LISTEN TO US.
...
HUH? YOUR FATHER'S FIELDS?
WHAT'S THAT ABOUT?
KAA (BLUSH)
...!

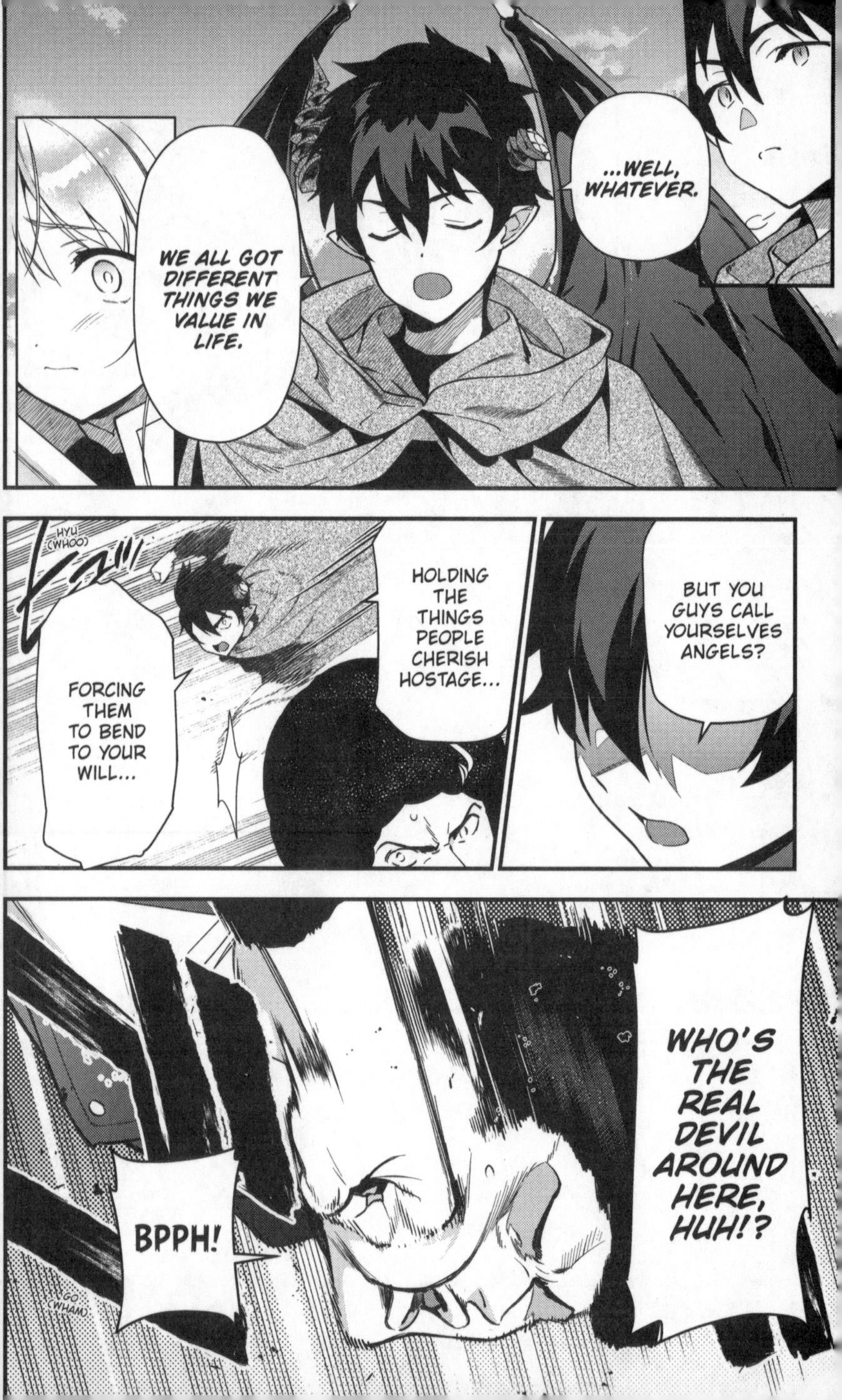
...WELL, WHATEVER.
WE ALL GOT DIFFERENT THINGS WE VALUE IN LIFE.
BUT YOU GUYS CALL YOURSELVES ANGELS?
HOLDING THE THINGS PEOPLE CHERISH HOSTAGE...
HYU (WHOO)
FORCING THEM TO BEND TO YOUR WILL...
WHO'S THE REAL DEVIL AROUND HERE, HUH!?
BPPH!
GO (WHAM)

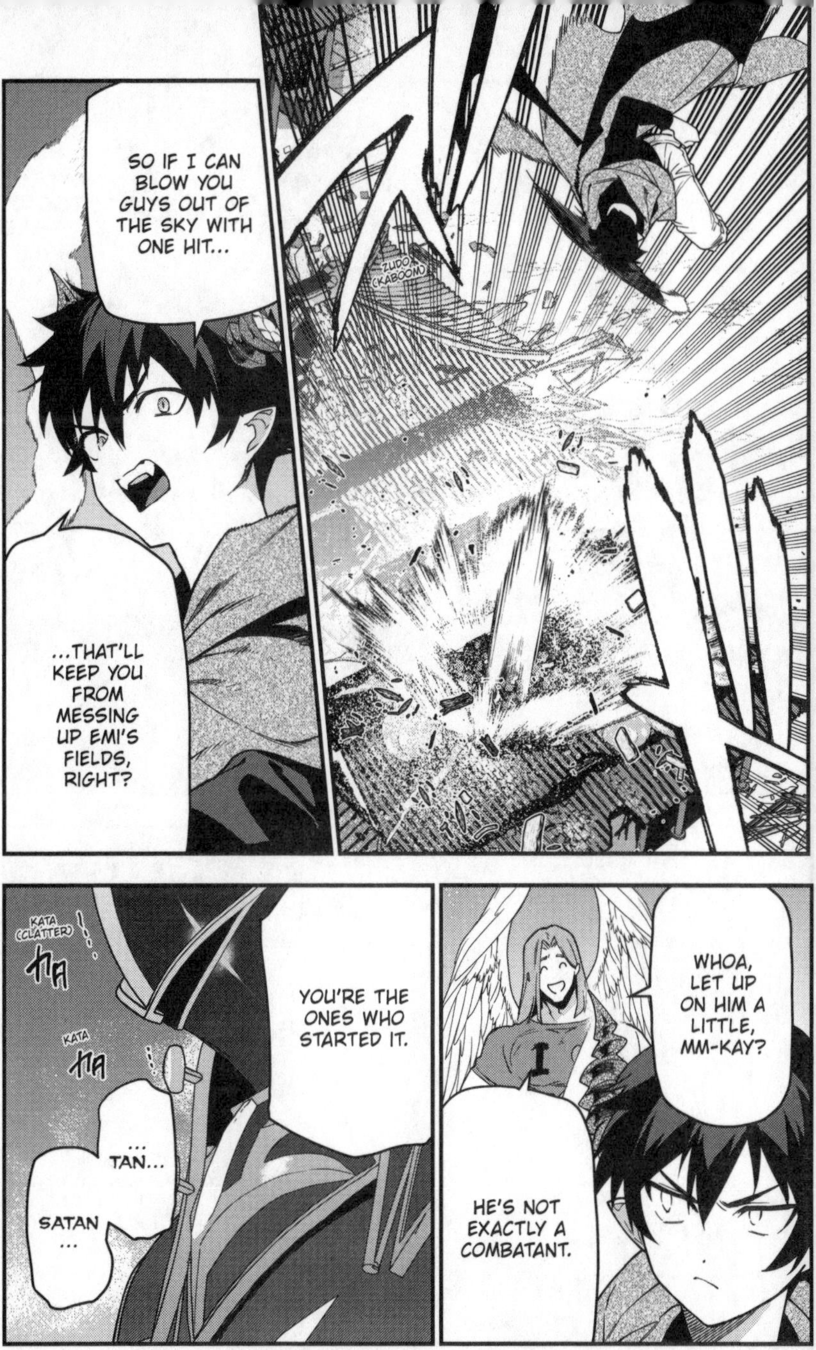
ZUDO (KABOOM)
SO IF I CAN BLOW YOU GUYS OUT OF THE SKY WITH ONE HIT...
...THAT'LL KEEP YOU FROM MESSING UP EMI'S FIELDS, RIGHT?
WHOA, LET UP ON HIM A LITTLE, MM-KAY?
HE'S NOT EXACTLY A COMBATANT.
YOU'RE THE ONES WHO STARTED IT.
KATA (CLATTER)
KATA
... TAN...
SATAN ...

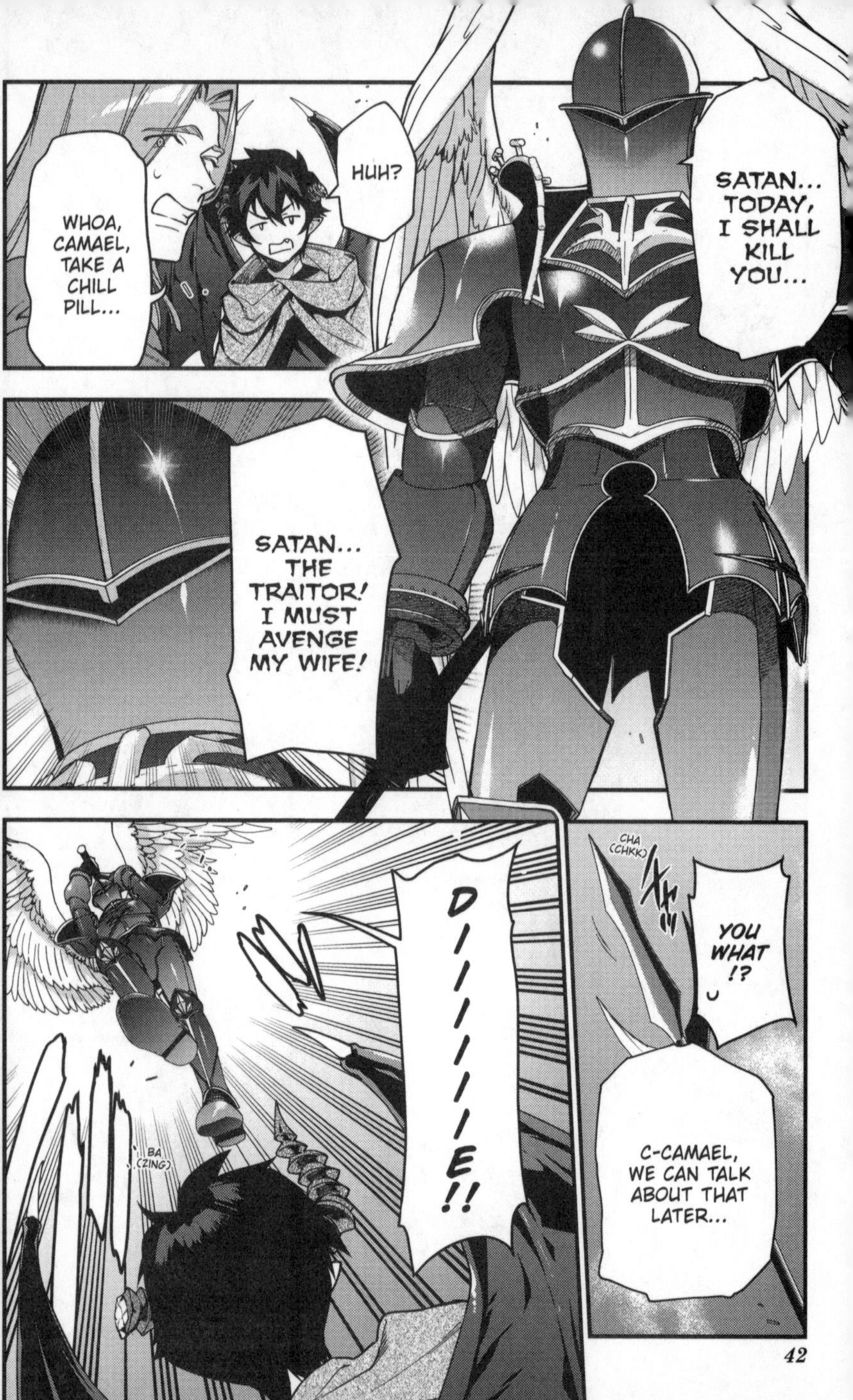
SATAN... TODAY, I SHALL KILL YOU...
HUH?
WHOA, CAMAEL, TAKE A CHILL PILL...
SATAN... THE TRAITOR! I MUST AVENGE MY WIFE!
CHA (CHKK)
YOU WHAT!?
C-CAMAEL, WE CAN TALK ABOUT THAT LATER...
DIIIIIIIE!!
BA (ZING)

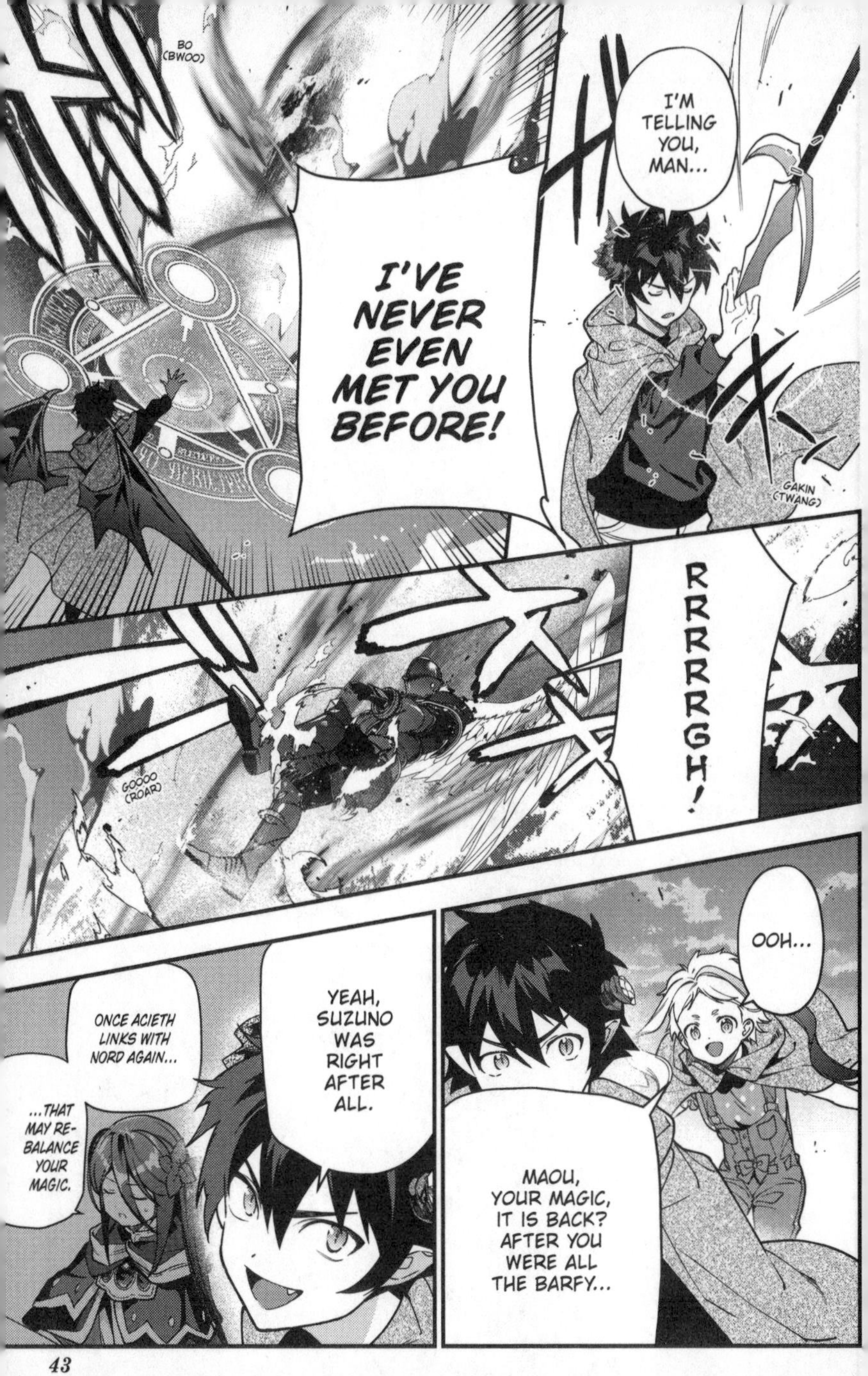
I'M TELLING YOU, MAN...
I'VE NEVER EVEN MET YOU BEFORE!
GAKIN (TWANG)
BO (BWOO)
RRRRRGH!
GOOOO (ROAR)
OOH...
MAOU, YOUR MAGIC, IT IS BACK? AFTER YOU WERE ALL THE BARFY...
YEAH, SUZUNO WAS RIGHT AFTER ALL.
ONCE ACIETH LINKS WITH NORD AGAIN...
...THAT MAY RE-BALANCE YOUR MAGIC.

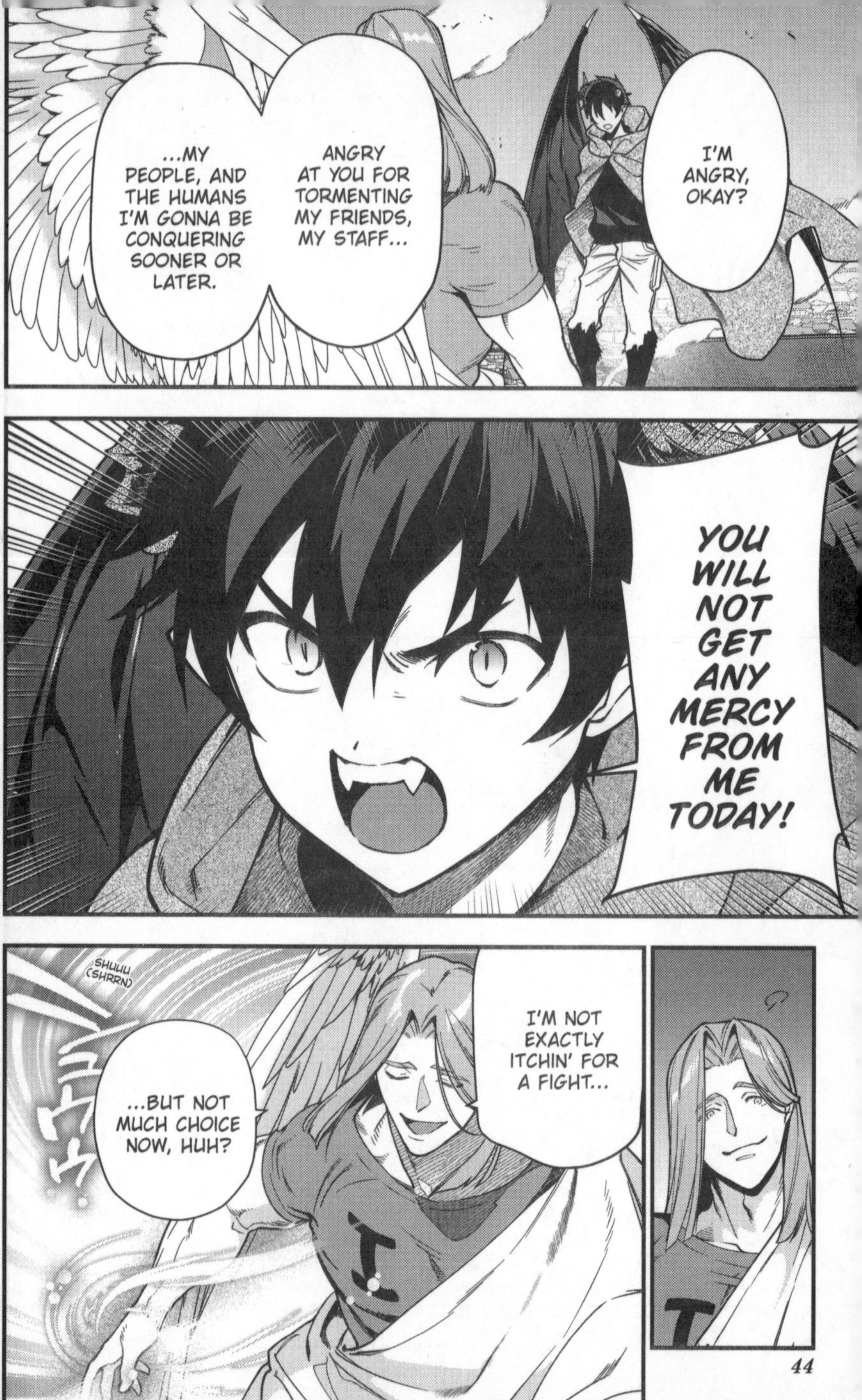
I'M ANGRY, OKAY?
ANGRY AT YOU FOR TORMENTING MY FRIENDS, MY STAFF...
...MY PEOPLE, AND THE HUMANS I'M GONNA BE CONQUERING SOONER OR LATER.
YOU WILL NOT GET ANY MERCY FROM ME TODAY!
I'M NOT EXACTLY ITCHIN' FOR A FIGHT...
SHUUU (SHRRN)
...BUT NOT MUCH CHOICE NOW, HUH?

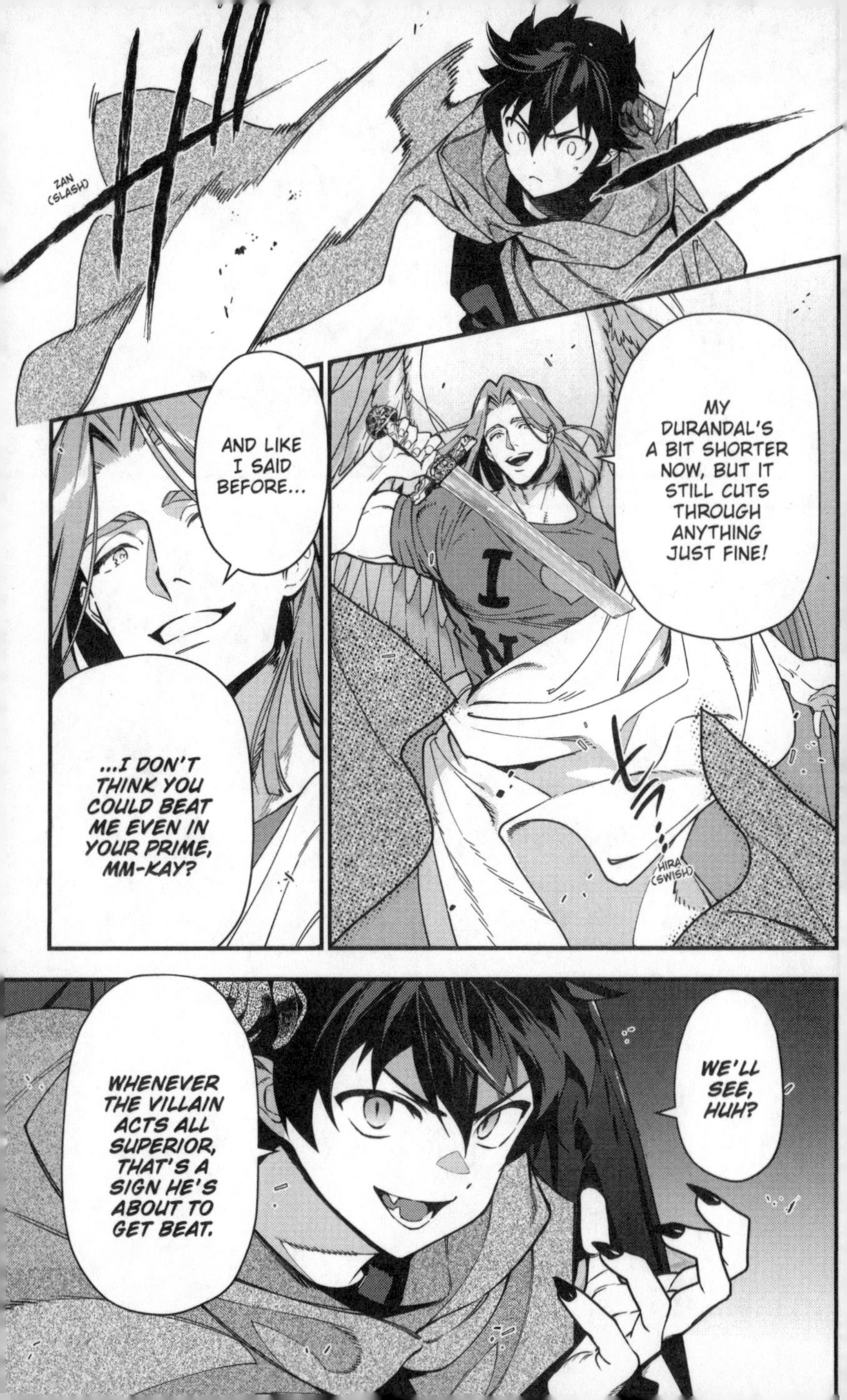
ZAN (SLASH)
MY DURANDAL'S A BIT SHORTER NOW, BUT IT STILL CUTS THROUGH ANYTHING JUST FINE!
HIRA (SWISH)
AND LIKE I SAID BEFORE...
...I DON'T THINK YOU COULD BEAT ME EVEN IN YOUR PRIME, MM-KAY?
WE'LL SEE, HUH?
WHENEVER THE VILLAIN ACTS ALL SUPERIOR, THAT'S A SIGN HE'S ABOUT TO GET BEAT.

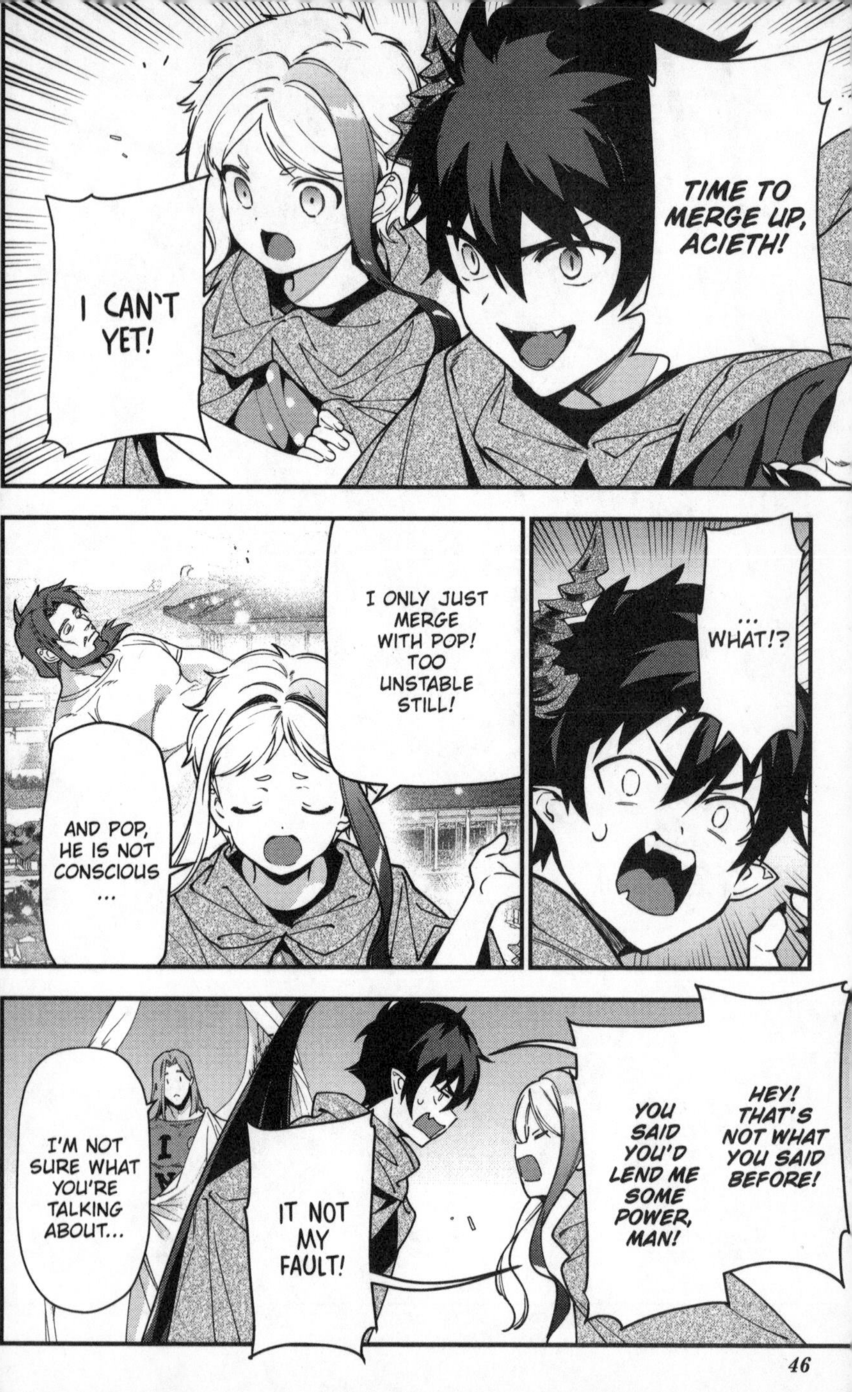
TIME TO MERGE UP, ACIETH!
I CAN'T YET!
... WHAT!?
I ONLY JUST MERGE WITH POP! TOO UNSTABLE STILL!
AND POP, HE IS NOT CONSCIOUS ...
HEY! THAT'S NOT WHAT YOU SAID BEFORE!
YOU SAID YOU'D LEND ME SOME POWER, MAN!
IT NOT MY FAULT!
I'M NOT SURE WHAT YOU'RE TALKING ABOUT...

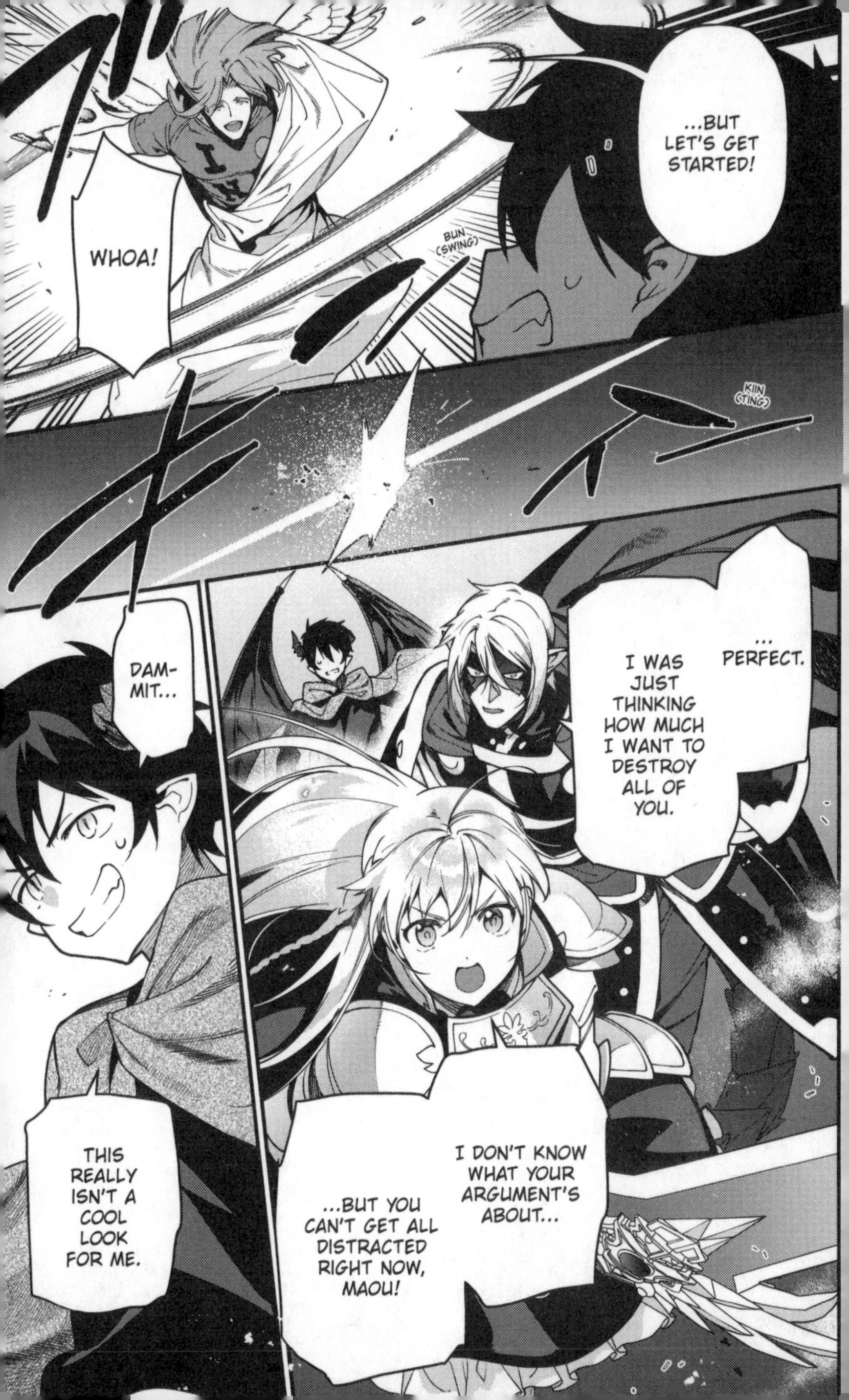
...BUT LET'S GET STARTED!
BUN (SWING)
WHOA!
KIIN (TING)
...PERFECT.
I WAS JUST THINKING HOW MUCH I WANT TO DESTROY ALL OF YOU.
I DON'T KNOW WHAT YOUR ARGUMENT'S ABOUT...
...BUT YOU CAN'T GET ALL DISTRACTED RIGHT NOW, MAOU!
DAM-MIT...
THIS REALLY ISN'T A COOL LOOK FOR ME.

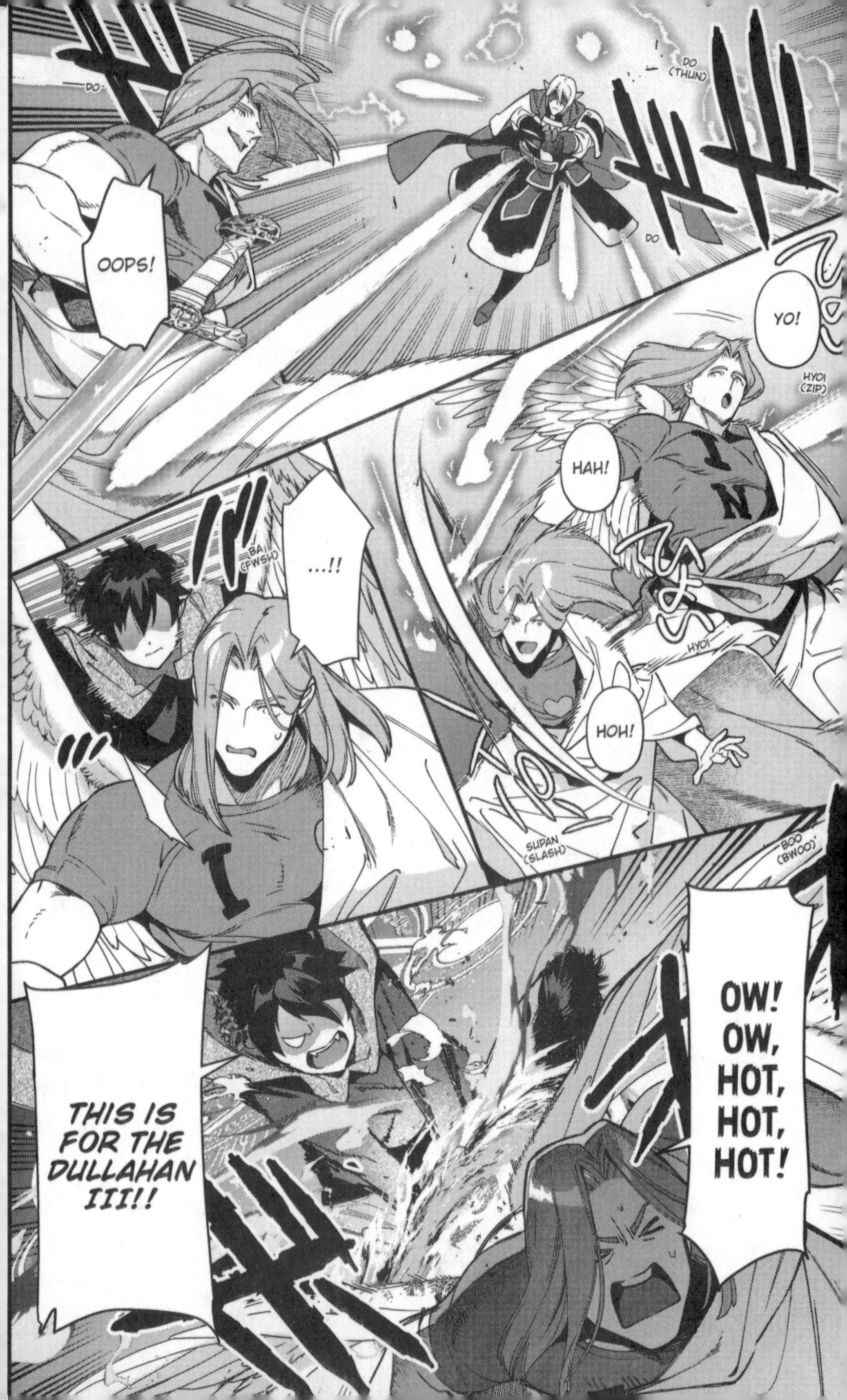
DO (THUNK)
DO
DO
OOPS!
YO!
HYOI (ZIP)
HAH!
HYOI
HOH!
SUPAN (SLASH)
BOO (BWOO)
BA (FWSH)
...!!
OW! OW, HOT, HOT, HOT!
THIS IS FOR THE DULLAHAN III!!

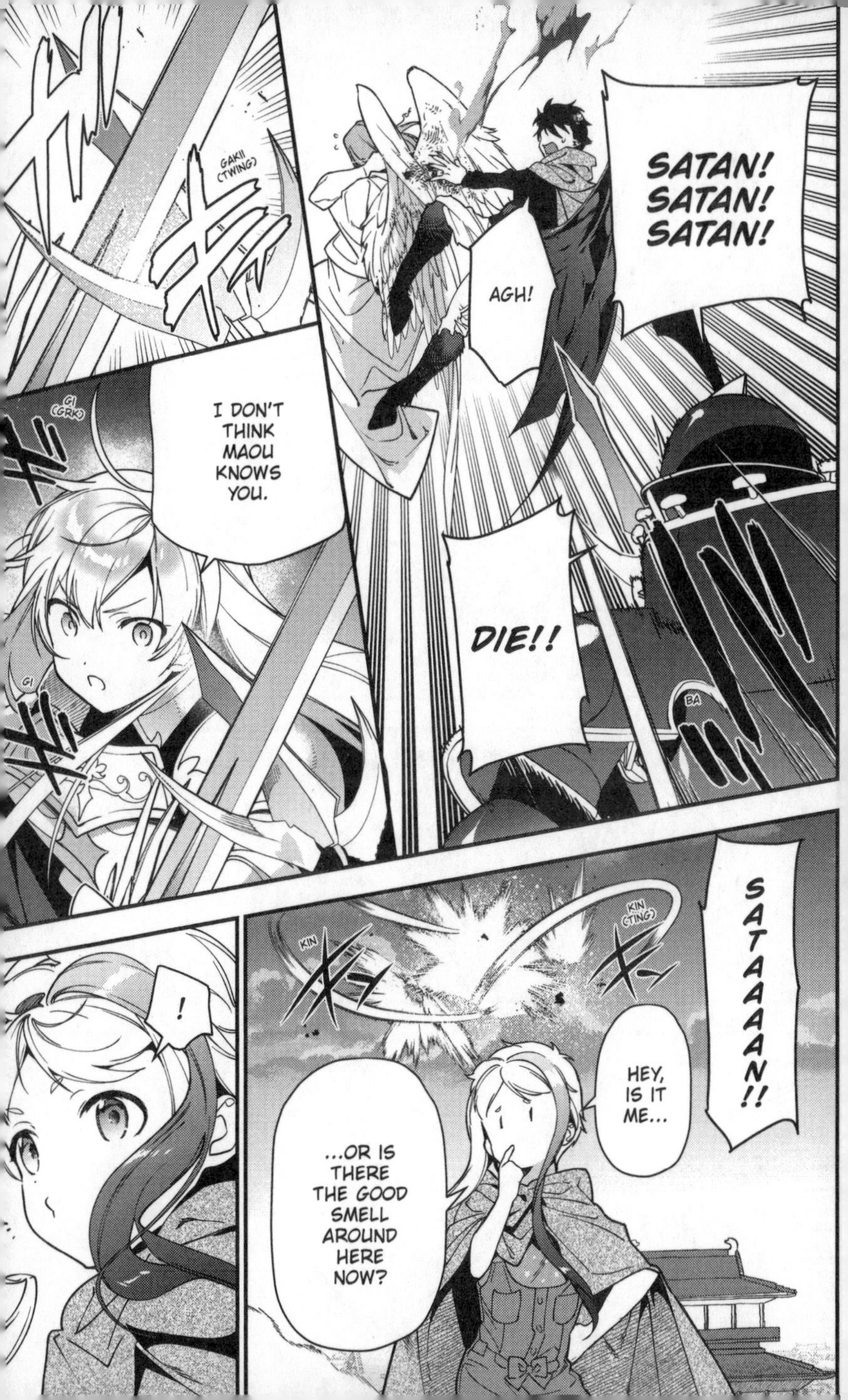

SATAN! SATAN! SATAN!
AGH!
DIE!!
BA
GAKII (TWING)
I DON'T THINK MAOU KNOWS YOU.
GI (GRK)
GI
SATAAAAAN!!
KIN (TING)
KIN
HEY, IS IT ME...
...OR IS THERE THE GOOD SMELL AROUND HERE NOW?
!

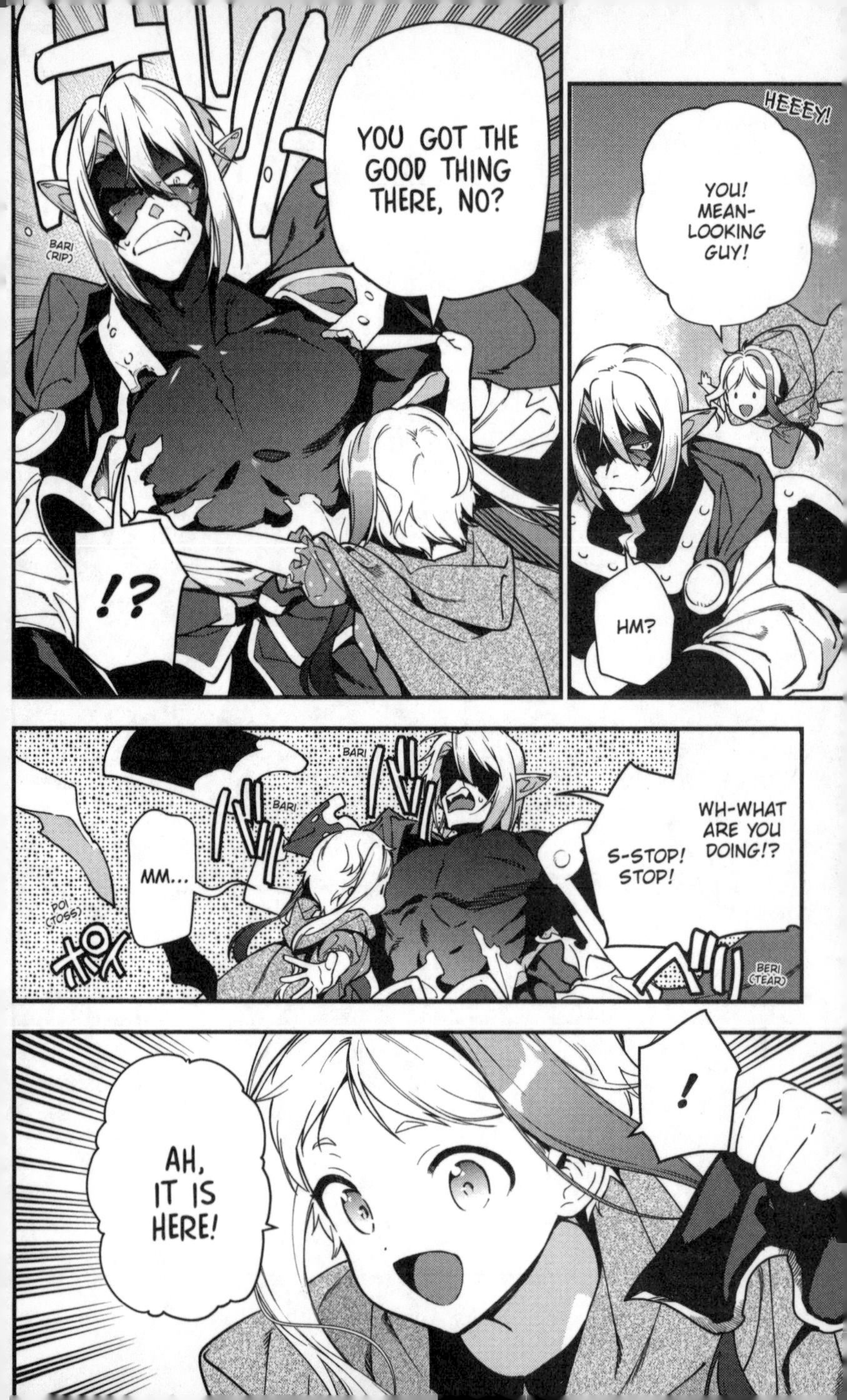
HEEEY!
YOU! MEAN-LOOKING GUY!
HM?
YOU GOT THE GOOD THING THERE, NO?
BARI (RIP)
!?
BERI (TEAR)
WH-WHAT ARE YOU DOING!?
S-STOP! STOP!
BARI
BARI
MM...
POI (TOSS)
!
AH, IT IS HERE!

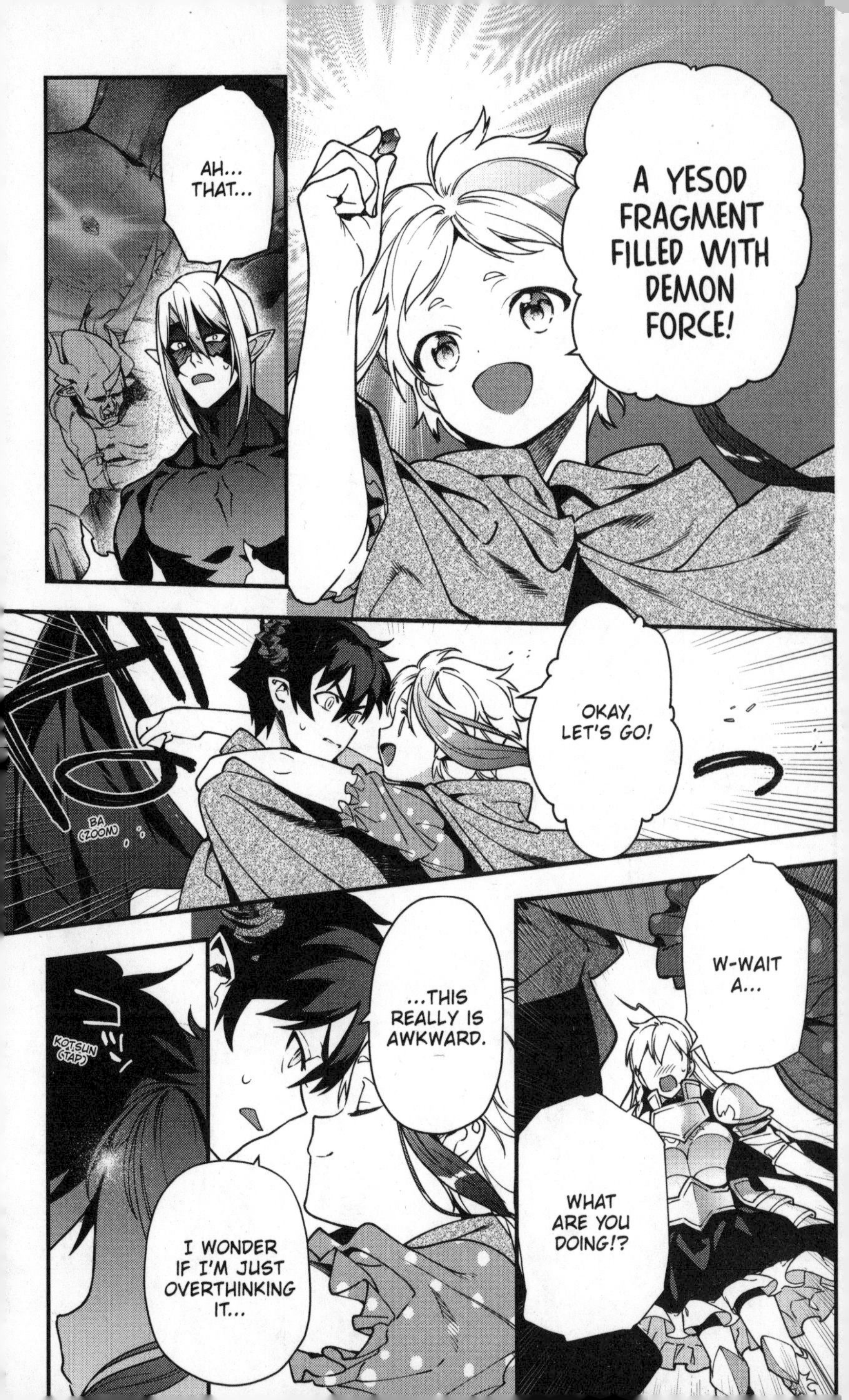
A YESOD FRAGMENT FILLED WITH DEMON FORCE!
AH... THAT...
OKAY, LET'S GO!
BA (ZOOM)
W-WAIT A...
WHAT ARE YOU DOING!?
...THIS REALLY IS AWKWARD.
I WONDER IF I'M JUST OVERTHINKING IT...
KOTSUN (TAP)

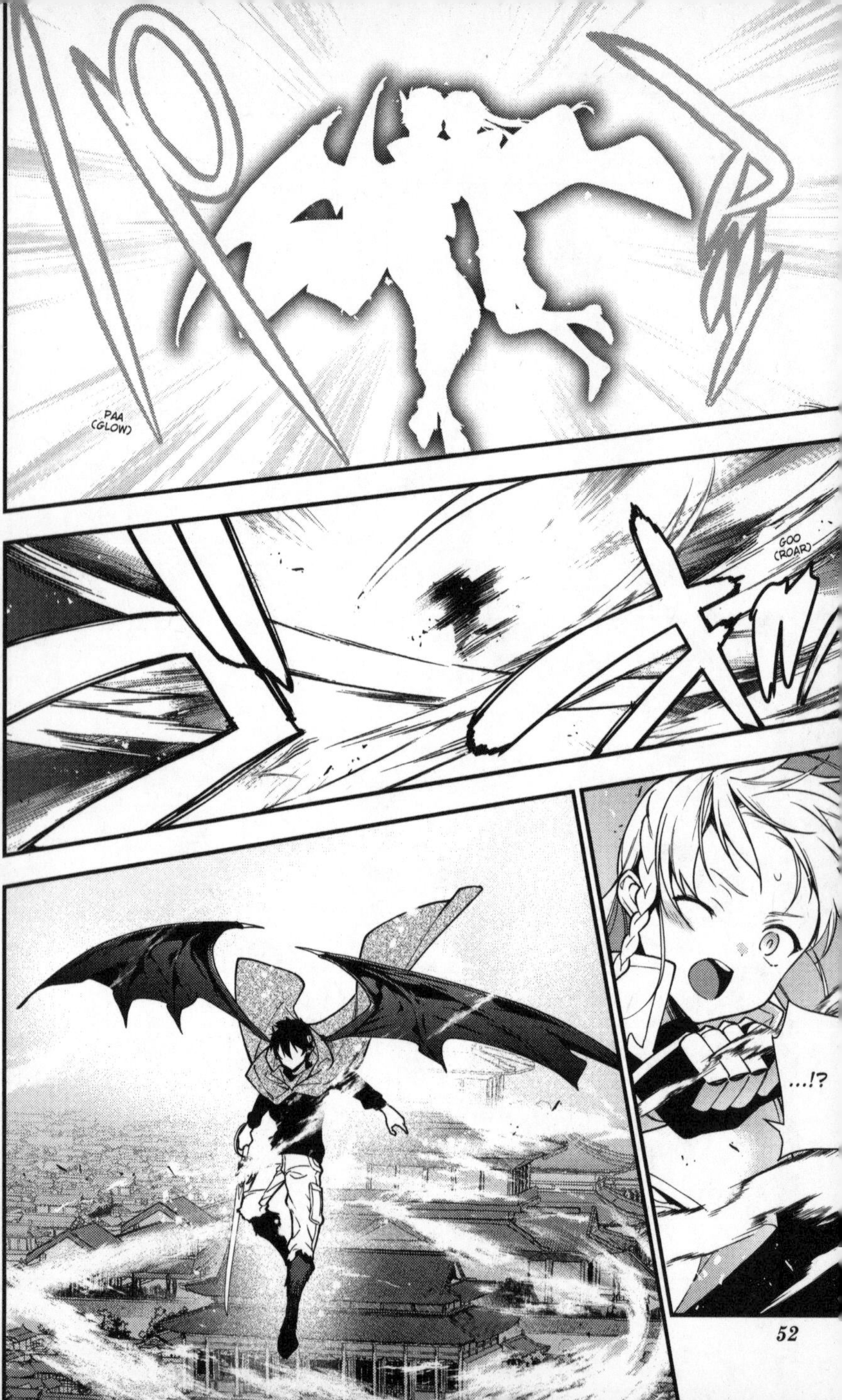
PAA
(GLOW)
GOO
(ROAR)
...!?

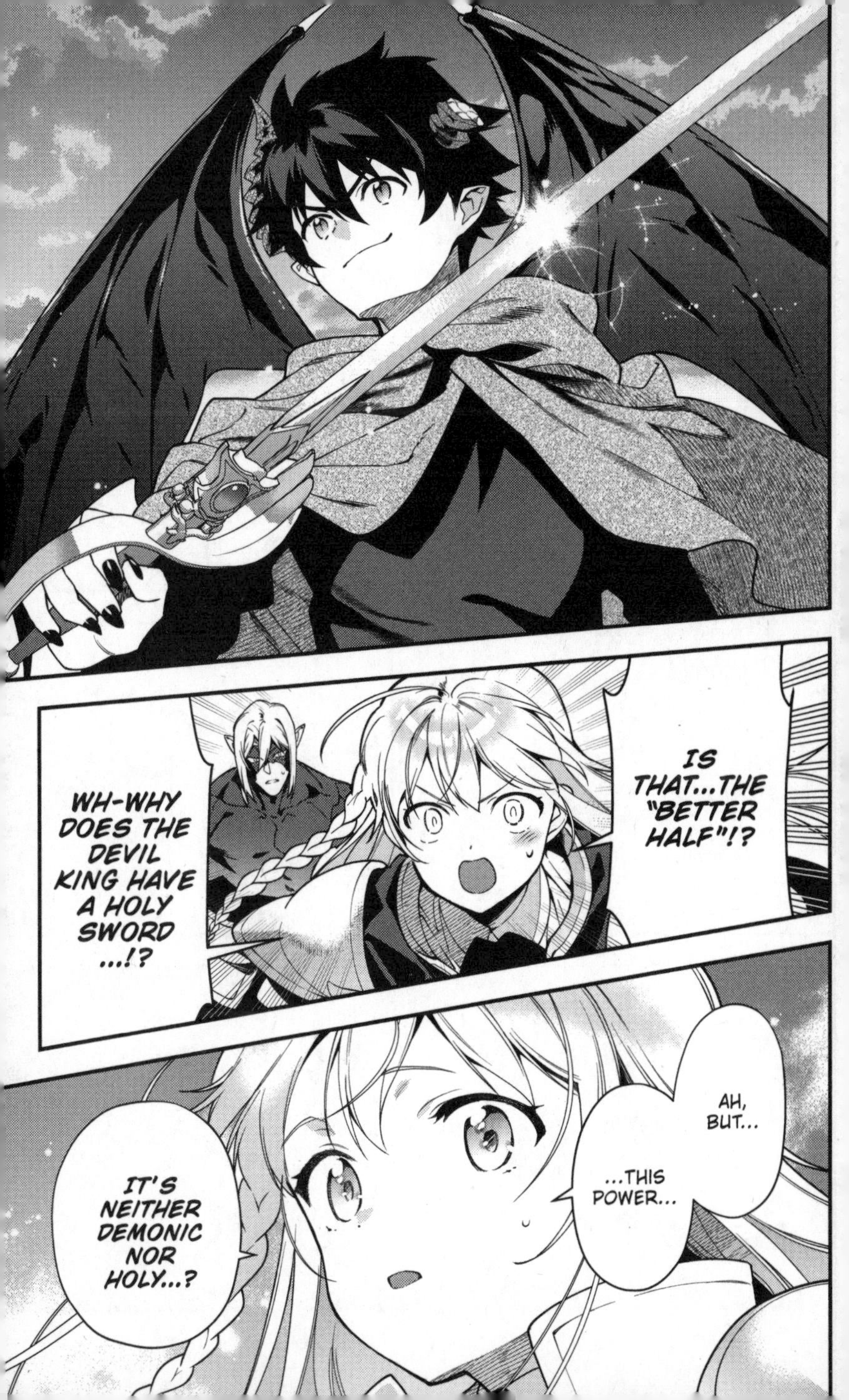
IS THAT...THE "BETTER HALF"!?
WH-WHY DOES THE DEVIL KING HAVE A HOLY SWORD ...!?
AH, BUT...
...THIS POWER...
IT'S NEITHER DEMONIC NOR HOLY...?

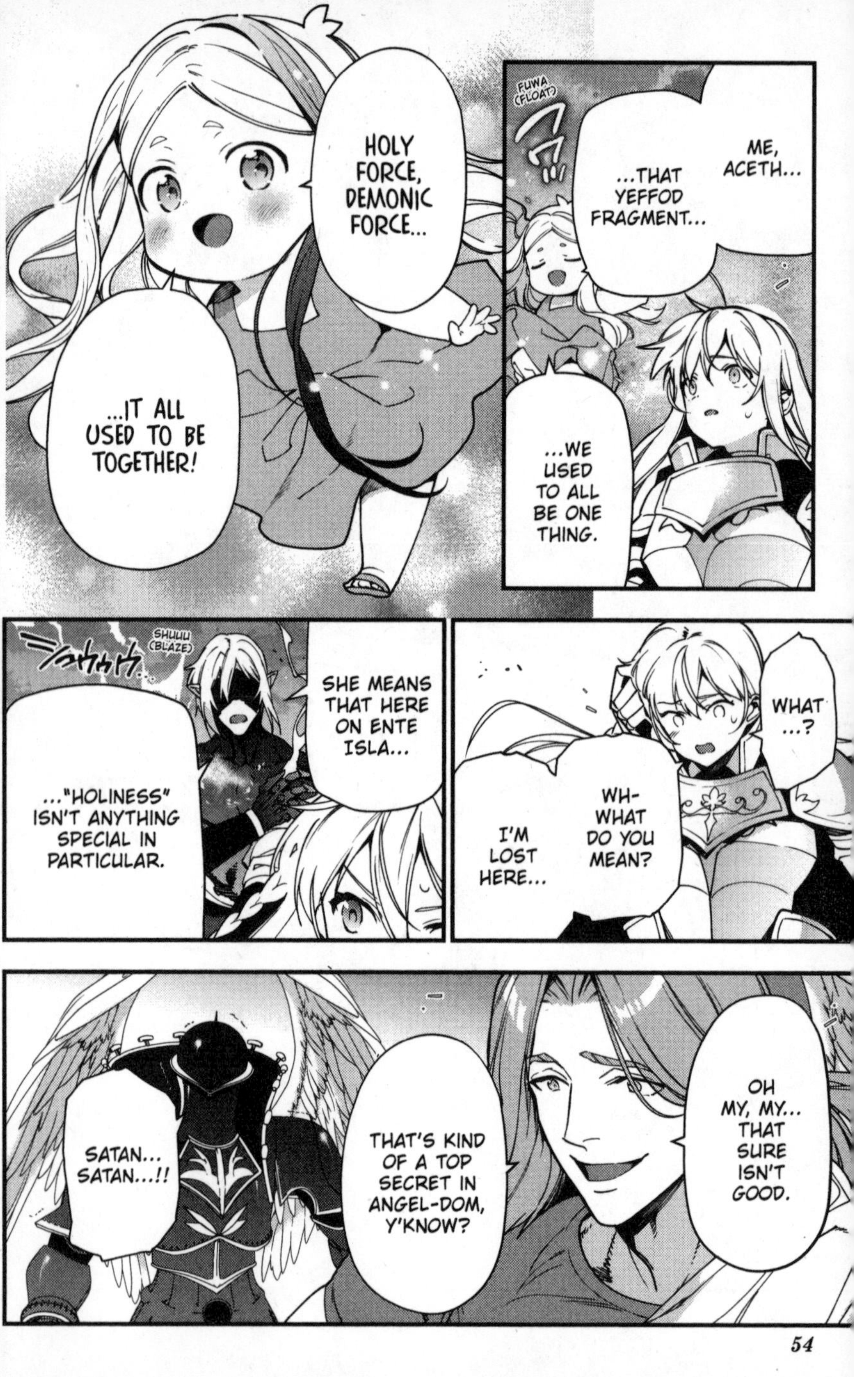
FUWA (FLOAT)
ME, ACETH...
...THAT YEFFOD FRAGMENT...
...WE USED TO ALL BE ONE THING.
HOLY FORCE, DEMONIC FORCE...
...IT ALL USED TO BE TOGETHER!
WHAT ...?
WH- WHAT DO YOU MEAN?
I'M LOST HERE...
SHUUU (BLAZE)
SHE MEANS THAT HERE ON ENTE ISLA...
..."HOLINESS" ISN'T ANYTHING SPECIAL IN PARTICULAR.
OH MY, MY... THAT SURE ISN'T GOOD.
THAT'S KIND OF A TOP SECRET IN ANGEL-DOM, Y'KNOW?
SATAN... SATAN...!!

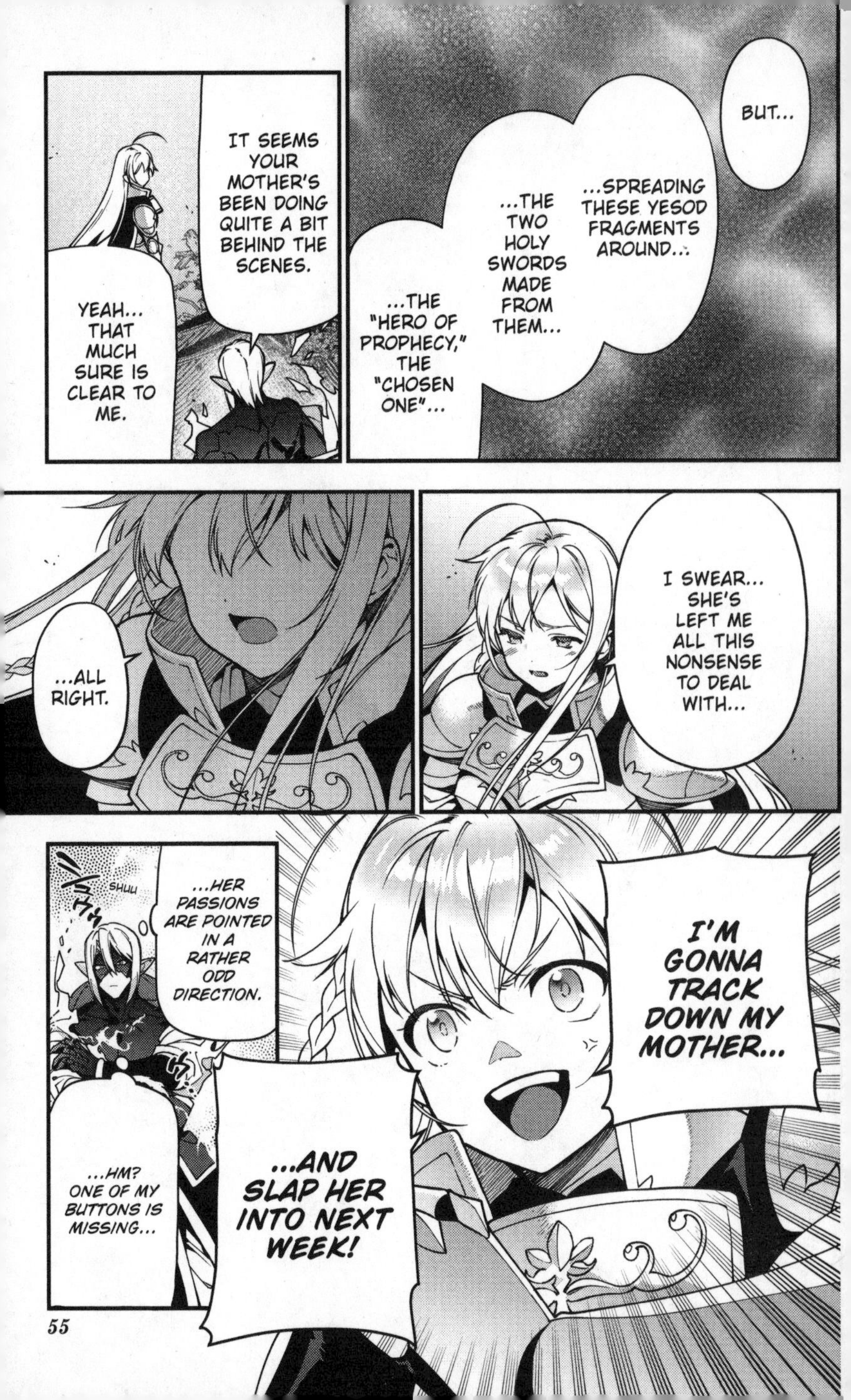
BUT...
...SPREADING THESE YESOD FRAGMENTS AROUND...
...THE TWO HOLY SWORDS MADE FROM THEM...
...THE "HERO OF PROPHECY," THE "CHOSEN ONE"...
IT SEEMS YOUR MOTHER'S BEEN DOING QUITE A BIT BEHIND THE SCENES.
YEAH... THAT MUCH SURE IS CLEAR TO ME.
I SWEAR... SHE'S LEFT ME ALL THIS NONSENSE TO DEAL WITH...
...ALL RIGHT.
I'M GONNA TRACK DOWN MY MOTHER...
...AND SLAP HER INTO NEXT WEEK!
SHUU
...HER PASSIONS ARE POINTED IN A RATHER ODD DIRECTION.
...HM? ONE OF MY BUTTONS IS MISSING...

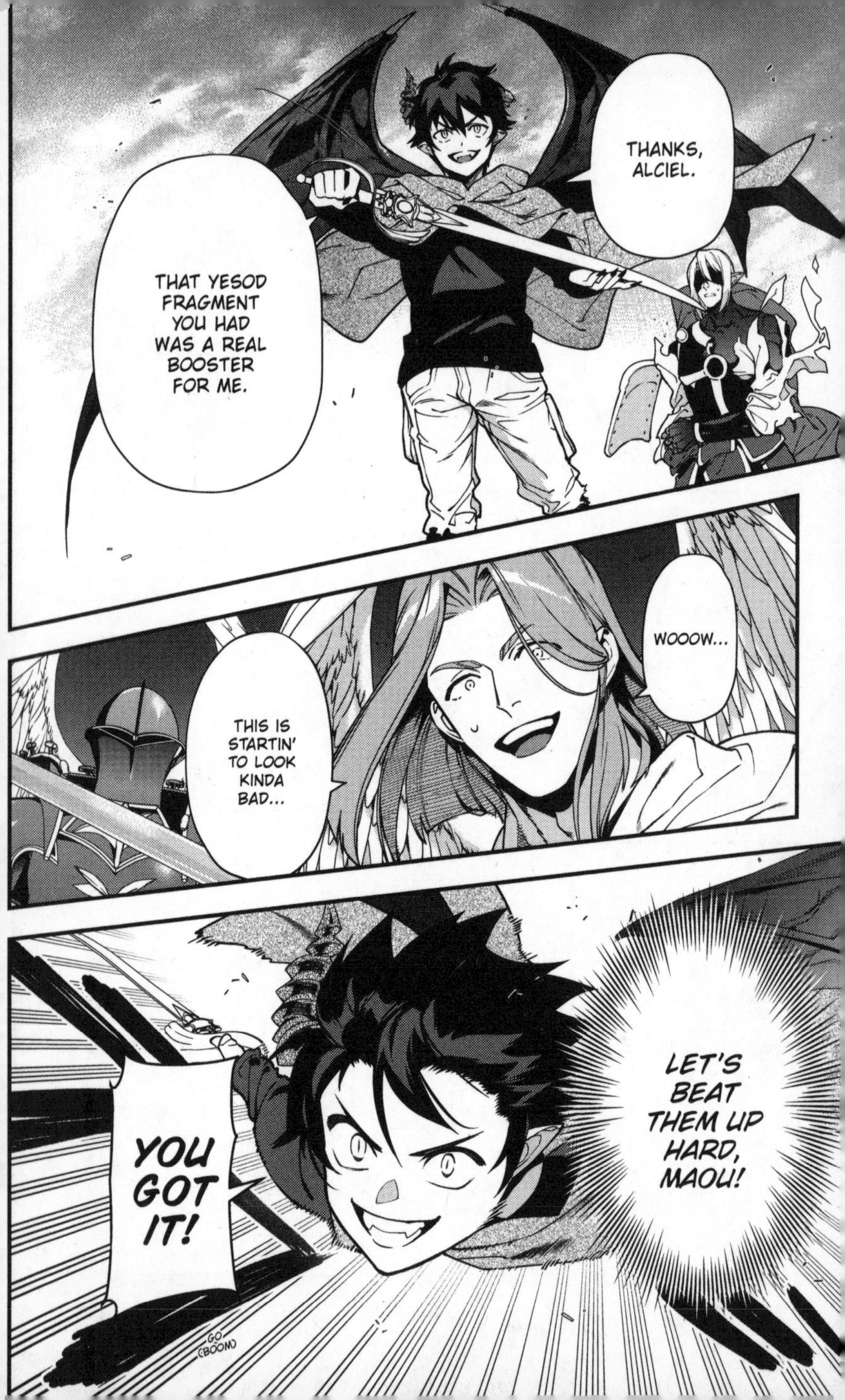
THANKS, ALCIEL.
THAT YESOD FRAGMENT YOU HAD WAS A REAL BOOSTER FOR ME.
WOOOW...
THIS IS STARTIN' TO LOOK KINDA BAD...
LET'S BEAT THEM UP HARD, MAOU!
YOU GOT IT!
GO (BOOM)

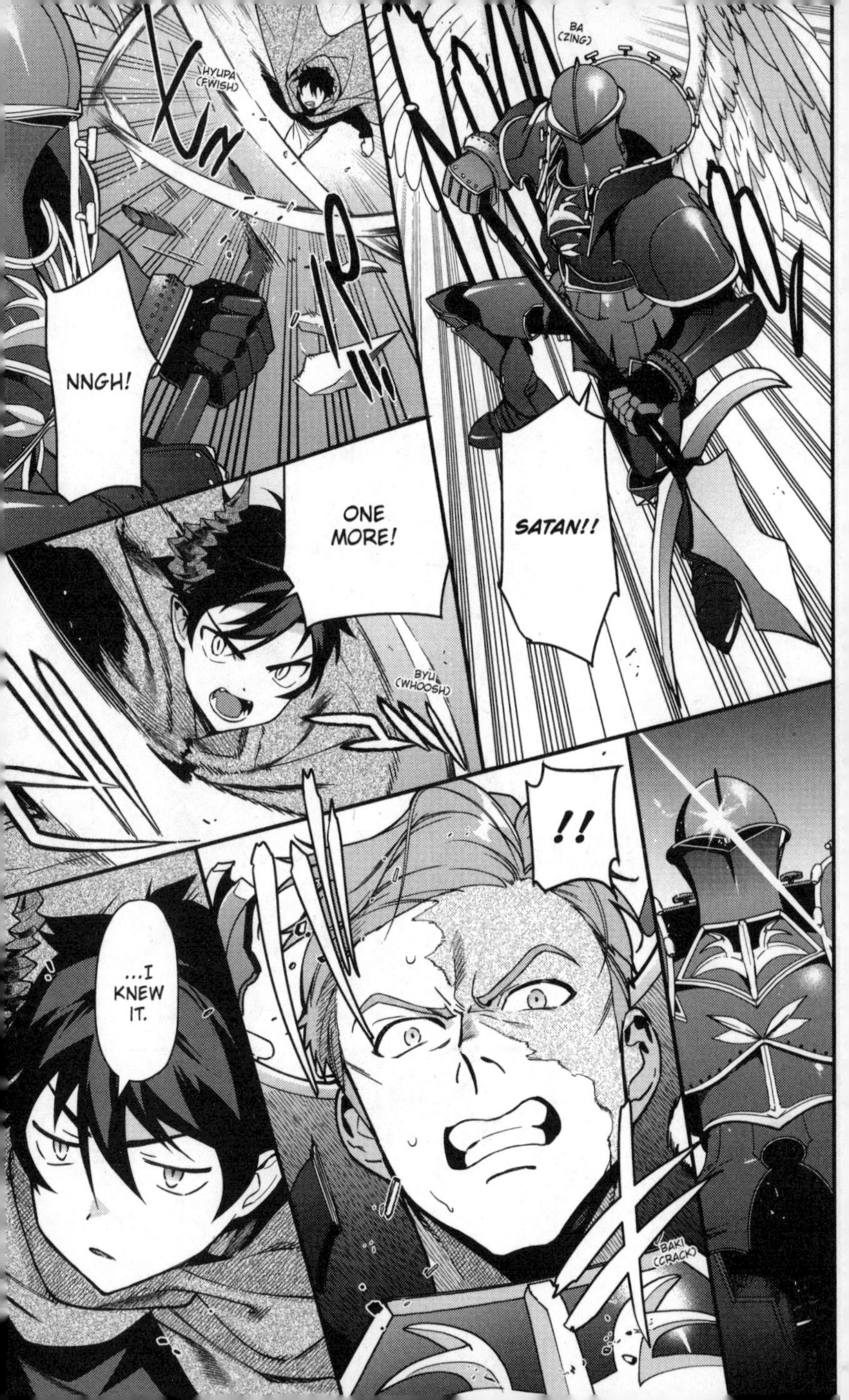
BA (ZING)
SATAN!!
HYUPA (FWISH)
NNGH!
ONE MORE!
BYU (WHOOSH)
!!
BAKI (CRACK)
...I KNEW IT.

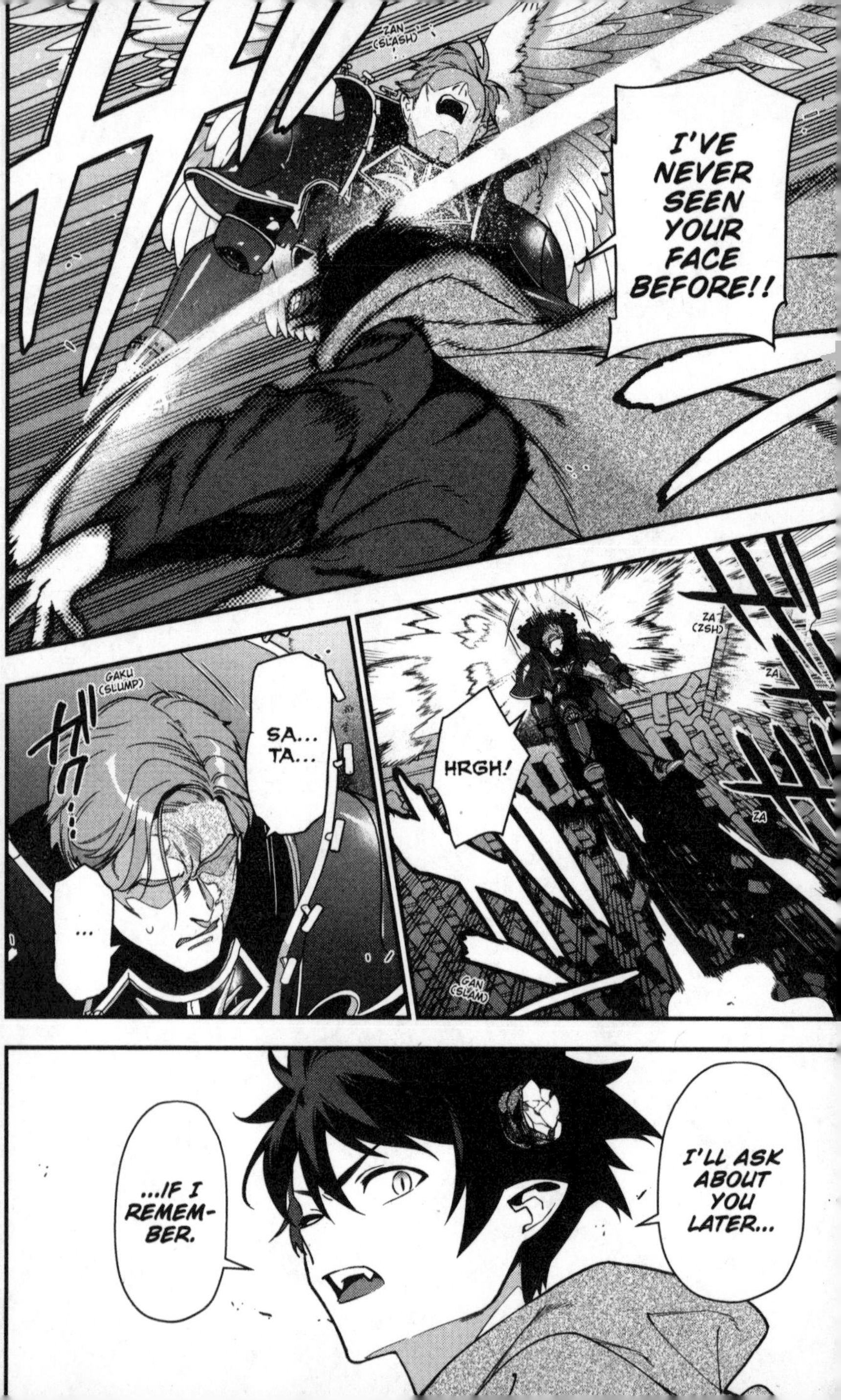
ZAN (SLASH)
I'VE NEVER SEEN YOUR FACE BEFORE!!
ZA (ZSH)
ZA
ZA
HRGH!
GAN (SLAM)
GAKU (SLUMP)
SA... TA...
...
I'LL ASK ABOUT YOU LATER...
...IF I REMEM-BER.

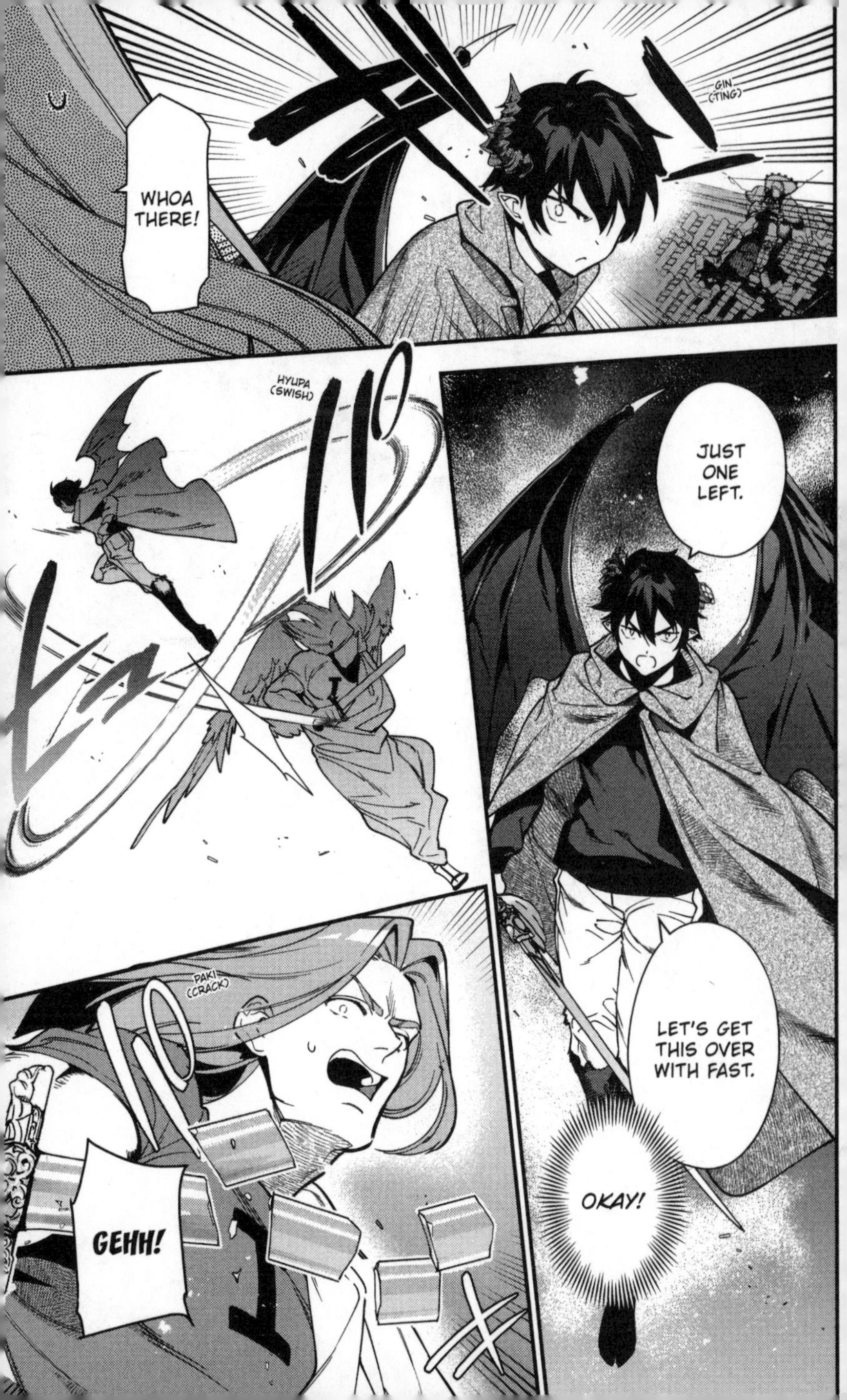
GIN (TING)
WHOA THERE!
JUST ONE LEFT.
LET'S GET THIS OVER WITH FAST.
OKAY!
HYUPA (SWISH)
PAKI (CRACK)
GEHH!

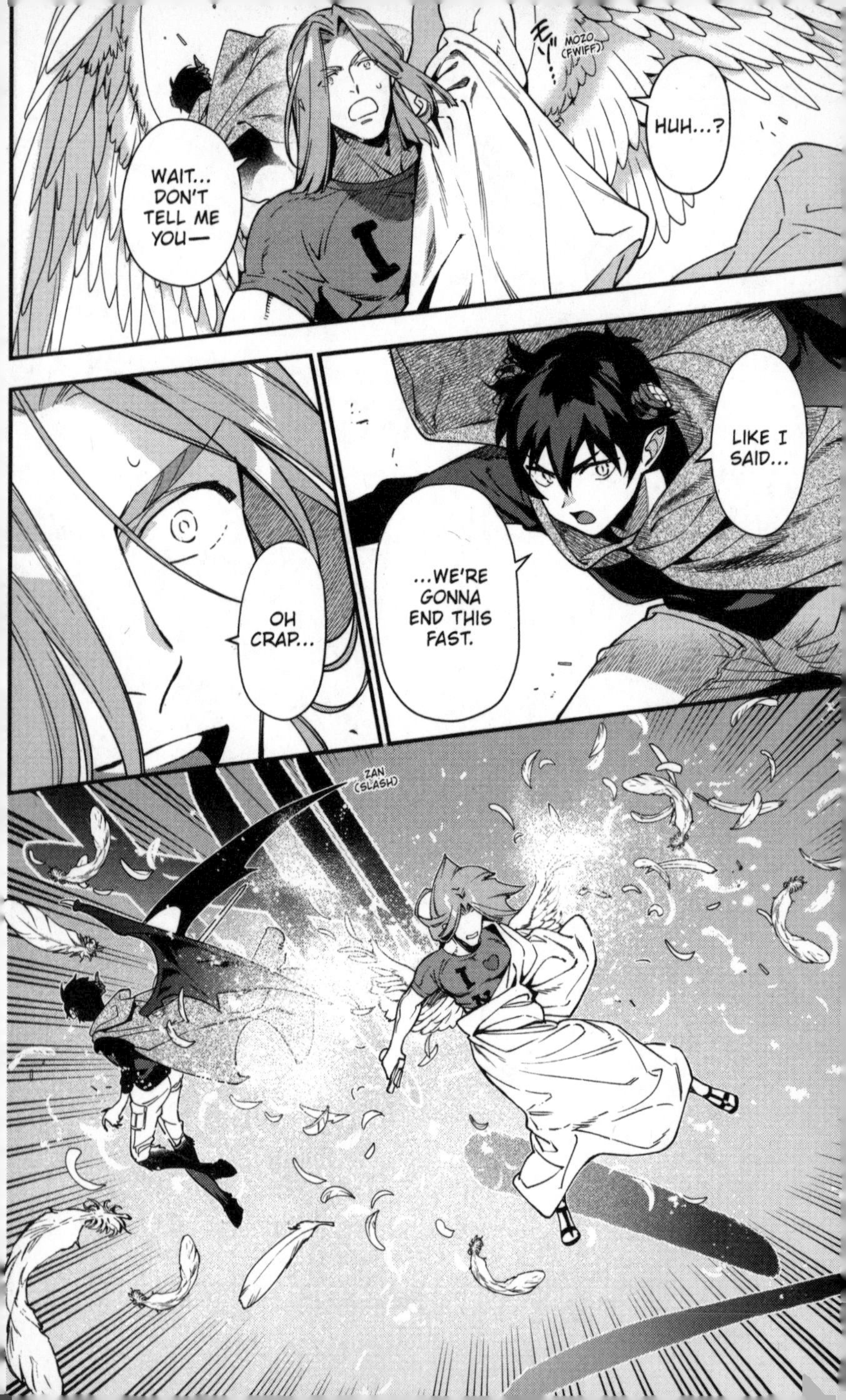
MOZO (FWIFF)
HUH...?
WAIT... DON'T TELL ME YOU—
LIKE I SAID...
...WE'RE GONNA END THIS FAST.
OH CRAP...
ZAN (SLASH)

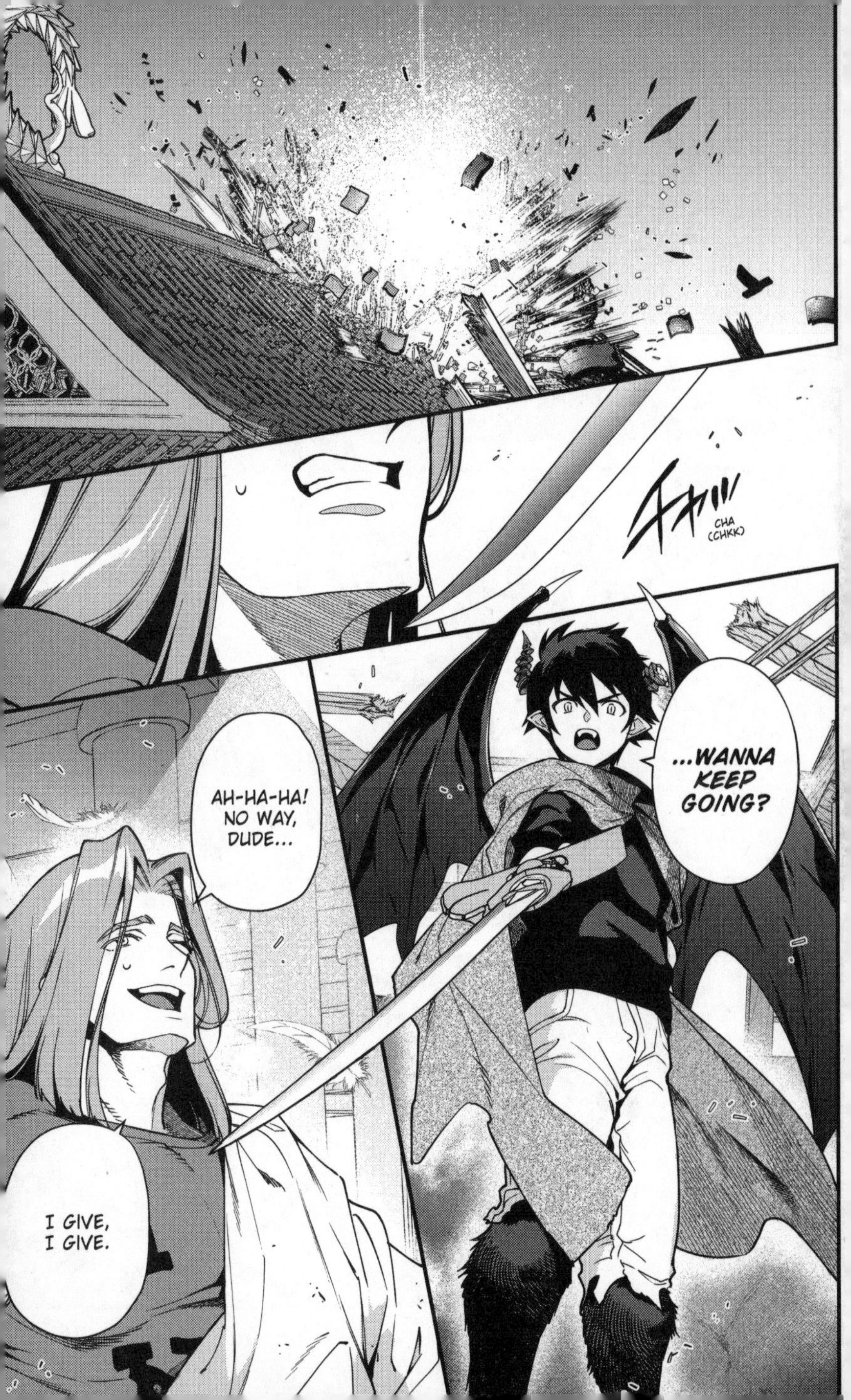
CHA (CHKK)
...WANNA KEEP GOING?
AH-HA-HA! NO WAY, DUDE...
I GIVE, I GIVE.

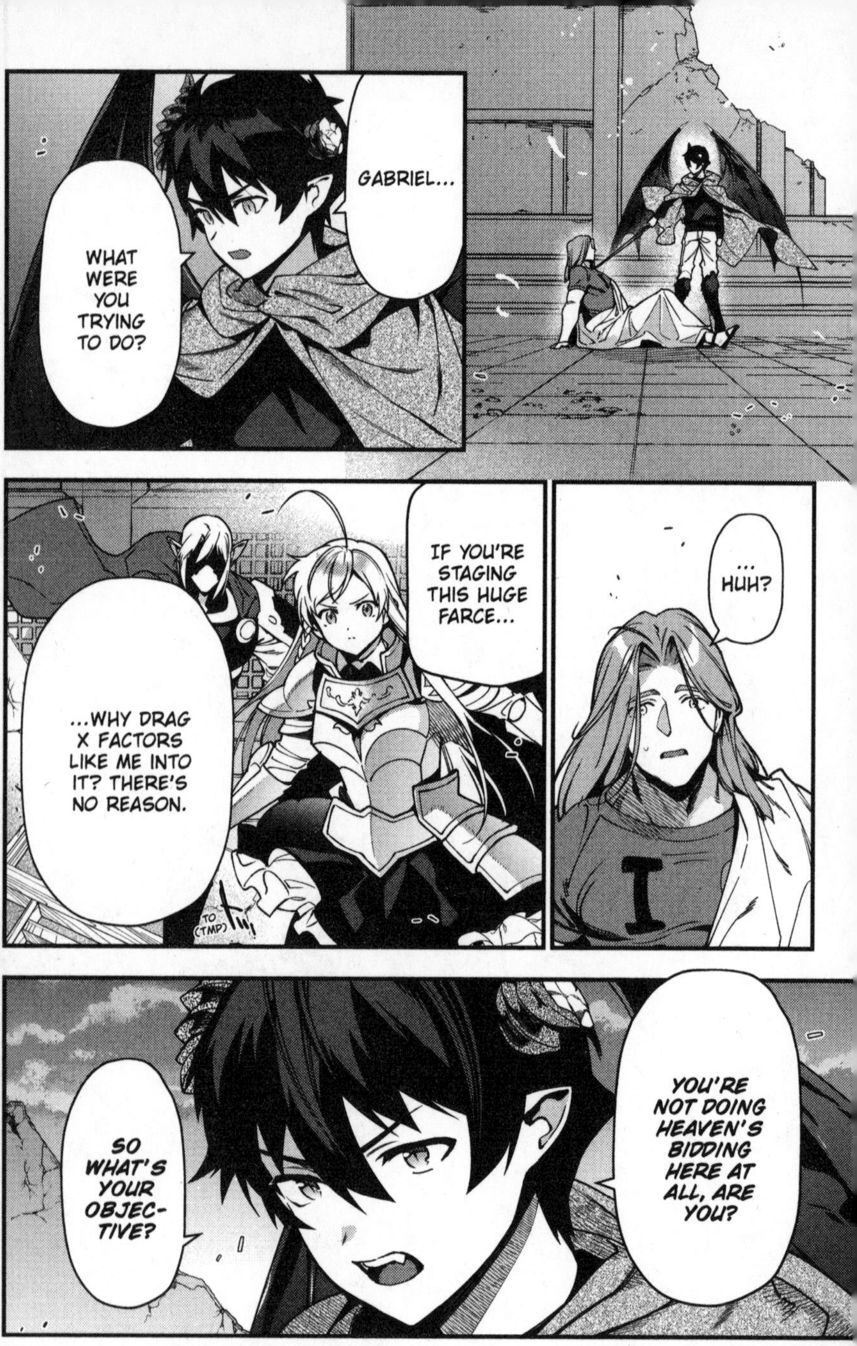
GABRIEL...
WHAT WERE YOU TRYING TO DO?
... HUH?
IF YOU'RE STAGING THIS HUGE FARCE...
...WHY DRAG X FACTORS LIKE ME INTO IT? THERE'S NO REASON.
TO (TMP)
YOU'RE NOT DOING HEAVEN'S BIDDING HERE AT ALL, ARE YOU?
SO WHAT'S YOUR OBJEC-TIVE?

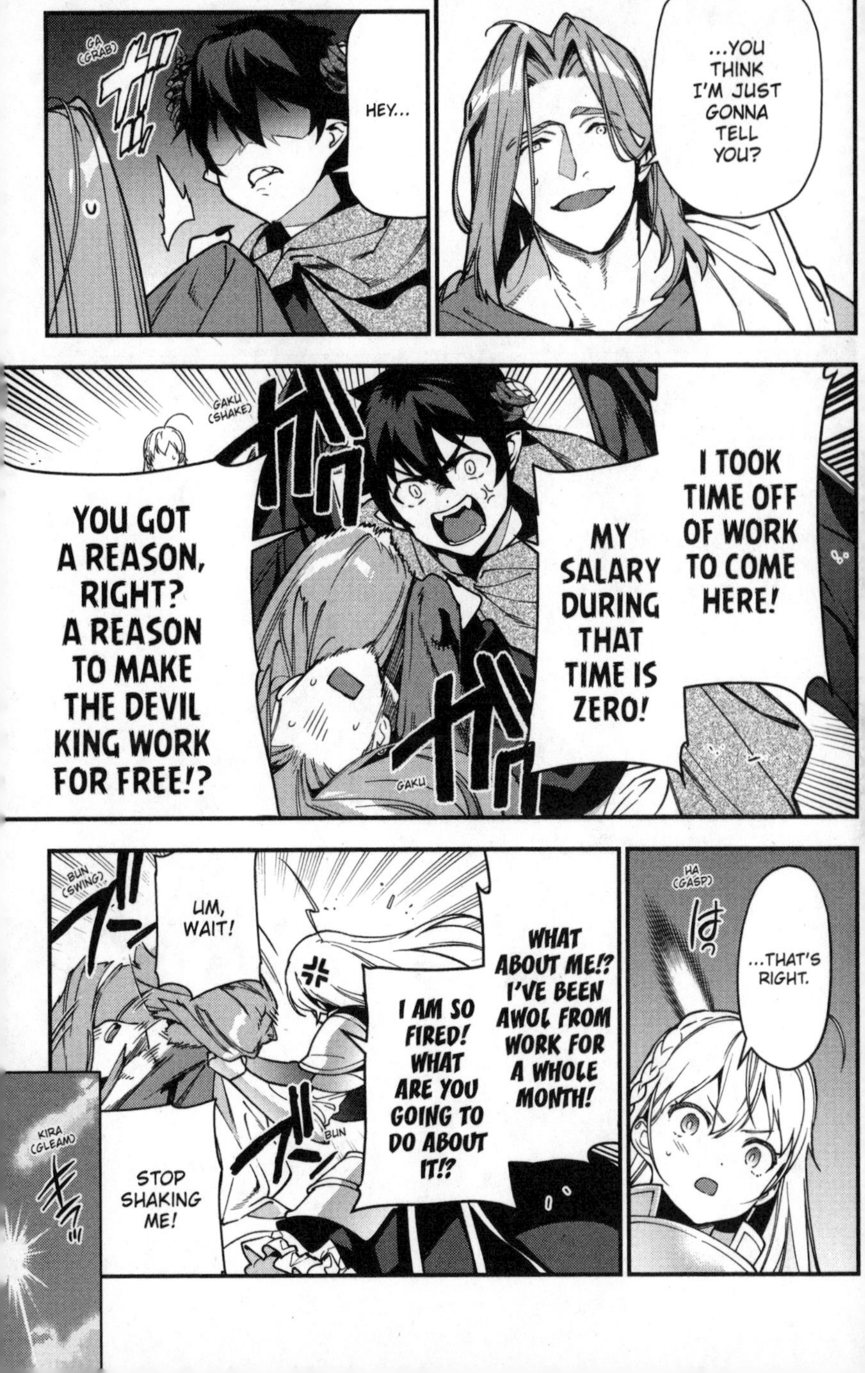
...YOU THINK I'M JUST GONNA TELL YOU?
GA (GRAB)
HEY...
I TOOK TIME OFF OF WORK TO COME HERE!
MY SALARY DURING THAT TIME IS ZERO!
GAKU (SHAKE)
YOU GOT A REASON, RIGHT? A REASON TO MAKE THE DEVIL KING WORK FOR FREE!?
GAKU
HA (GASP)
...THAT'S RIGHT.
WHAT ABOUT ME!? I'VE BEEN AWOL FROM WORK FOR A WHOLE MONTH!
I AM SO FIRED! WHAT ARE YOU GOING TO DO ABOUT IT!?
BUN (SWING)
UM, WAIT!
BUN
KIRA (GLEAM)
STOP SHAKING ME!

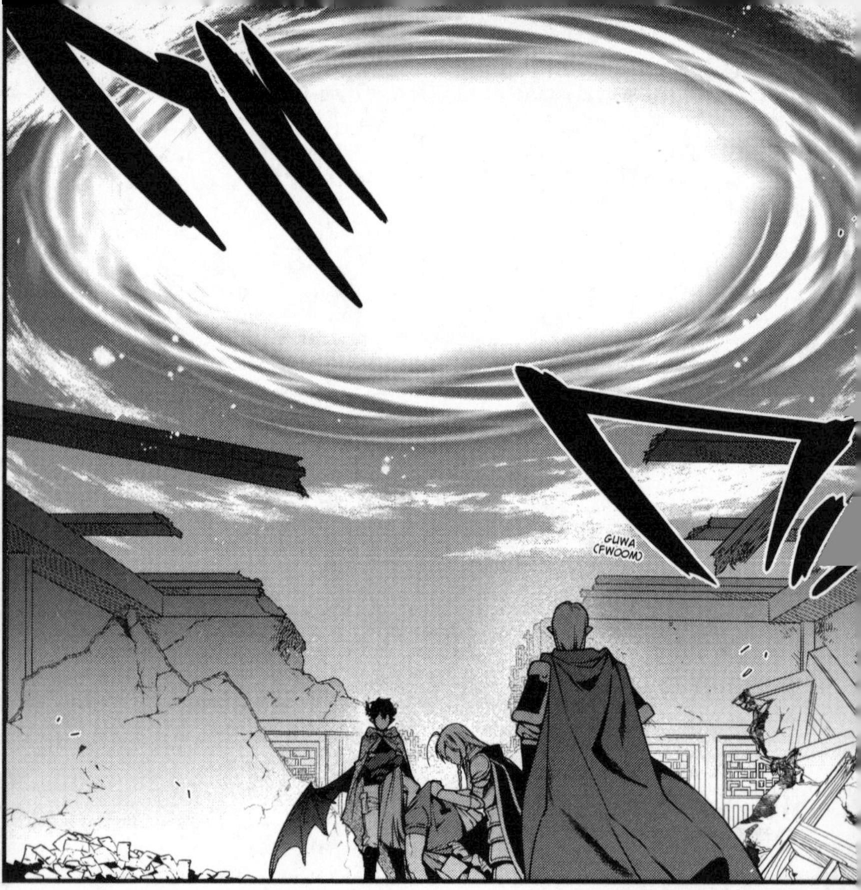
GUWA
(FWOOM)
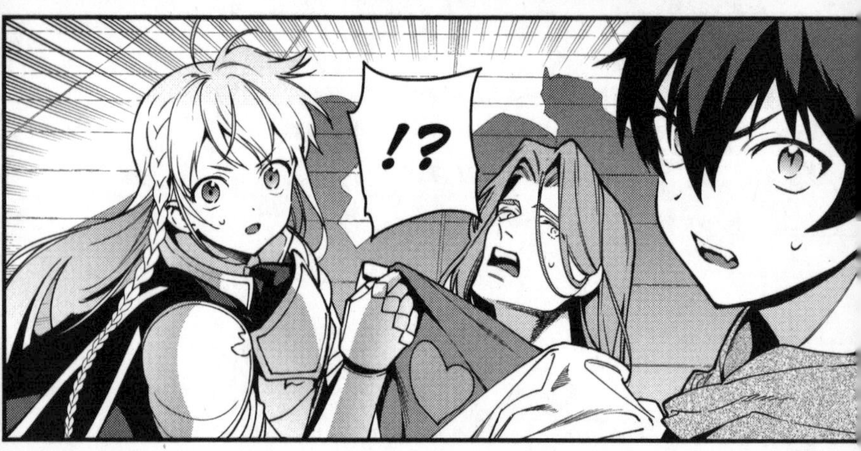
!?

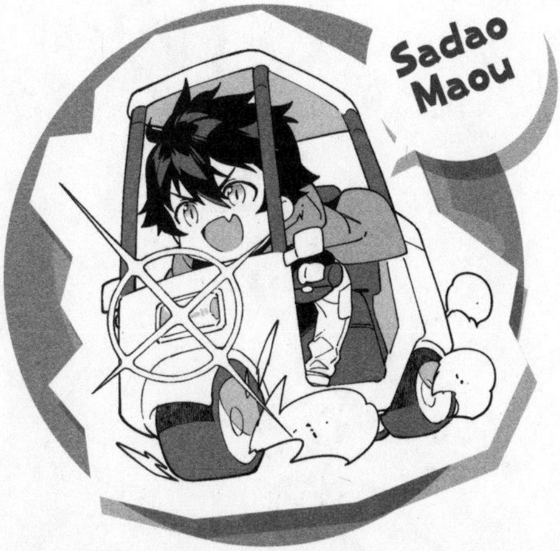
Sadao
Maou

THE DEVIL IS A PART-TIMER!

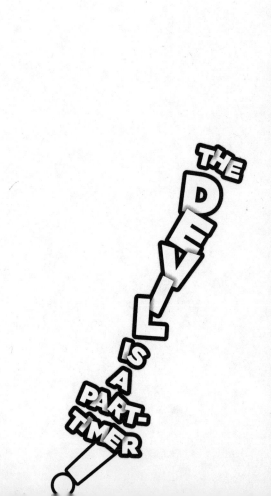

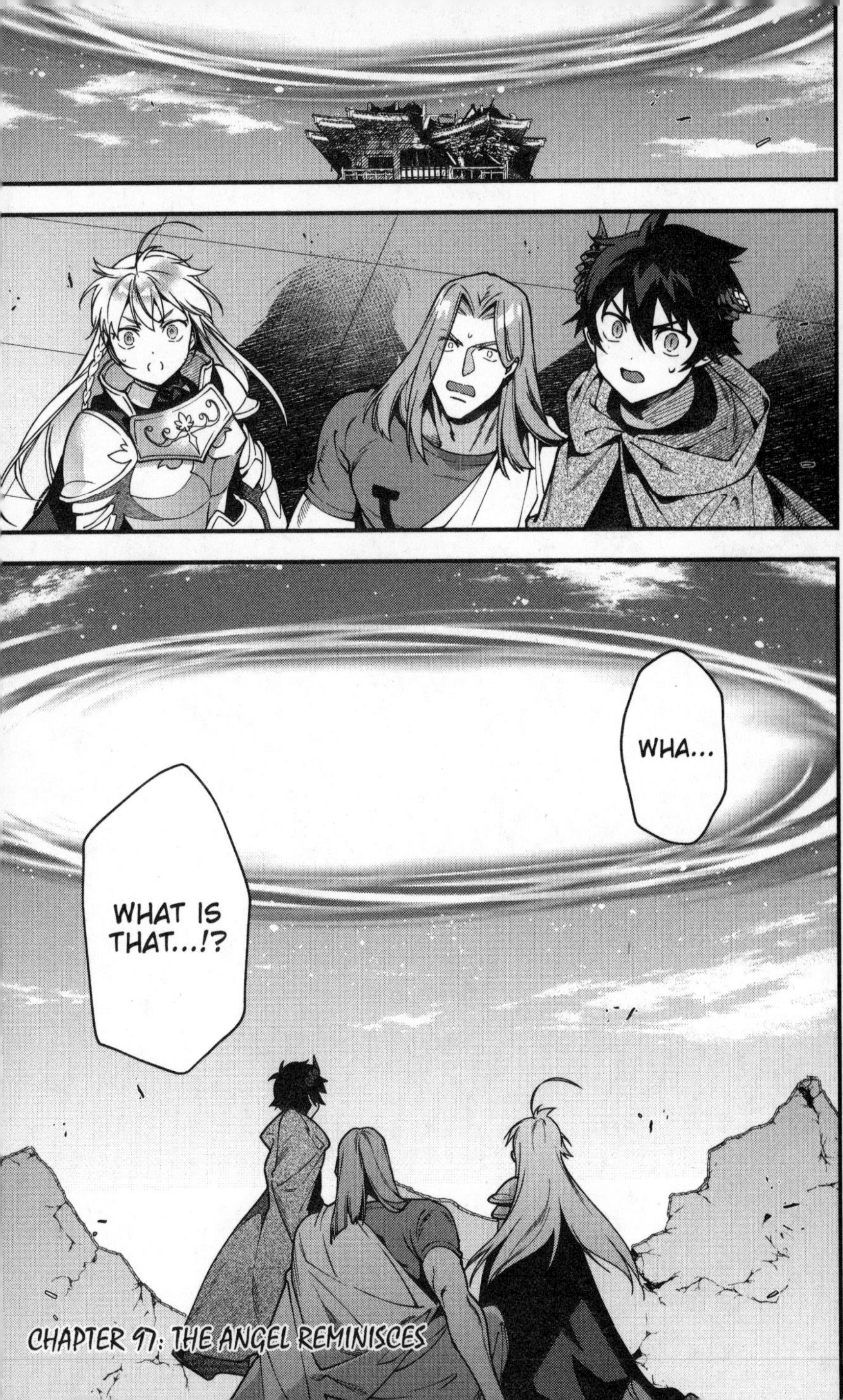
WHA...
WHAT IS THAT...!?
CHAPTER 97: THE ANGEL REMINISCES

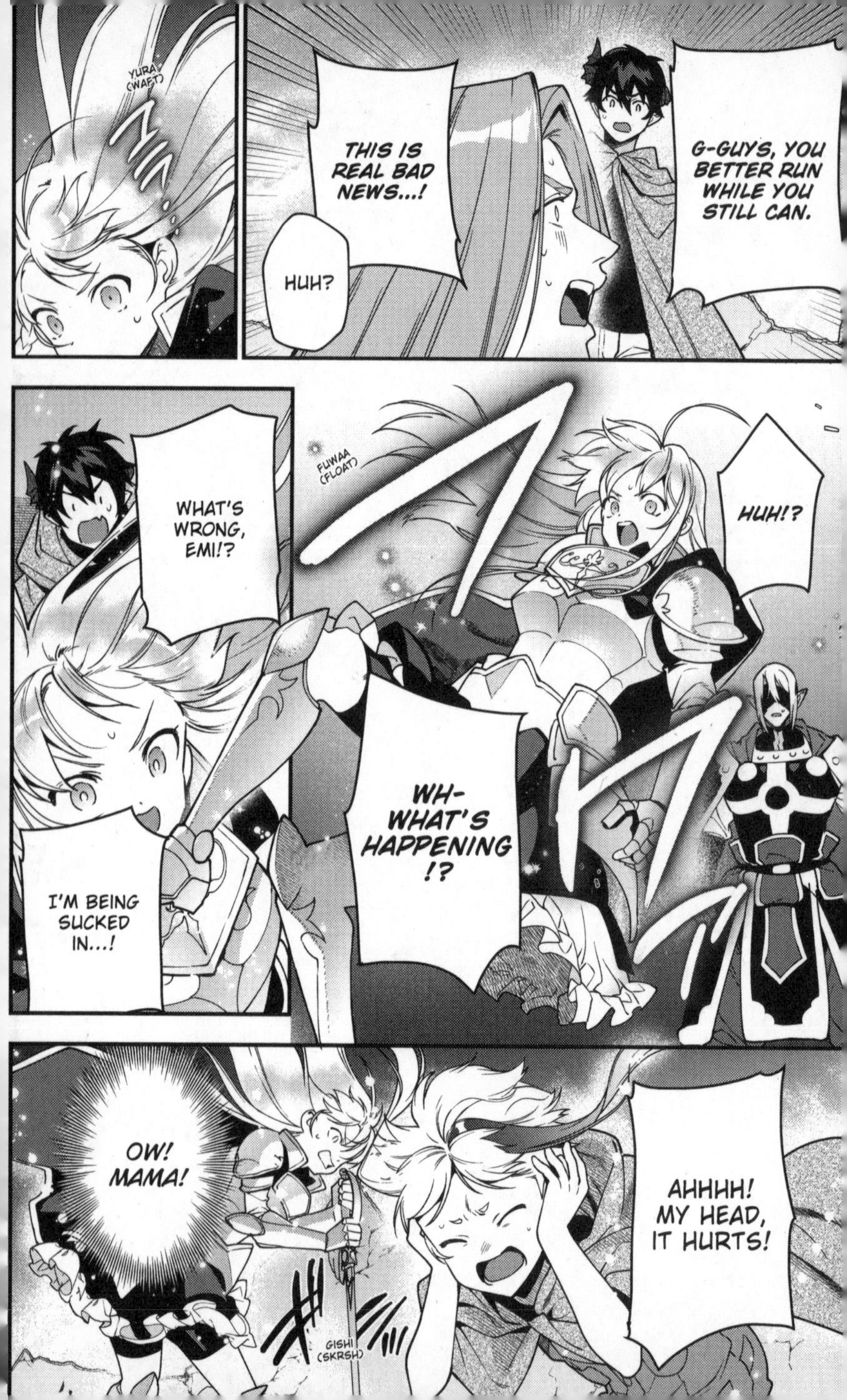
G-GUYS, YOU BETTER RUN WHILE YOU STILL CAN.
THIS IS REAL BAD NEWS...!
HUH?
YURA (WAFT)
HUH!?
FUWAA (FLOAT)
WH-WHAT'S HAPPENING!?
WHAT'S WRONG, EMI!?
I'M BEING SUCKED IN...!
AHHHH! MY HEAD, IT HURTS!
OW! MAMA!
GISHI (SKRSH)

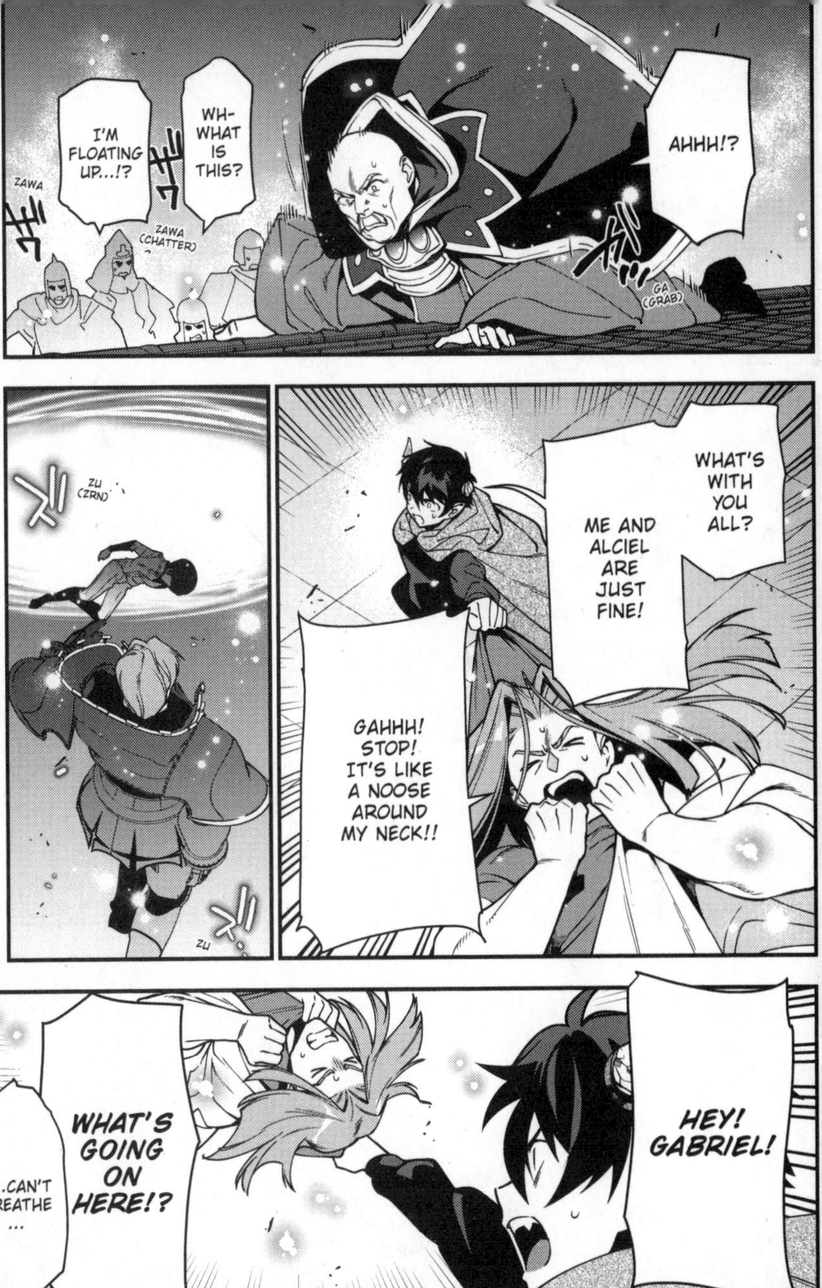
AHHH!?
GA (GRAB)
WH-WHAT IS THIS?
I'M FLOATING UP...!?
ZAWA (CHATTER)
ZAWA
WHAT'S WITH YOU ALL?
ME AND ALCIEL ARE JUST FINE!
GAHHH! STOP! IT'S LIKE A NOOSE AROUND MY NECK!!
ZU (ZRN)
ZU
HEY! GABRIEL!
WHAT'S GOING ON HERE!?
I...CAN'T BREATHE ...

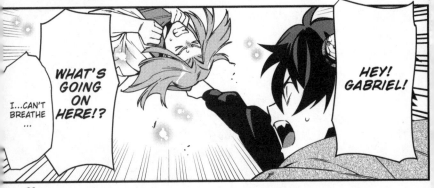

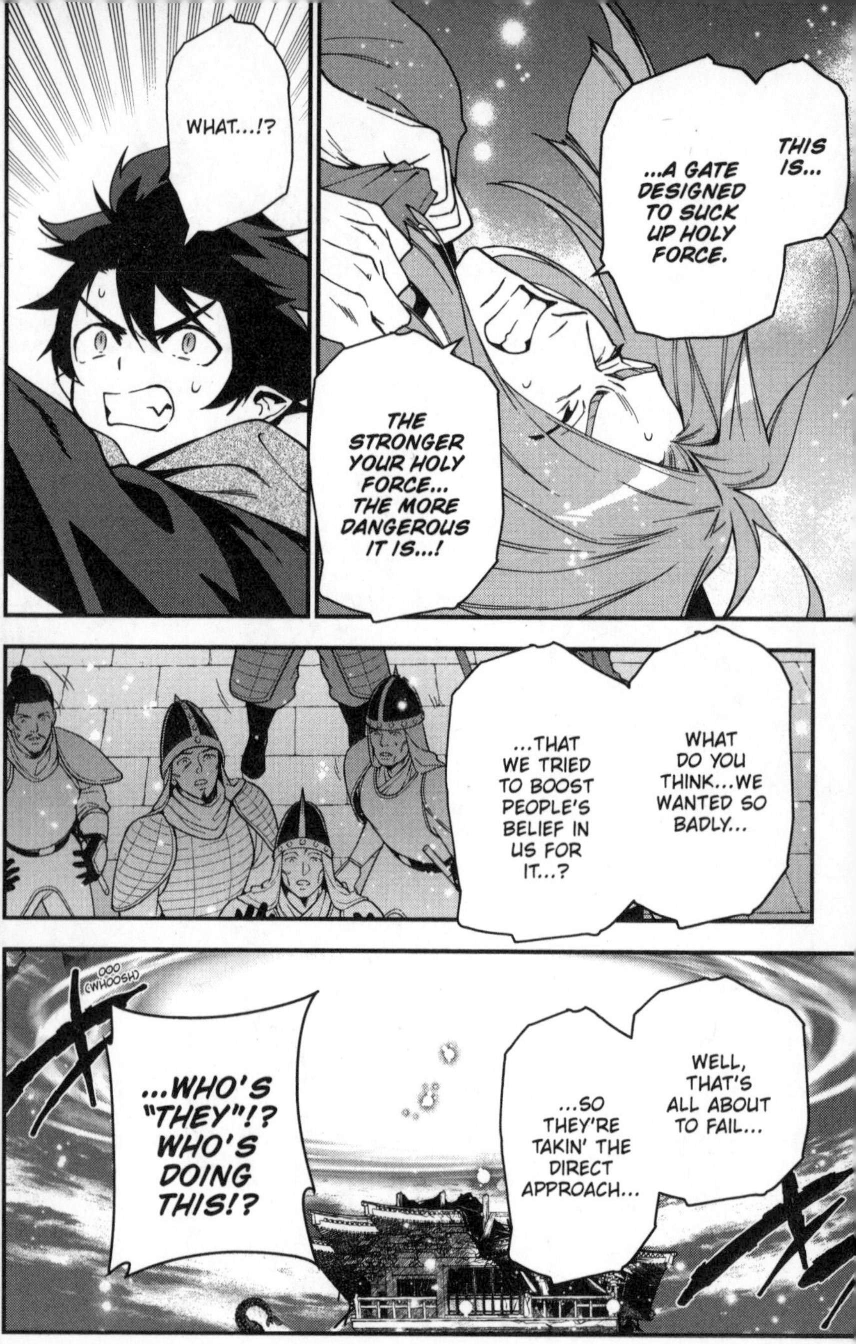
THIS IS...
...A GATE DESIGNED TO SUCK UP HOLY FORCE.
THE STRONGER YOUR HOLY FORCE... THE MORE DANGEROUS IT IS...!
WHAT...!?
WHAT DO YOU THINK...WE WANTED SO BADLY...
...THAT WE TRIED TO BOOST PEOPLE'S BELIEF IN US FOR IT...?
(WHOOSH)
WELL, THAT'S ALL ABOUT TO FAIL...
...SO THEY'RE TAKIN' THE DIRECT APPROACH...
...WHO'S "THEY"!? WHO'S DOING THIS!?

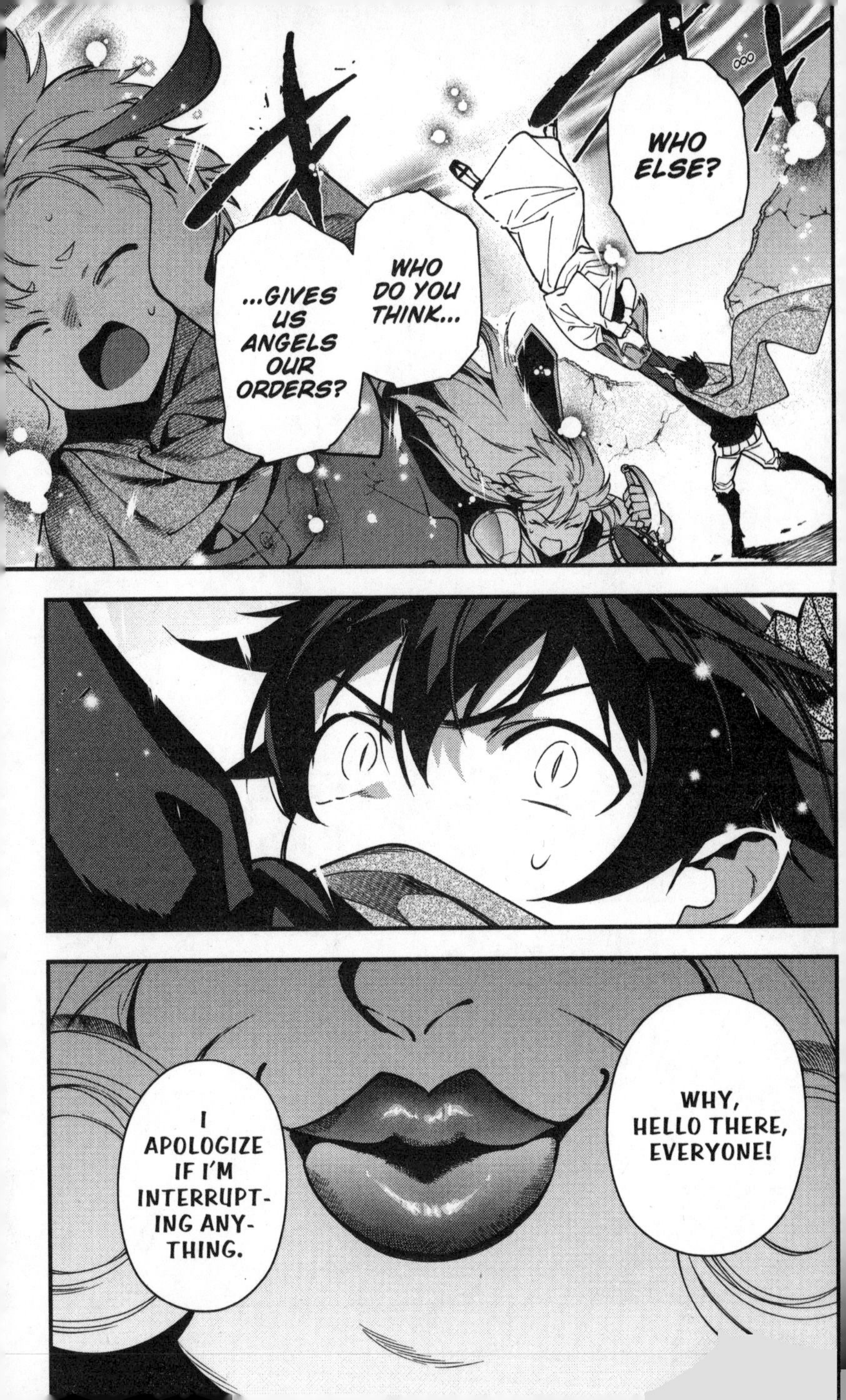
WHO ELSE?
WHO DO YOU THINK...
...GIVES US ANGELS OUR ORDERS?
WHY, HELLO THERE, EVERYONE!
I APOLOGIZE IF I'M INTERRUPT-ING ANY-THING.

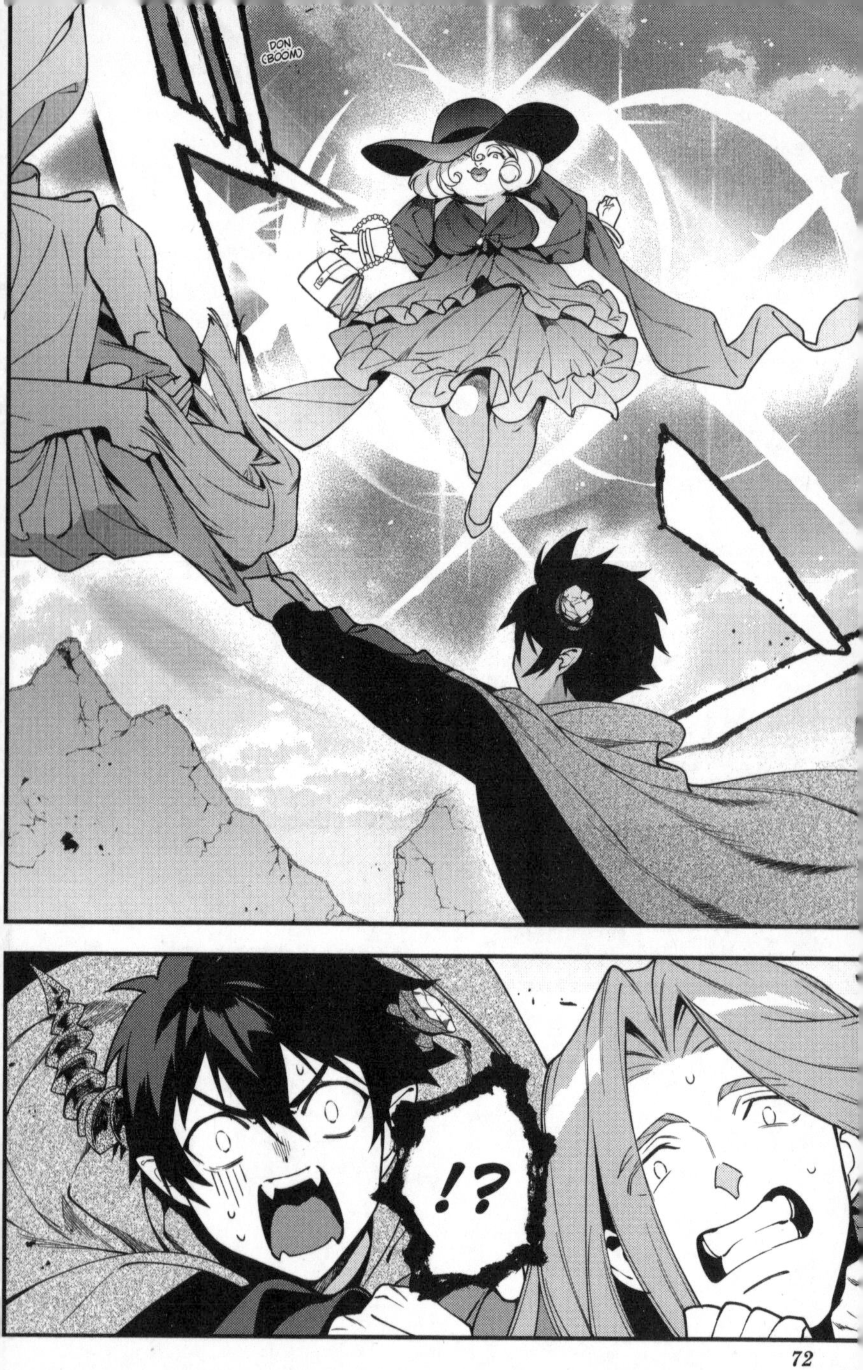
DON (BOOM)
!?

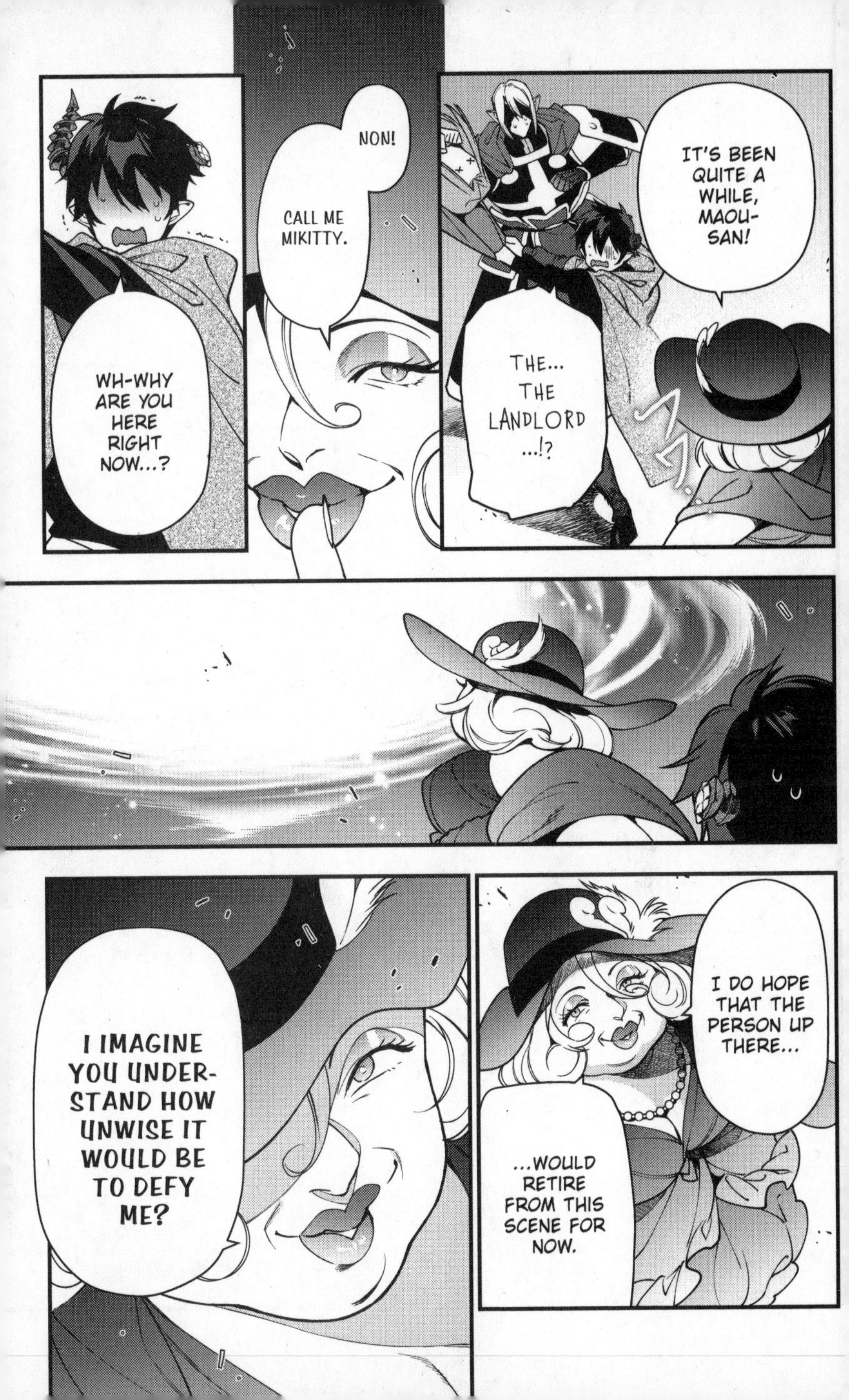
IT'S BEEN QUITE A WHILE, MAOU-SAN!
THE... THE LANDLORD ...!?
NON!
CALL ME MIKITTY.
WH-WHY ARE YOU HERE RIGHT NOW...?
I DO HOPE THAT THE PERSON UP THERE...
...WOULD RETIRE FROM THIS SCENE FOR NOW.
I IMAGINE YOU UNDERSTAND HOW UNWISE IT WOULD BE TO DEFY ME?

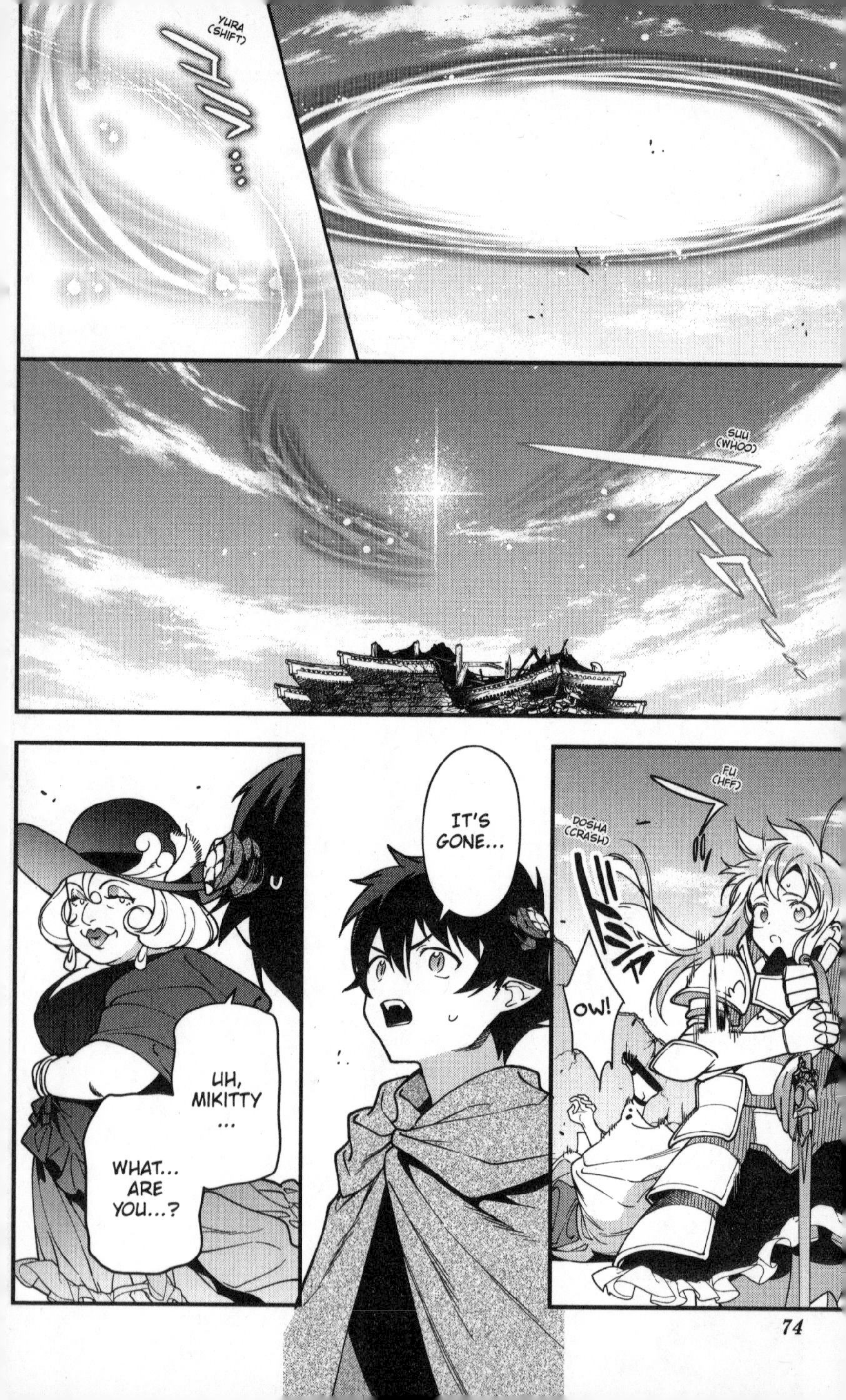
YURA (SHIFT)
SUU (WHOO)
FU (HFF)
DOSHA (CRASH)
OW!
IT'S GONE...
UH, MIKITTY ...
WHAT... ARE YOU...?

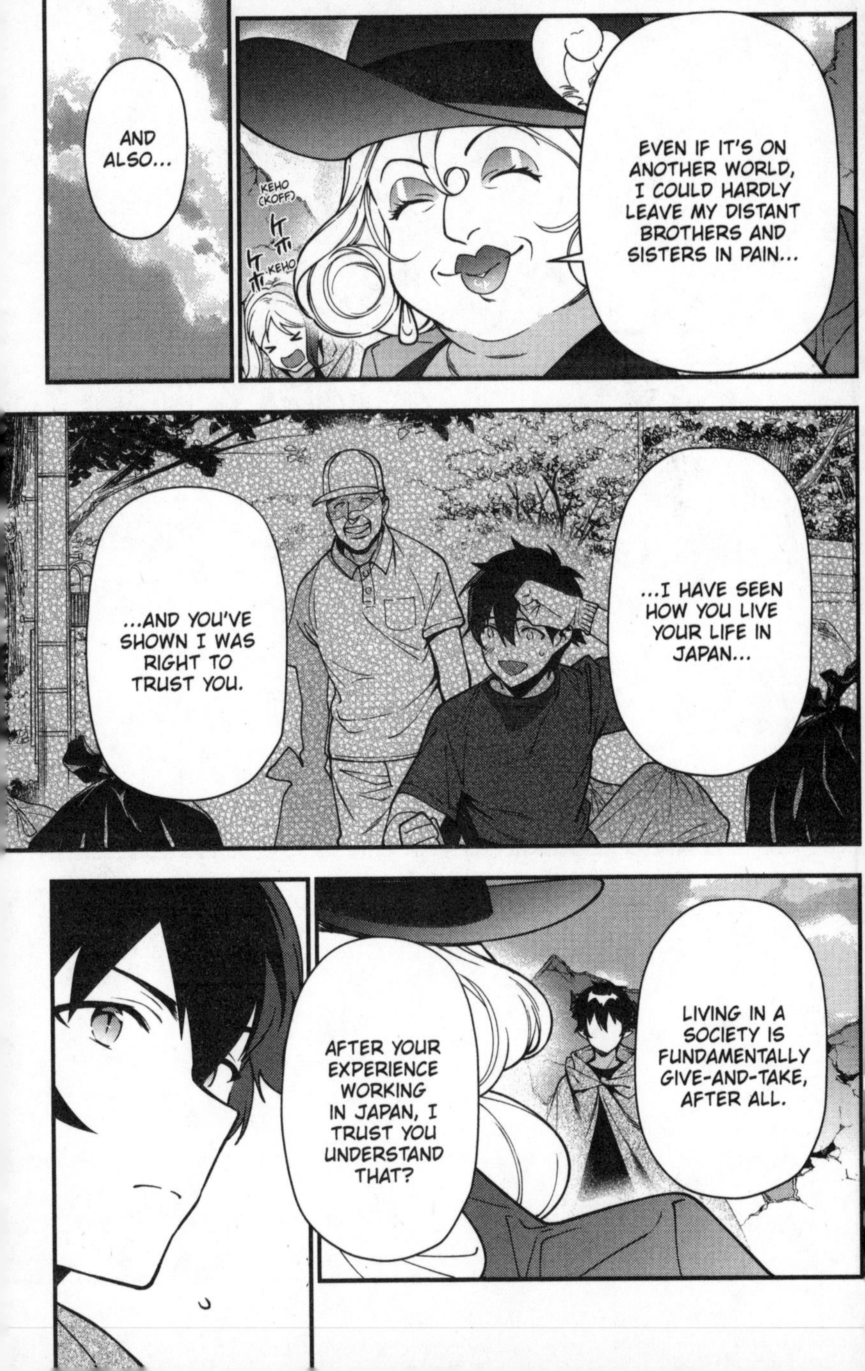
EVEN IF IT'S ON ANOTHER WORLD, I COULD HARDLY LEAVE MY DISTANT BROTHERS AND SISTERS IN PAIN...
KEHO (KOFF)
ケホ
ケホ
KEHO
AND ALSO...
...I HAVE SEEN HOW YOU LIVE YOUR LIFE IN JAPAN...
...AND YOU'VE SHOWN I WAS RIGHT TO TRUST YOU.
LIVING IN A SOCIETY IS FUNDAMENTALLY GIVE-AND-TAKE, AFTER ALL.
AFTER YOUR EXPERIENCE WORKING IN JAPAN, I TRUST YOU UNDERSTAND THAT?

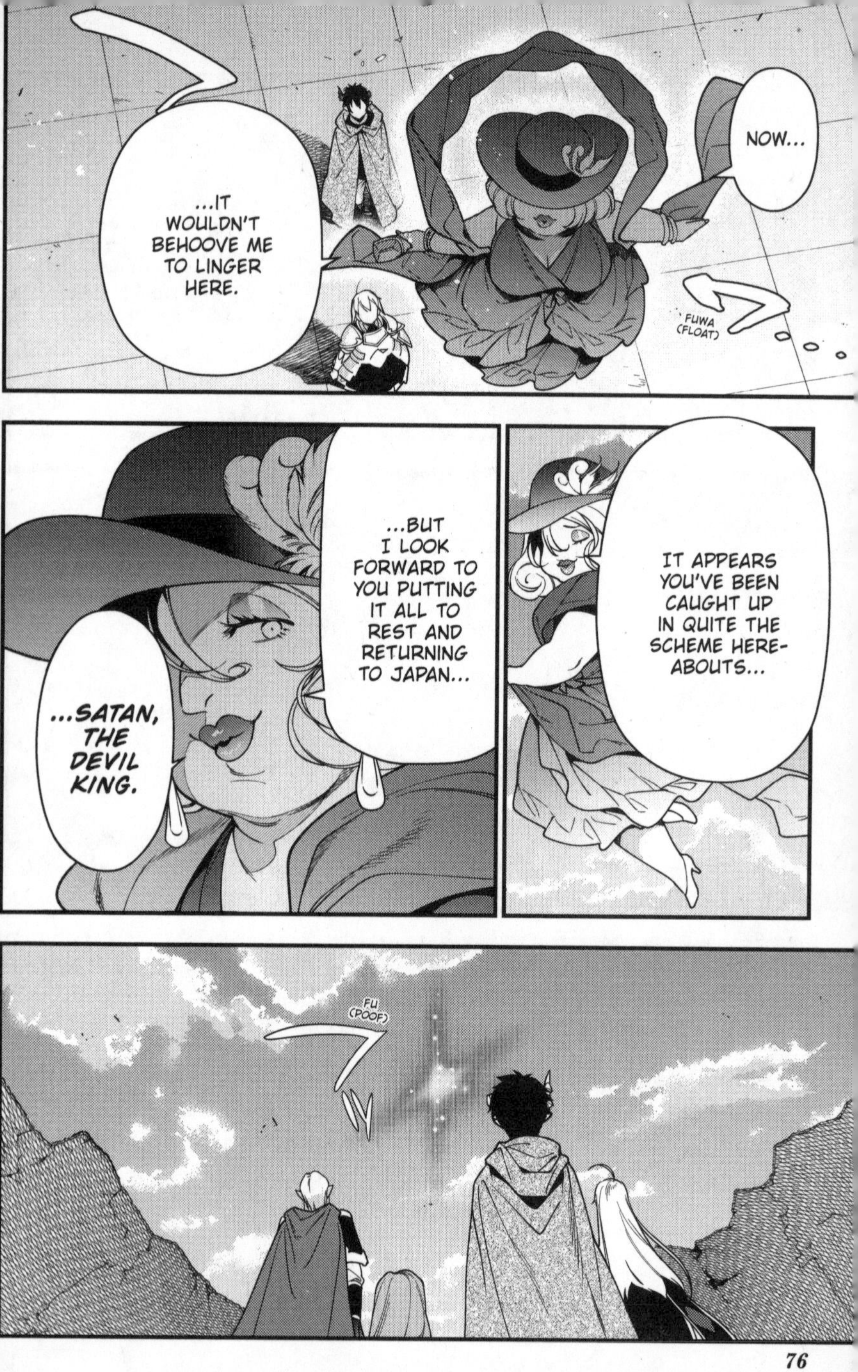
NOW...
...IT WOULDN'T BEHOOVE ME TO LINGER HERE.
FUWA (FLOAT)
IT APPEARS YOU'VE BEEN CAUGHT UP IN QUITE THE SCHEME HERE-ABOUTS...
...BUT I LOOK FORWARD TO YOU PUTTING IT ALL TO REST AND RETURNING TO JAPAN...
...SATAN, THE DEVIL KING.
FU (POOF)

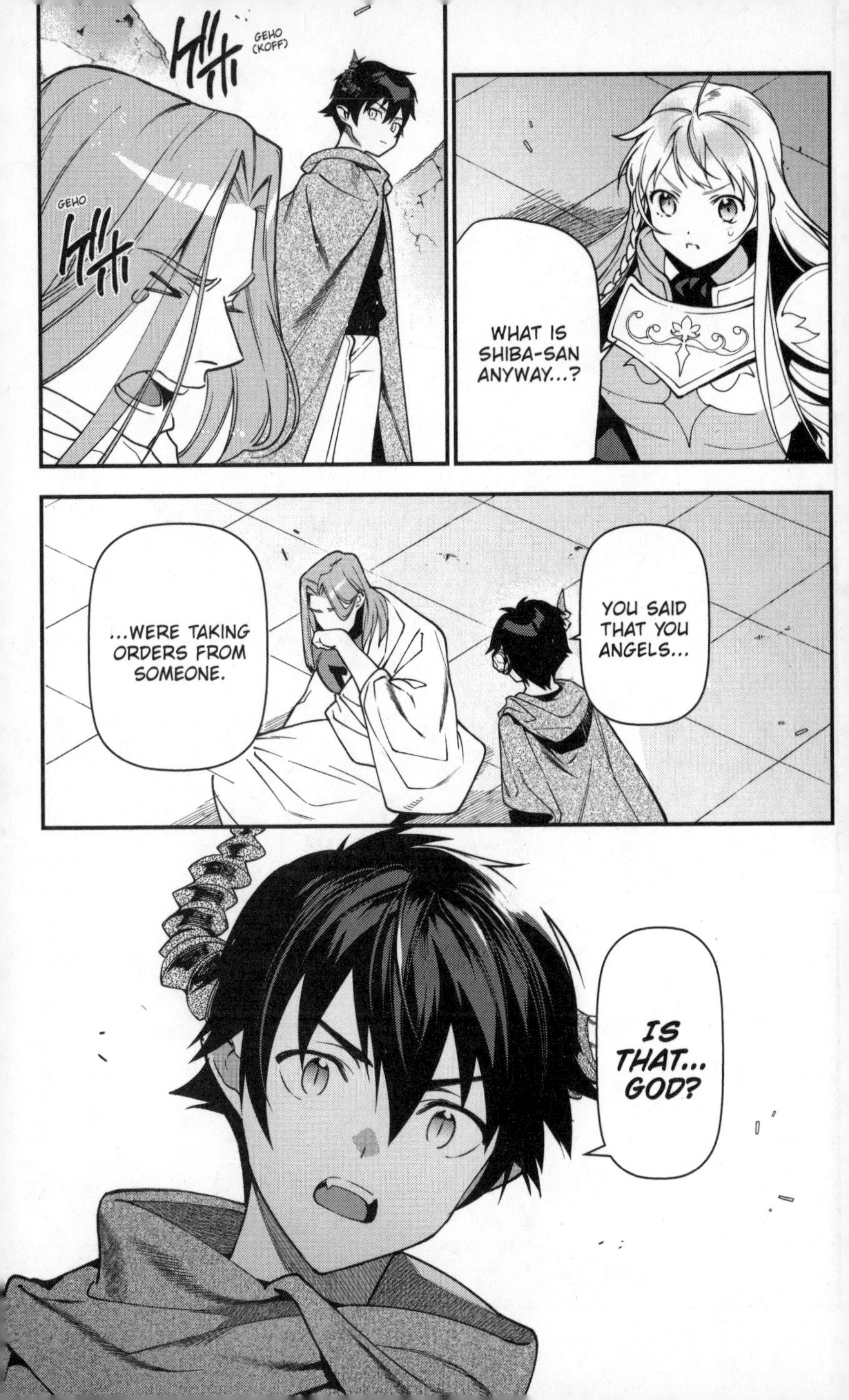
WHAT IS SHIBA-SAN ANYWAY...?
GEHO (KOFF)
GEHO
YOU SAID THAT YOU ANGELS...
...WERE TAKING ORDERS FROM SOMEONE.
IS THAT... GOD?

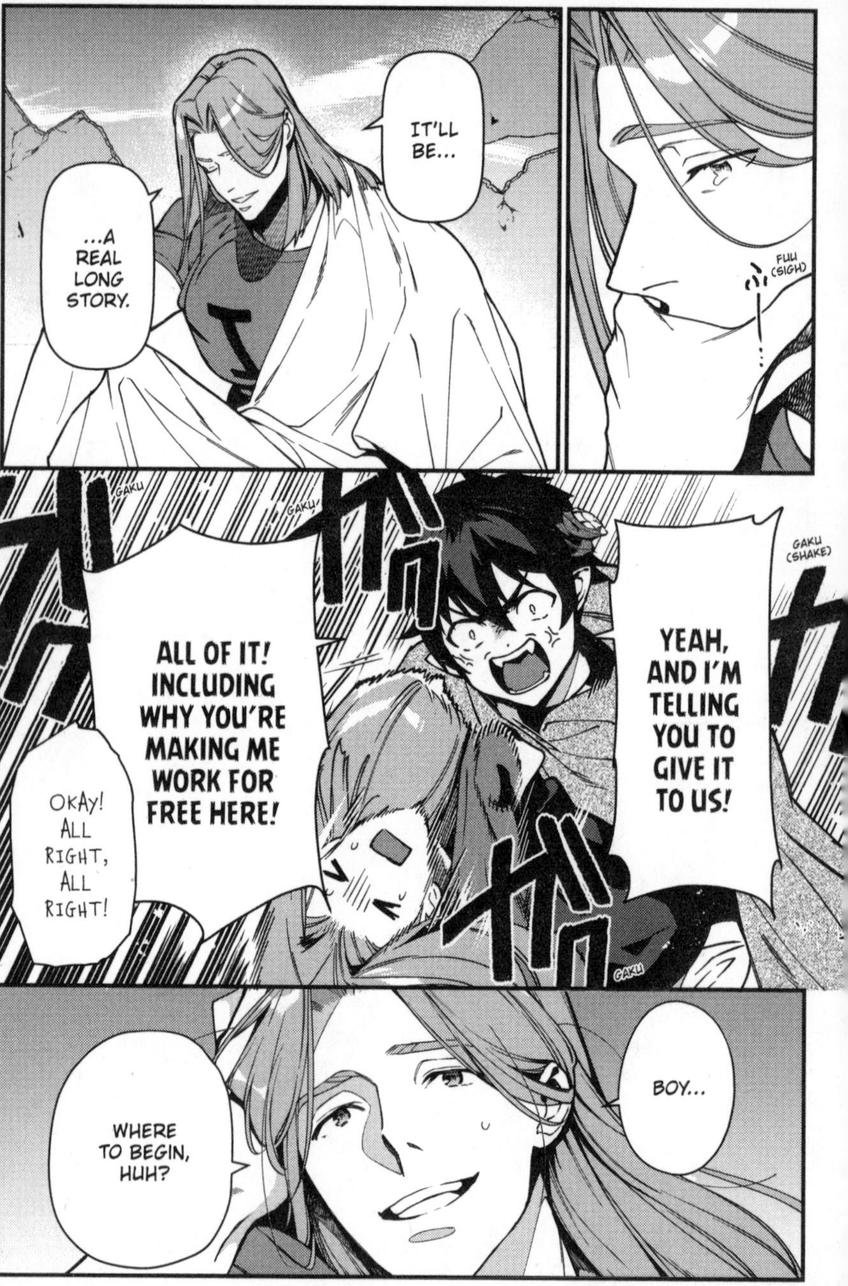
FUU (SIGH)
IT'LL BE...
...A REAL LONG STORY.
GAKU (SHAKE)
YEAH, AND I'M TELLING YOU TO GIVE IT TO US!
GAKU
ALL OF IT! INCLUDING WHY YOU'RE MAKING ME WORK FOR FREE HERE!
GAKU
OKAY! ALL RIGHT, ALL RIGHT!
GAKU
BOY...
WHERE TO BEGIN, HUH?

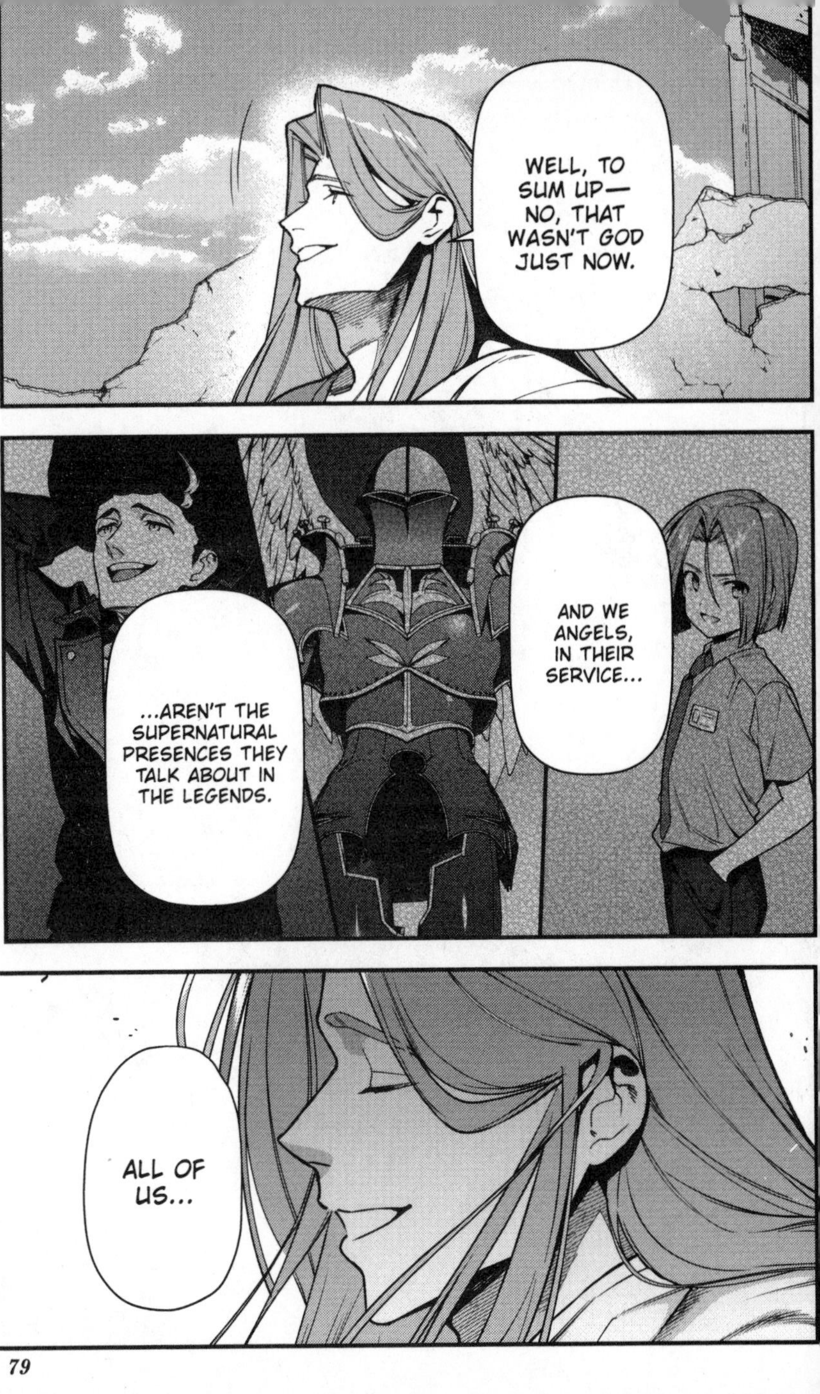
WELL, TO SUM UP— NO, THAT WASN'T GOD JUST NOW.
AND WE ANGELS, IN THEIR SERVICE...
...AREN'T THE SUPERNATURAL PRESENCES THEY TALK ABOUT IN THE LEGENDS.
ALL OF US...

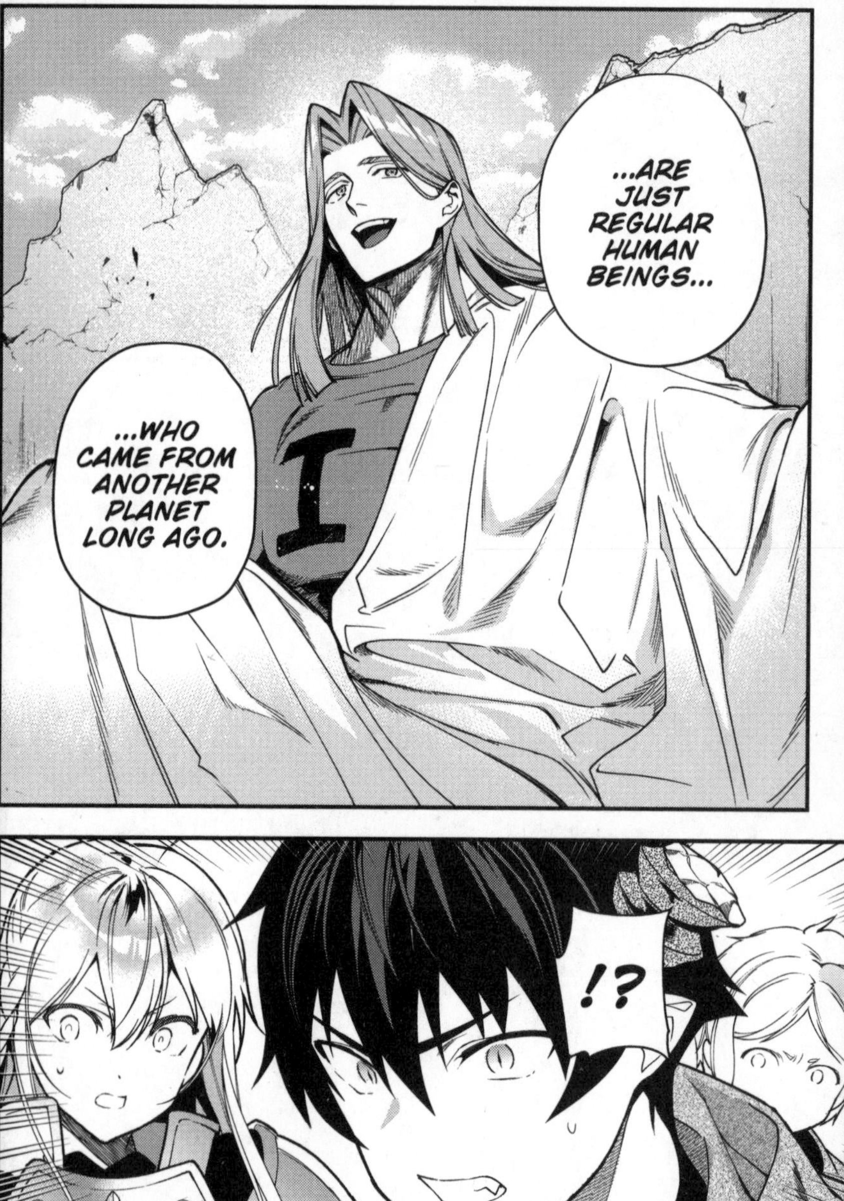
...ARE JUST REGULAR HUMAN BEINGS...
...WHO CAME FROM ANOTHER PLANET LONG AGO.
!?

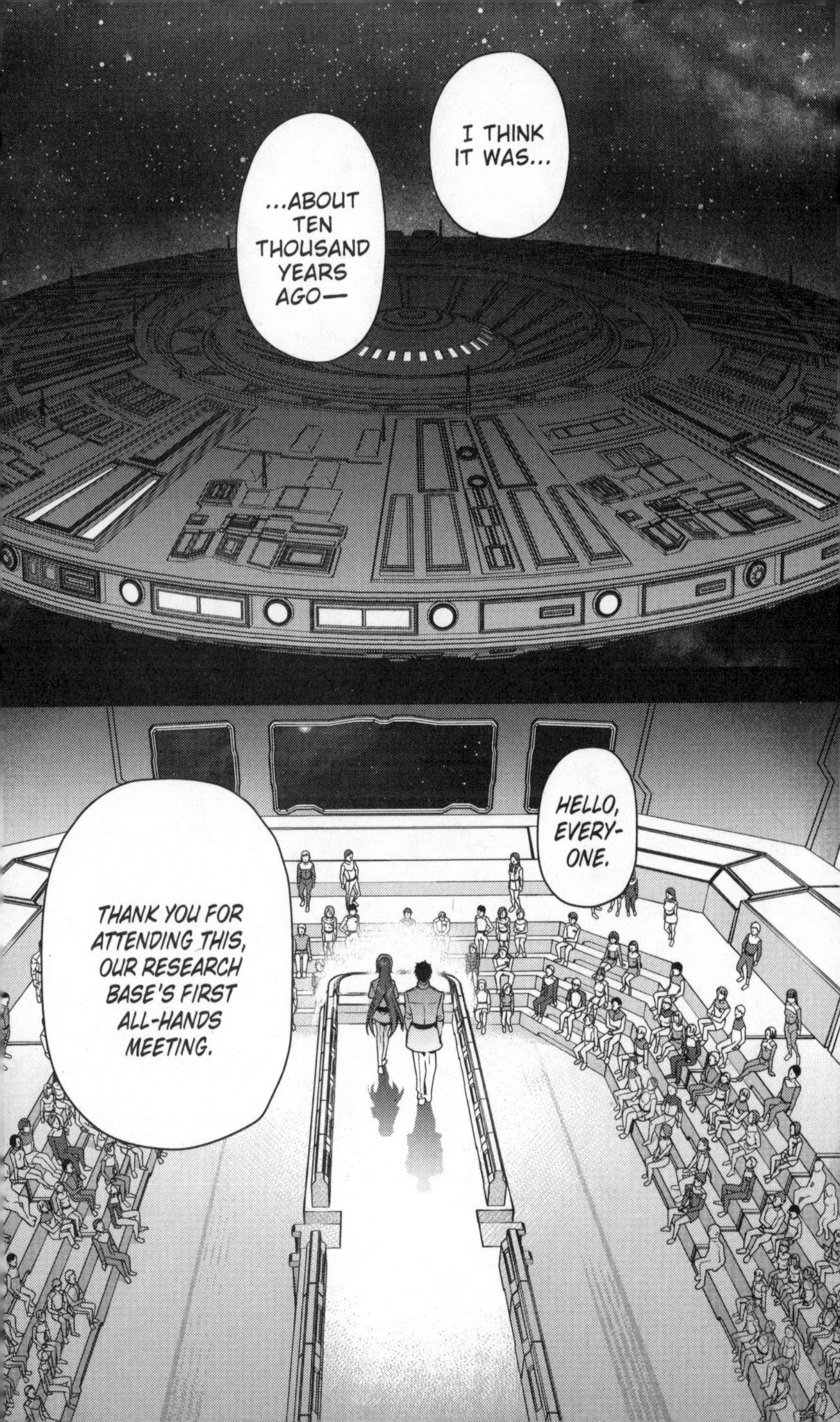
I THINK IT WAS...
...ABOUT TEN THOUSAND YEARS AGO—
HELLO, EVERY-ONE.
THANK YOU FOR ATTENDING THIS, OUR RESEARCH BASE'S FIRST ALL-HANDS MEETING.

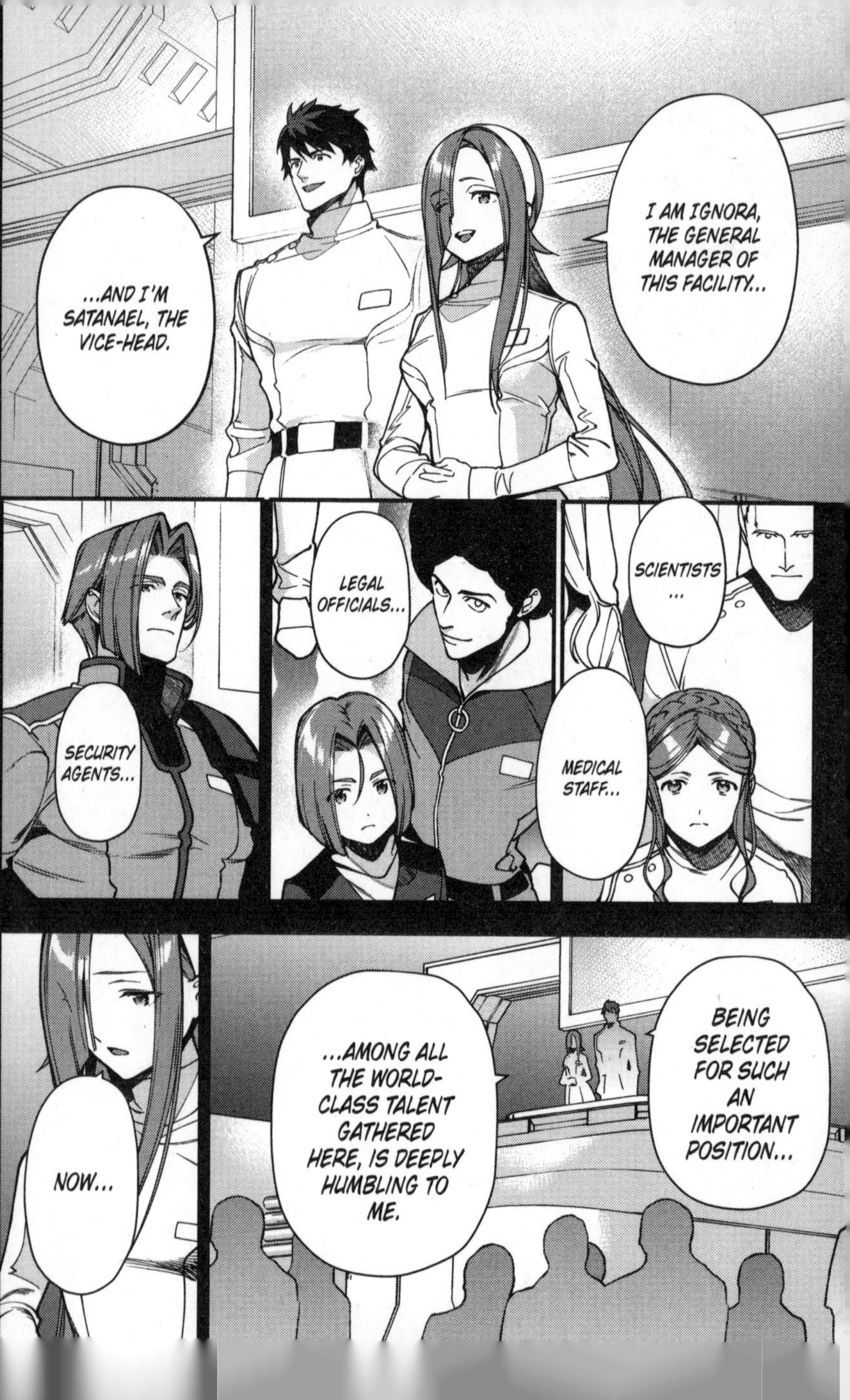
I AM IGNORA, THE GENERAL MANAGER OF THIS FACILITY...
...AND I'M SATANAEL, THE VICE-HEAD.
SCIENTISTS...
MEDICAL STAFF...
LEGAL OFFICIALS...
SECURITY AGENTS...
BEING SELECTED FOR SUCH AN IMPORTANT POSITION...
...AMONG ALL THE WORLD-CLASS TALENT GATHERED HERE, IS DEEPLY HUMBLING TO ME.
NOW...

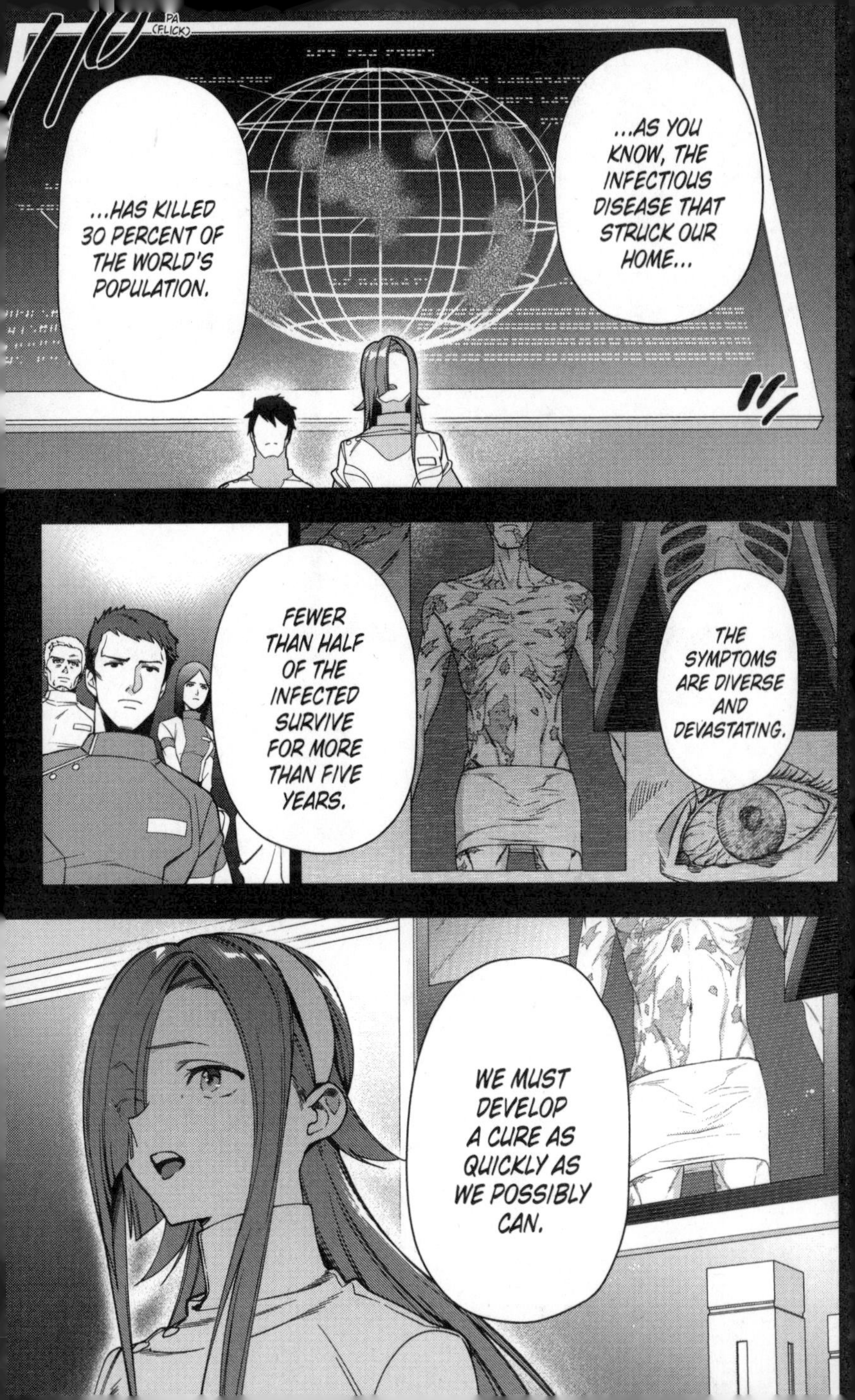
PA (FLICK)
...AS YOU KNOW, THE INFECTIOUS DISEASE THAT STRUCK OUR HOME...
...HAS KILLED 30 PERCENT OF THE WORLD'S POPULATION.
THE SYMPTOMS ARE DIVERSE AND DEVASTATING.
FEWER THAN HALF OF THE INFECTED SURVIVE FOR MORE THAN FIVE YEARS.
WE MUST DEVELOP A CURE AS QUICKLY AS WE POSSIBLY CAN.

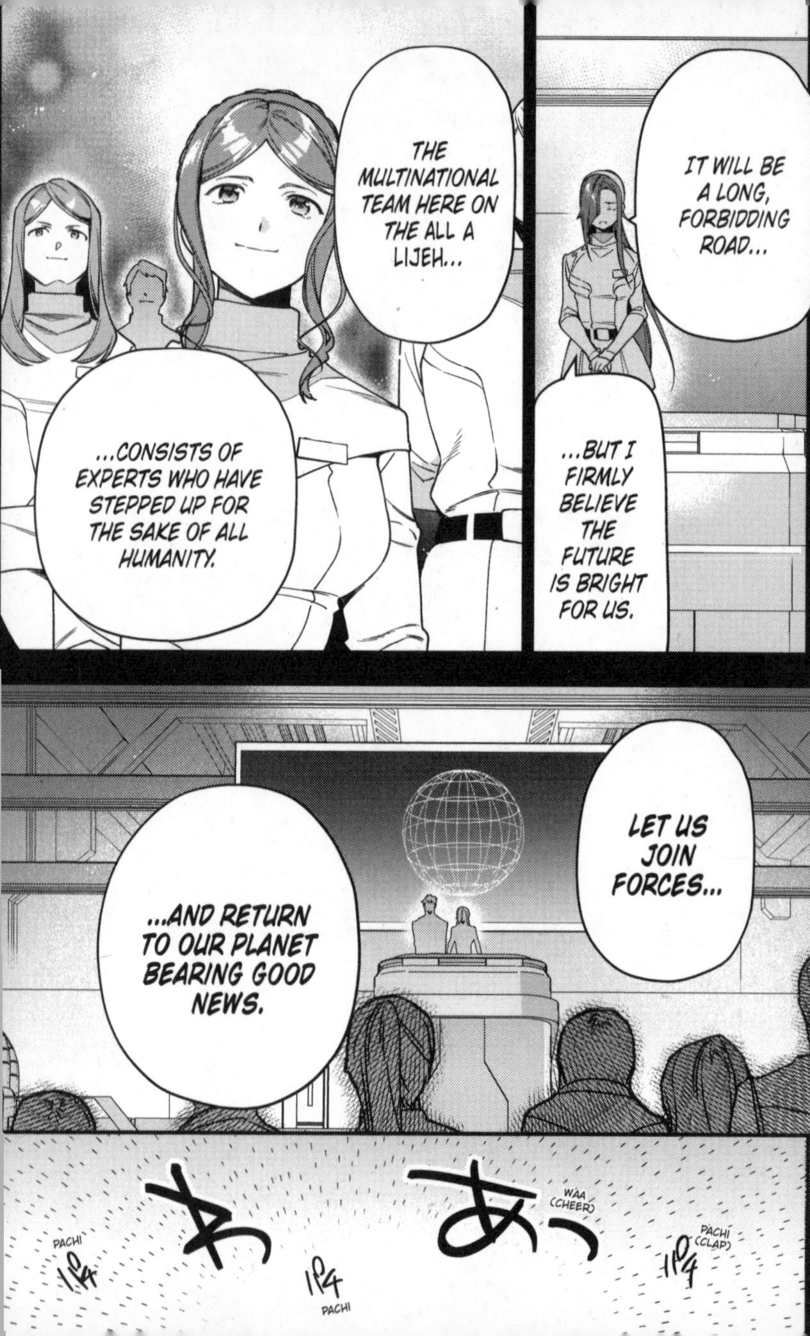
IT WILL BE A LONG, FORBIDDING ROAD...
...BUT I FIRMLY BELIEVE THE FUTURE IS BRIGHT FOR US.
THE MULTINATIONAL TEAM HERE ON THE ALL A LIJEH...
...CONSISTS OF EXPERTS WHO HAVE STEPPED UP FOR THE SAKE OF ALL HUMANITY.
LET US JOIN FORCES...
...AND RETURN TO OUR PLANET BEARING GOOD NEWS.
わあっ
WAA (CHEER)
PACHI (CLAP)
PACHI
PACHI

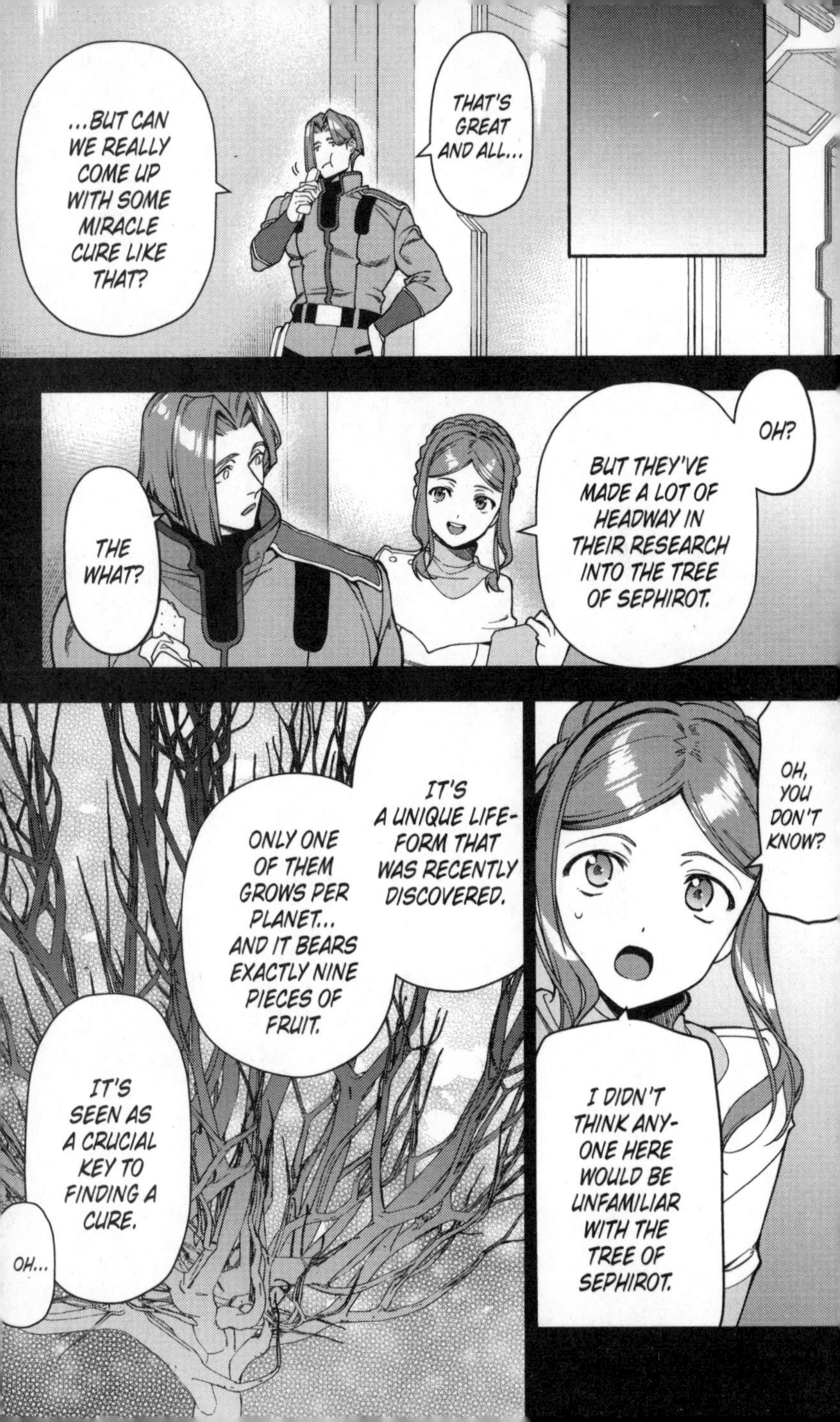
THAT'S GREAT AND ALL...
...BUT CAN WE REALLY COME UP WITH SOME MIRACLE CURE LIKE THAT?
OH?
BUT THEY'VE MADE A LOT OF HEADWAY IN THEIR RESEARCH INTO THE TREE OF SEPHIROT.
THE WHAT?
OH, YOU DON'T KNOW?
I DIDN'T THINK ANY-ONE HERE WOULD BE UNFAMILIAR WITH THE TREE OF SEPHIROT.
IT'S A UNIQUE LIFE-FORM THAT WAS RECENTLY DISCOVERED.
ONLY ONE OF THEM GROWS PER PLANET... AND IT BEARS EXACTLY NINE PIECES OF FRUIT.
IT'S SEEN AS A CRUCIAL KEY TO FINDING A CURE.
OH...

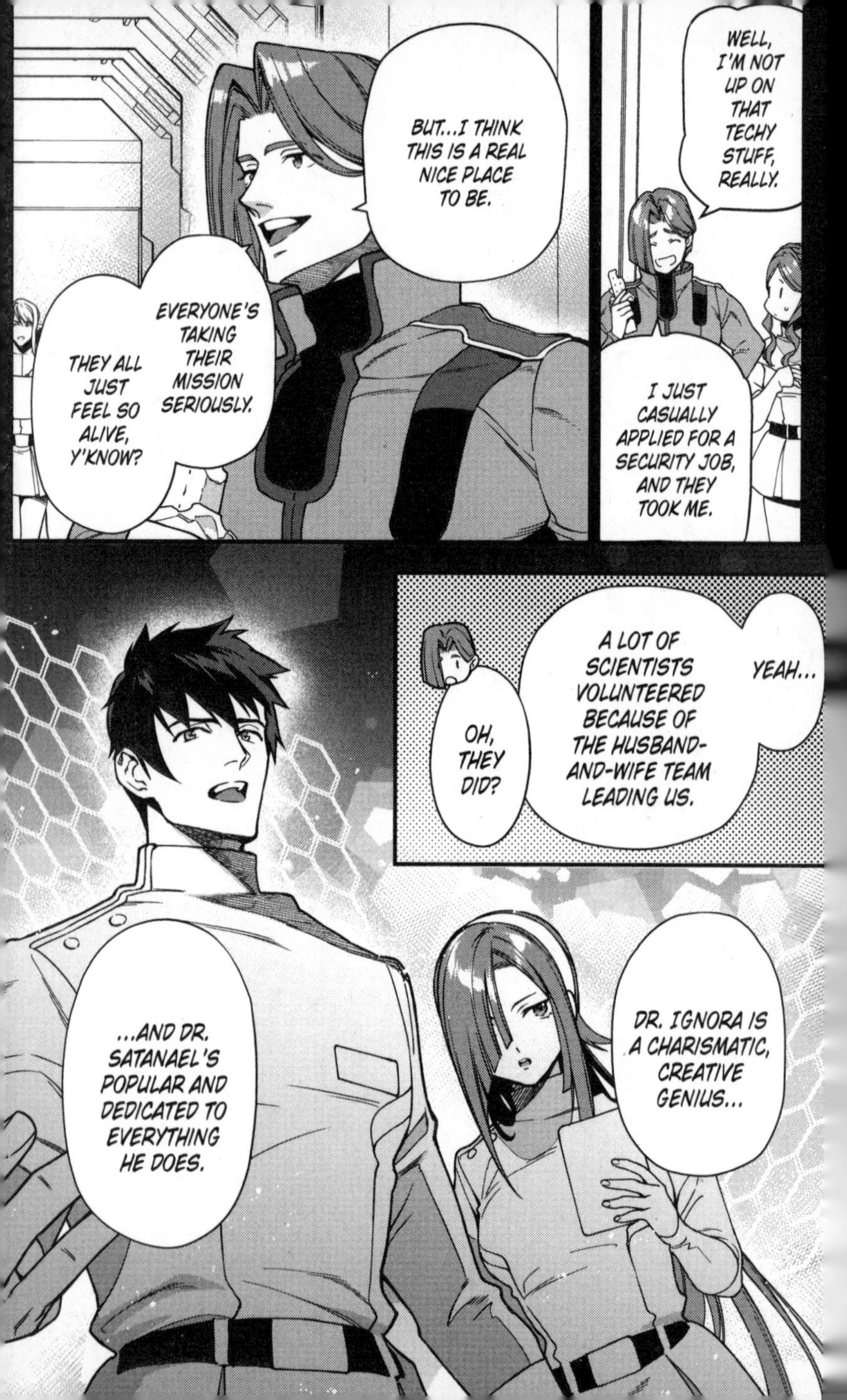
WELL, I'M NOT UP ON THAT TECHY STUFF, REALLY.
I JUST CASUALLY APPLIED FOR A SECURITY JOB, AND THEY TOOK ME.
BUT...I THINK THIS IS A REAL NICE PLACE TO BE.
EVERYONE'S TAKING THEIR MISSION SERIOUSLY.
THEY ALL JUST FEEL SO ALIVE, Y'KNOW?
YEAH...
A LOT OF SCIENTISTS VOLUNTEERED BECAUSE OF THE HUSBAND-AND-WIFE TEAM LEADING US.
OH, THEY DID?
DR. IGNORA IS A CHARISMATIC, CREATIVE GENIUS...
...AND DR. SATANAEL'S POPULAR AND DEDICATED TO EVERYTHING HE DOES.

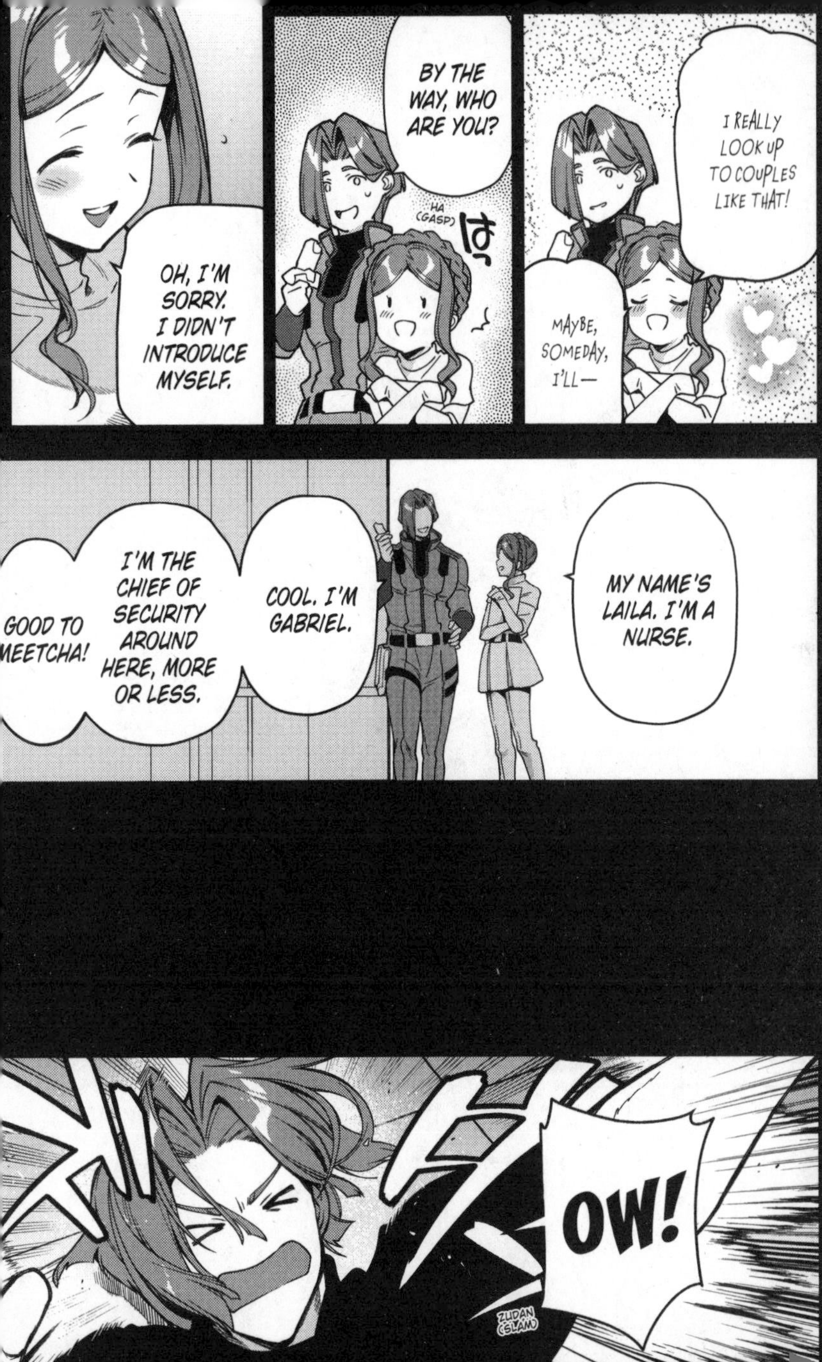
I REALLY LOOK UP TO COUPLES LIKE THAT!
MAYBE, SOMEDAY, I'LL—
BY THE WAY, WHO ARE YOU?
は
HA (GASP)
OH, I'M SORRY. I DIDN'T INTRODUCE MYSELF.
MY NAME'S LAILA. I'M A NURSE.
COOL. I'M GABRIEL.
I'M THE CHIEF OF SECURITY AROUND HERE, MORE OR LESS.
GOOD TO MEETCHA!
OW!
ZUDAN (SLAM)

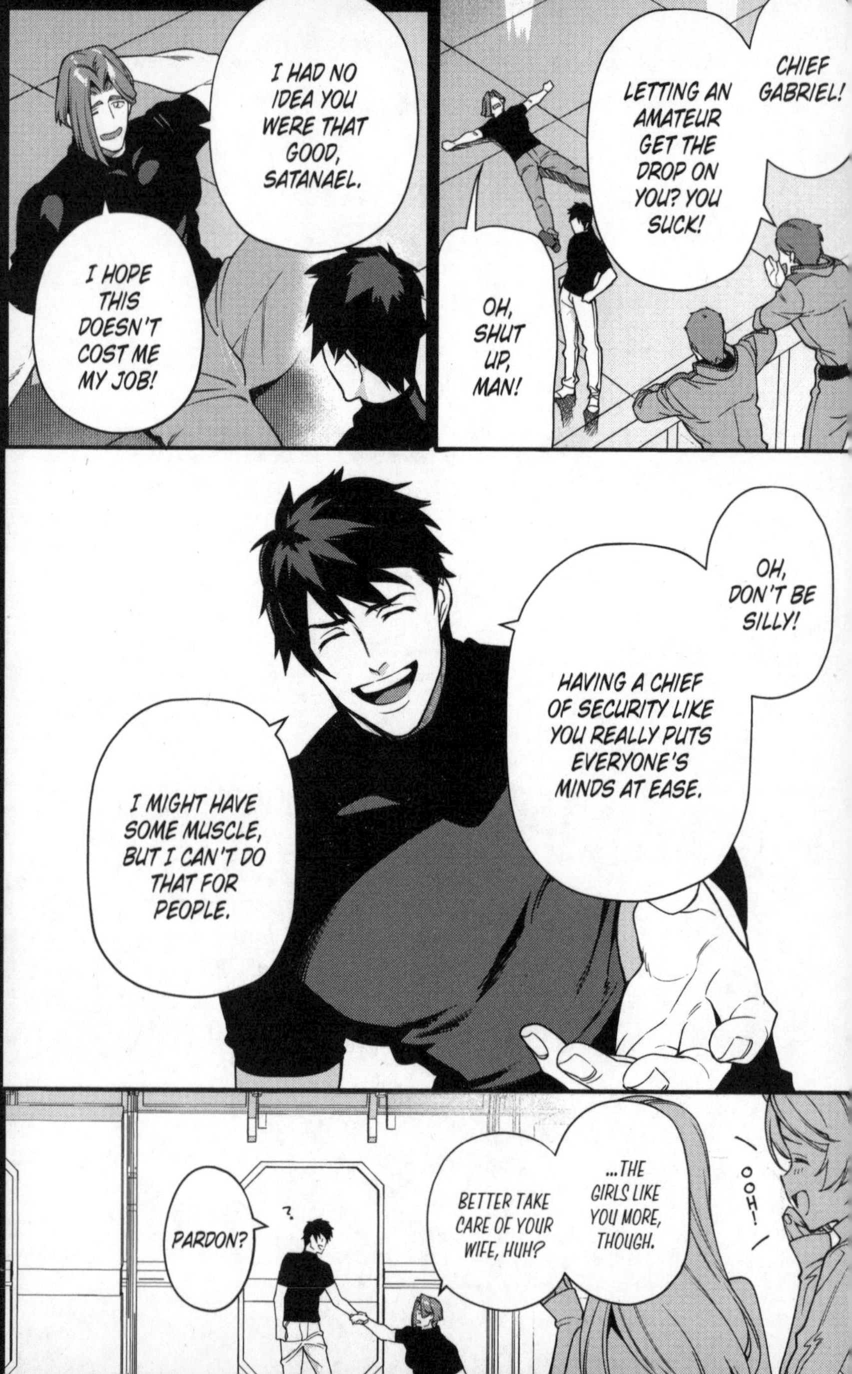
CHIEF GABRIEL!
LETTING AN AMATEUR GET THE DROP ON YOU? YOU SUCK!
OH, SHUT UP, MAN!
I HAD NO IDEA YOU WERE THAT GOOD, SATANAEL.
I HOPE THIS DOESN'T COST ME MY JOB!
OH, DON'T BE SILLY!
HAVING A CHIEF OF SECURITY LIKE YOU REALLY PUTS EVERYONE'S MINDS AT EASE.
I MIGHT HAVE SOME MUSCLE, BUT I CAN'T DO THAT FOR PEOPLE.
OOH!
...THE GIRLS LIKE YOU MORE, THOUGH.
BETTER TAKE CARE OF YOUR WIFE, HUH?
?
PARDON?

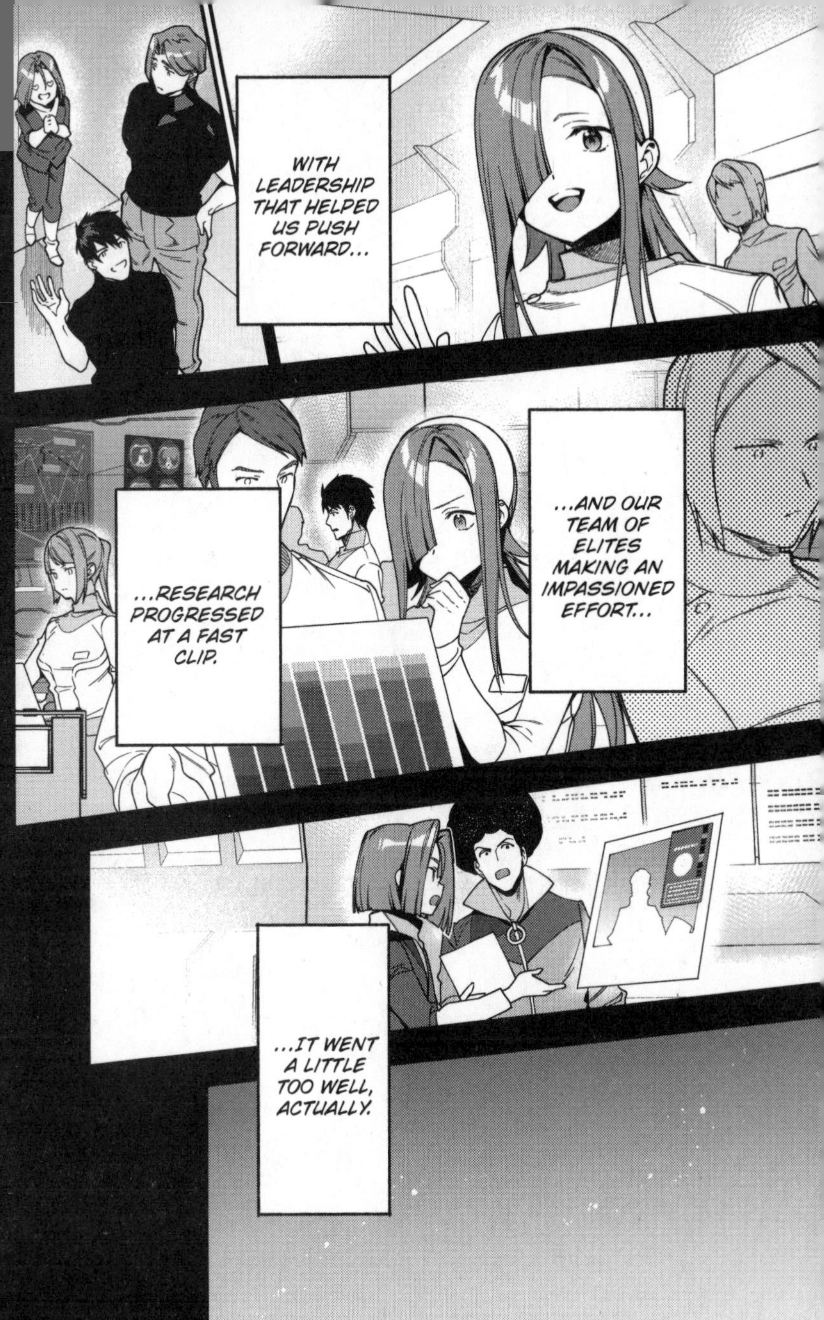
WITH LEADERSHIP THAT HELPED US PUSH FORWARD...
...AND OUR TEAM OF ELITES MAKING AN IMPASSIONED EFFORT...
...RESEARCH PROGRESSED AT A FAST CLIP.
...IT WENT A LITTLE TOO WELL, ACTUALLY.

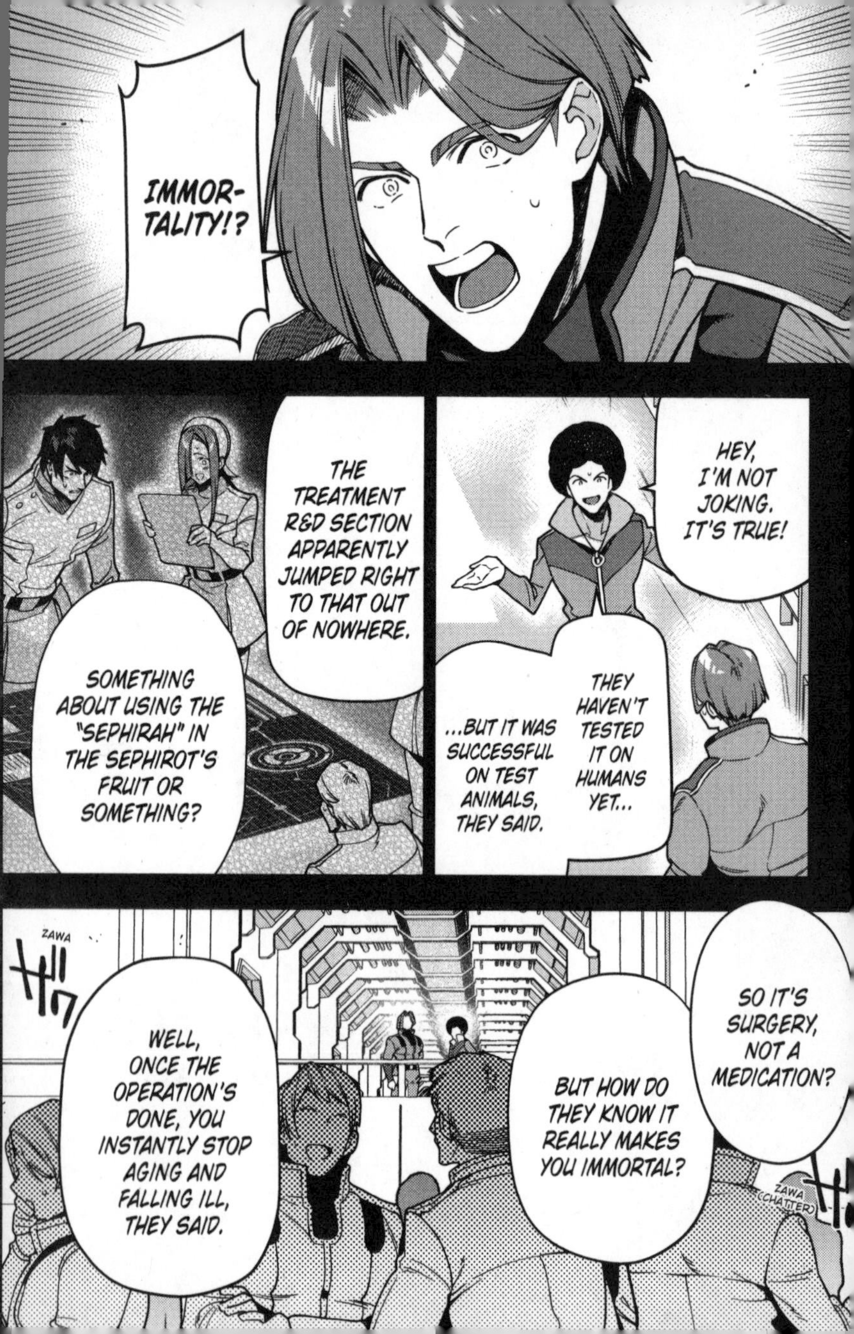
IMMORTALITY!?
HEY, I'M NOT JOKING. IT'S TRUE!
THEY HAVEN'T TESTED IT ON HUMANS YET...
...BUT IT WAS SUCCESSFUL ON TEST ANIMALS, THEY SAID.
THE TREATMENT R&D SECTION APPARENTLY JUMPED RIGHT TO THAT OUT OF NOWHERE.
SOMETHING ABOUT USING THE "SEPHIRAH" IN THE SEPHIROT'S FRUIT OR SOMETHING?
ZAWA (CHATTER)
SO IT'S SURGERY, NOT A MEDICATION?
BUT HOW DO THEY KNOW IT REALLY MAKES YOU IMMORTAL?
WELL, ONCE THE OPERATION'S DONE, YOU INSTANTLY STOP AGING AND FALLING ILL, THEY SAID.
ZAWA

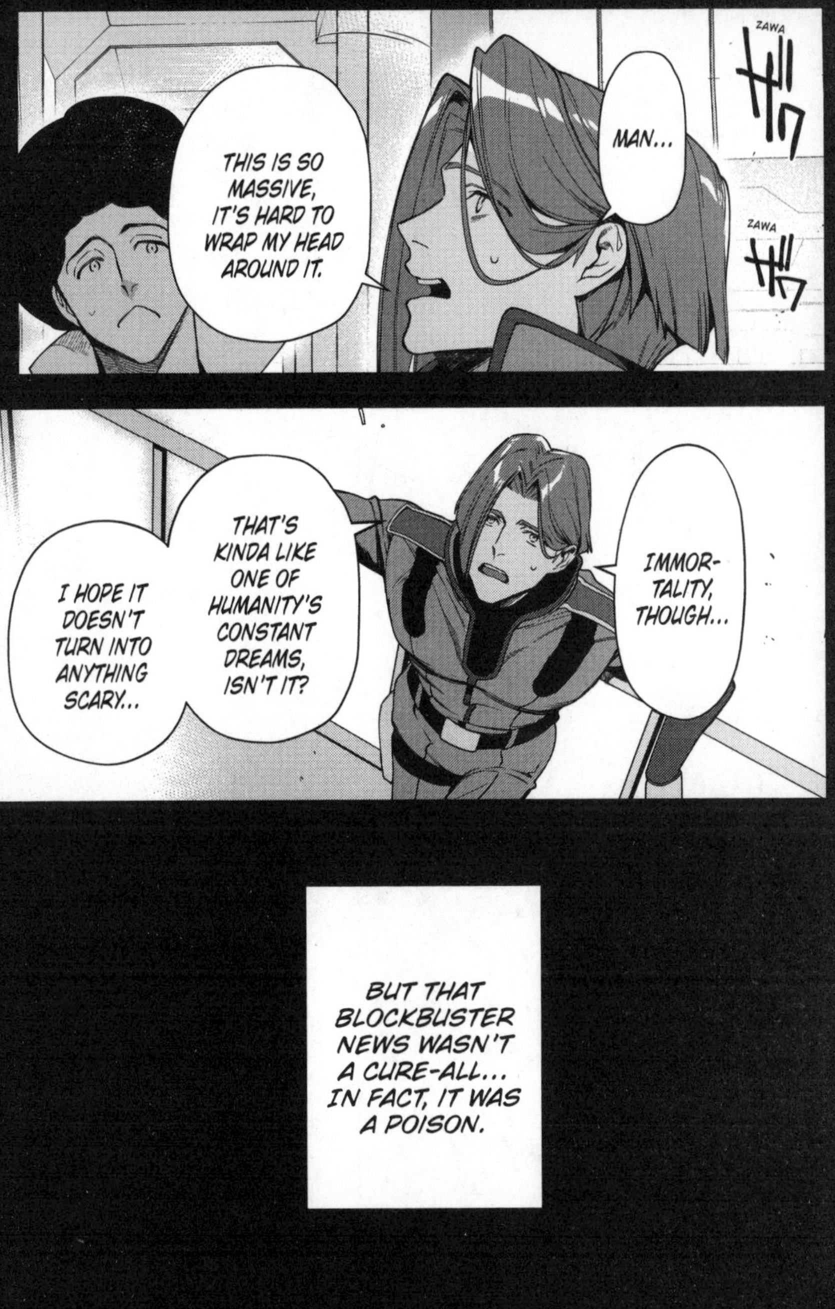
ZAWA
ZAWA
MAN…
THIS IS SO MASSIVE, IT'S HARD TO WRAP MY HEAD AROUND IT.
IMMOR-TALITY, THOUGH…
THAT'S KINDA LIKE ONE OF HUMANITY'S CONSTANT DREAMS, ISN'T IT?
I HOPE IT DOESN'T TURN INTO ANYTHING SCARY…
BUT THAT BLOCKBUSTER NEWS WASN'T A CURE-ALL… IN FACT, IT WAS A POISON.

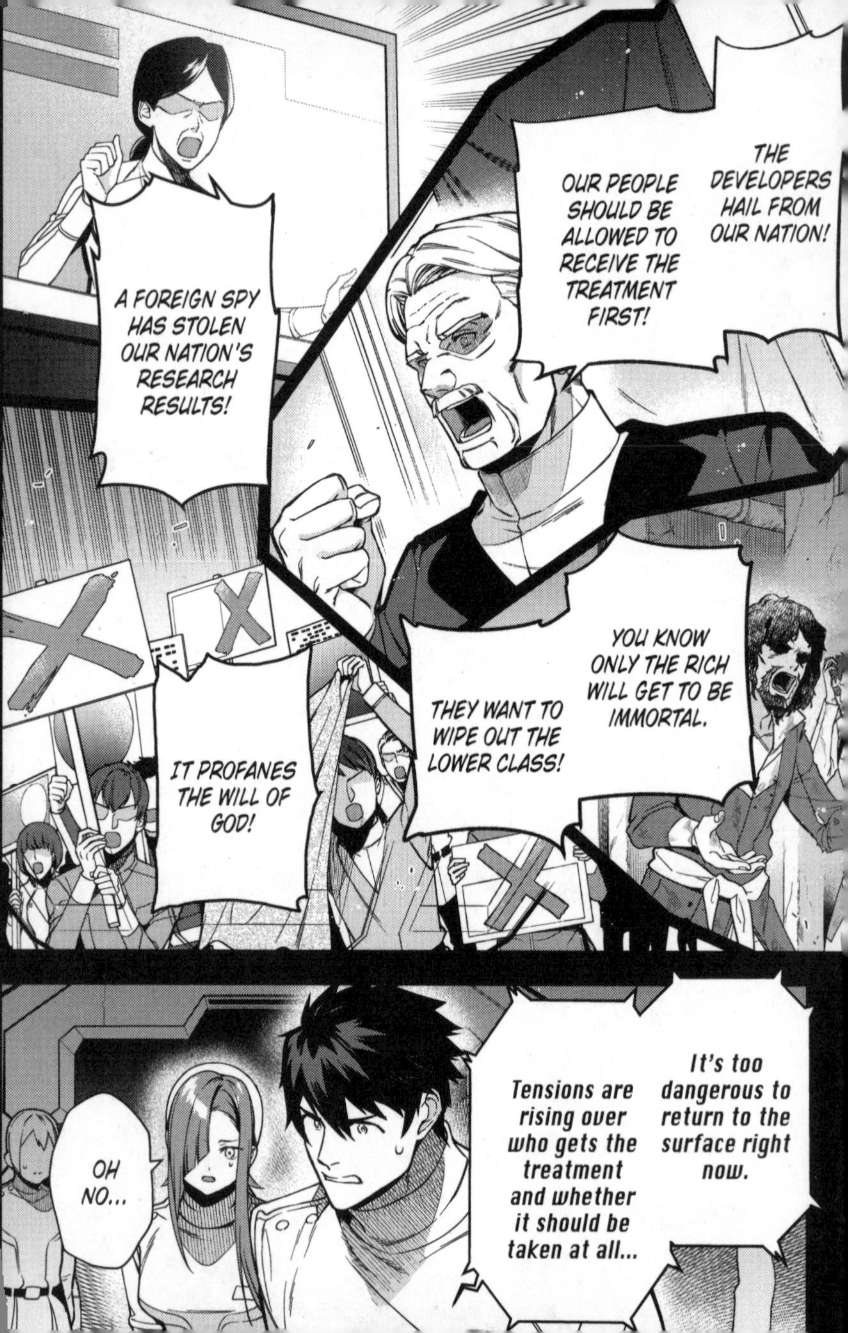
THE DEVELOPERS HAIL FROM OUR NATION!
OUR PEOPLE SHOULD BE ALLOWED TO RECEIVE THE TREATMENT FIRST!
A FOREIGN SPY HAS STOLEN OUR NATION'S RESEARCH RESULTS!
YOU KNOW ONLY THE RICH WILL GET TO BE IMMORTAL.
THEY WANT TO WIPE OUT THE LOWER CLASS!
IT PROFANES THE WILL OF GOD!
It's too dangerous to return to the surface right now.
Tensions are rising over who gets the treatment and whether it should be taken at all...
OH NO...

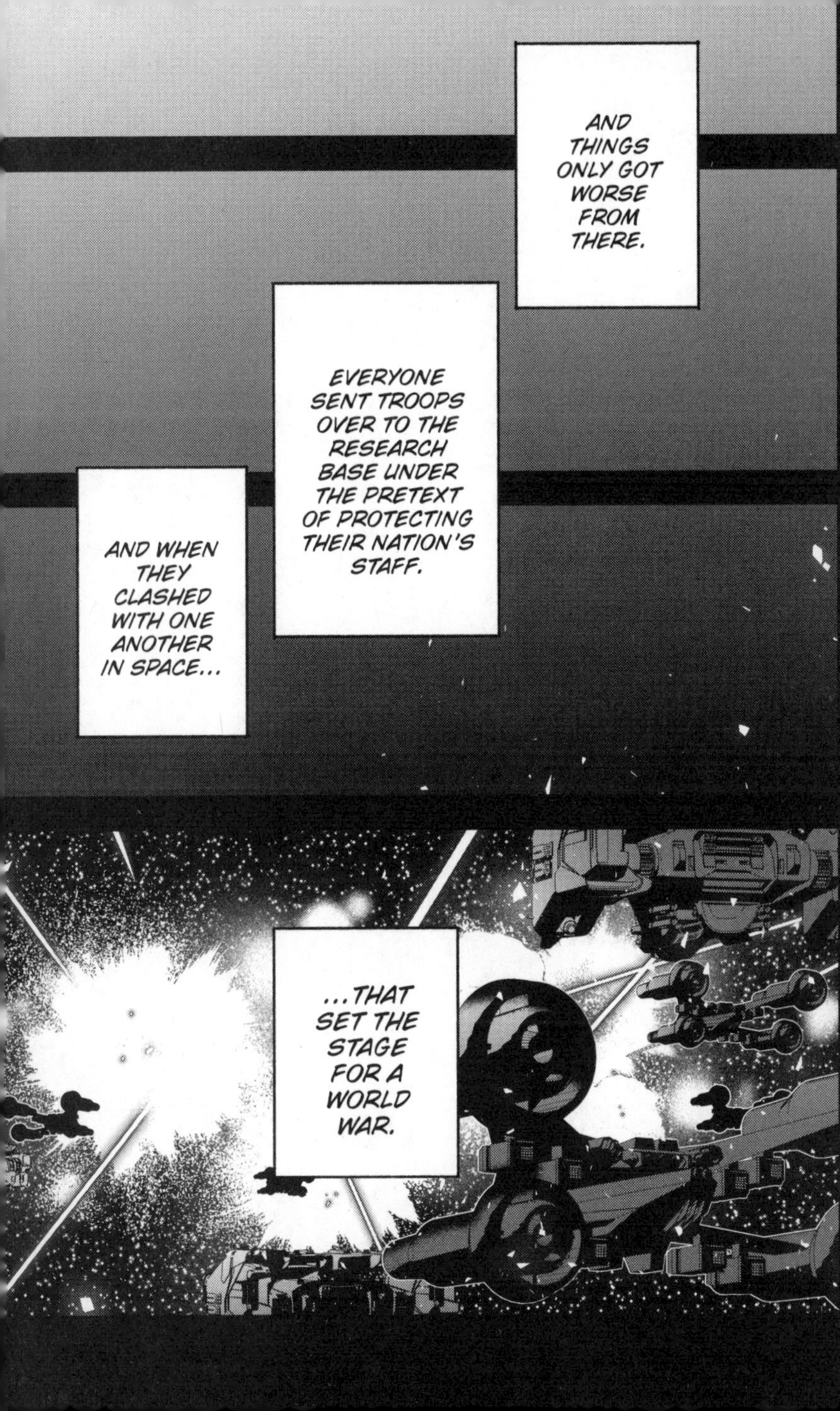
AND THINGS ONLY GOT WORSE FROM THERE.
EVERYONE SENT TROOPS OVER TO THE RESEARCH BASE UNDER THE PRETEXT OF PROTECTING THEIR NATION'S STAFF.
AND WHEN THEY CLASHED WITH ONE ANOTHER IN SPACE...
...THAT SET THE STAGE FOR A WORLD WAR.

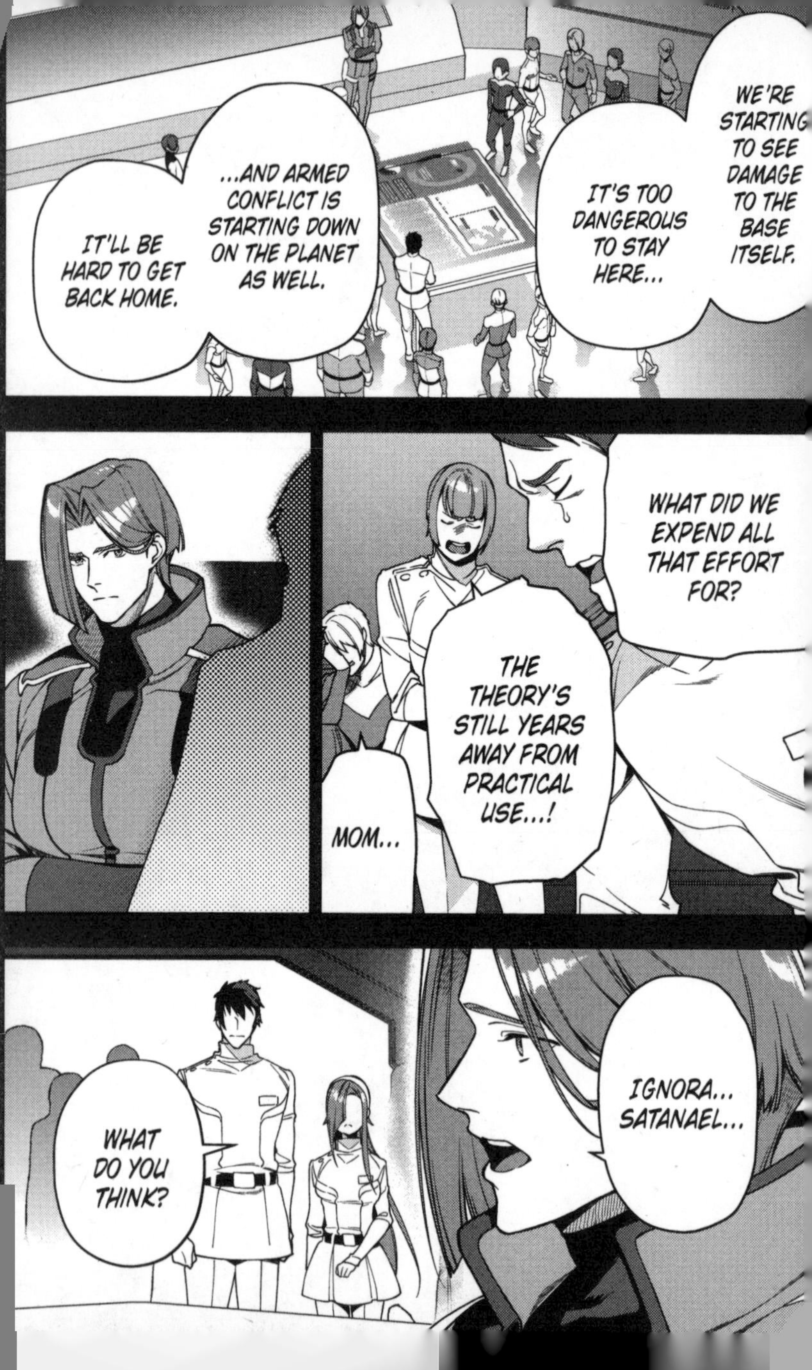
WE'RE STARTING TO SEE DAMAGE TO THE BASE ITSELF.
IT'S TOO DANGEROUS TO STAY HERE...
...AND ARMED CONFLICT IS STARTING DOWN ON THE PLANET AS WELL.
IT'LL BE HARD TO GET BACK HOME.
WHAT DID WE EXPEND ALL THAT EFFORT FOR?
THE THEORY'S STILL YEARS AWAY FROM PRACTICAL USE...!
MOM...
IGNORA... SATANAEL...
WHAT DO YOU THINK?

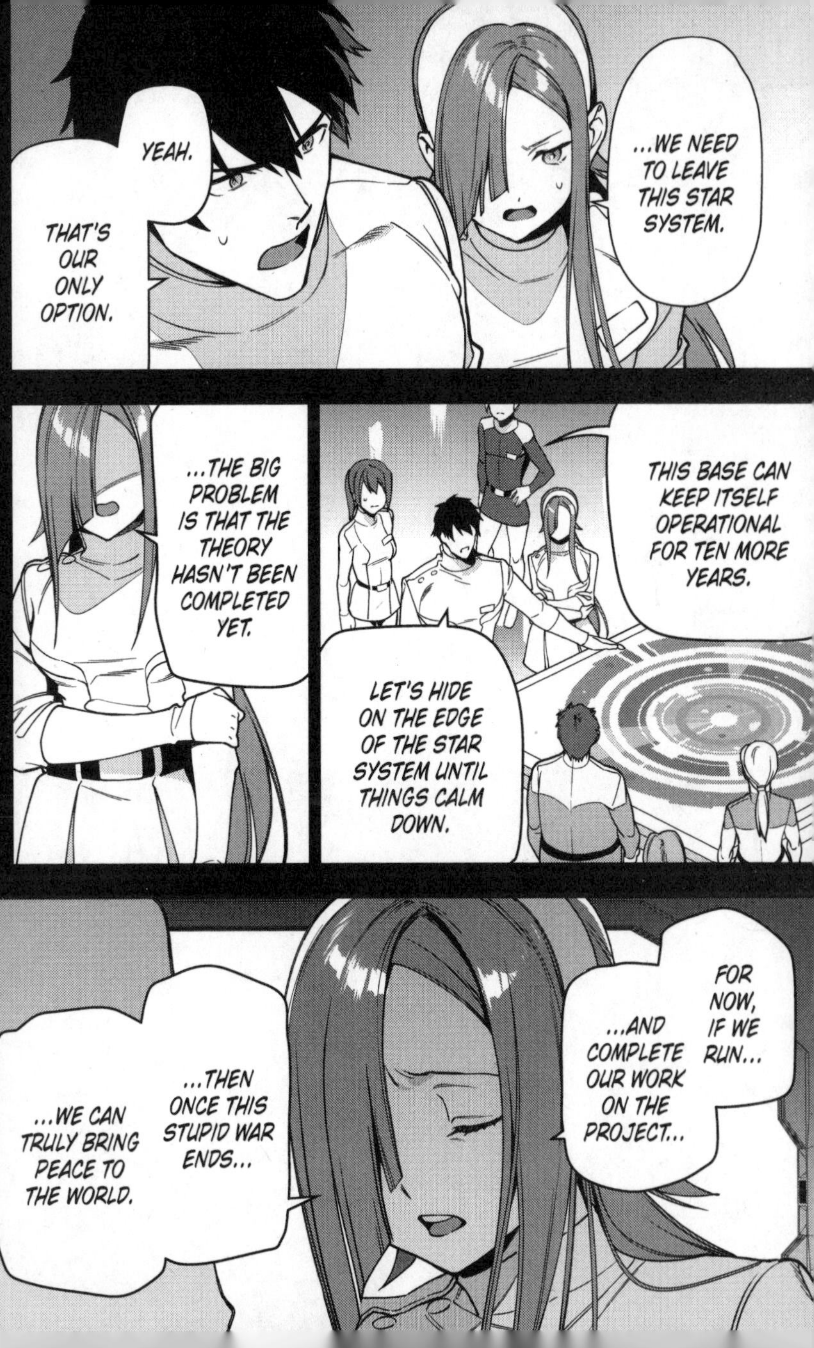
...WE NEED TO LEAVE THIS STAR SYSTEM.
YEAH.
THAT'S OUR ONLY OPTION.
THIS BASE CAN KEEP ITSELF OPERATIONAL FOR TEN MORE YEARS.
LET'S HIDE ON THE EDGE OF THE STAR SYSTEM UNTIL THINGS CALM DOWN.
...THE BIG PROBLEM IS THAT THE THEORY HASN'T BEEN COMPLETED YET.
FOR NOW, IF WE RUN...
...AND COMPLETE OUR WORK ON THE PROJECT...
...THEN ONCE THIS STUPID WAR ENDS...
...WE CAN TRULY BRING PEACE TO THE WORLD.

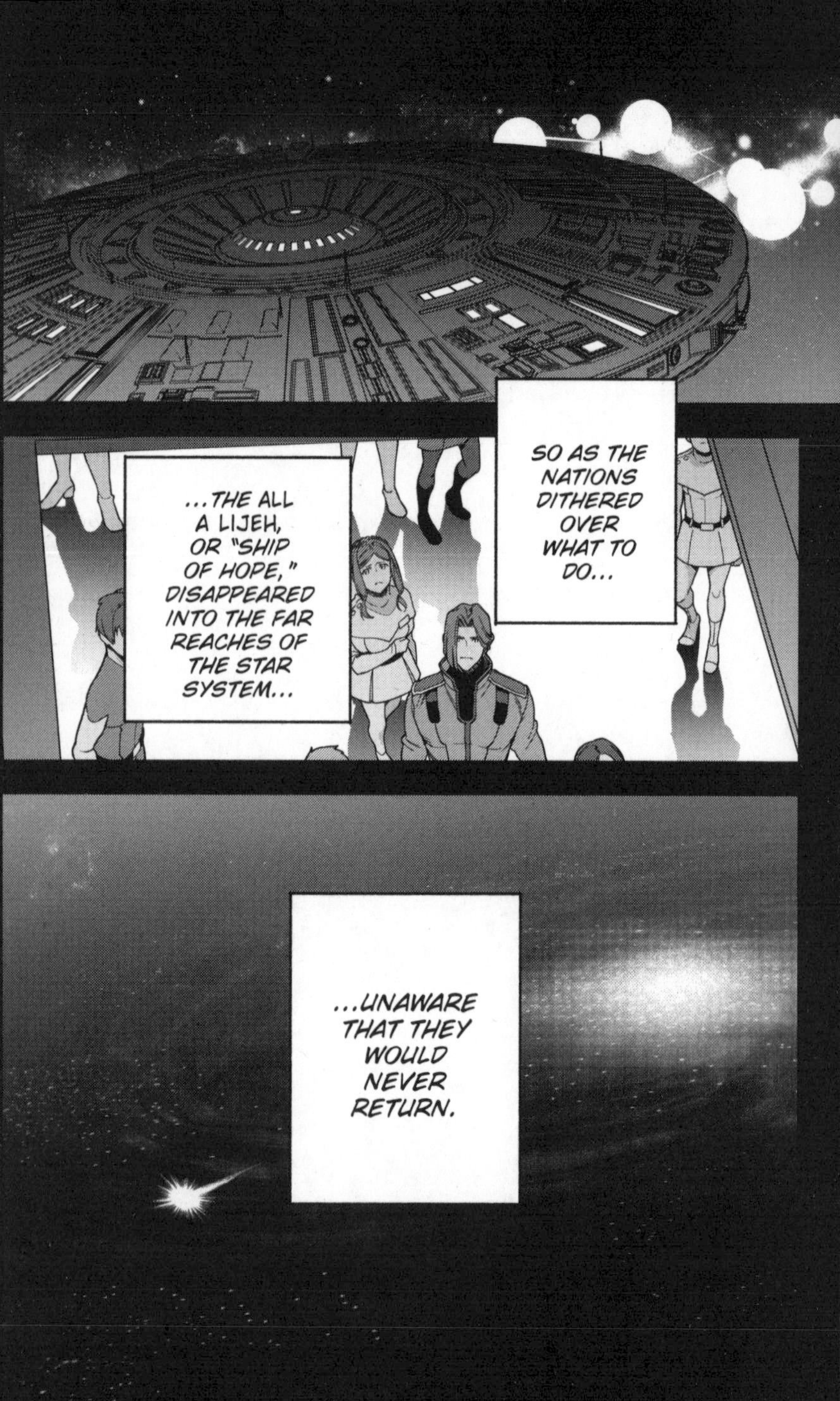
SO AS THE NATIONS DITHERED OVER WHAT TO DO...
...THE ALL A LIJEH, OR "SHIP OF HOPE," DISAPPEARED INTO THE FAR REACHES OF THE STAR SYSTEM...
...UNAWARE THAT THEY WOULD NEVER RETURN.

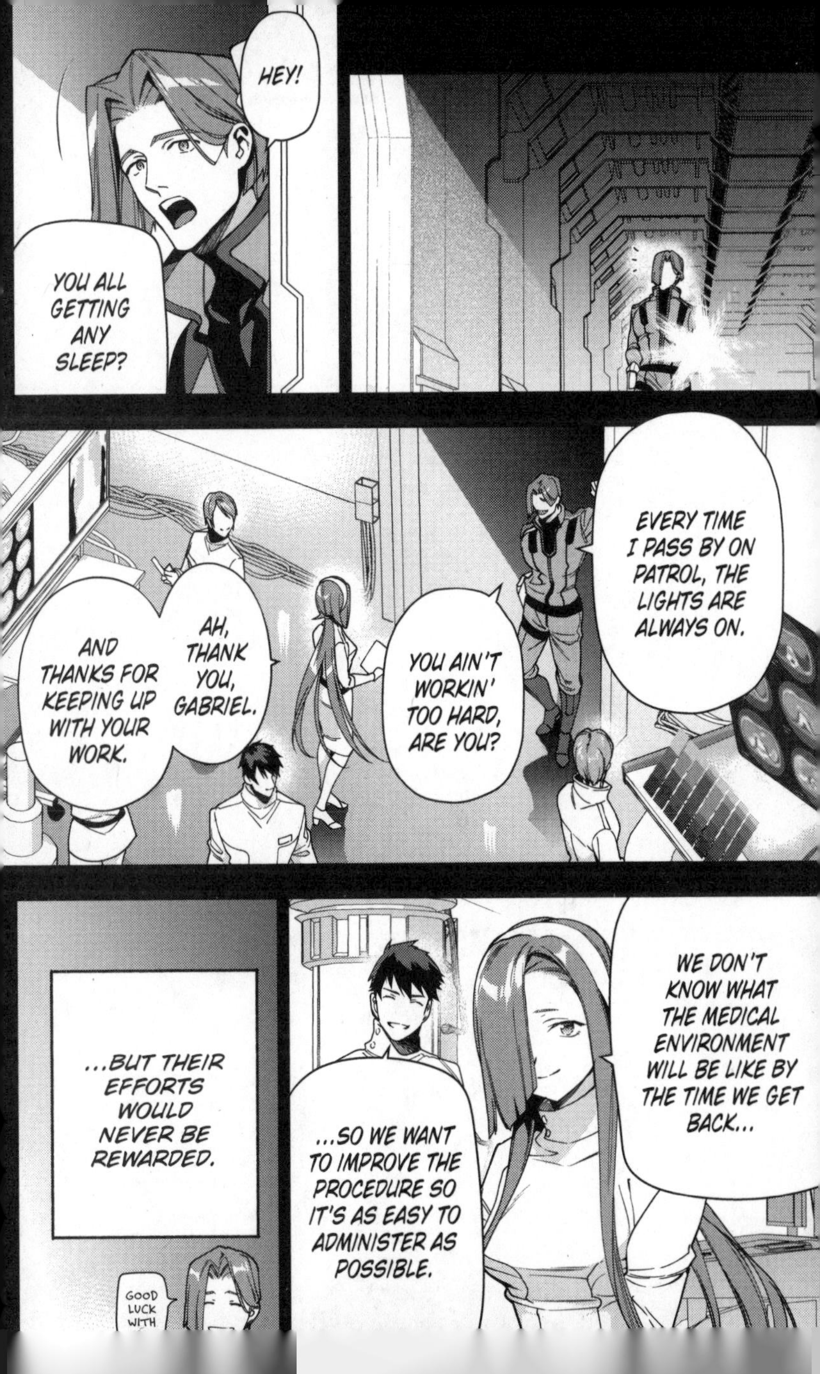
HEY!
YOU ALL GETTING ANY SLEEP?
EVERY TIME I PASS BY ON PATROL, THE LIGHTS ARE ALWAYS ON.
YOU AIN'T WORKIN' TOO HARD, ARE YOU?
AH, THANK YOU, GABRIEL.
AND THANKS FOR KEEPING UP WITH YOUR WORK.
WE DON'T KNOW WHAT THE MEDICAL ENVIRONMENT WILL BE LIKE BY THE TIME WE GET BACK...
...SO WE WANT TO IMPROVE THE PROCEDURE SO IT'S AS EASY TO ADMINISTER AS POSSIBLE.
...BUT THEIR EFFORTS WOULD NEVER BE REWARDED.
GOOD LUCK WITH

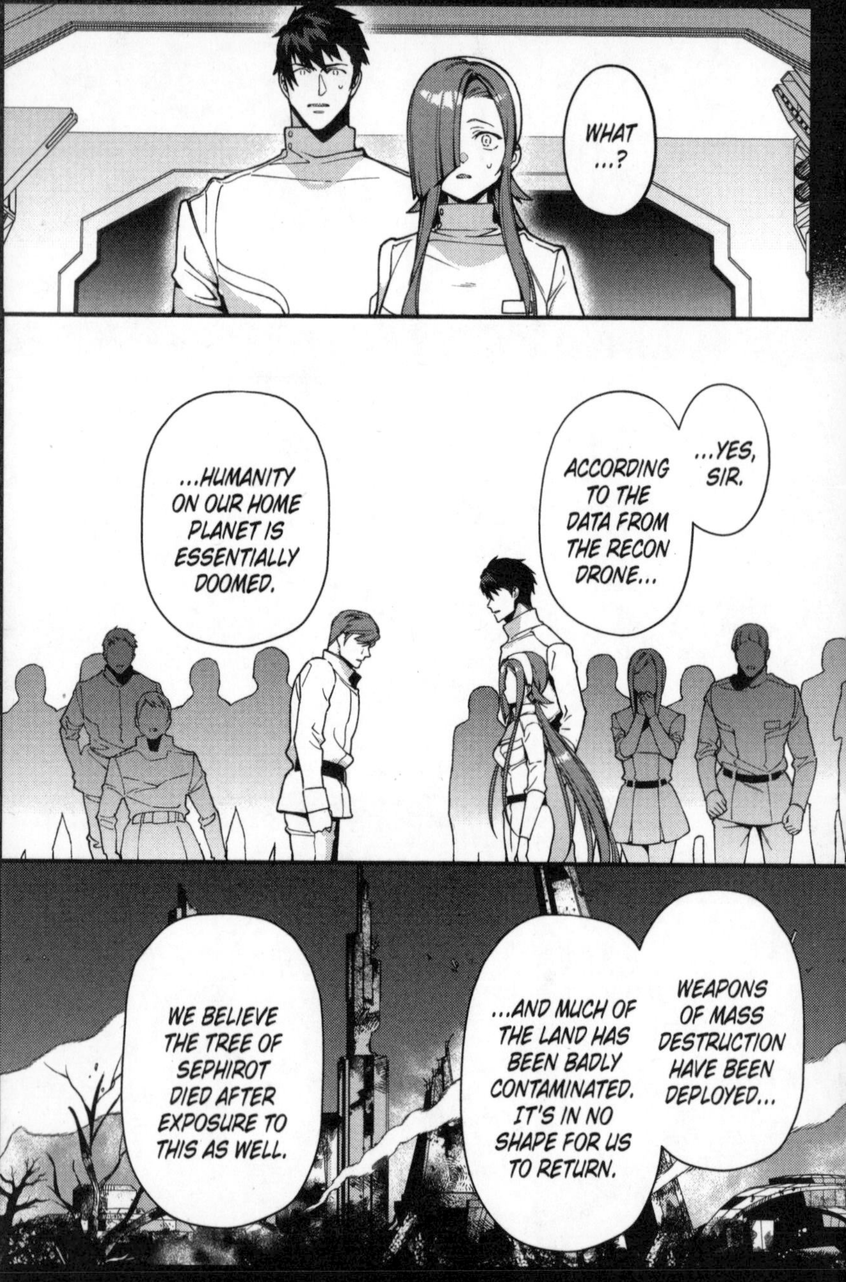
WHAT ...?
...YES, SIR.
ACCORDING TO THE DATA FROM THE RECON DRONE...
...HUMANITY ON OUR HOME PLANET IS ESSENTIALLY DOOMED.
WEAPONS OF MASS DESTRUCTION HAVE BEEN DEPLOYED...
...AND MUCH OF THE LAND HAS BEEN BADLY CONTAMINATED. IT'S IN NO SHAPE FOR US TO RETURN.
WE BELIEVE THE TREE OF SEPHIROT DIED AFTER EXPOSURE TO THIS AS WELL.

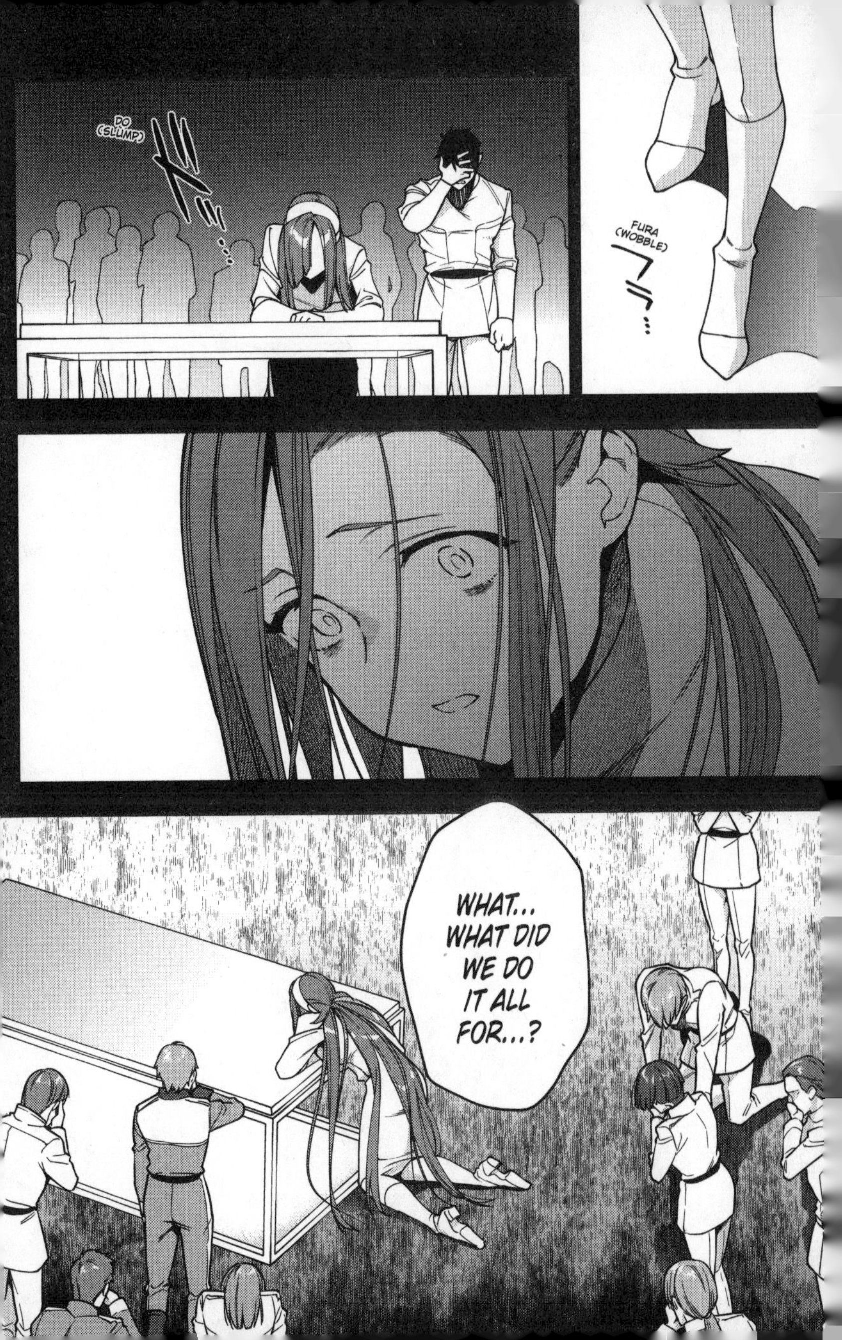
FURA (WOBBLE)
DO (SLUMP)
WHAT... WHAT DID WE DO IT ALL FOR...?

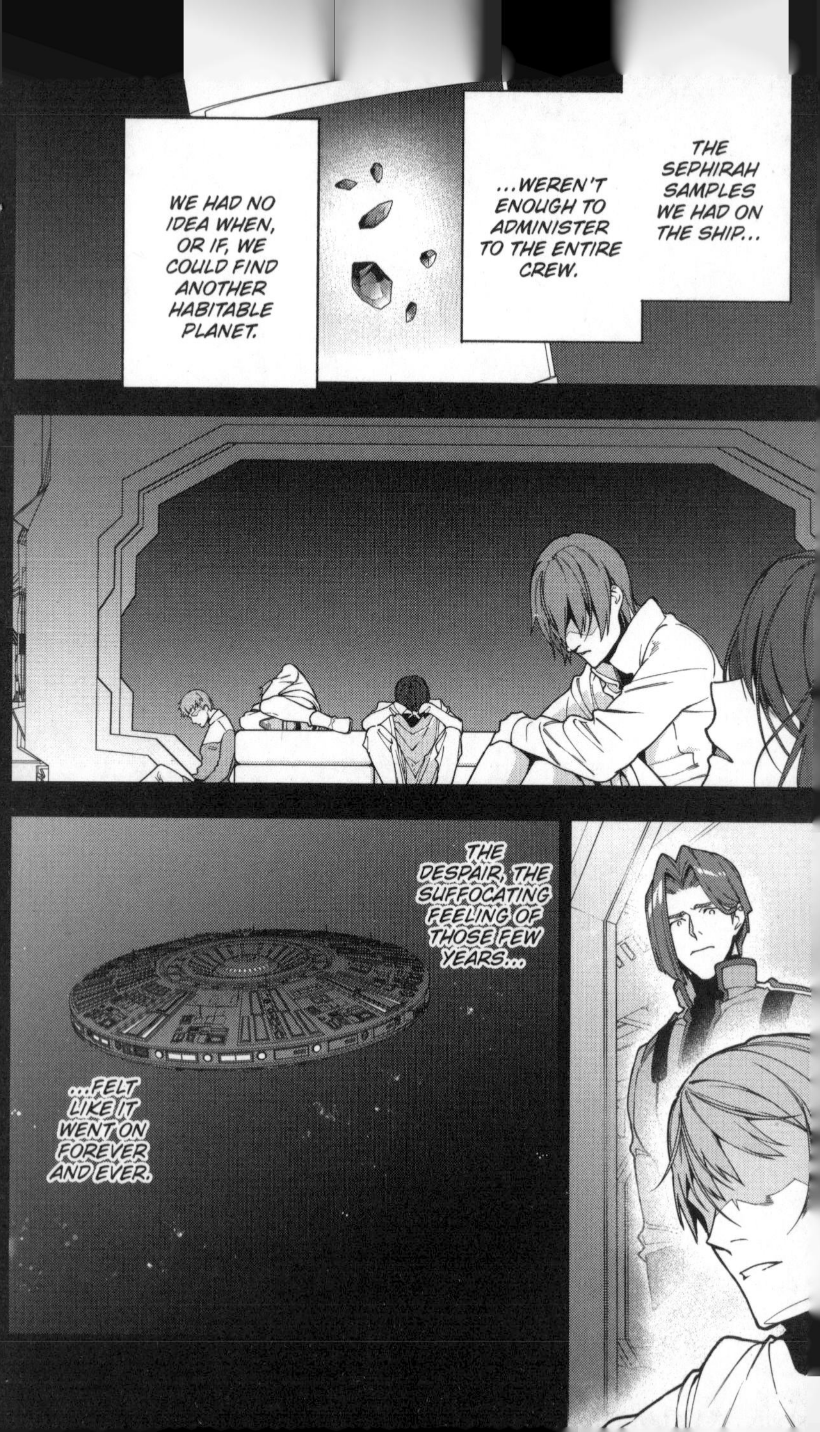
THE SEPHIRAH SAMPLES WE HAD ON THE SHIP...
...WEREN'T ENOUGH TO ADMINISTER TO THE ENTIRE CREW.
WE HAD NO IDEA WHEN, OR IF, WE COULD FIND ANOTHER HABITABLE PLANET.
THE DESPAIR, THE SUFFOCATING FEELING OF THOSE FEW YEARS...
...FELT LIKE IT WENT ON FOREVER AND EVER.

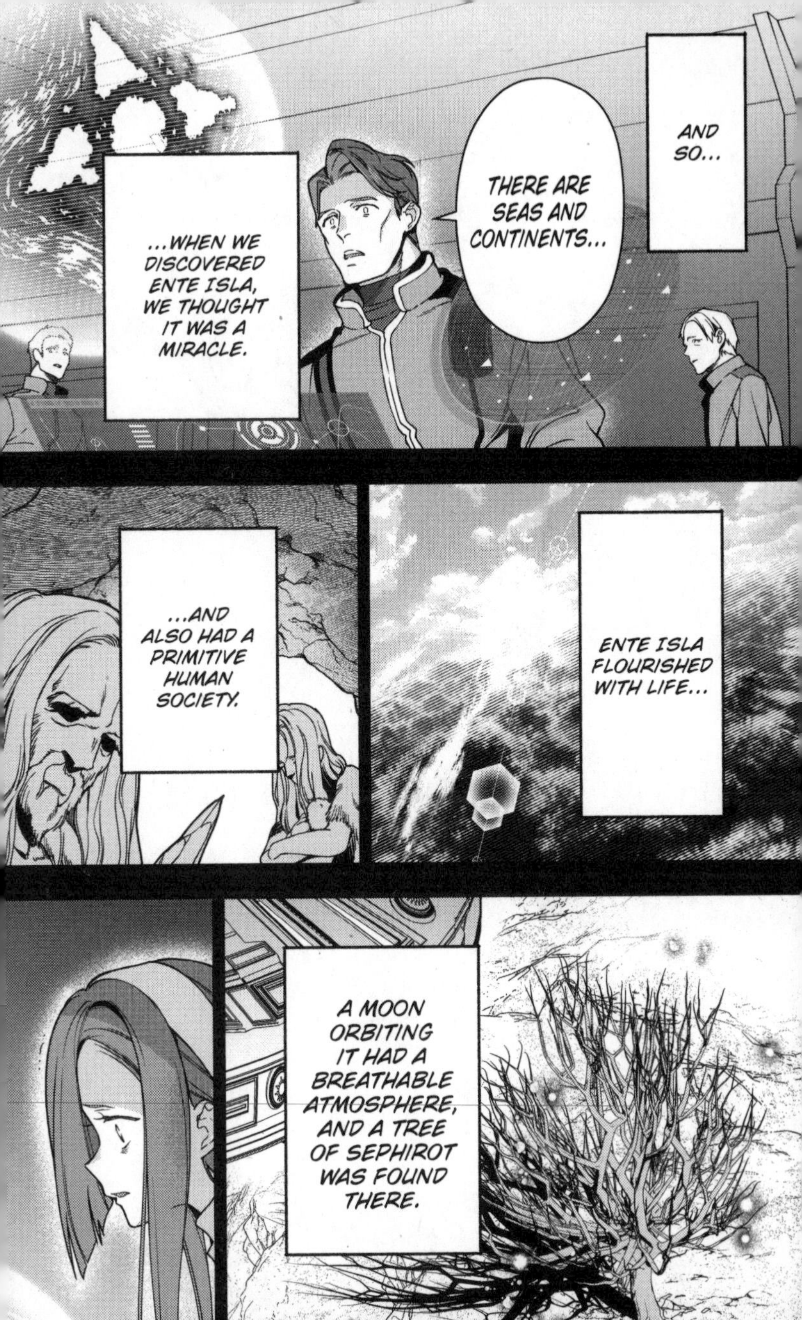
AND SO...
THERE ARE SEAS AND CONTINENTS...
...WHEN WE DISCOVERED ENTE ISLA, WE THOUGHT IT WAS A MIRACLE.
ENTE ISLA FLOURISHED WITH LIFE...
...AND ALSO HAD A PRIMITIVE HUMAN SOCIETY.
A MOON ORBITING IT HAD A BREATHABLE ATMOSPHERE, AND A TREE OF SEPHIROT WAS FOUND THERE.

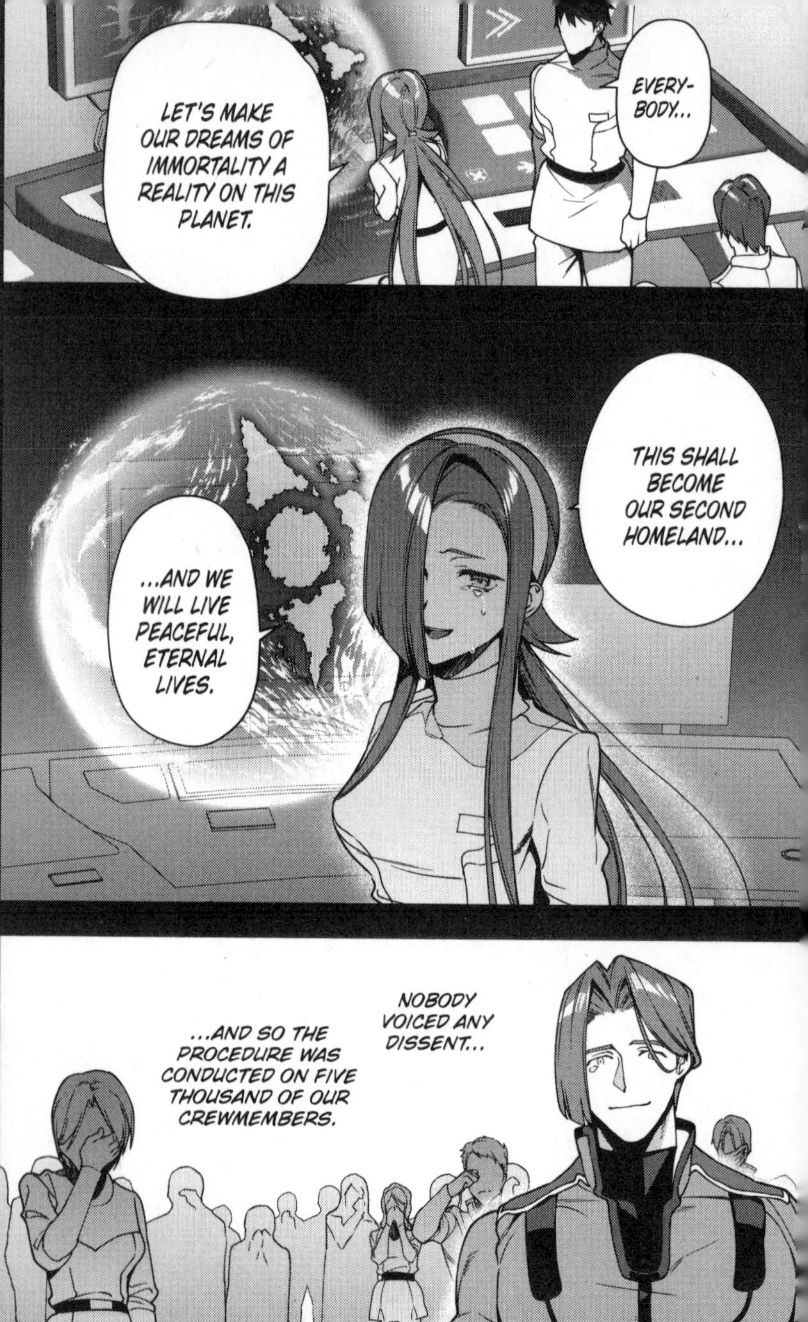
EVERY-BODY...
LET'S MAKE OUR DREAMS OF IMMORTALITY A REALITY ON THIS PLANET.
THIS SHALL BECOME OUR SECOND HOMELAND...
...AND WE WILL LIVE PEACEFUL, ETERNAL LIVES.
NOBODY VOICED ANY DISSENT...
...AND SO THE PROCEDURE WAS CONDUCTED ON FIVE THOUSAND OF OUR CREWMEMBERS.

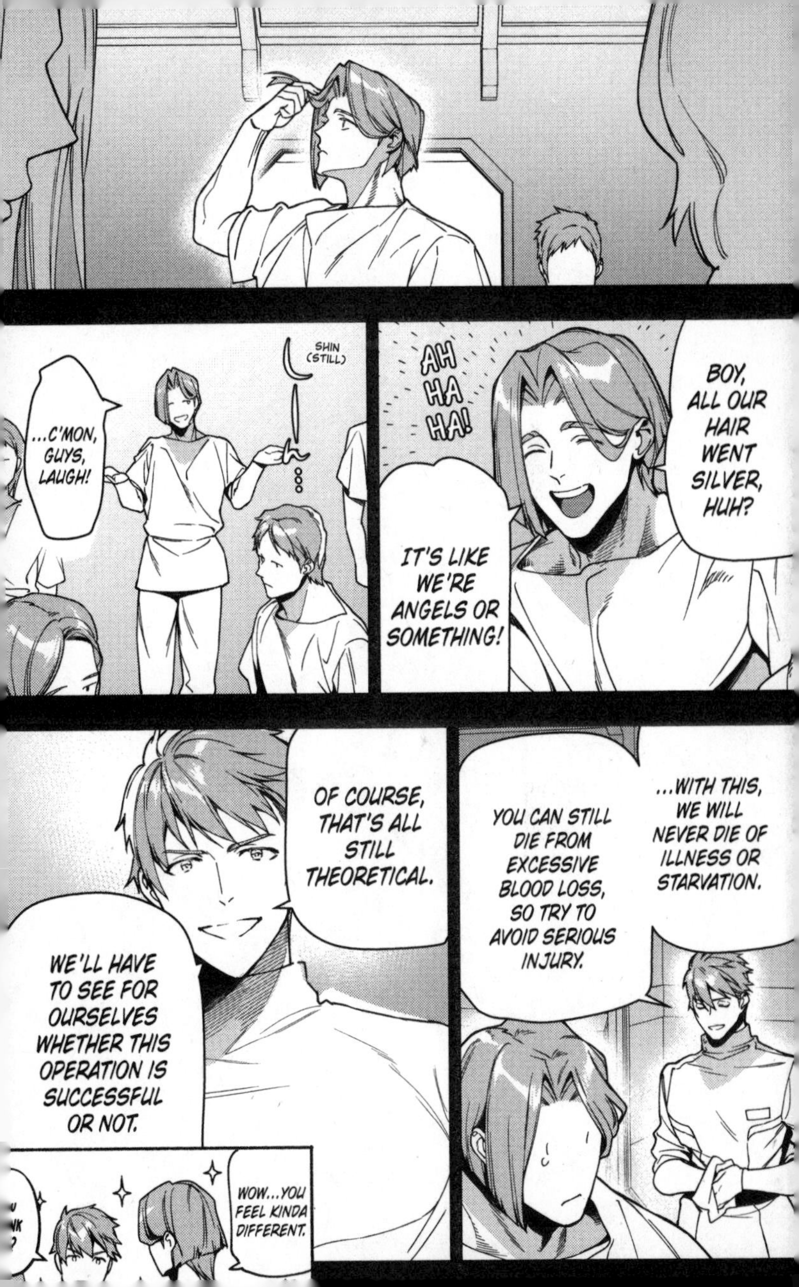
BOY, ALL OUR HAIR WENT SILVER, HUH?
AH HA HA!
IT'S LIKE WE'RE ANGELS OR SOMETHING!
SHIN (STILL)
...C'MON, GUYS, LAUGH!
...WITH THIS, WE WILL NEVER DIE OF ILLNESS OR STARVATION.
YOU CAN STILL DIE FROM EXCESSIVE BLOOD LOSS, SO TRY TO AVOID SERIOUS INJURY.
OF COURSE, THAT'S ALL STILL THEORETICAL.
WE'LL HAVE TO SEE FOR OURSELVES WHETHER THIS OPERATION IS SUCCESSFUL OR NOT.
WOW...YOU FEEL KINDA DIFFERENT.

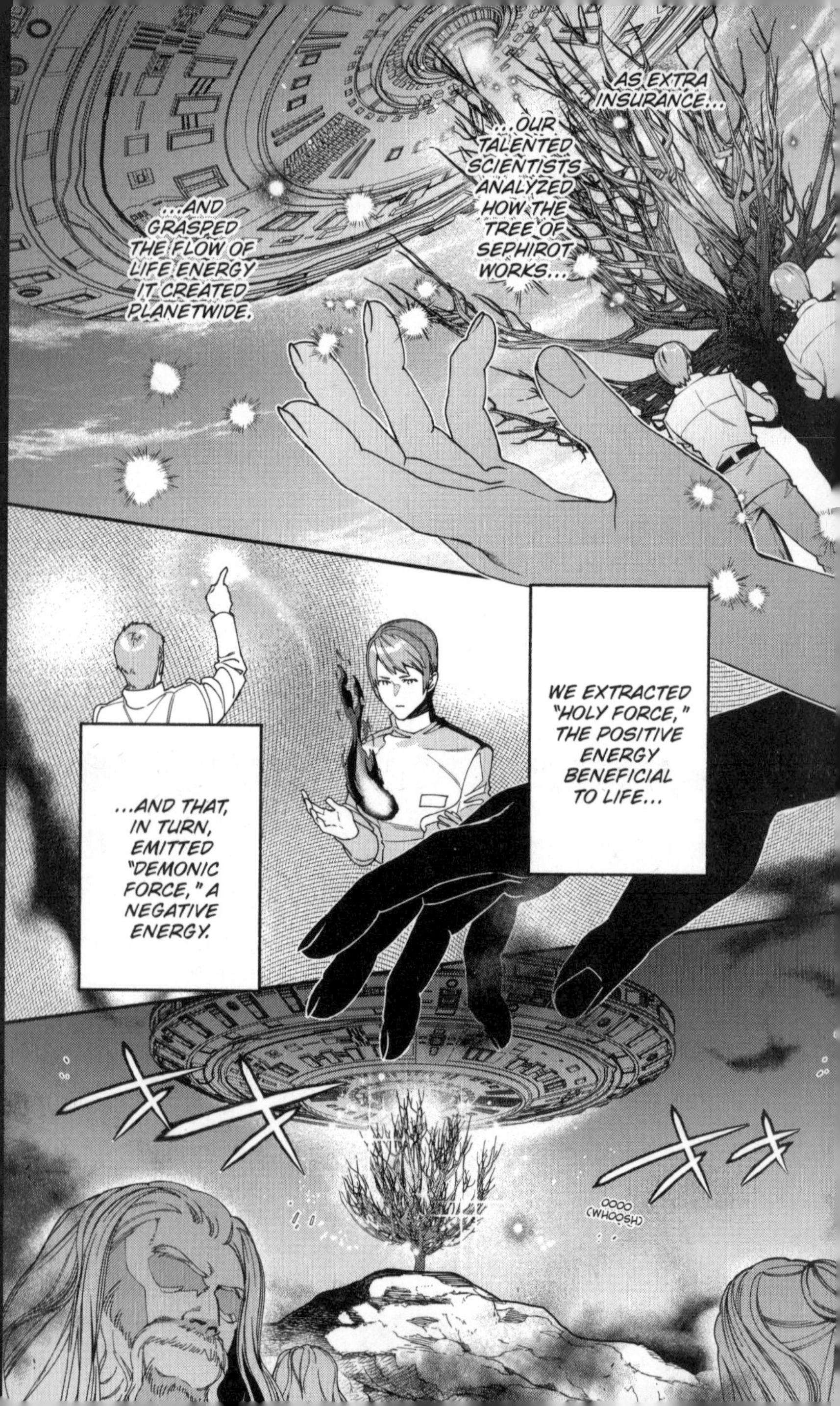
AS EXTRA INSURANCE...
...OUR TALENTED SCIENTISTS ANALYZED HOW THE TREE OF SEPHIROT WORKS...
...AND GRASPED THE FLOW OF LIFE ENERGY IT CREATED PLANETWIDE.
WE EXTRACTED "HOLY FORCE," THE POSITIVE ENERGY BENEFICIAL TO LIFE...
...AND THAT, IN TURN, EMITTED "DEMONIC FORCE," A NEGATIVE ENERGY.
OOOO (WHOOSH)

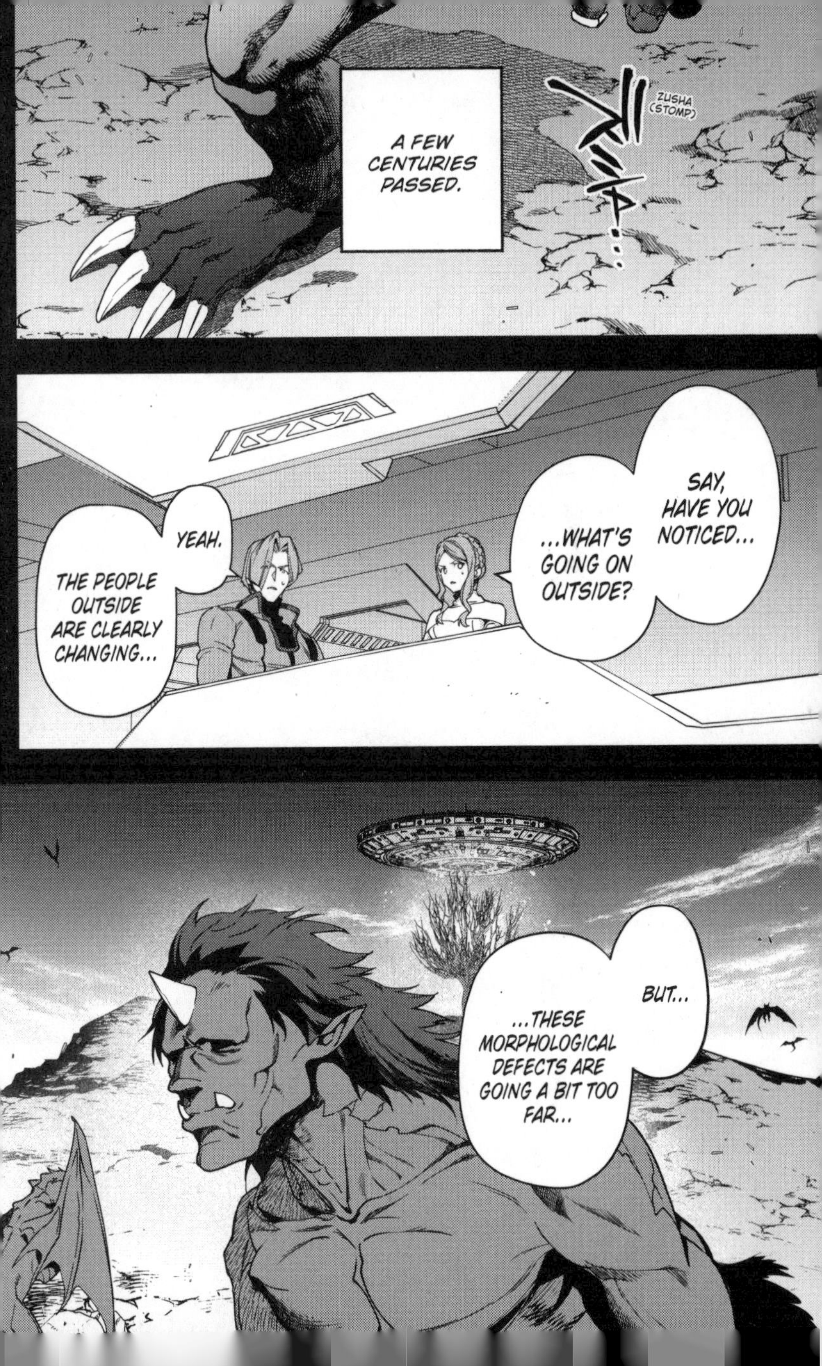
ZUSHA (STOMP)
A FEW CENTURIES PASSED.
SAY, HAVE YOU NOTICED...
...WHAT'S GOING ON OUTSIDE?
YEAH.
THE PEOPLE OUTSIDE ARE CLEARLY CHANGING...
BUT...
...THESE MORPHOLOGICAL DEFECTS ARE GOING A BIT TOO FAR...

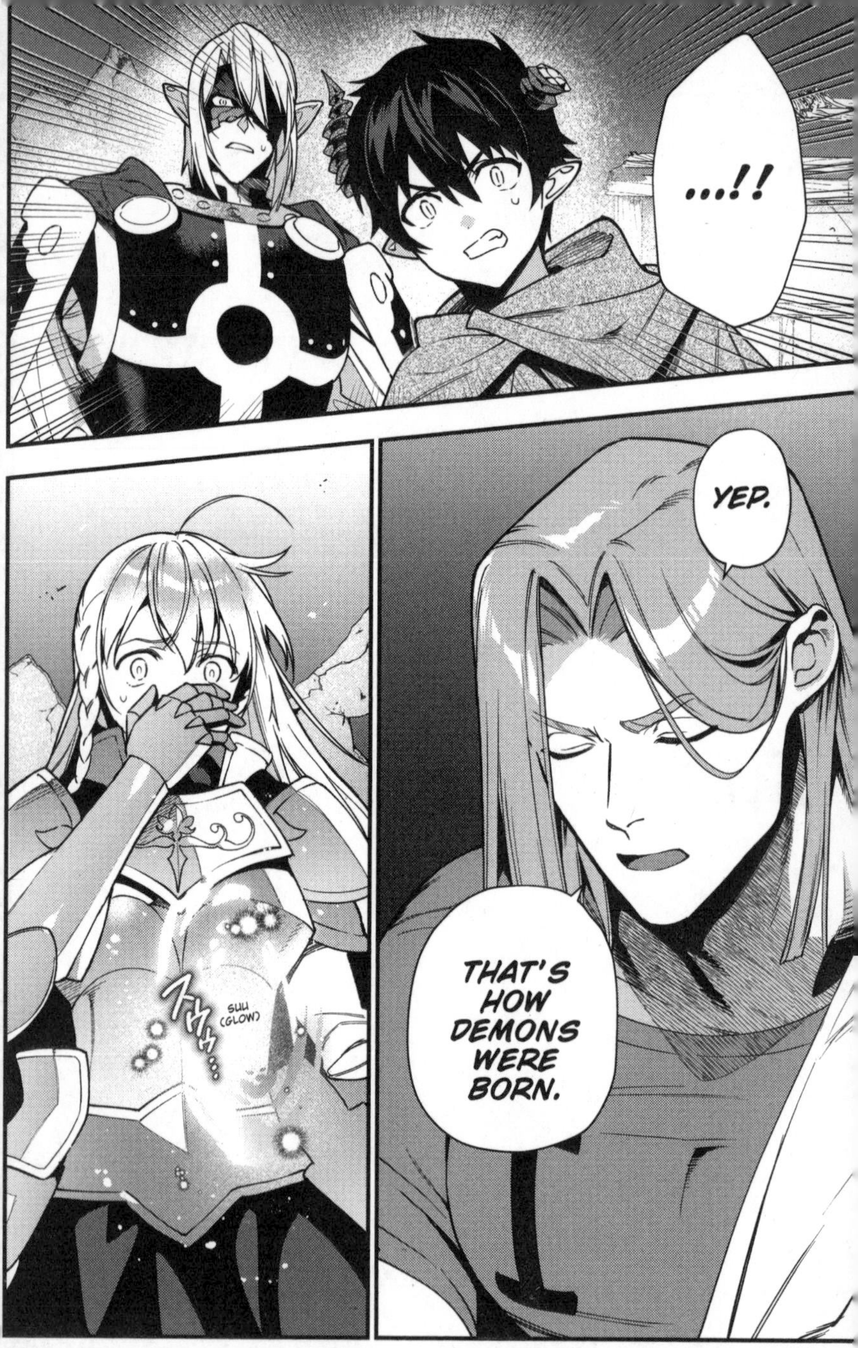
...!!
YEP.
THAT'S HOW DEMONS WERE BORN.
SUU (GLOW)

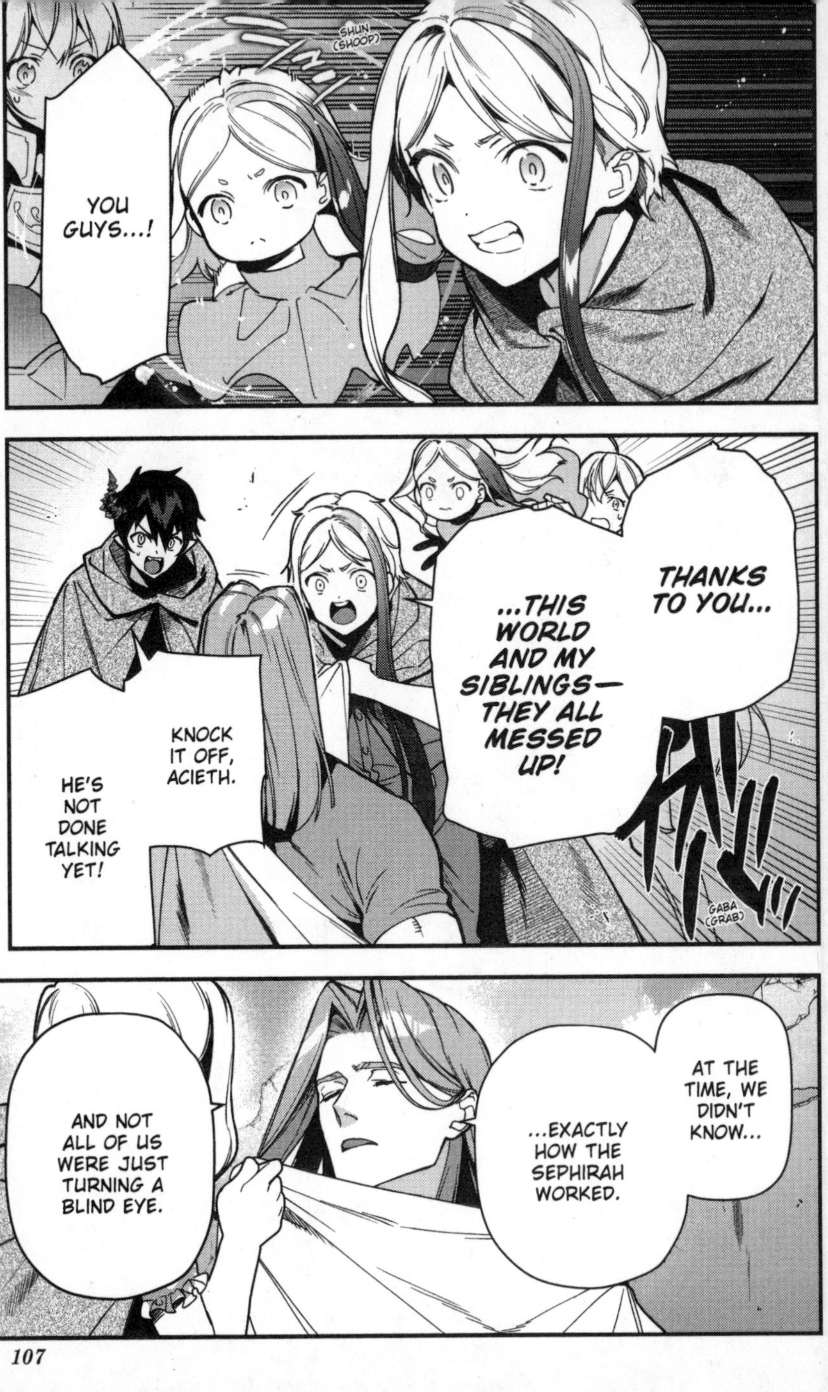
SHUN (SHOOP)
YOU GUYS...!
THANKS TO YOU...
...THIS WORLD AND MY SIBLINGS— THEY ALL MESSED UP!
GABA (GRAB)
KNOCK IT OFF, ACIETH.
HE'S NOT DONE TALKING YET!
AT THE TIME, WE DIDN'T KNOW...
...EXACTLY HOW THE SEPHIRAH WORKED.
AND NOT ALL OF US WERE JUST TURNING A BLIND EYE.

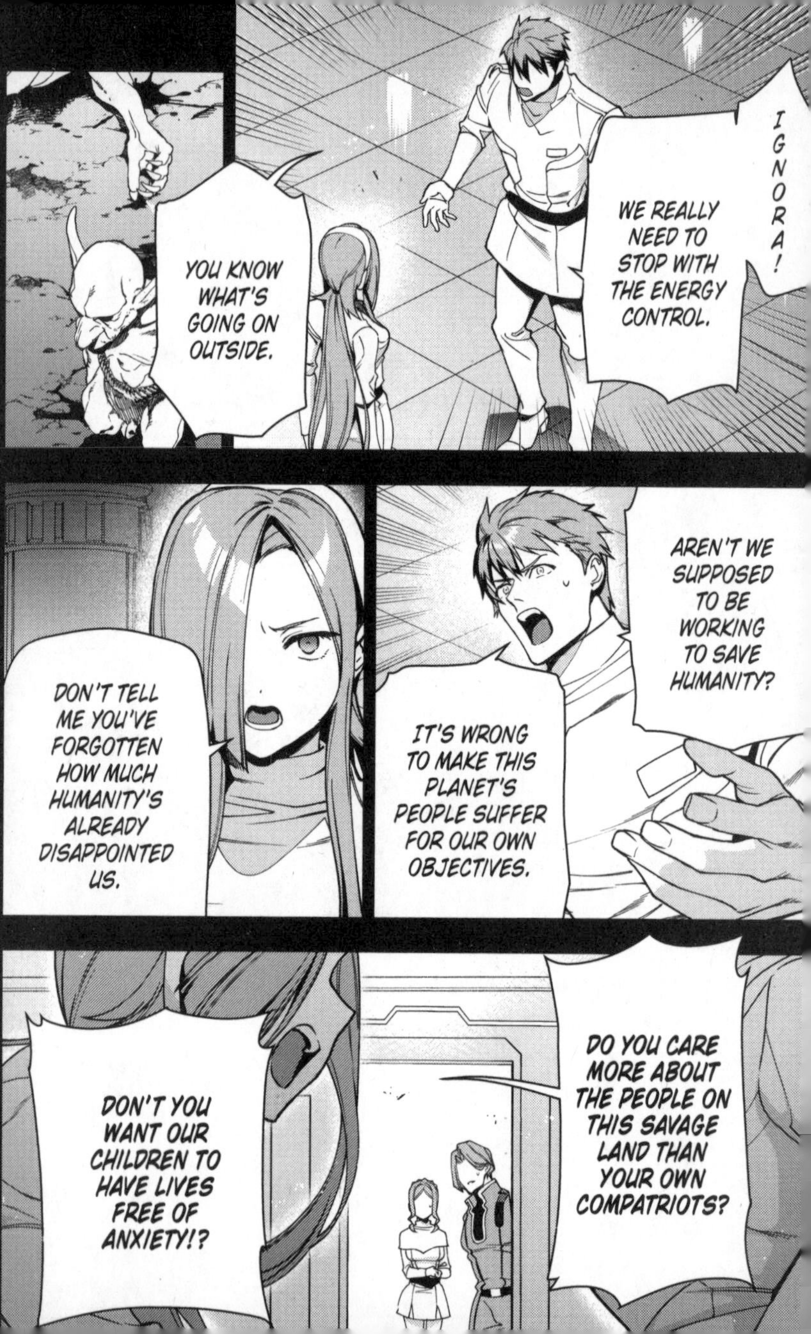
IGNORA!
WE REALLY NEED TO STOP WITH THE ENERGY CONTROL.
YOU KNOW WHAT'S GOING ON OUTSIDE.
AREN'T WE SUPPOSED TO BE WORKING TO SAVE HUMANITY?
IT'S WRONG TO MAKE THIS PLANET'S PEOPLE SUFFER FOR OUR OWN OBJECTIVES.
DON'T TELL ME YOU'VE FORGOTTEN HOW MUCH HUMANITY'S ALREADY DISAPPOINTED US.
DO YOU CARE MORE ABOUT THE PEOPLE ON THIS SAVAGE LAND THAN YOUR OWN COMPATRIOTS?
DON'T YOU WANT OUR CHILDREN TO HAVE LIVES FREE OF ANXIETY!?

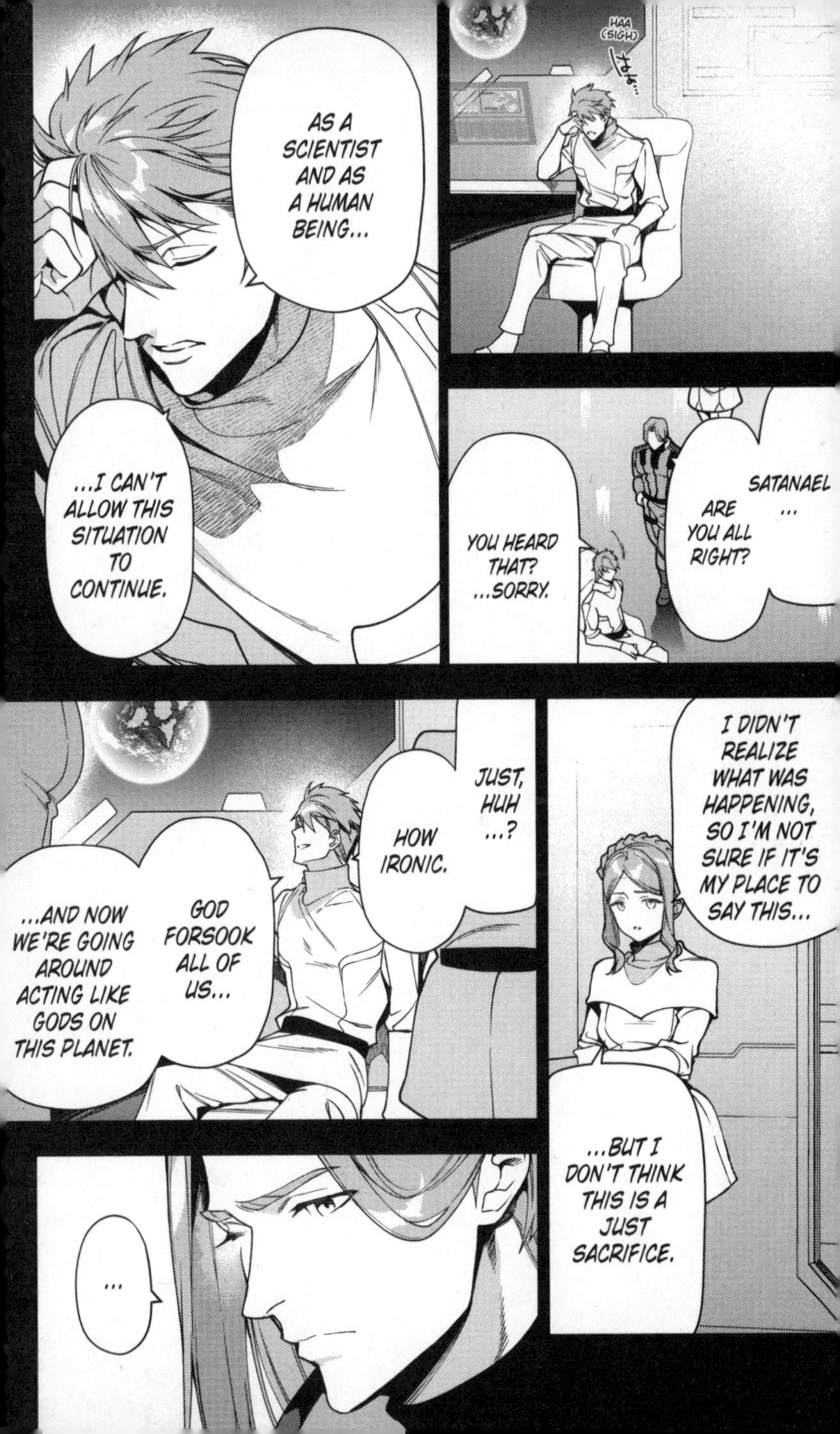
HAA (SIGH)
SATANAEL ... ARE YOU ALL RIGHT?
YOU HEARD THAT? ...SORRY.
AS A SCIENTIST AND AS A HUMAN BEING...
...I CAN'T ALLOW THIS SITUATION TO CONTINUE.
I DIDN'T REALIZE WHAT WAS HAPPENING, SO I'M NOT SURE IF IT'S MY PLACE TO SAY THIS...
...BUT I DON'T THINK THIS IS A JUST SACRIFICE.
JUST, HUH ...?
HOW IRONIC.
GOD FORSOOK ALL OF US...
...AND NOW WE'RE GOING AROUND ACTING LIKE GODS ON THIS PLANET.
...

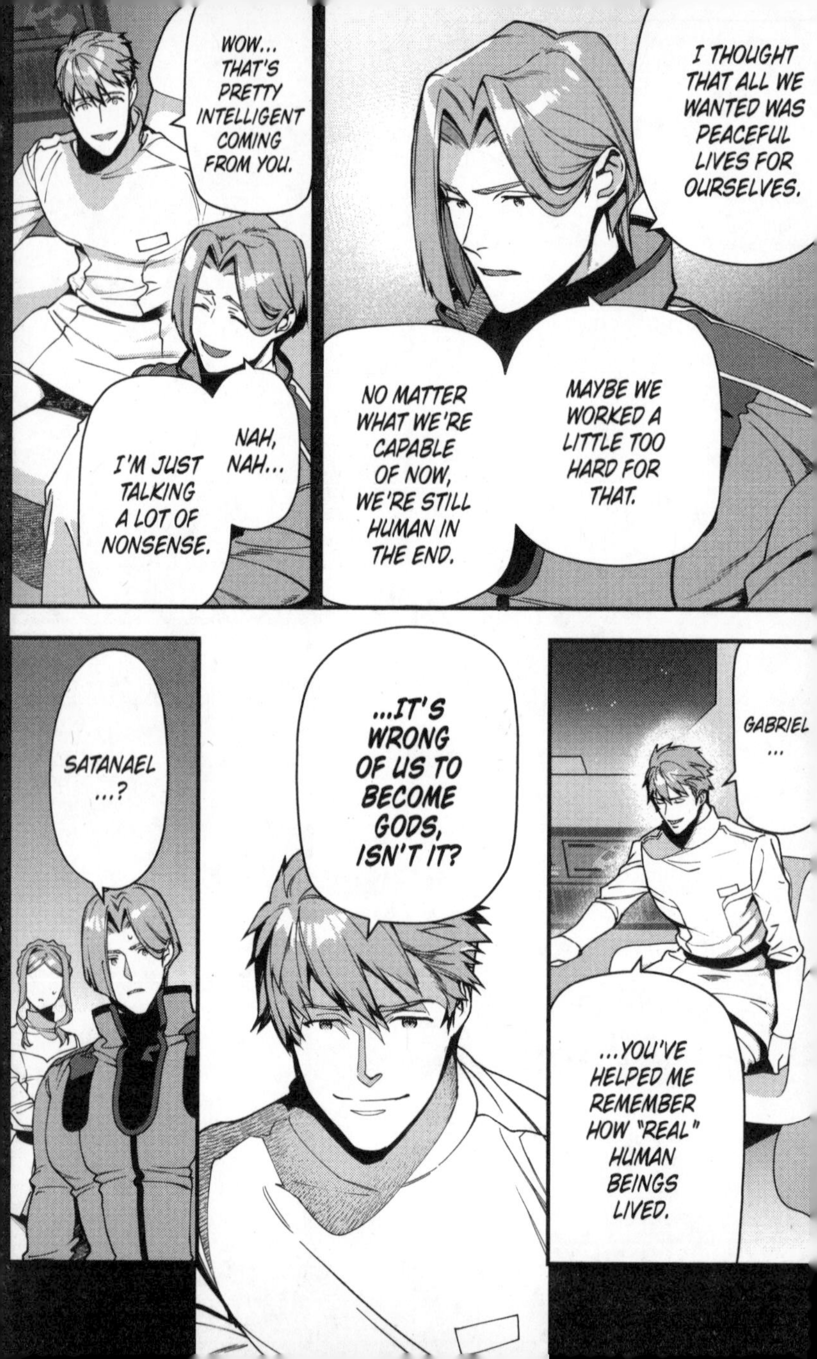
I THOUGHT THAT ALL WE WANTED WAS PEACEFUL LIVES FOR OURSELVES.
MAYBE WE WORKED A LITTLE TOO HARD FOR THAT.
NO MATTER WHAT WE'RE CAPABLE OF NOW, WE'RE STILL HUMAN IN THE END.
WOW... THAT'S PRETTY INTELLIGENT COMING FROM YOU.
NAH, NAH...
I'M JUST TALKING A LOT OF NONSENSE.
GABRIEL...
...YOU'VE HELPED ME REMEMBER HOW "REAL" HUMAN BEINGS LIVED.
...IT'S WRONG OF US TO BECOME GODS, ISN'T IT?
SATANAEL...?

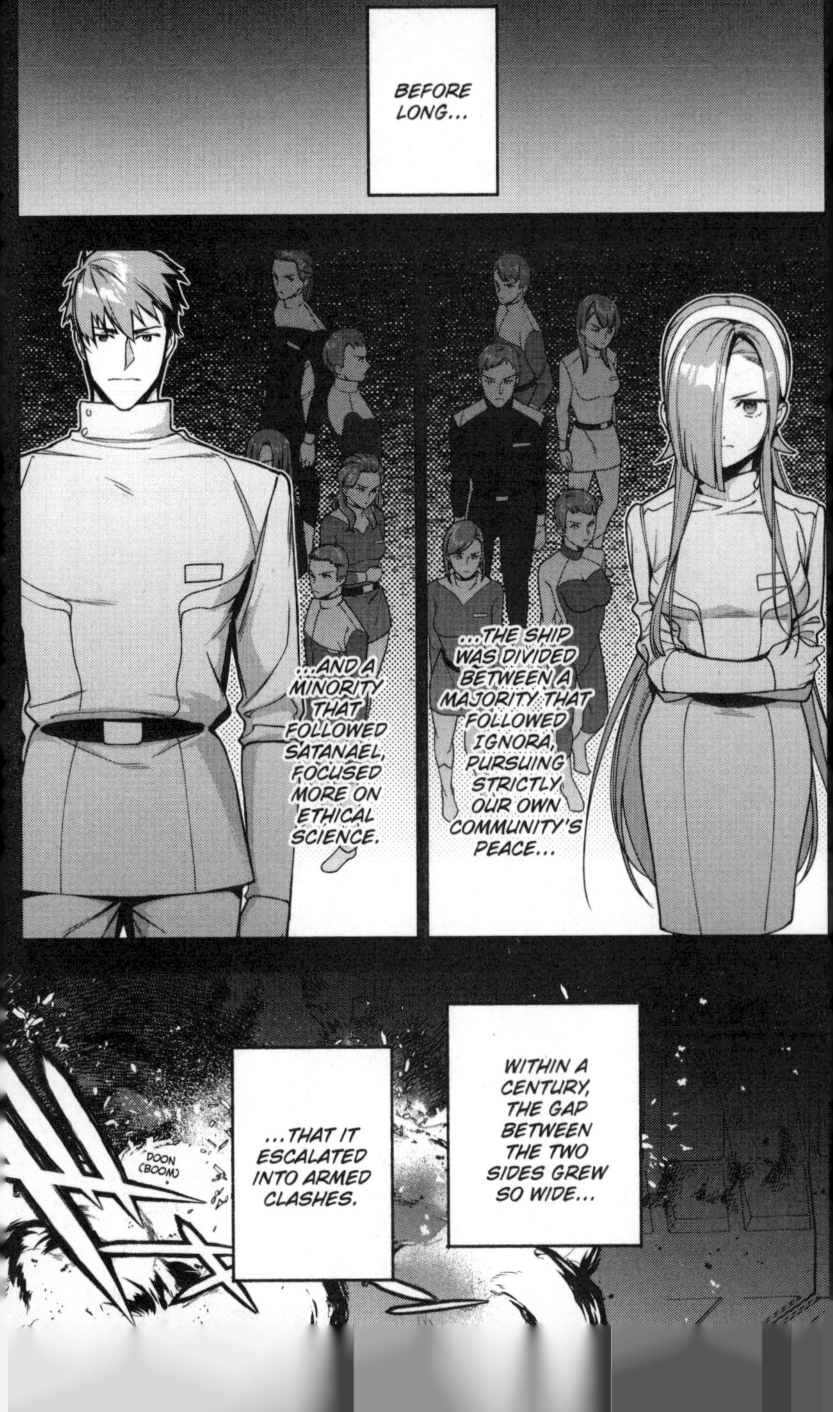
BEFORE LONG...
...THE SHIP WAS DIVIDED BETWEEN A MAJORITY THAT FOLLOWED IGNORA, PURSUING STRICTLY OUR OWN COMMUNITY'S PEACE...
...AND A MINORITY THAT FOLLOWED SATANAEL, FOCUSED MORE ON ETHICAL SCIENCE.
WITHIN A CENTURY, THE GAP BETWEEN THE TWO SIDES GREW SO WIDE...
...THAT IT ESCALATED INTO ARMED CLASHES.
DOON (BOOM)

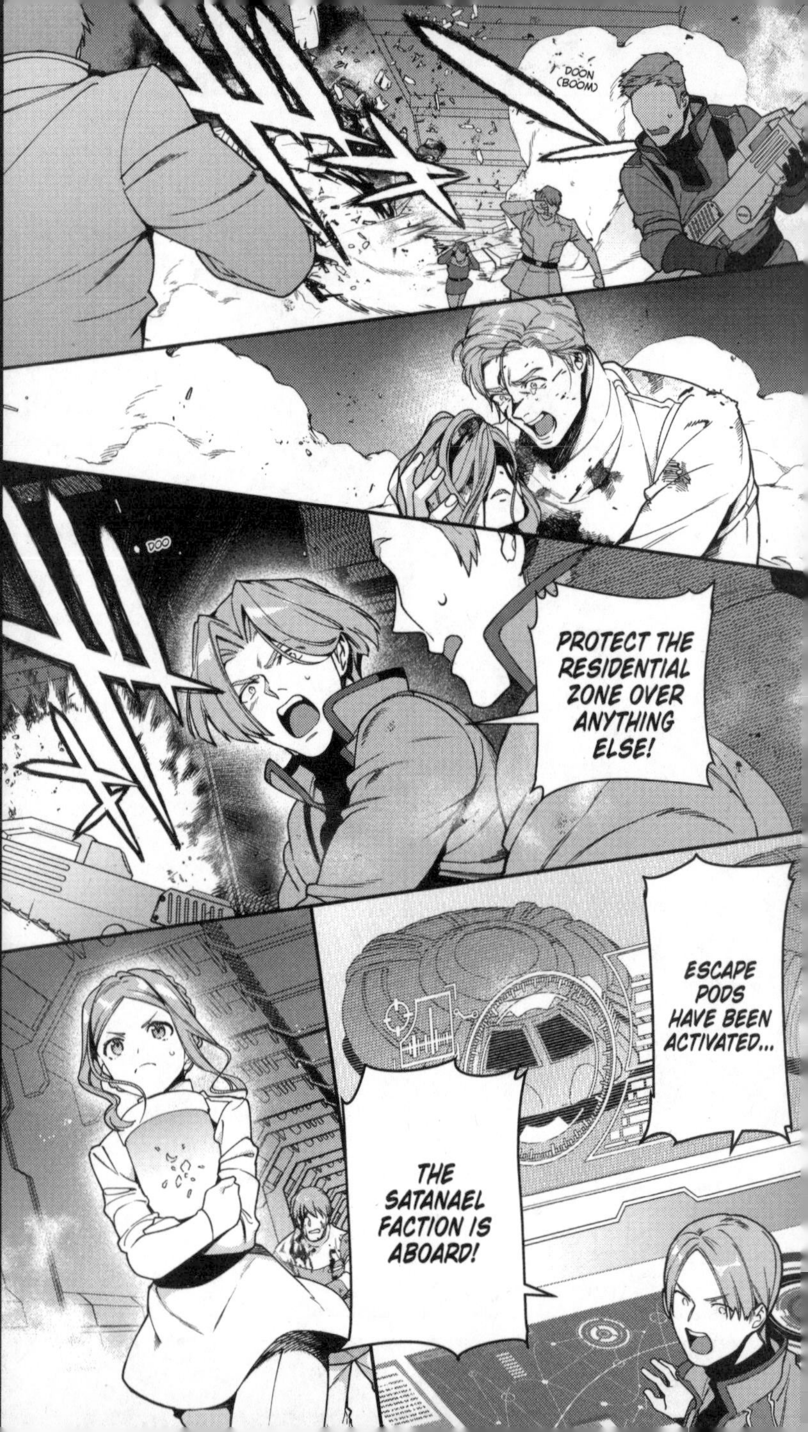
DOON (BOOM)
DOO
PROTECT THE RESIDENTIAL ZONE OVER ANYTHING ELSE!
ESCAPE PODS HAVE BEEN ACTIVATED...
THE SATANAEL FACTION IS ABOARD!

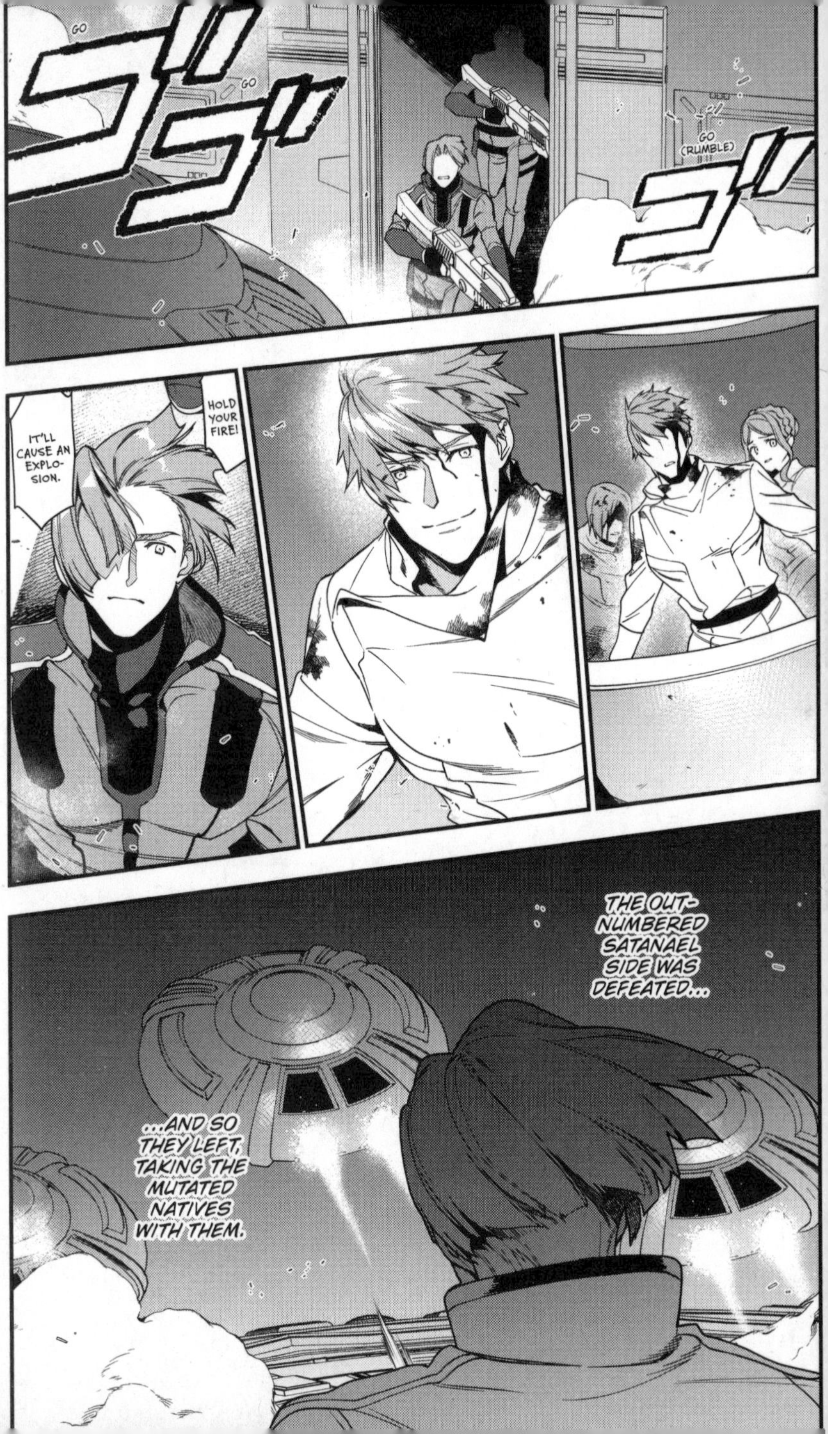
GO (RUMBLE)
GO
GO
HOLD YOUR FIRE!
IT'LL CAUSE AN EXPLOSION.
THE OUTNUMBERED SATANAEL SIDE WAS DEFEATED...
...AND SO THEY LEFT, TAKING THE MUTATED NATIVES WITH THEM.

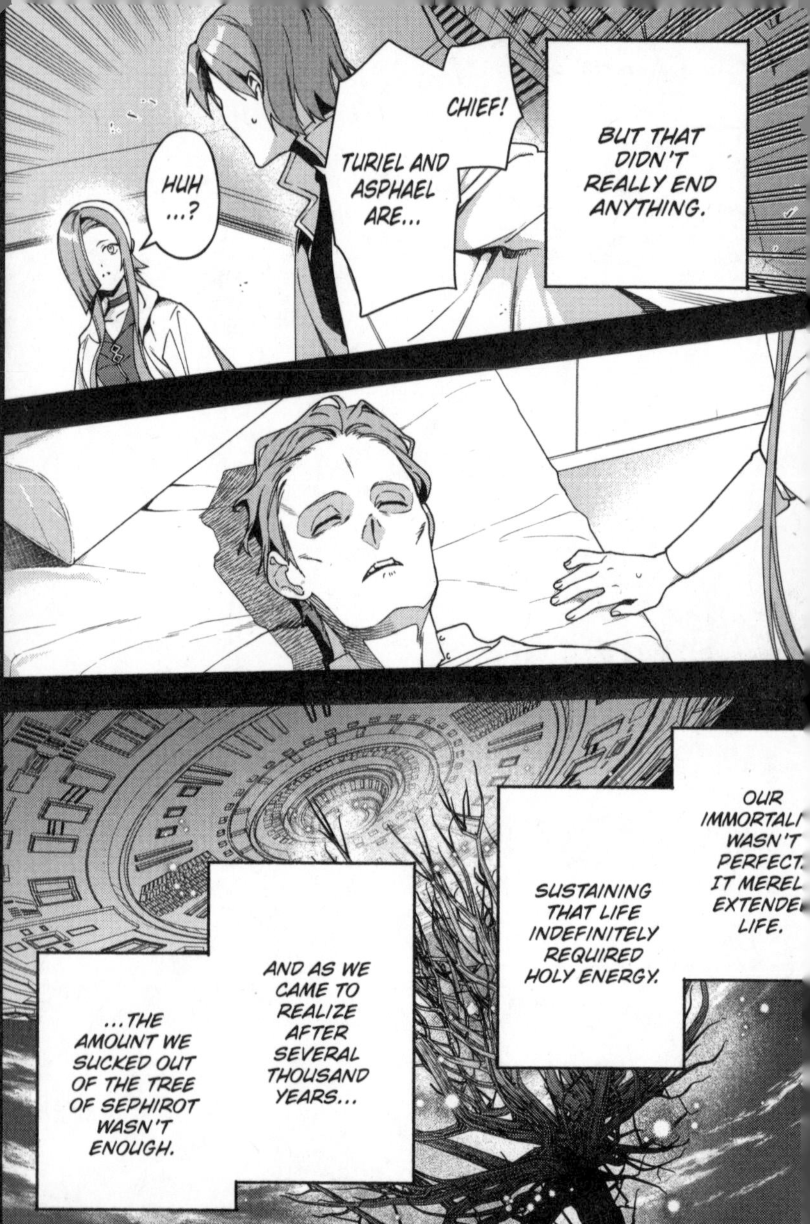
BUT THAT DIDN'T REALLY END ANYTHING.
CHIEF!
TURIEL AND ASPHAEL ARE...
HUH ...?
OUR IMMORTALI WASN'T PERFECT. IT MEREL EXTENDE LIFE.
SUSTAINING THAT LIFE INDEFINITELY REQUIRED HOLY ENERGY.
AND AS WE CAME TO REALIZE AFTER SEVERAL THOUSAND YEARS...
...THE AMOUNT WE SUCKED OUT OF THE TREE OF SEPHIROT WASN'T ENOUGH.

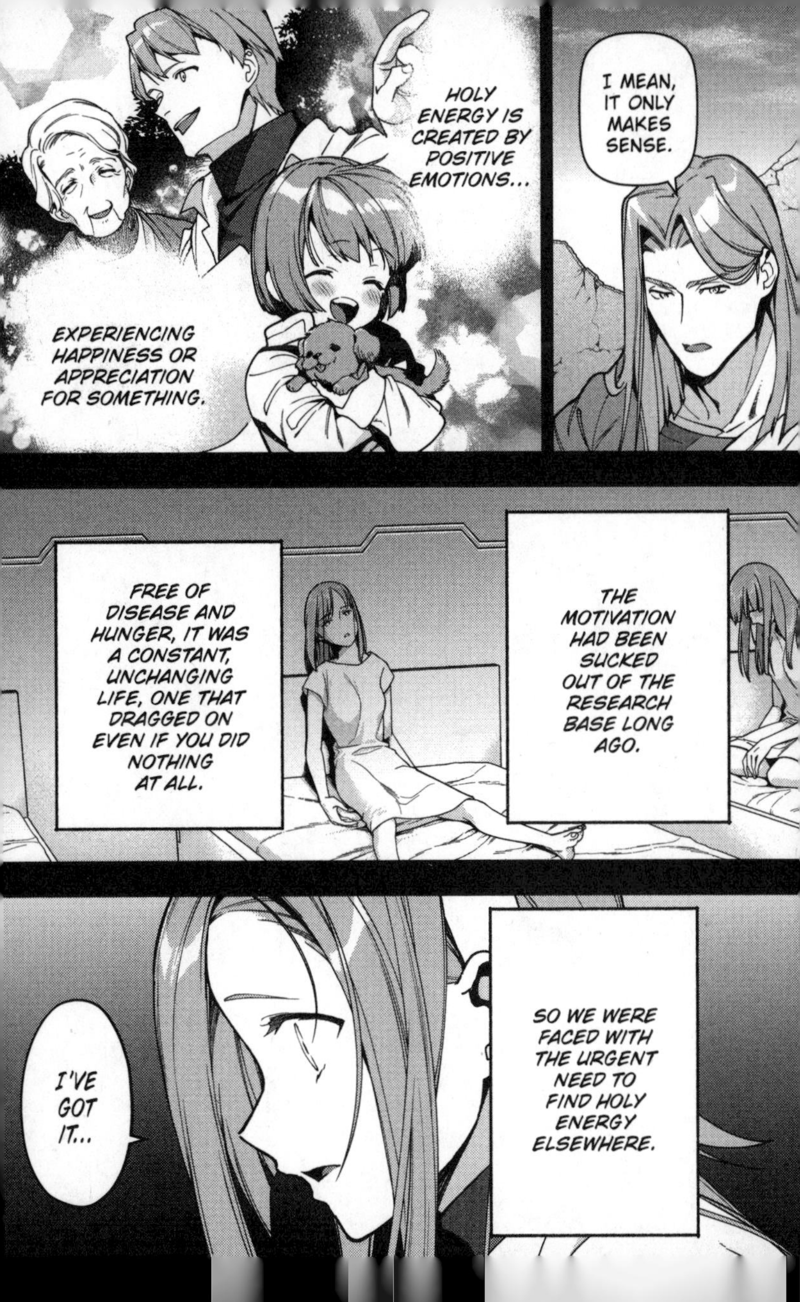
I MEAN, IT ONLY MAKES SENSE.
HOLY ENERGY IS CREATED BY POSITIVE EMOTIONS...
EXPERIENCING HAPPINESS OR APPRECIATION FOR SOMETHING.
THE MOTIVATION HAD BEEN SUCKED OUT OF THE RESEARCH BASE LONG AGO.
FREE OF DISEASE AND HUNGER, IT WAS A CONSTANT, UNCHANGING LIFE, ONE THAT DRAGGED ON EVEN IF YOU DID NOTHING AT ALL.
SO WE WERE FACED WITH THE URGENT NEED TO FIND HOLY ENERGY ELSEWHERE.
I'VE GOT IT...

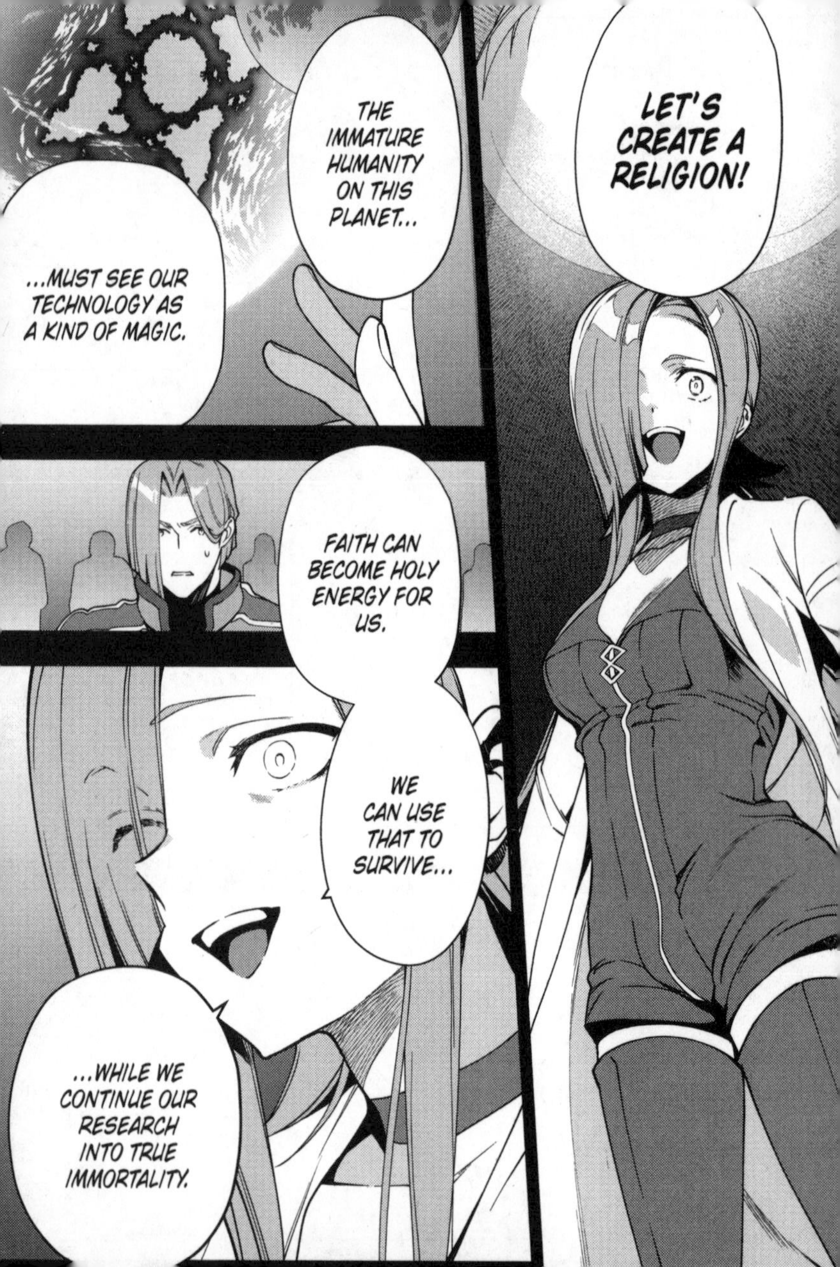
LET'S CREATE A RELIGION!
THE IMMATURE HUMANITY ON THIS PLANET...
...MUST SEE OUR TECHNOLOGY AS A KIND OF MAGIC.
FAITH CAN BECOME HOLY ENERGY FOR US.
WE CAN USE THAT TO SURVIVE...
...WHILE WE CONTINUE OUR RESEARCH INTO TRUE IMMORTALITY.

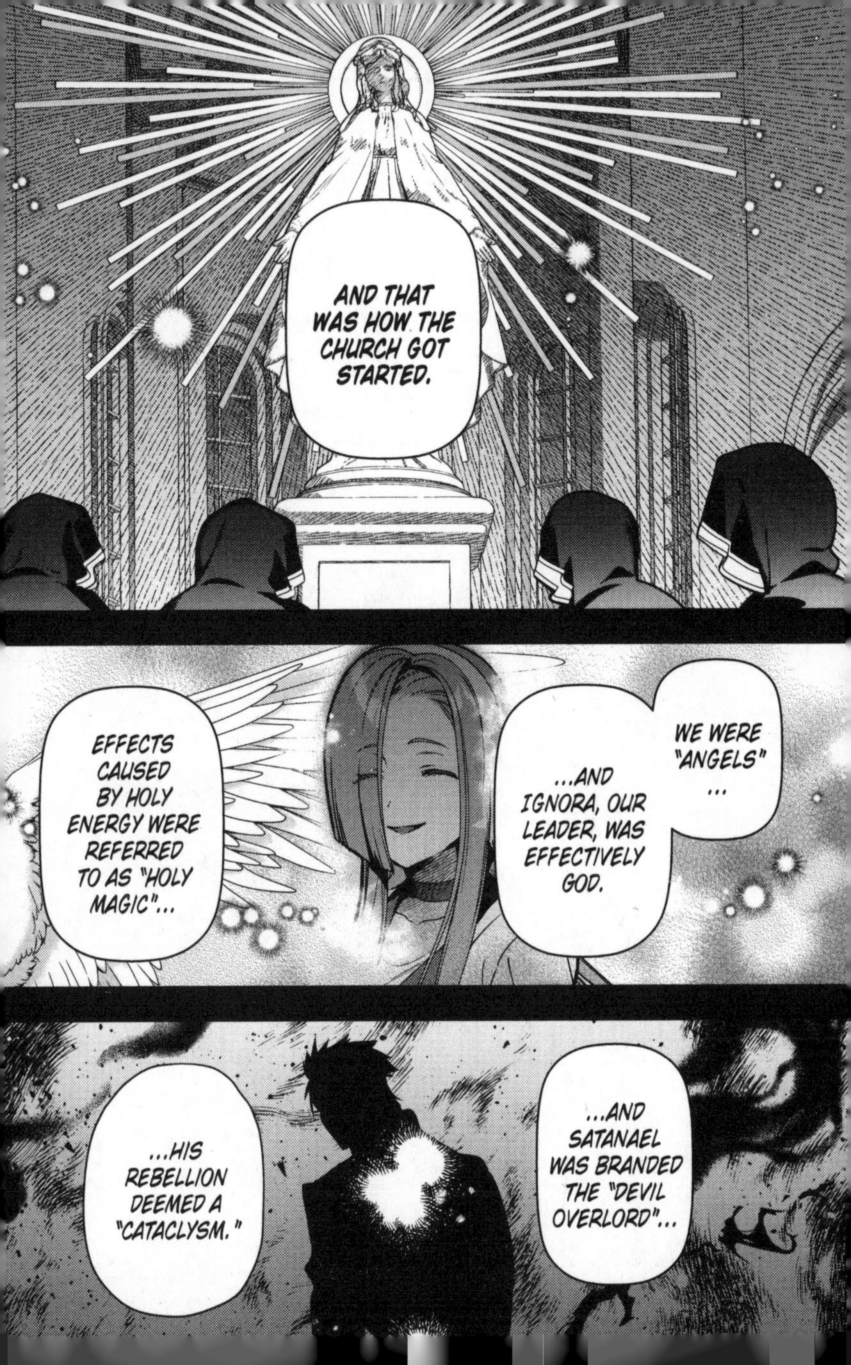
AND THAT WAS HOW THE CHURCH GOT STARTED.
WE WERE "ANGELS"...
...AND IGNORA, OUR LEADER, WAS EFFECTIVELY GOD.
EFFECTS CAUSED BY HOLY ENERGY WERE REFERRED TO AS "HOLY MAGIC"...
...AND SATANAEL WAS BRANDED THE "DEVIL OVERLORD"...
...HIS REBELLION DEEMED A "CATACLYSM."

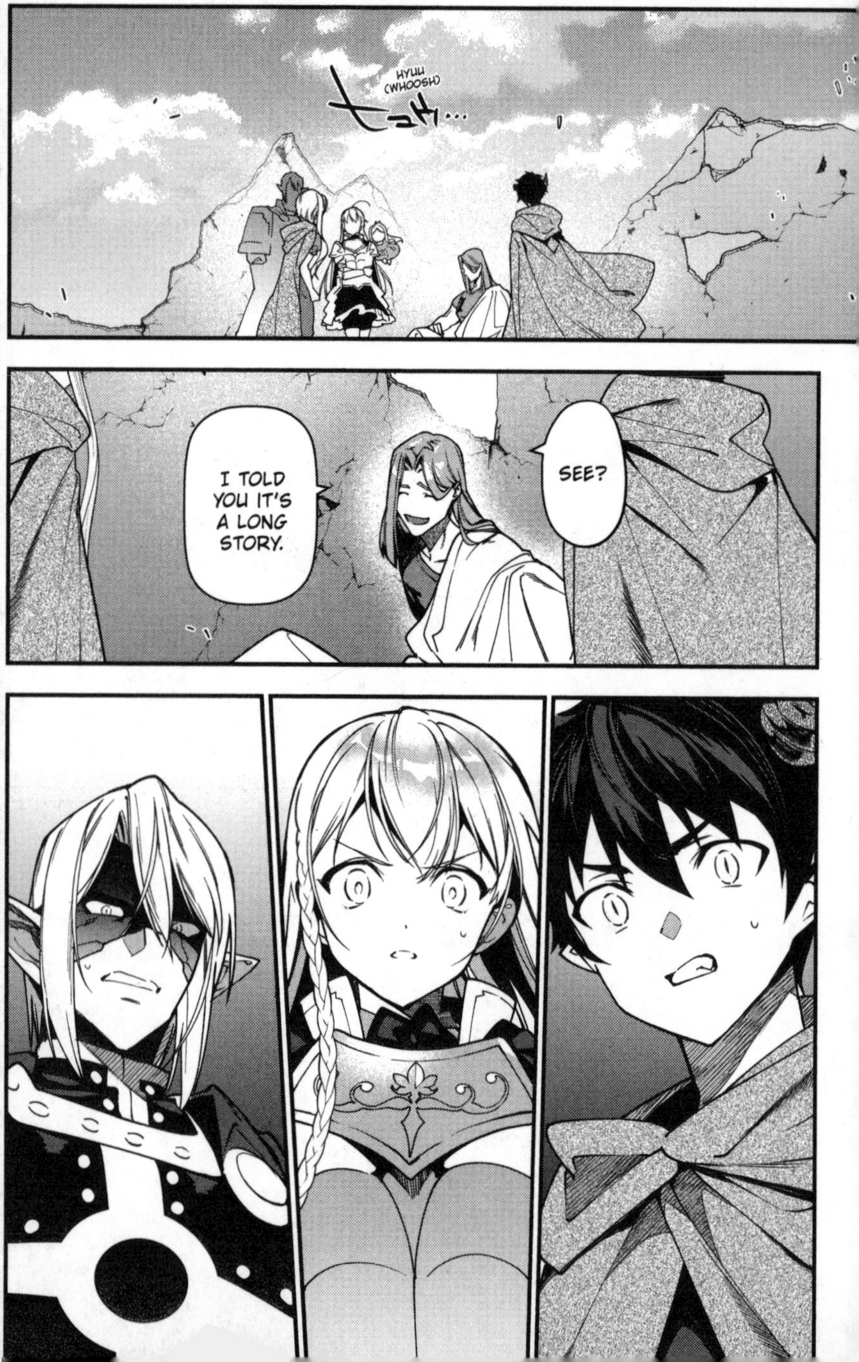
HYUU (WHOOSH)
SEE?
I TOLD YOU IT'S A LONG STORY.

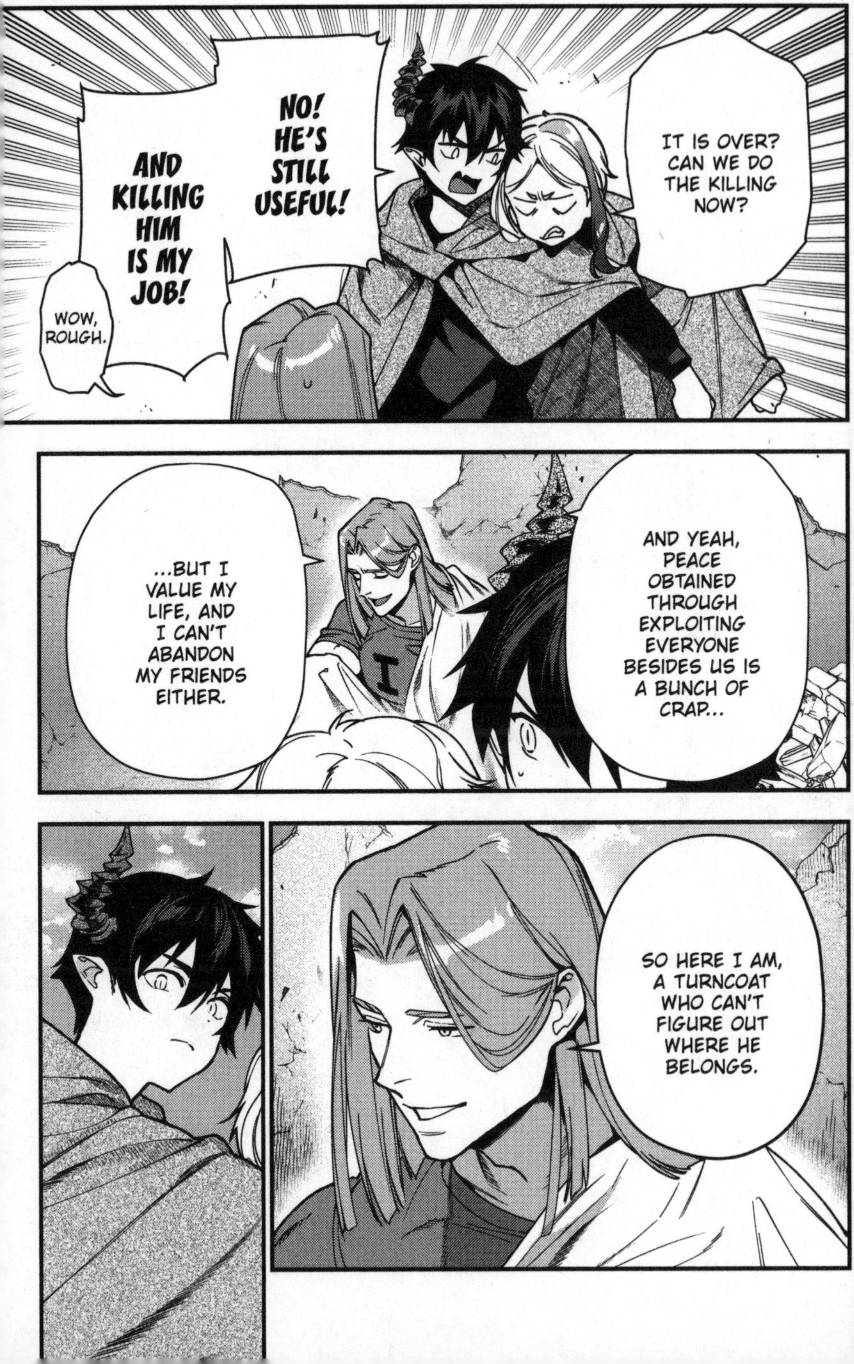
IT IS OVER? CAN WE DO THE KILLING NOW?
NO! HE'S STILL USEFUL!
AND KILLING HIM IS MY JOB!
WOW, ROUGH.
AND YEAH, PEACE OBTAINED THROUGH EXPLOITING EVERYONE BESIDES US IS A BUNCH OF CRAP...
...BUT I VALUE MY LIFE, AND I CAN'T ABANDON MY FRIENDS EITHER.
SO HERE I AM, A TURNCOAT WHO CAN'T FIGURE OUT WHERE HE BELONGS.

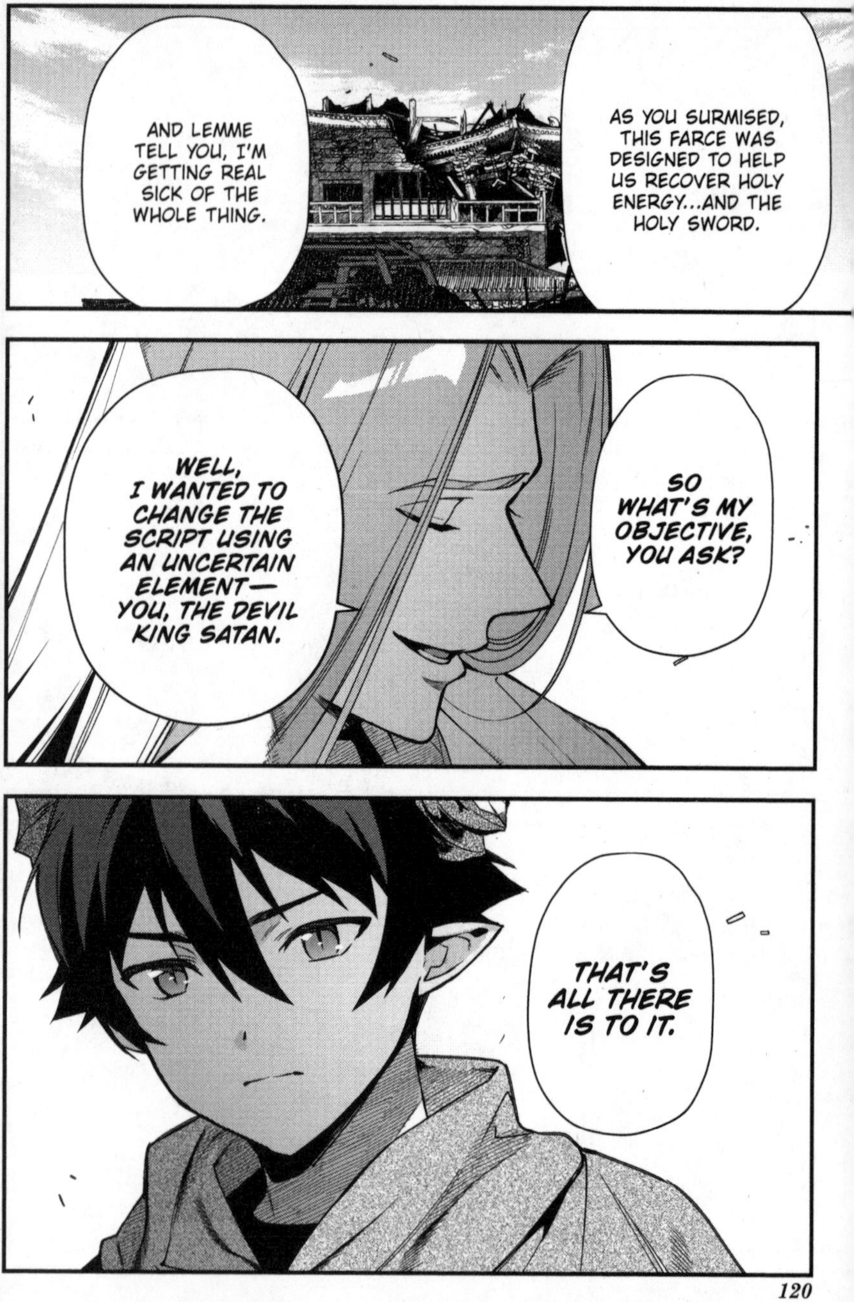
AS YOU SURMISED, THIS FARCE WAS DESIGNED TO HELP US RECOVER HOLY ENERGY...AND THE HOLY SWORD.
AND LEMME TELL YOU, I'M GETTING REAL SICK OF THE WHOLE THING.
SO WHAT'S MY OBJECTIVE, YOU ASK?
WELL, I WANTED TO CHANGE THE SCRIPT USING AN UNCERTAIN ELEMENT—YOU, THE DEVIL KING SATAN.
THAT'S ALL THERE IS TO IT.

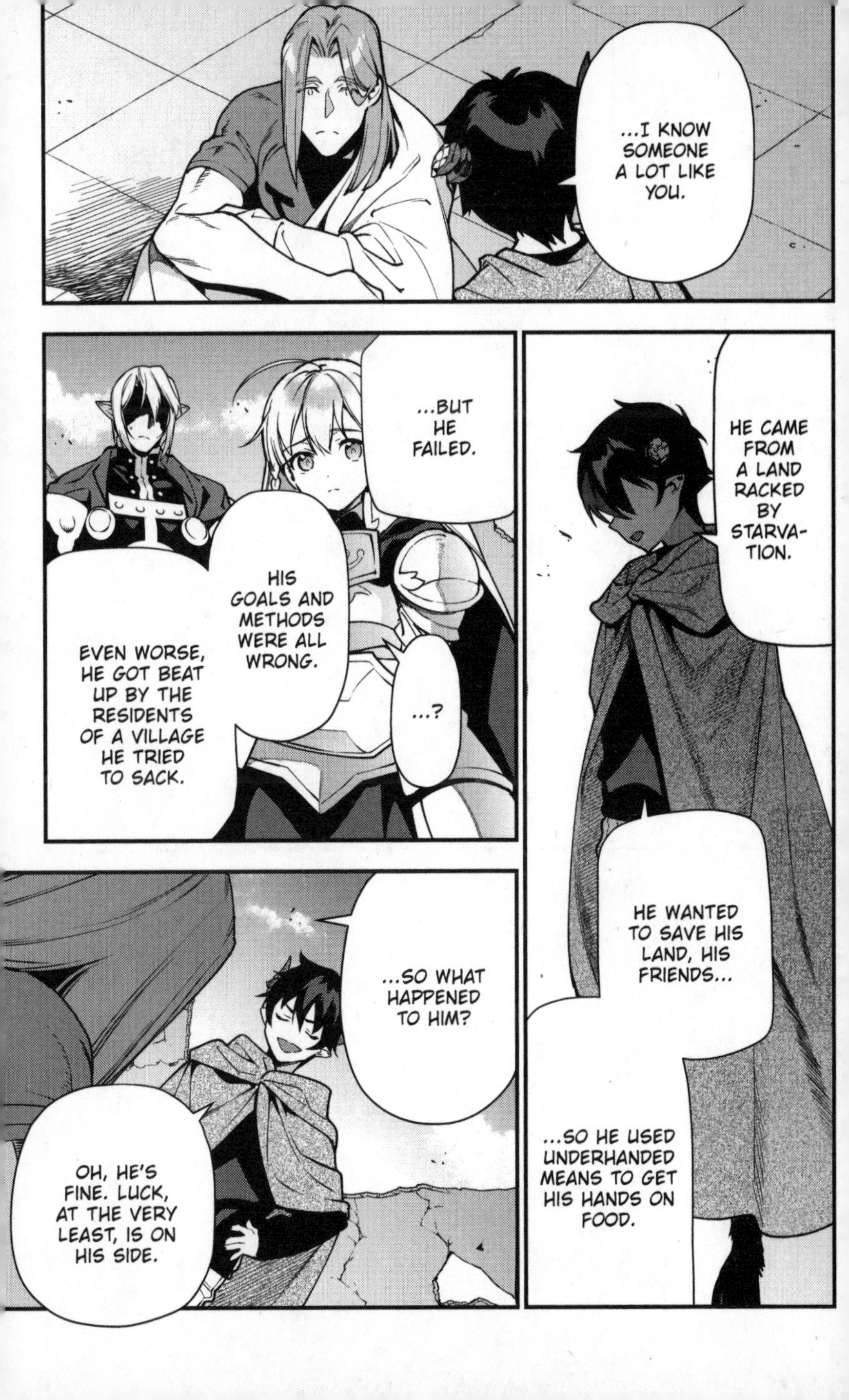
...I KNOW SOMEONE A LOT LIKE YOU.
HE CAME FROM A LAND RACKED BY STARVATION.
HE WANTED TO SAVE HIS LAND, HIS FRIENDS...
...SO HE USED UNDERHANDED MEANS TO GET HIS HANDS ON FOOD.
...BUT HE FAILED.
HIS GOALS AND METHODS WERE ALL WRONG.
EVEN WORSE, HE GOT BEAT UP BY THE RESIDENTS OF A VILLAGE HE TRIED TO SACK.
...?
...SO WHAT HAPPENED TO HIM?
OH, HE'S FINE. LUCK, AT THE VERY LEAST, IS ON HIS SIDE.

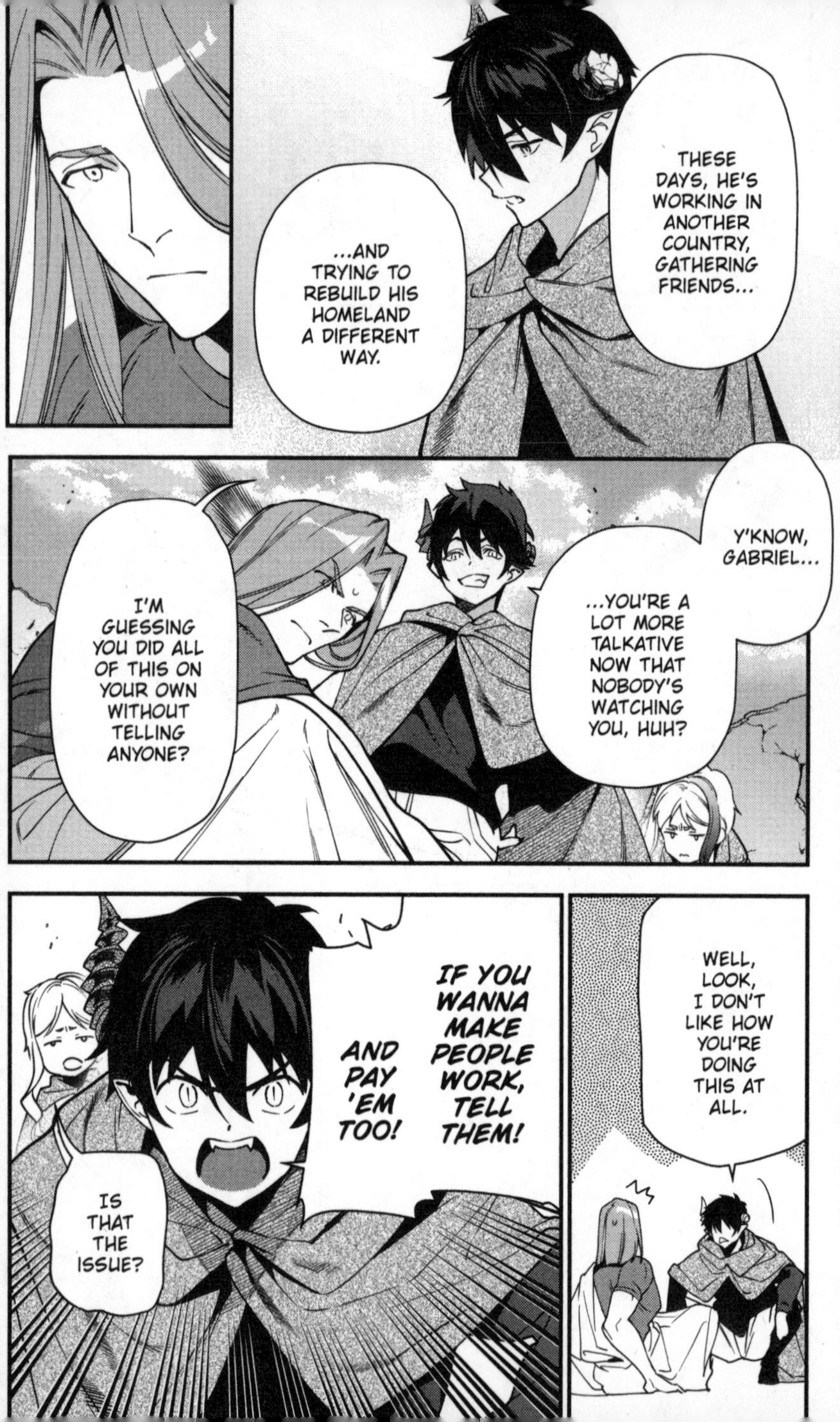
THESE DAYS, HE'S WORKING IN ANOTHER COUNTRY, GATHERING FRIENDS...
...AND TRYING TO REBUILD HIS HOMELAND A DIFFERENT WAY.
Y'KNOW, GABRIEL...
...YOU'RE A LOT MORE TALKATIVE NOW THAT NOBODY'S WATCHING YOU, HUH?
I'M GUESSING YOU DID ALL OF THIS ON YOUR OWN WITHOUT TELLING ANYONE?
WELL, LOOK, I DON'T LIKE HOW YOU'RE DOING THIS AT ALL.
IF YOU WANNA MAKE PEOPLE WORK, TELL THEM!
AND PAY 'EM TOO!
IS THAT THE ISSUE?

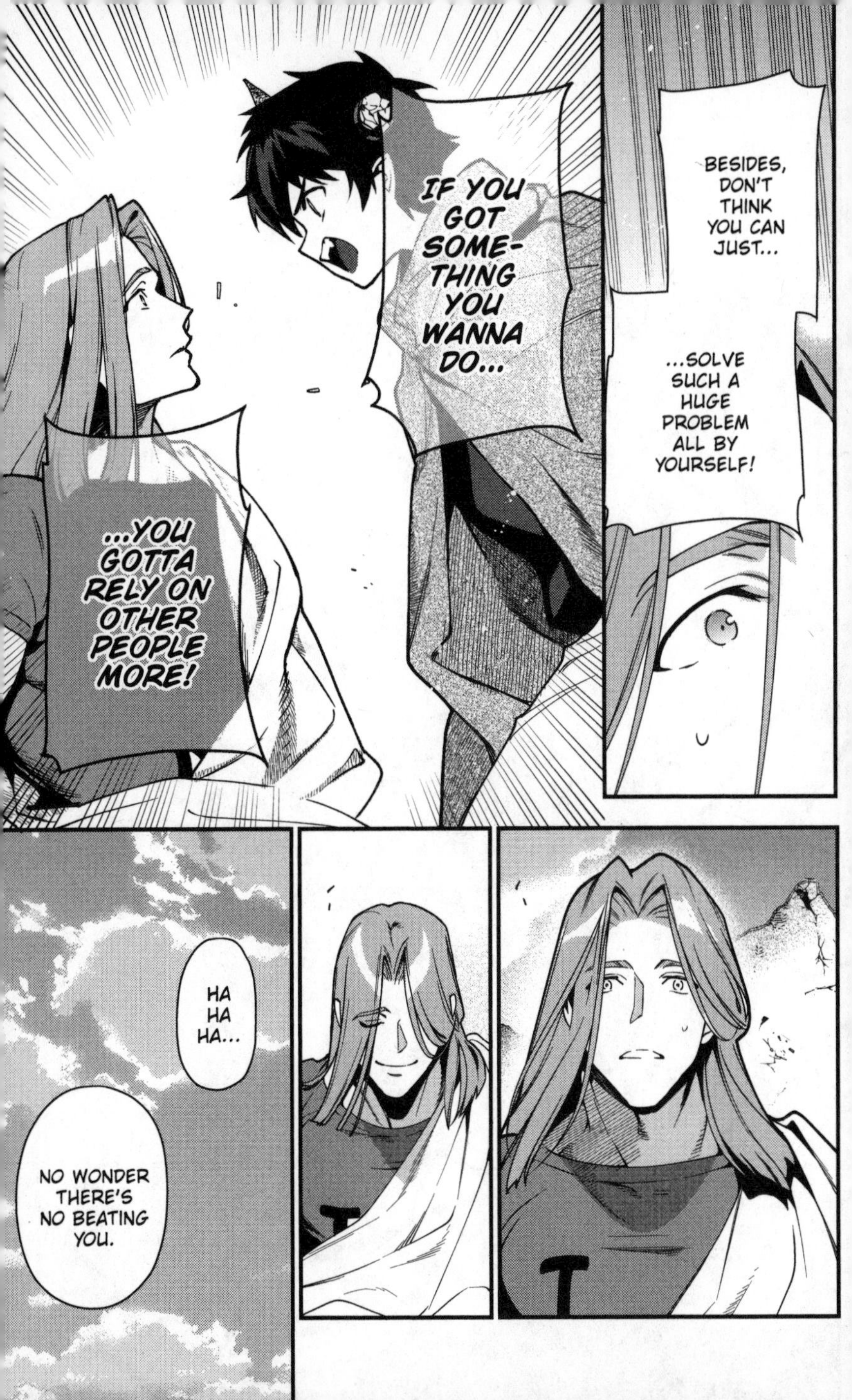
BESIDES, DON'T THINK YOU CAN JUST...
...SOLVE SUCH A HUGE PROBLEM ALL BY YOURSELF!
IF YOU GOT SOME-THING YOU WANNA DO...
...YOU GOTTA RELY ON OTHER PEOPLE MORE!
HA HA HA...
NO WONDER THERE'S NO BEATING YOU.

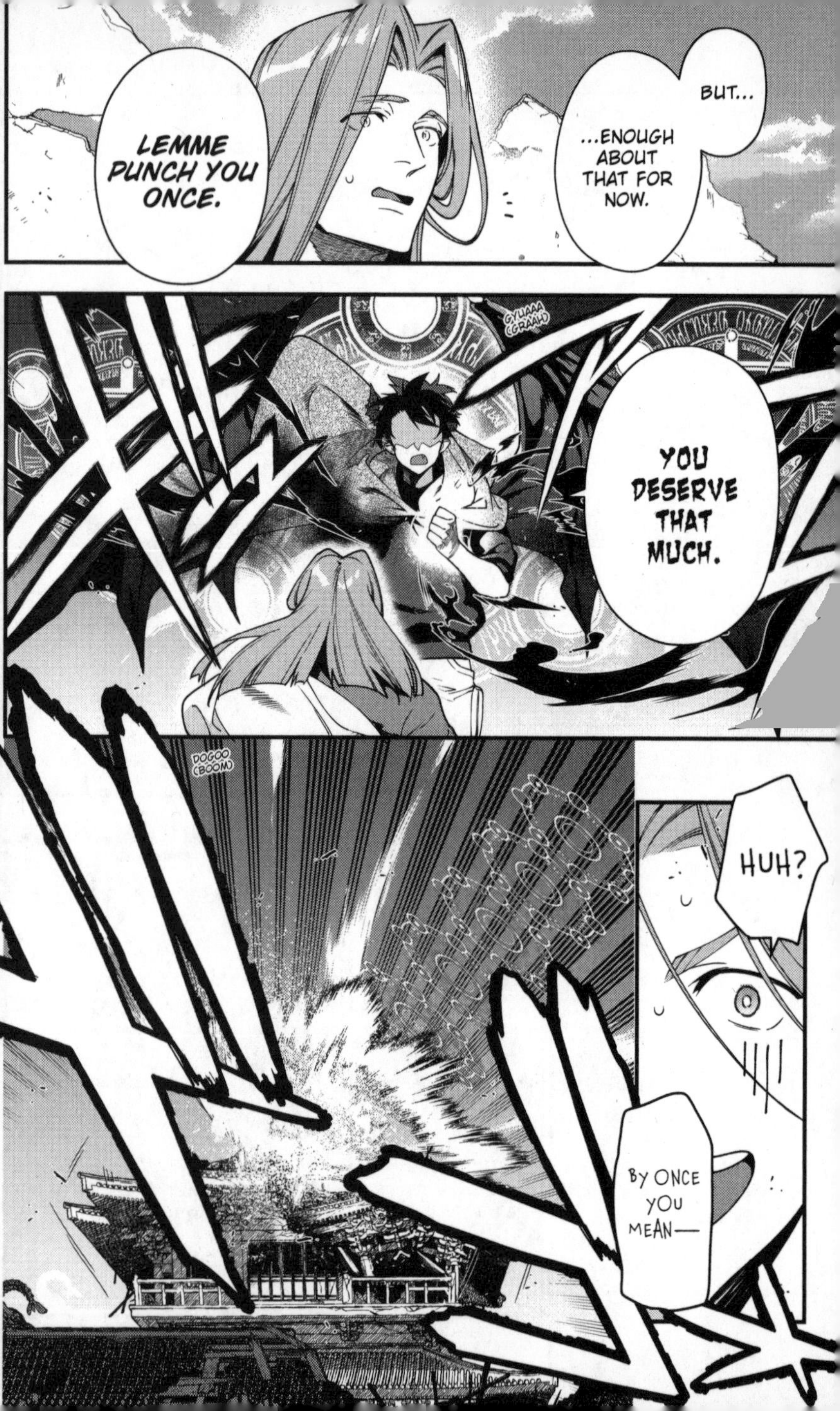
BUT...
...ENOUGH ABOUT THAT FOR NOW.
LEMME PUNCH YOU ONCE.
GYUAAA (GRAAH)
YOU DESERVE THAT MUCH.
HUH?
BY ONCE YOU MEAN—
DOGOO (BOOM)

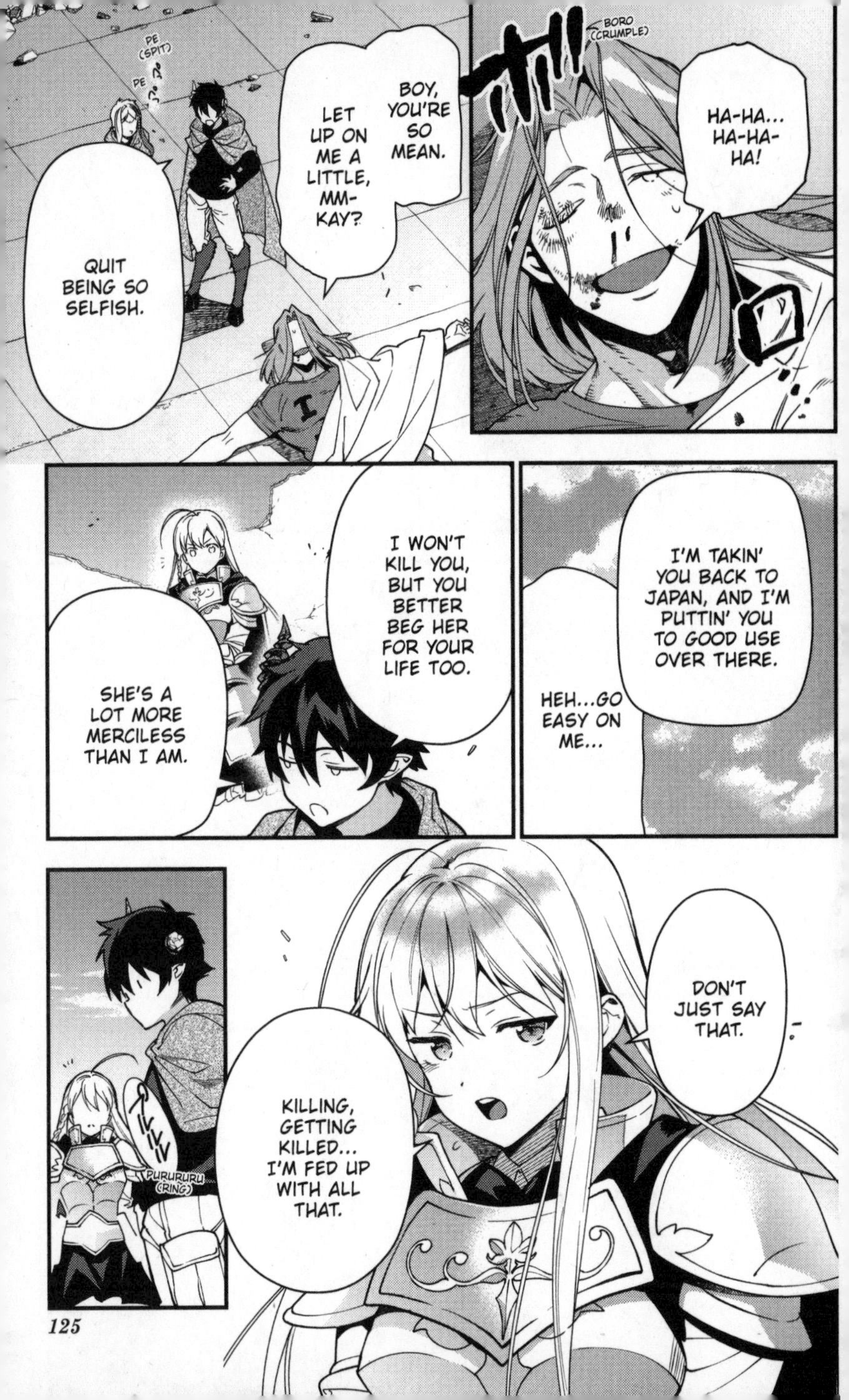
BORO (CRUMPLE)
HA-HA... HA-HA-HA!
BOY, YOU'RE SO MEAN.
LET UP ON ME A LITTLE, MM-KAY?
PE (SPIT) PE
QUIT BEING SO SELFISH.
I'M TAKIN' YOU BACK TO JAPAN, AND I'M PUTTIN' YOU TO GOOD USE OVER THERE.
HEH...GO EASY ON ME...
I WON'T KILL YOU, BUT YOU BETTER BEG HER FOR YOUR LIFE TOO.
SHE'S A LOT MORE MERCILESS THAN I AM.
DON'T JUST SAY THAT.
KILLING, GETTING KILLED... I'M FED UP WITH ALL THAT.
PURURURU (RING)

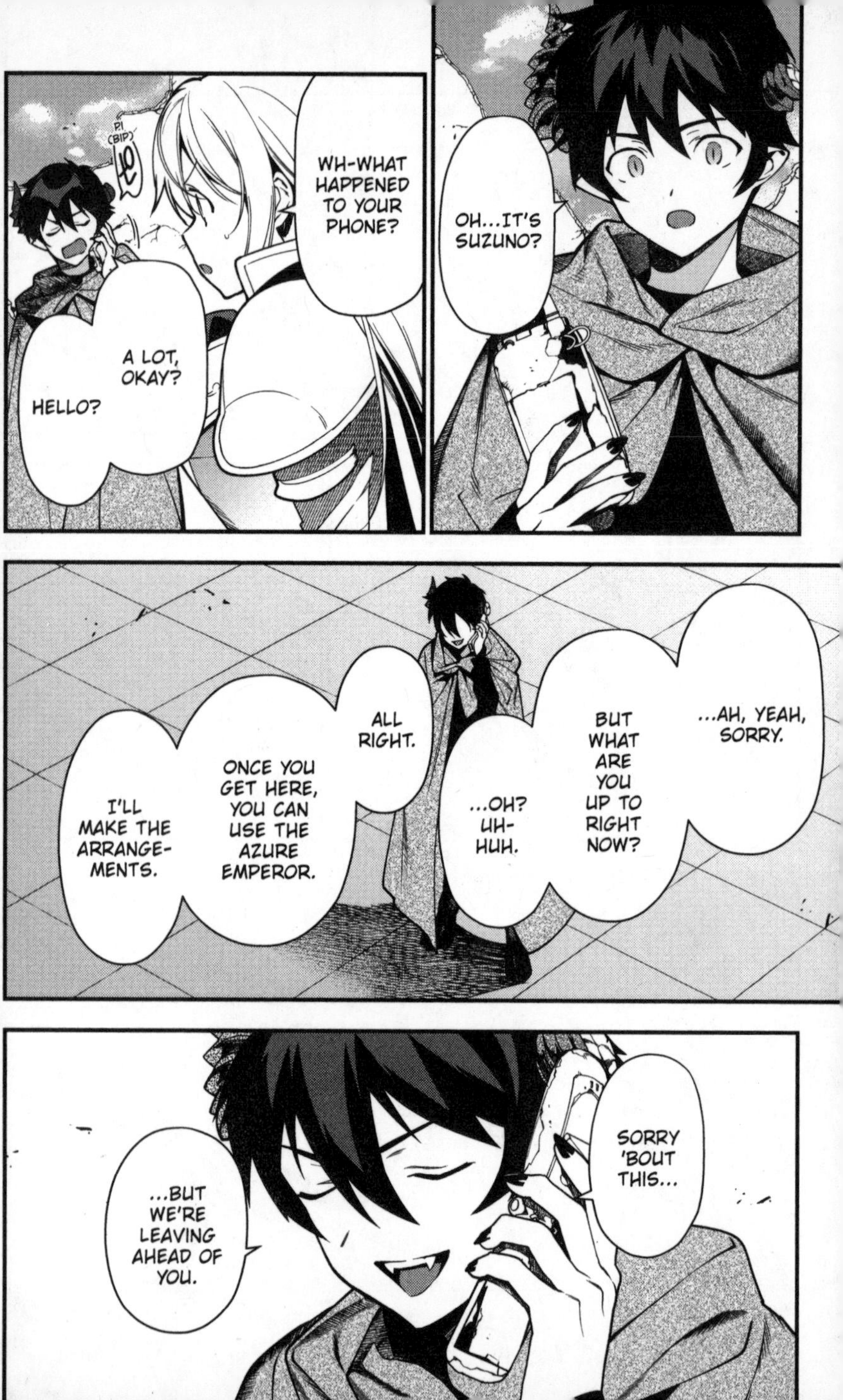
OH...IT'S SUZUNO?
WH-WHAT HAPPENED TO YOUR PHONE?
PI (BIP)
A LOT, OKAY?
HELLO?
...AH, YEAH, SORRY.
BUT WHAT ARE YOU UP TO RIGHT NOW?
...OH? UH-HUH.
ALL RIGHT.
ONCE YOU GET HERE, YOU CAN USE THE AZURE EMPEROR.
I'LL MAKE THE ARRANGE-MENTS.
SORRY 'BOUT THIS...
...BUT WE'RE LEAVING AHEAD OF YOU.

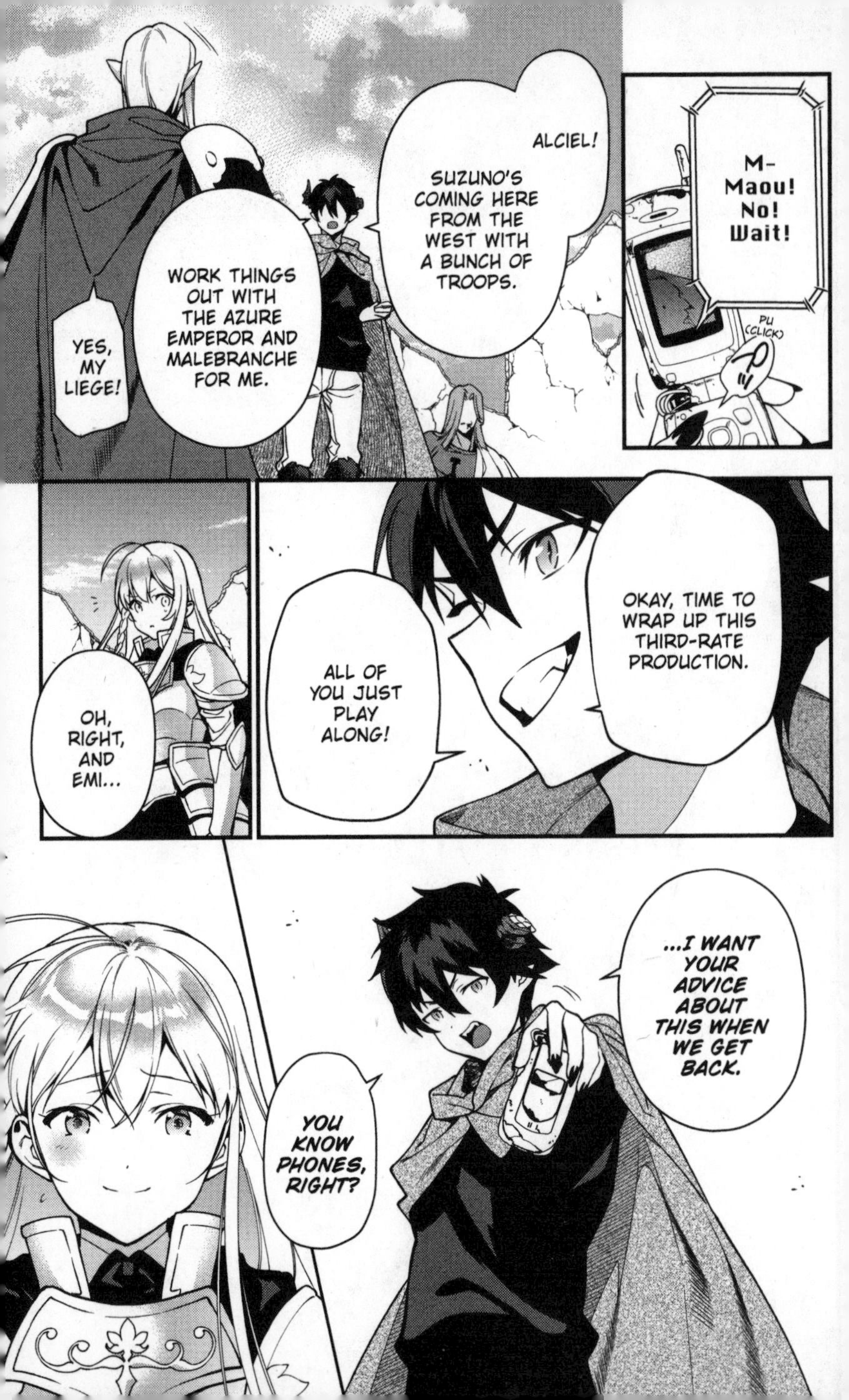
M-Maou! No! Wait!
PU (CLICK)
ALCIEL!
SUZUNO'S COMING HERE FROM THE WEST WITH A BUNCH OF TROOPS.
WORK THINGS OUT WITH THE AZURE EMPEROR AND MALEBRANCHE FOR ME.
YES, MY LIEGE!
OKAY, TIME TO WRAP UP THIS THIRD-RATE PRODUCTION.
ALL OF YOU JUST PLAY ALONG!
OH, RIGHT, AND EMI...
...I WANT YOUR ADVICE ABOUT THIS WHEN WE GET BACK.
YOU KNOW PHONES, RIGHT?

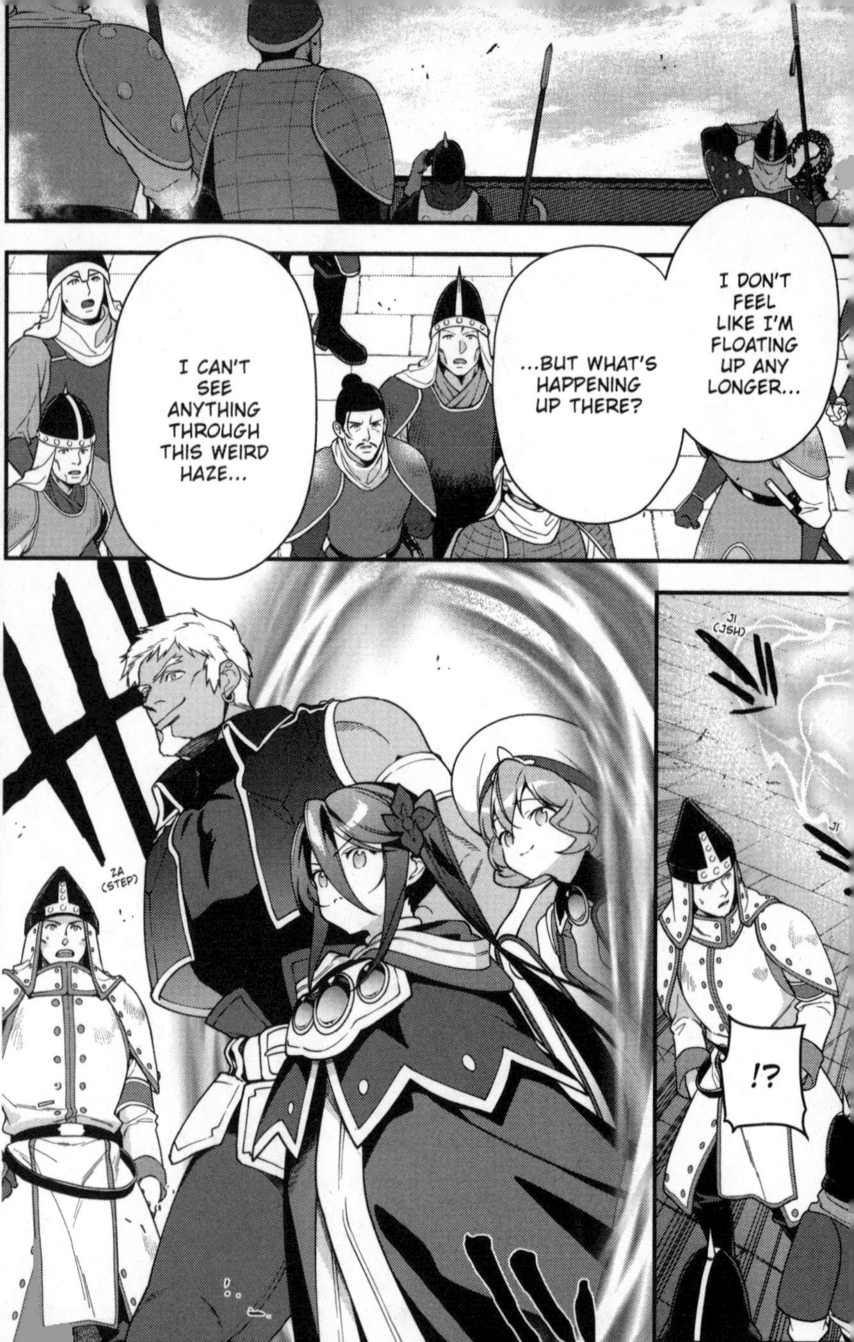
I DON'T FEEL LIKE I'M FLOATING UP ANY LONGER...
...BUT WHAT'S HAPPENING UP THERE?
I CAN'T SEE ANYTHING THROUGH THIS WEIRD HAZE...
JI (JSH)
JI
!?
ZA (STEP)

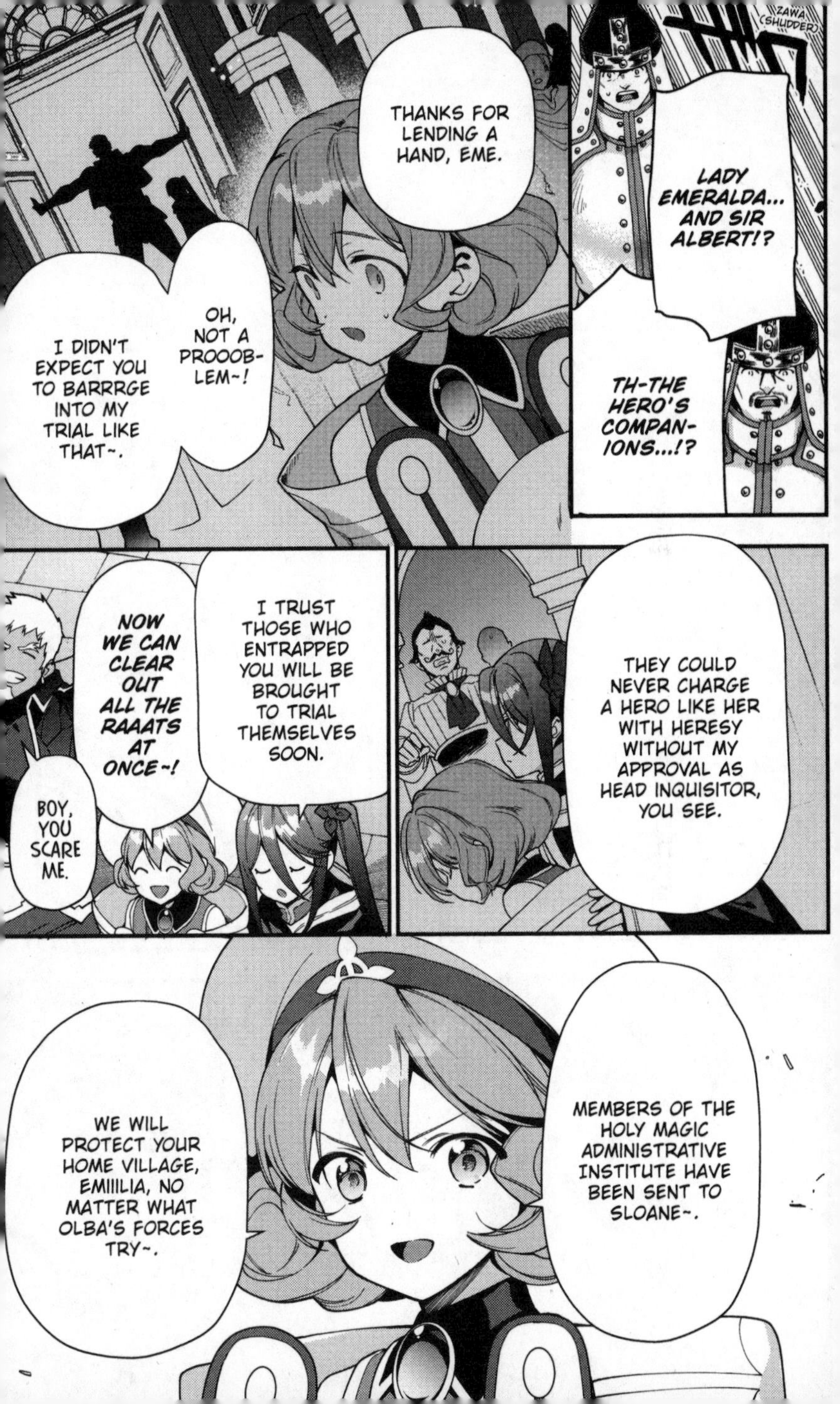

ZAWA (SHUDDER)
LADY EMERALDA... AND SIR ALBERT!?
TH-THE HERO'S COMPANIONS...!?
THANKS FOR LENDING A HAND, EME.
OH, NOT A PROOOBLEM~!
I DIDN'T EXPECT YOU TO BARRRGE INTO MY TRIAL LIKE THAT~.
THEY COULD NEVER CHARGE A HERO LIKE HER WITH HERESY WITHOUT MY APPROVAL AS HEAD INQUISITOR, YOU SEE.
I TRUST THOSE WHO ENTRAPPED YOU WILL BE BROUGHT TO TRIAL THEMSELVES SOON.
NOW WE CAN CLEAR OUT ALL THE RAAATS AT ONCE~!
BOY, YOU SCARE ME.
MEMBERS OF THE HOLY MAGIC ADMINISTRATIVE INSTITUTE HAVE BEEN SENT TO SLOANE~.
WE WILL PROTECT YOUR HOME VILLAGE, EMIIILIA, NO MATTER WHAT OLBA'S FORCES TRY~.

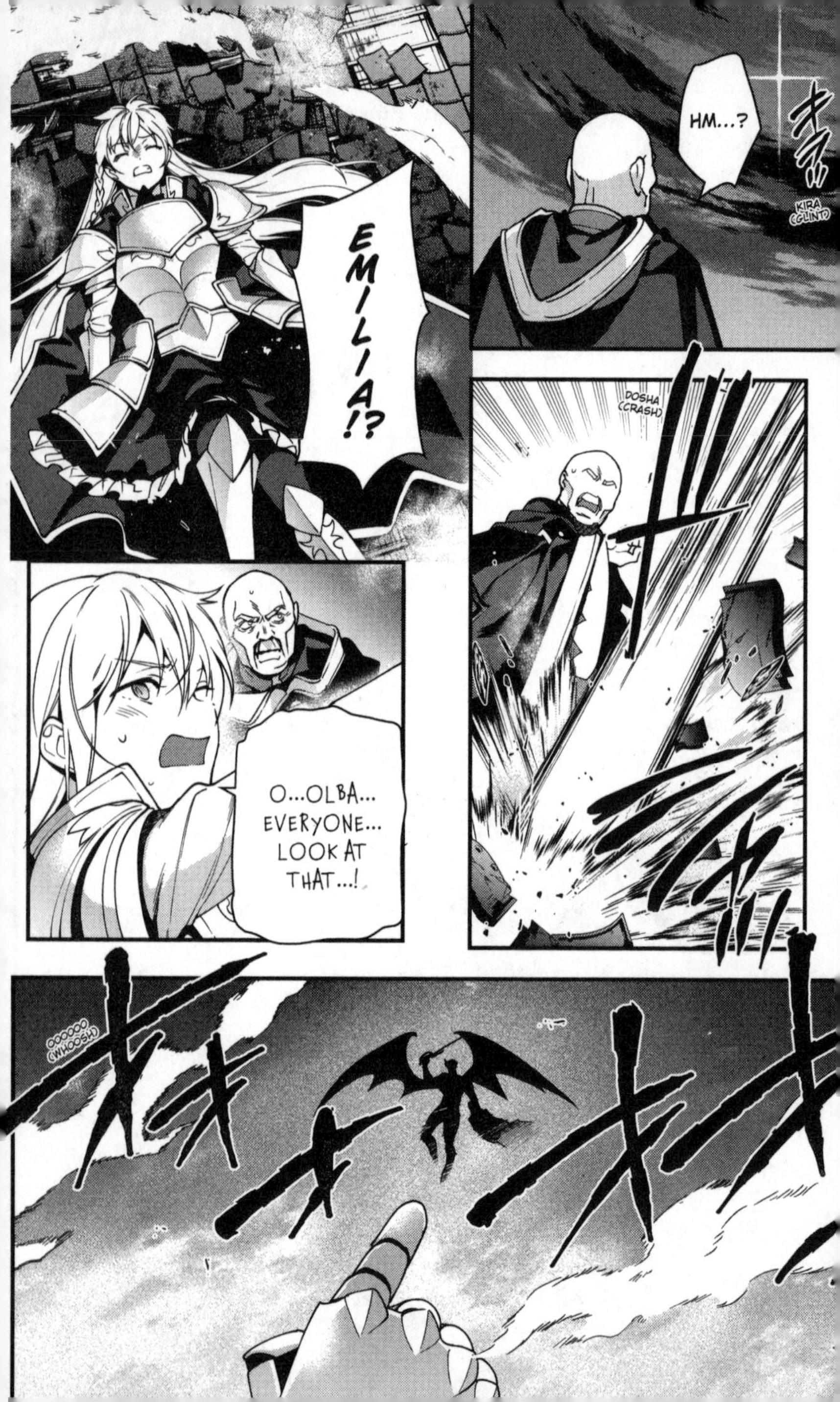
HM...?
KIRA (GLINT)
EMILIA!?
DOSHA (CRASH)
O...OLBA... EVERYONE... LOOK AT THAT...!
OOOOOO (WHOOSH)

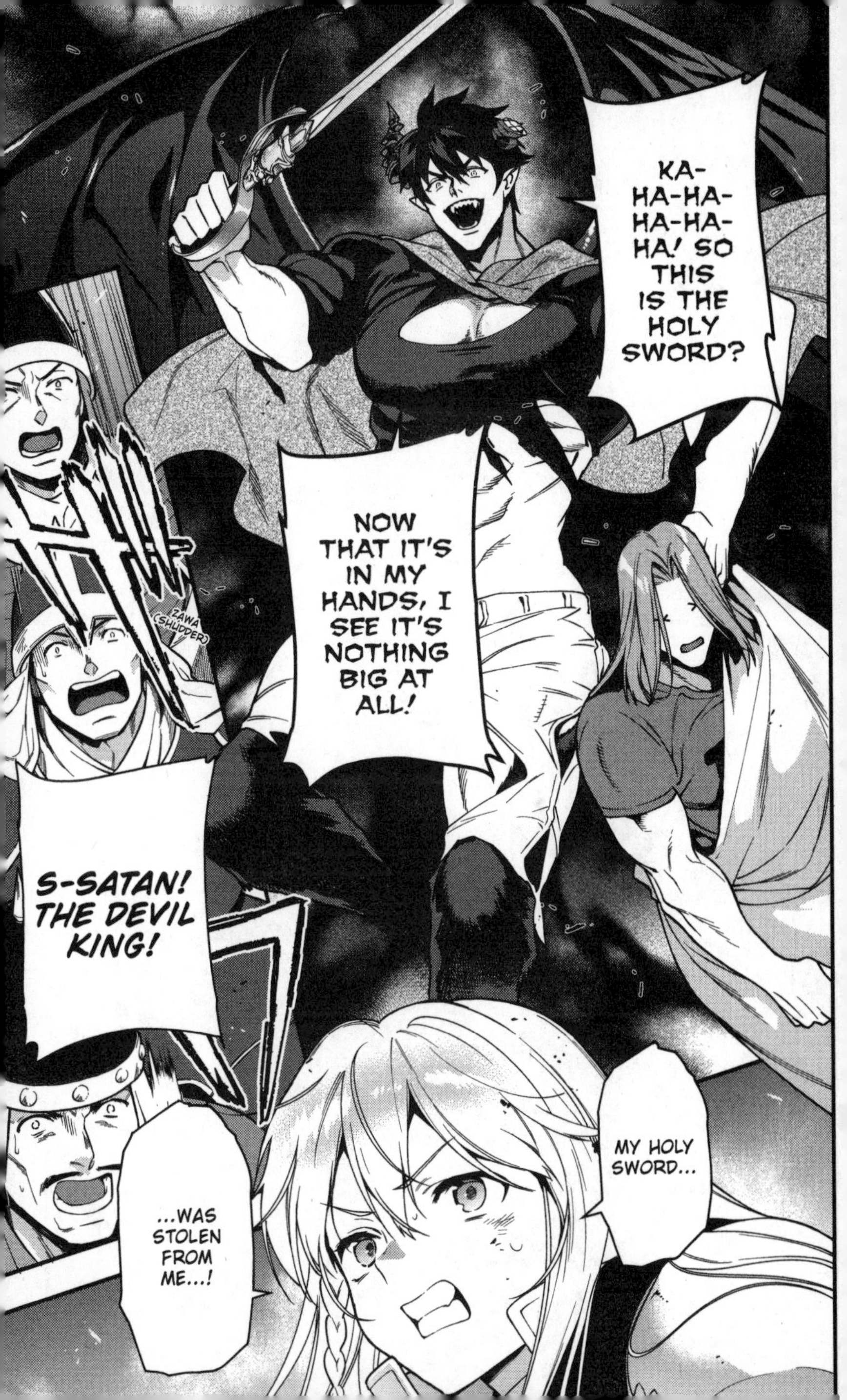
KA-HA-HA-HA-HA-HA! SO THIS IS THE HOLY SWORD?
NOW THAT IT'S IN MY HANDS, I SEE IT'S NOTHING BIG AT ALL!
ZAWA (SHUDDER)
S-SATAN! THE DEVIL KING!
MY HOLY SWORD...
...WAS STOLEN FROM ME...!

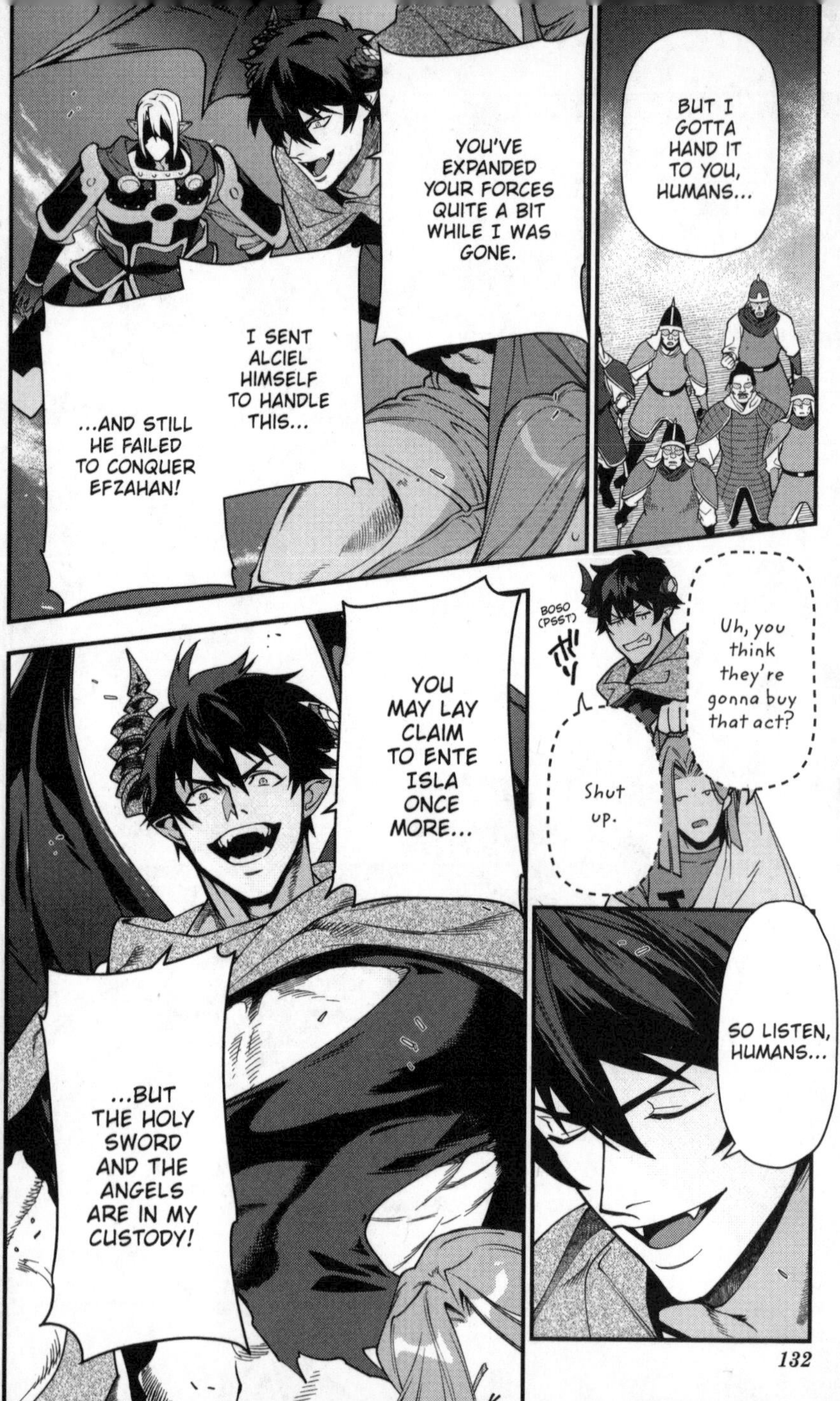
BUT I GOTTA HAND IT TO YOU, HUMANS...
YOU'VE EXPANDED YOUR FORCES QUITE A BIT WHILE I WAS GONE.
I SENT ALCIEL HIMSELF TO HANDLE THIS...
...AND STILL HE FAILED TO CONQUER EFZAHAN!
BOSO (PSST)
Uh, you think they're gonna buy that act?
Shut up.
SO LISTEN, HUMANS...
YOU MAY LAY CLAIM TO ENTE ISLA ONCE MORE...
...BUT THE HOLY SWORD AND THE ANGELS ARE IN MY CUSTODY!

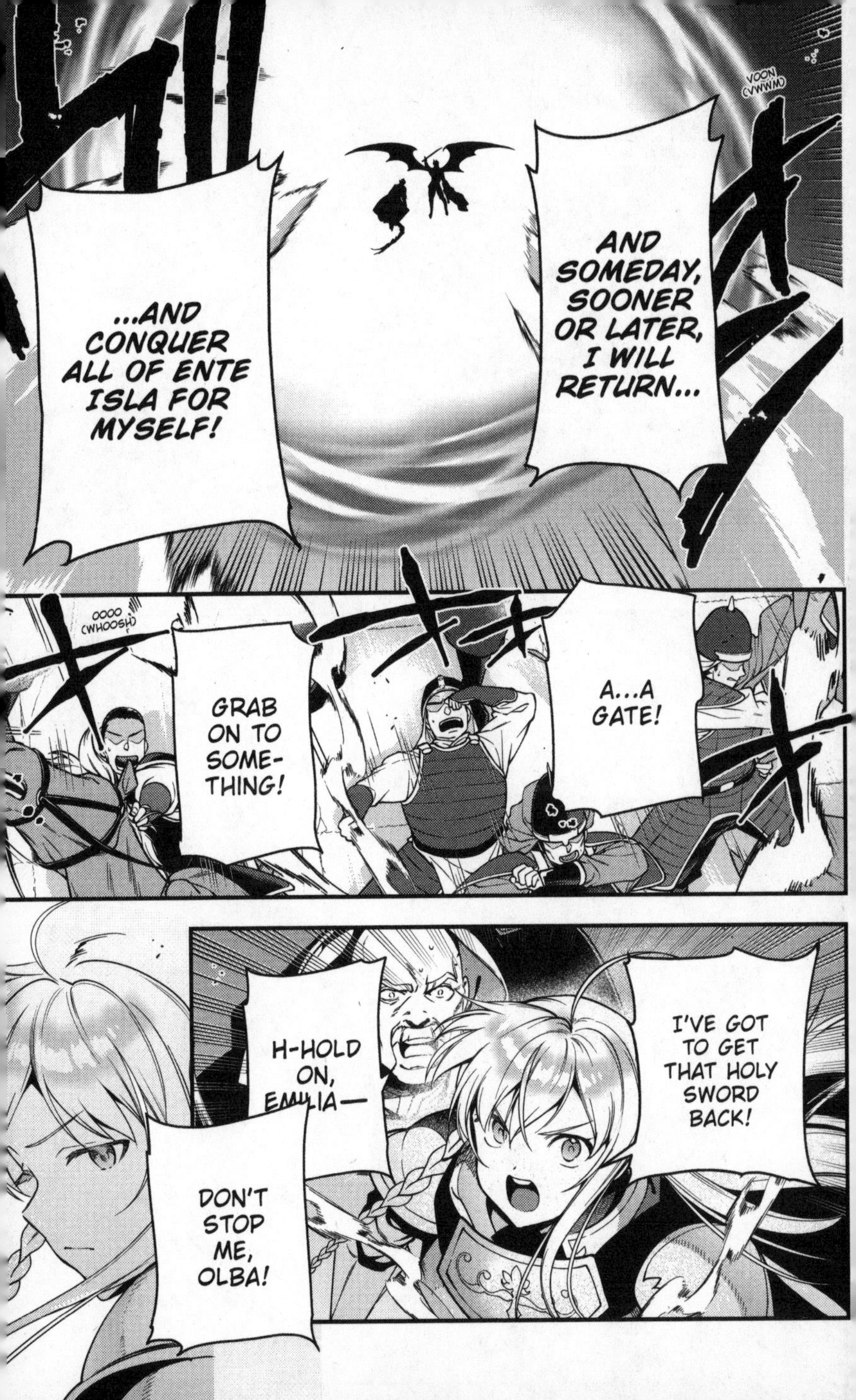
VOON (VWWM)
AND SOMEDAY, SOONER OR LATER, I WILL RETURN...
...AND CONQUER ALL OF ENTE ISLA FOR MYSELF!
A...A GATE!
GRAB ON TO SOME-THING!
OOOO (WHOOSH)
I'VE GOT TO GET THAT HOLY SWORD BACK!
H-HOLD ON, EMILIA—
DON'T STOP ME, OLBA!

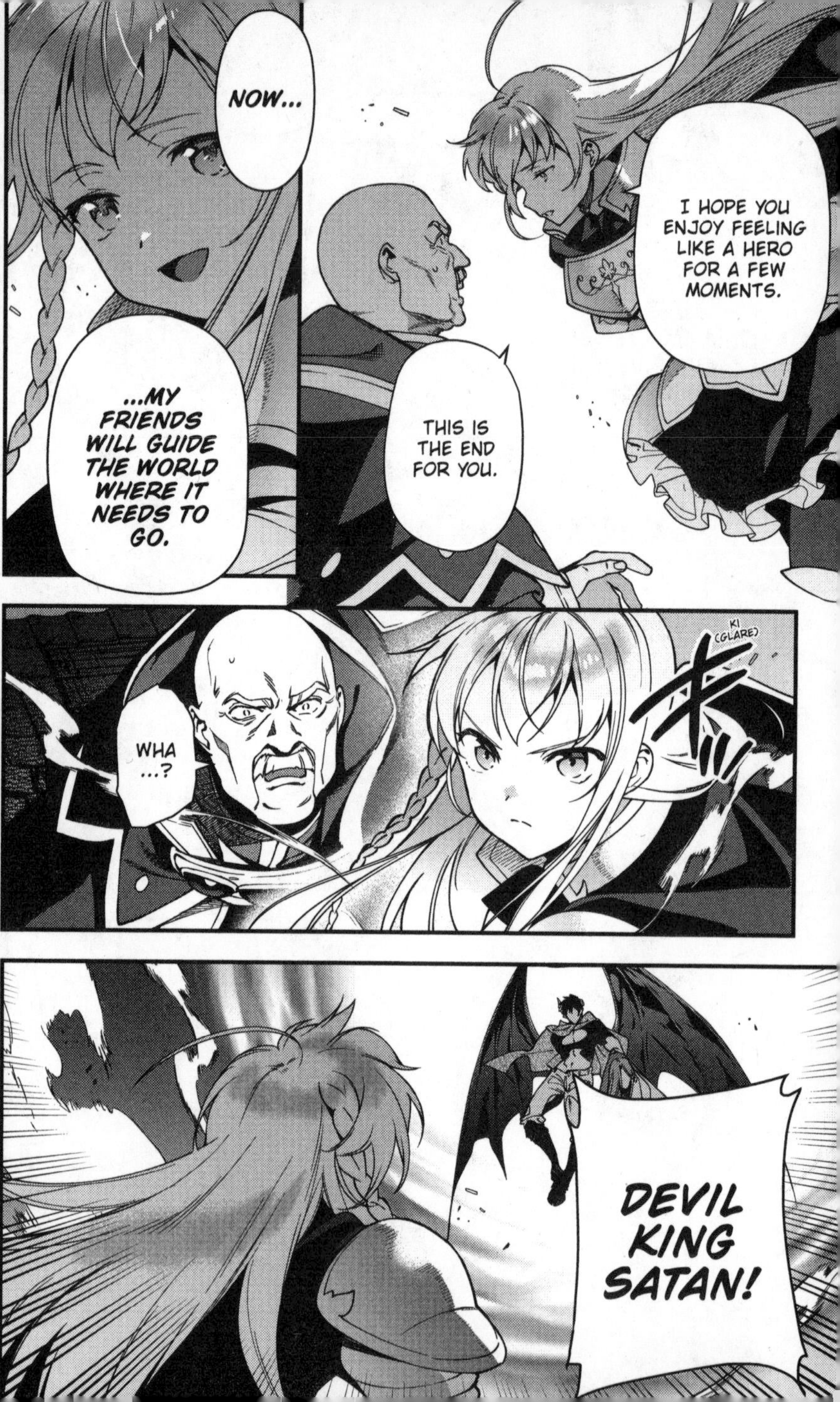
I HOPE YOU ENJOY FEELING LIKE A HERO FOR A FEW MOMENTS.
THIS IS THE END FOR YOU.
NOW...
...MY FRIENDS WILL GUIDE THE WORLD WHERE IT NEEDS TO GO.
KI (GLARE)
WHA ...?
DEVIL KING SATAN!

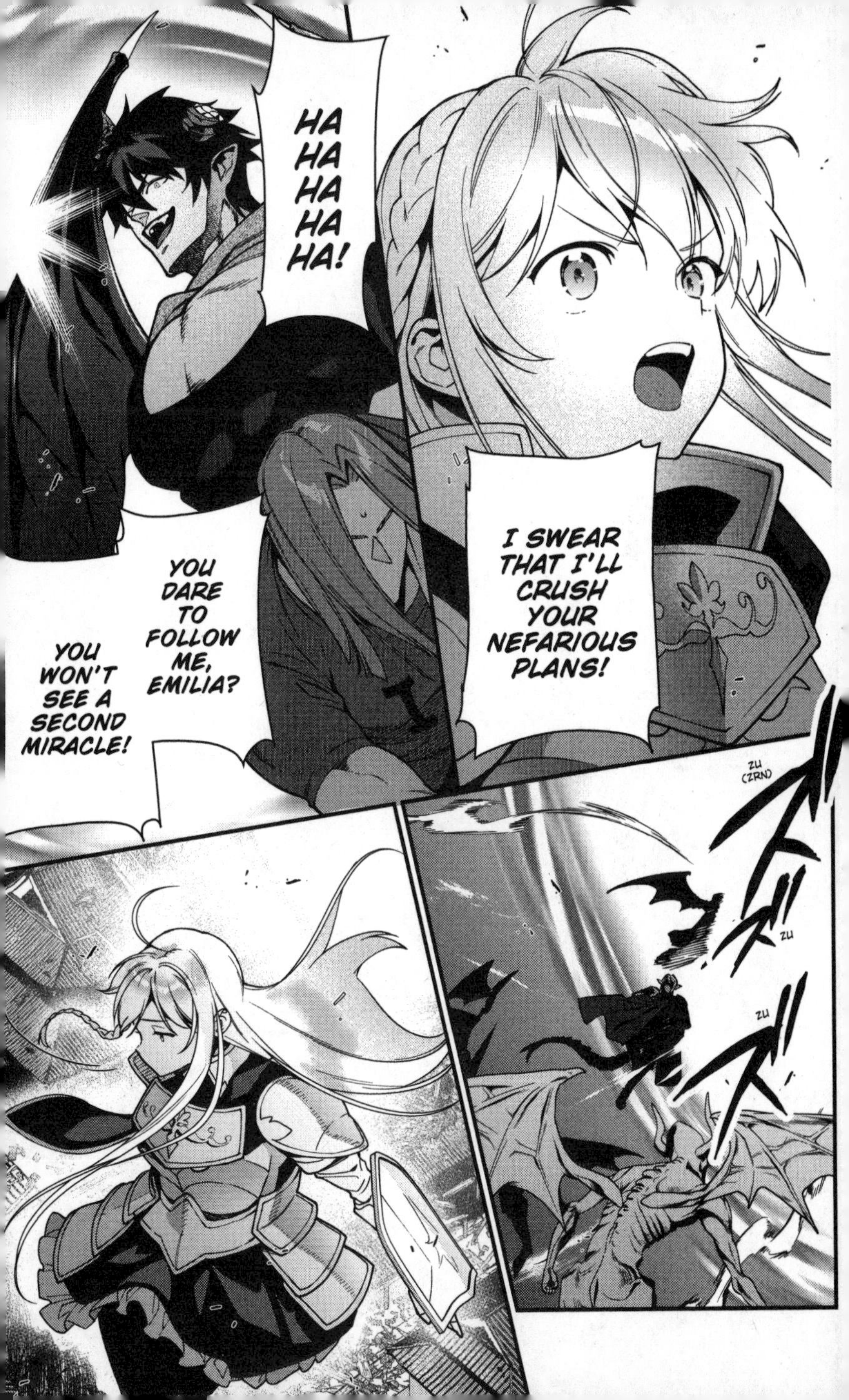
I SWEAR THAT I'LL CRUSH YOUR NEFARIOUS PLANS!
HA HA HA HA HA!
YOU DARE TO FOLLOW ME, EMILIA?
YOU WON'T SEE A SECOND MIRACLE!
ZU (ZRN)
ZU
ZU

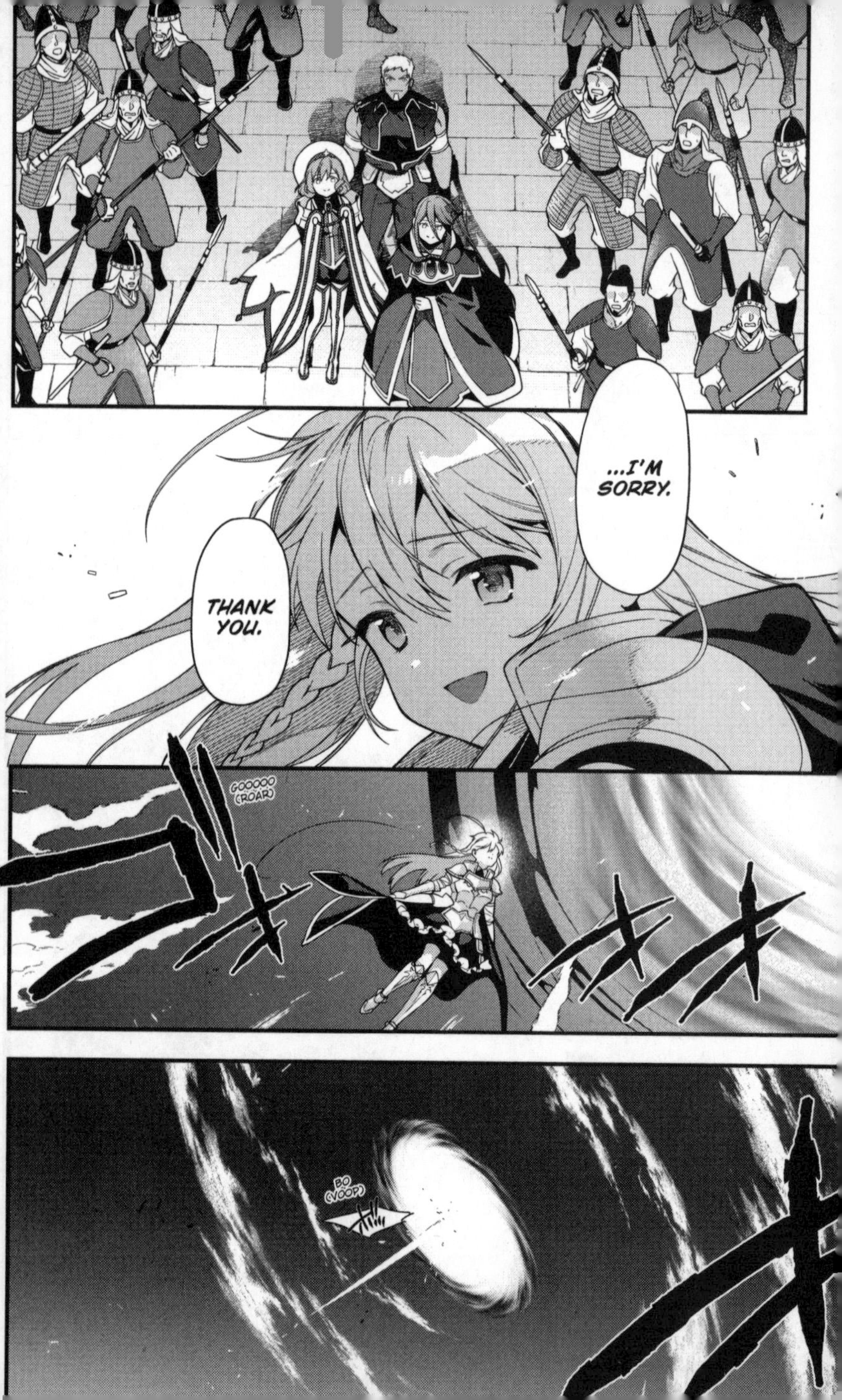
...I'M SORRY.
THANK YOU.
GOOOOO (ROAR)
BO (VOOP)

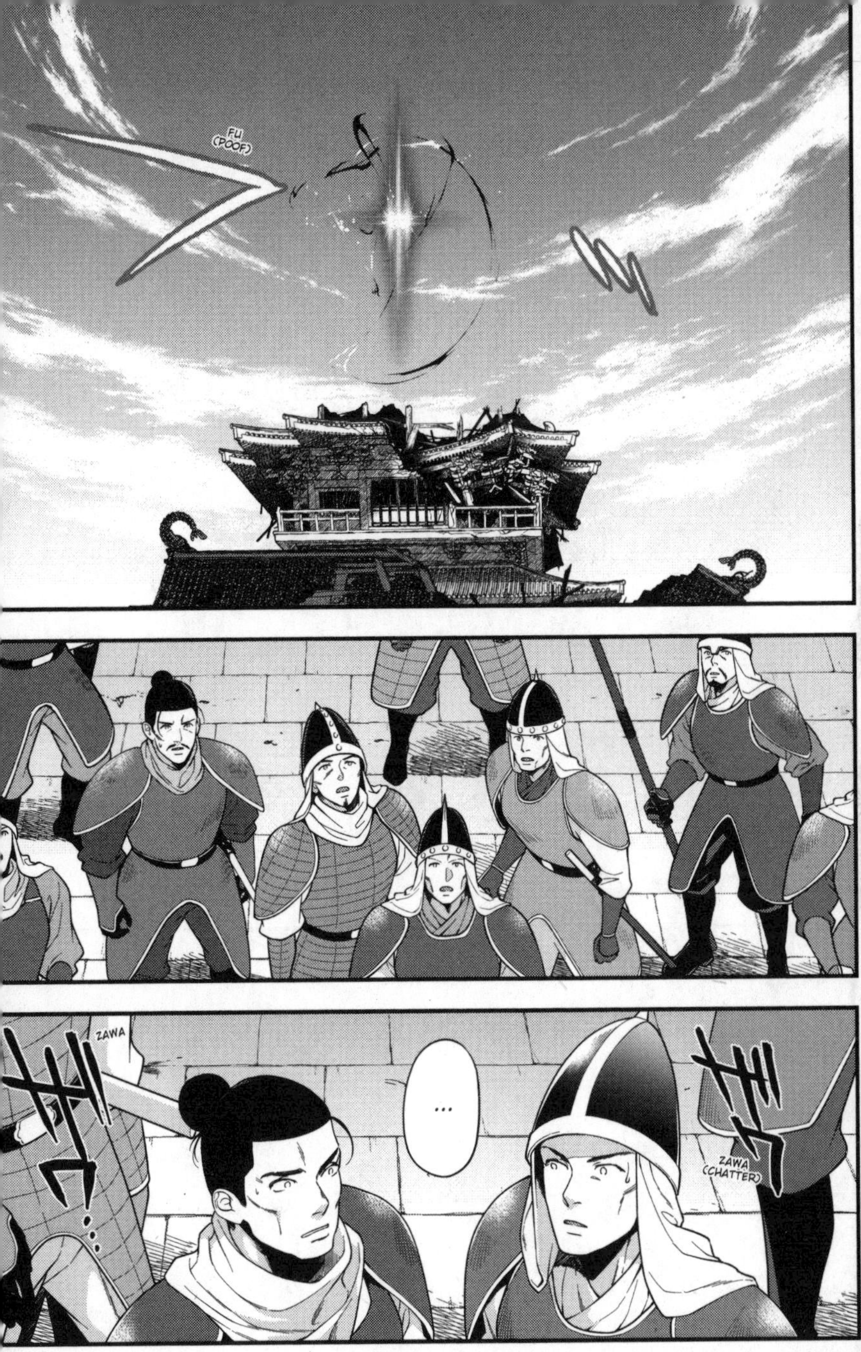
FU
(POOF)
ZAWA
(CHATTER)
...
ZAWA

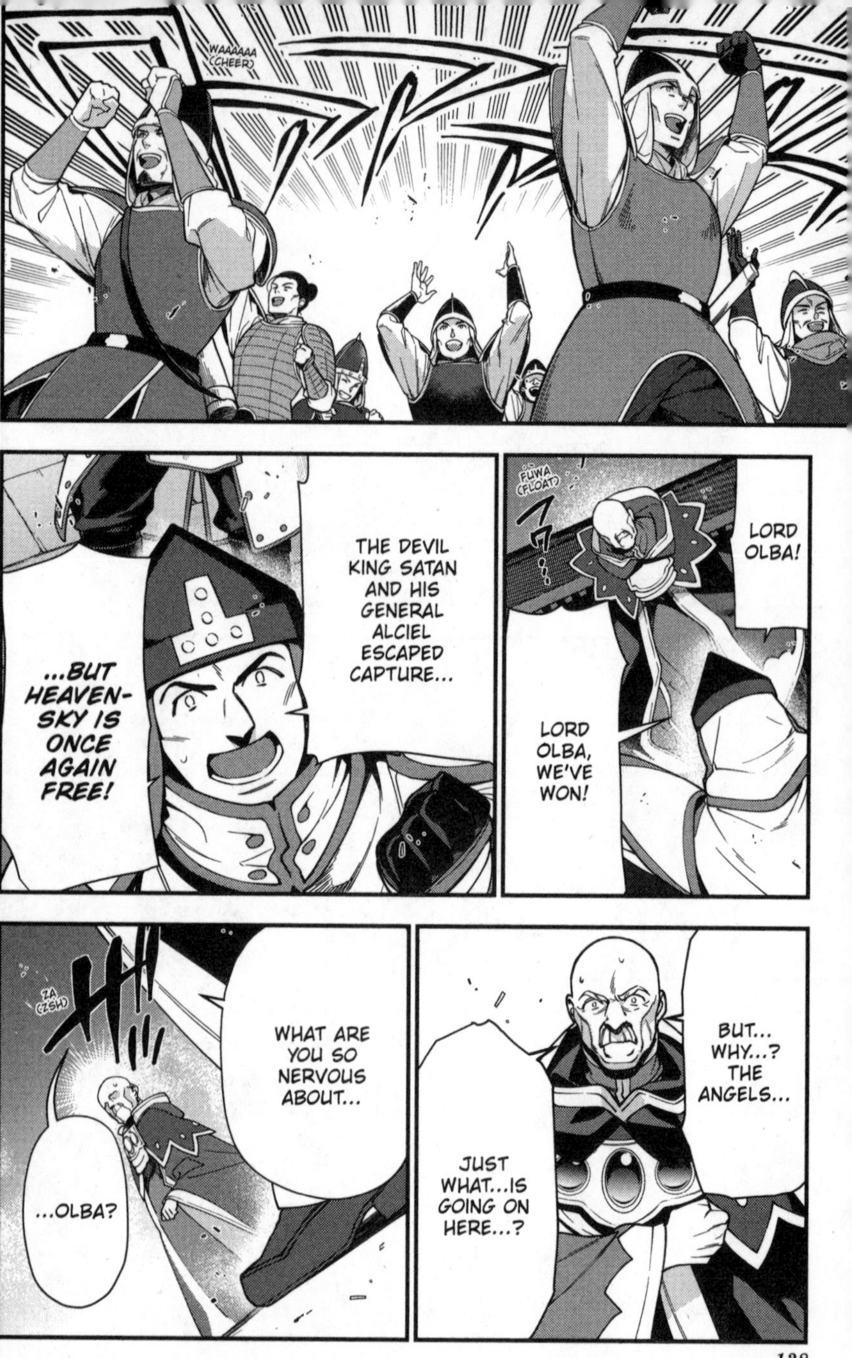

WAAAAAA (CHEER)
FUWA (FLOAT)
LORD OLBA!
LORD OLBA, WE'VE WON!
THE DEVIL KING SATAN AND HIS GENERAL ALCIEL ESCAPED CAPTURE...
...BUT HEAVEN-SKY IS ONCE AGAIN FREE!
BUT... WHY...? THE ANGELS...
JUST WHAT...IS GOING ON HERE...?
ZA (ZSH)
WHAT ARE YOU SO NERVOUS ABOUT...
...OLBA?

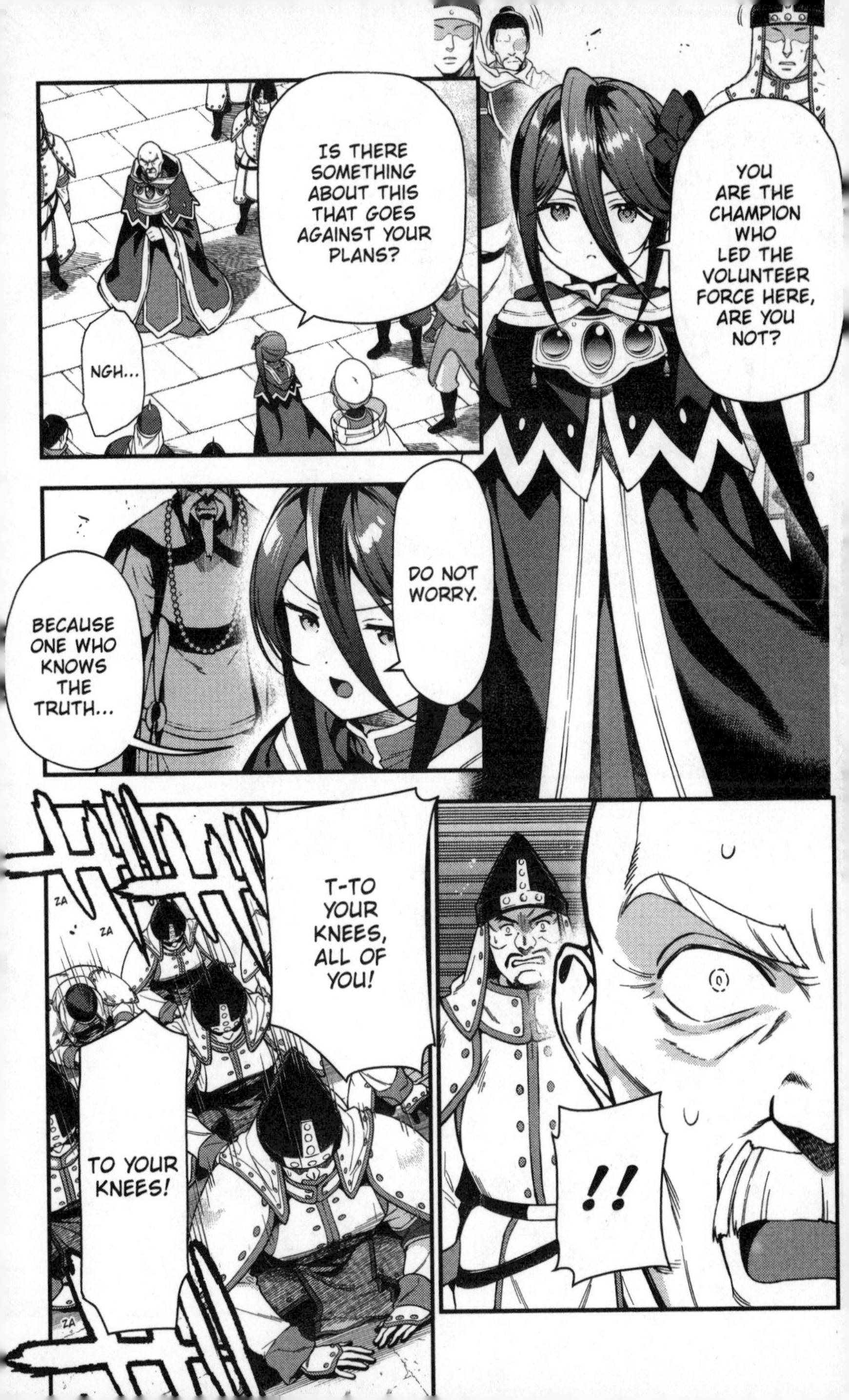
YOU ARE THE CHAMPION WHO LED THE VOLUNTEER FORCE HERE, ARE YOU NOT?
IS THERE SOMETHING ABOUT THIS THAT GOES AGAINST YOUR PLANS?
NGH...
DO NOT WORRY.
BECAUSE ONE WHO KNOWS THE TRUTH...
!!
T-TO YOUR KNEES, ALL OF YOU!
ZA
ZA
TO YOUR KNEES!
ZA

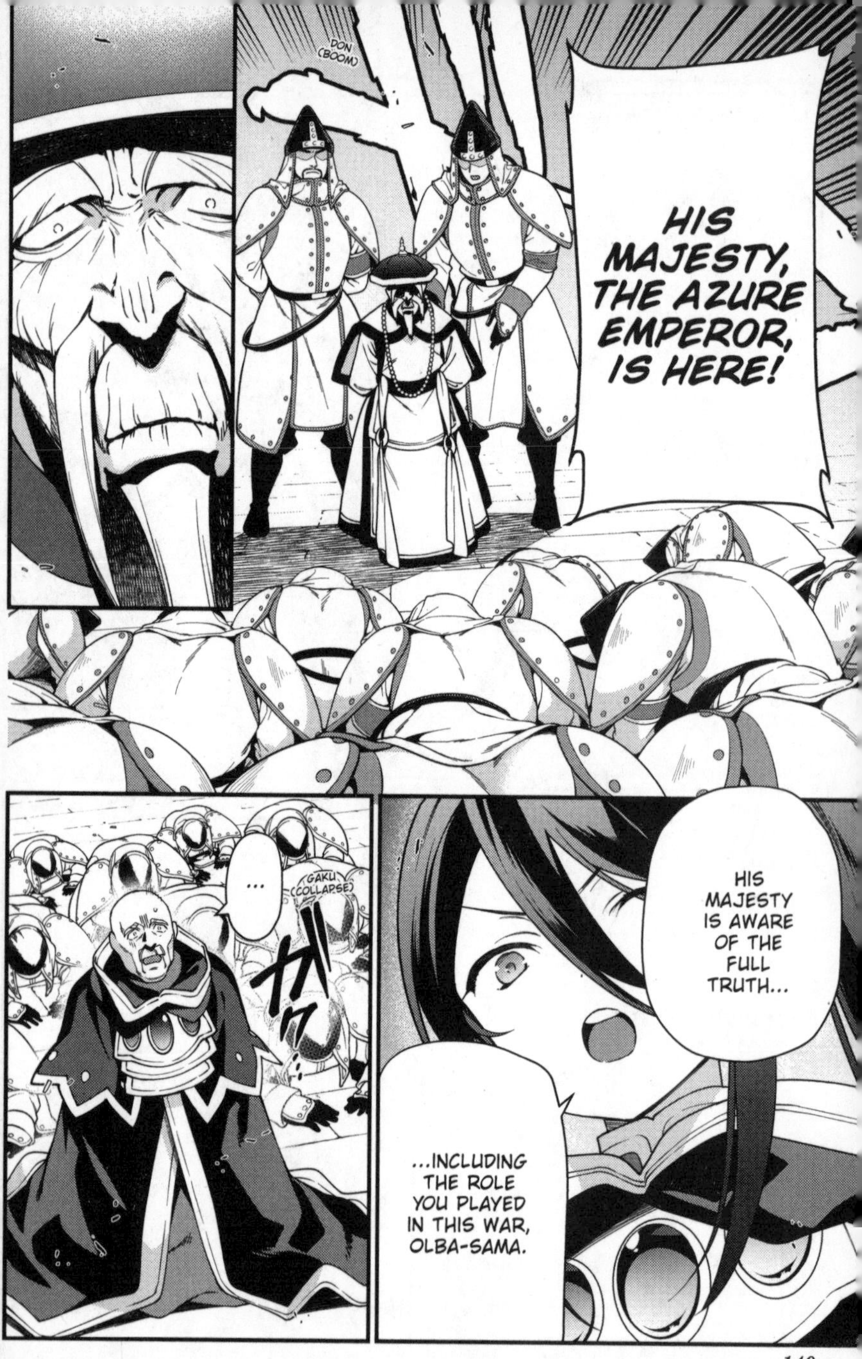
DON (BOOM)
HIS MAJESTY, THE AZURE EMPEROR, IS HERE!
HIS MAJESTY IS AWARE OF THE FULL TRUTH...
...INCLUDING THE ROLE YOU PLAYED IN THIS WAR, OLBA-SAMA.
...
GAKU (COLLAPSE)

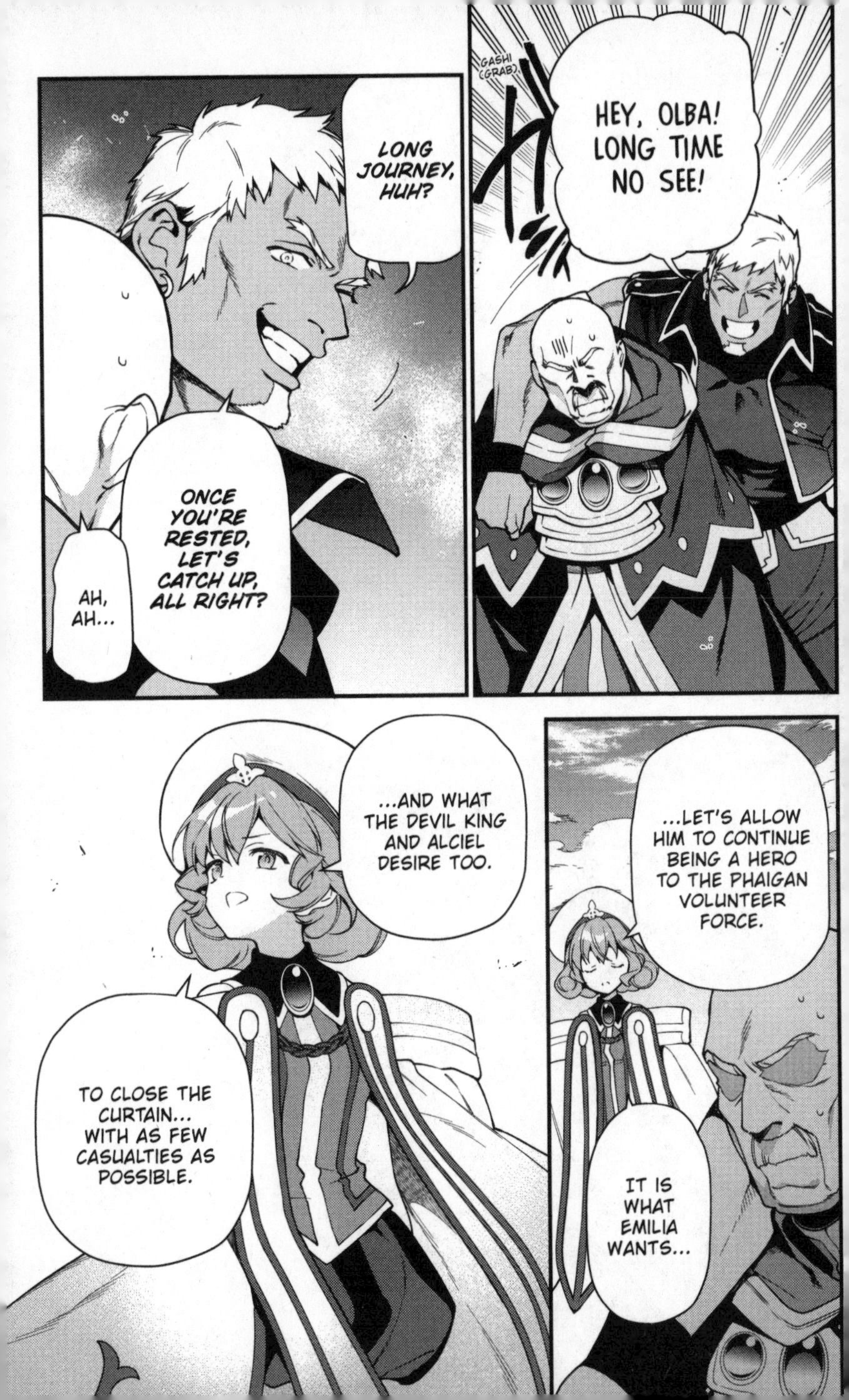
GASHI (GRAB)
HEY, OLBA! LONG TIME NO SEE!
LONG JOURNEY, HUH?
ONCE YOU'RE RESTED, LET'S CATCH UP, ALL RIGHT?
AH, AH...
...LET'S ALLOW HIM TO CONTINUE BEING A HERO TO THE PHAIGAN VOLUNTEER FORCE.
IT IS WHAT EMILIA WANTS...
...AND WHAT THE DEVIL KING AND ALCIEL DESIRE TOO.
TO CLOSE THE CURTAIN... WITH AS FEW CASUALTIES AS POSSIBLE.

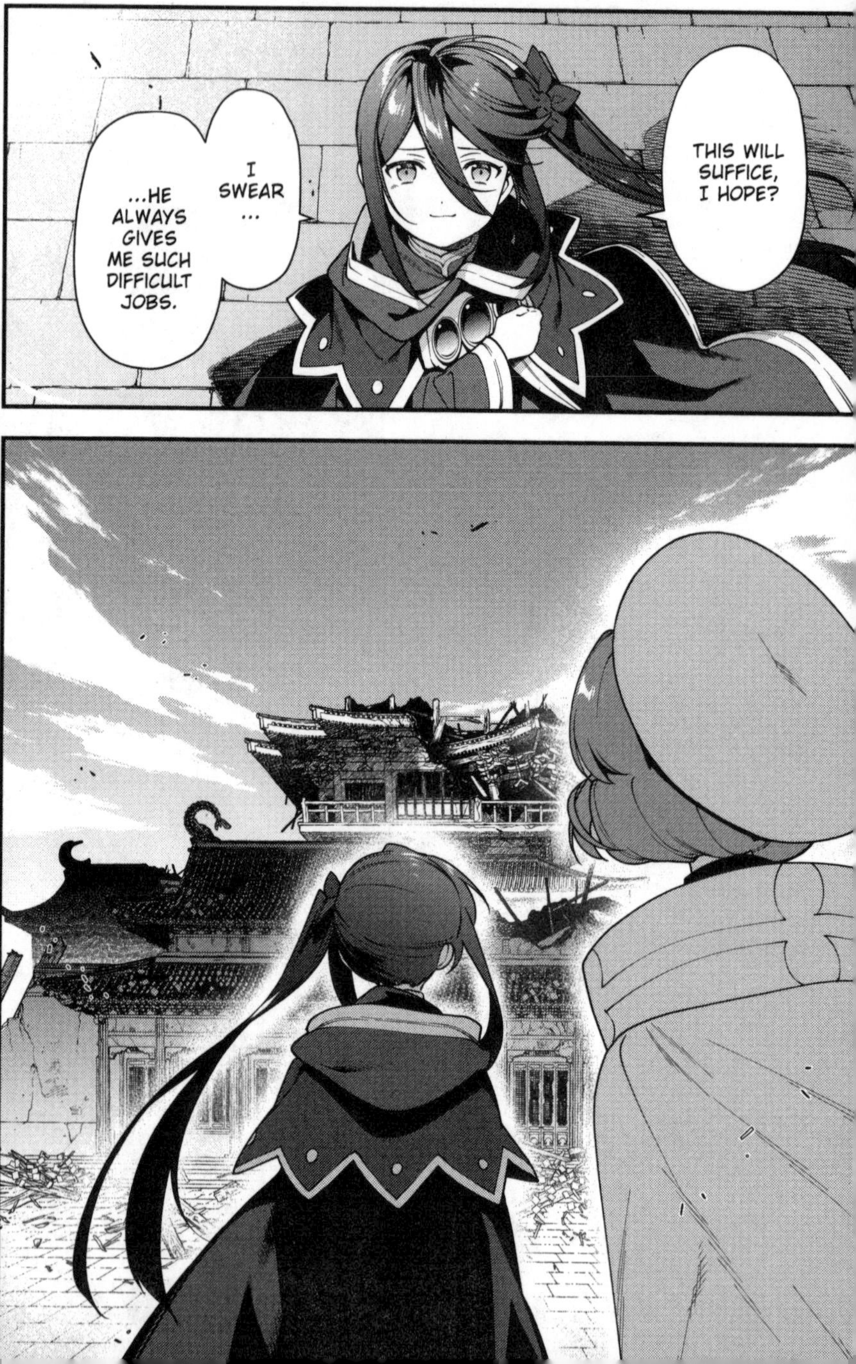
THIS WILL SUFFICE, I HOPE?
I SWEAR ...
...HE ALWAYS GIVES ME SUCH DIFFICULT JOBS.

Emi Yusa

THE DEVIL IS A PART-TIMER!

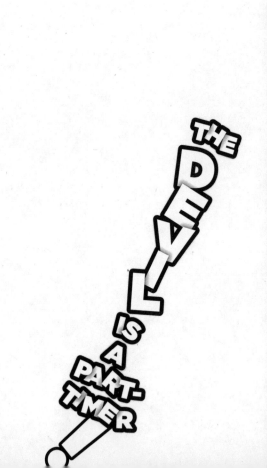

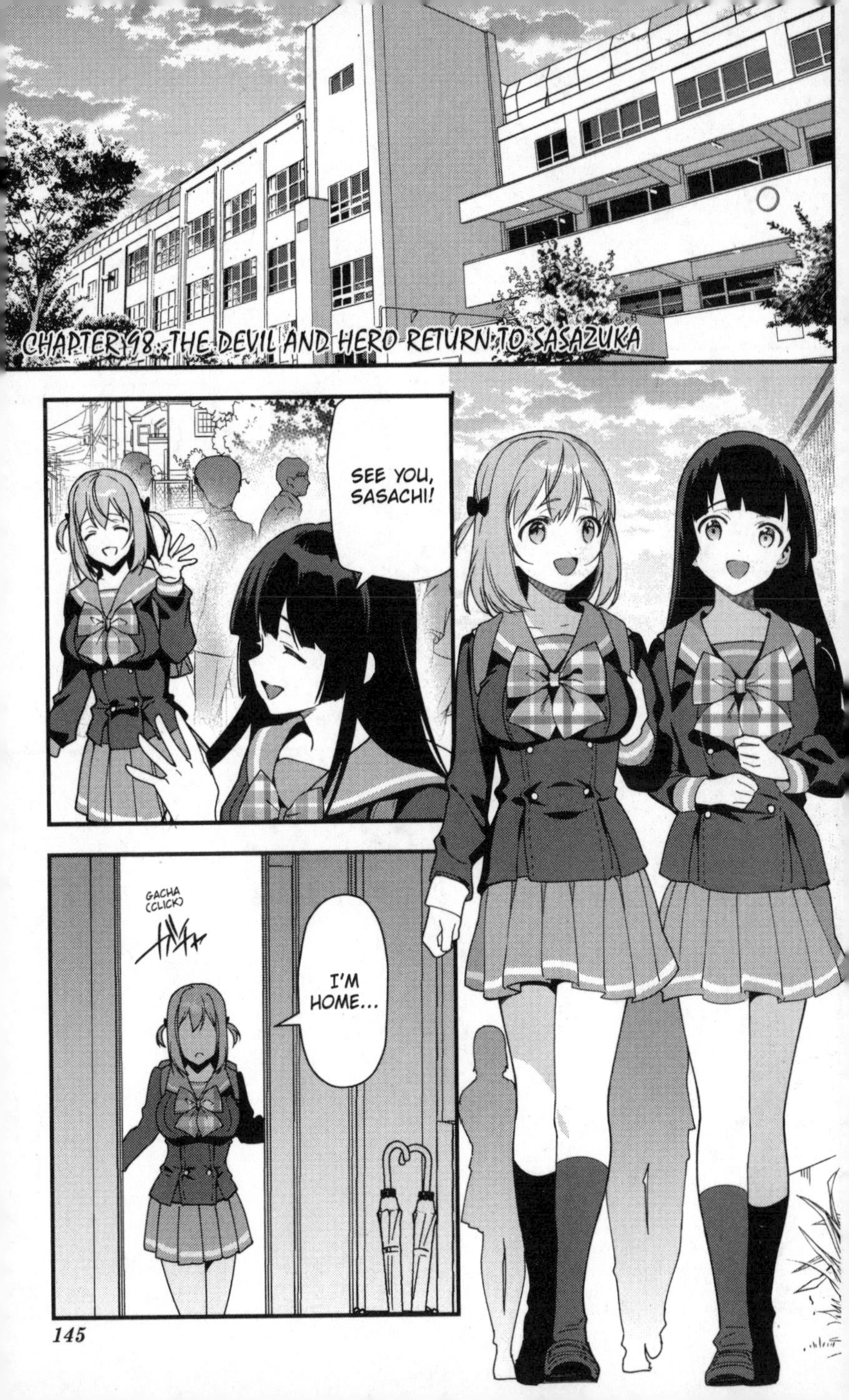
CHAPTER 98: THE DEVIL AND HERO RETURN TO SASAZUKA
SEE YOU, SASACHI!
I'M HOME...
GACHA (CLICK)

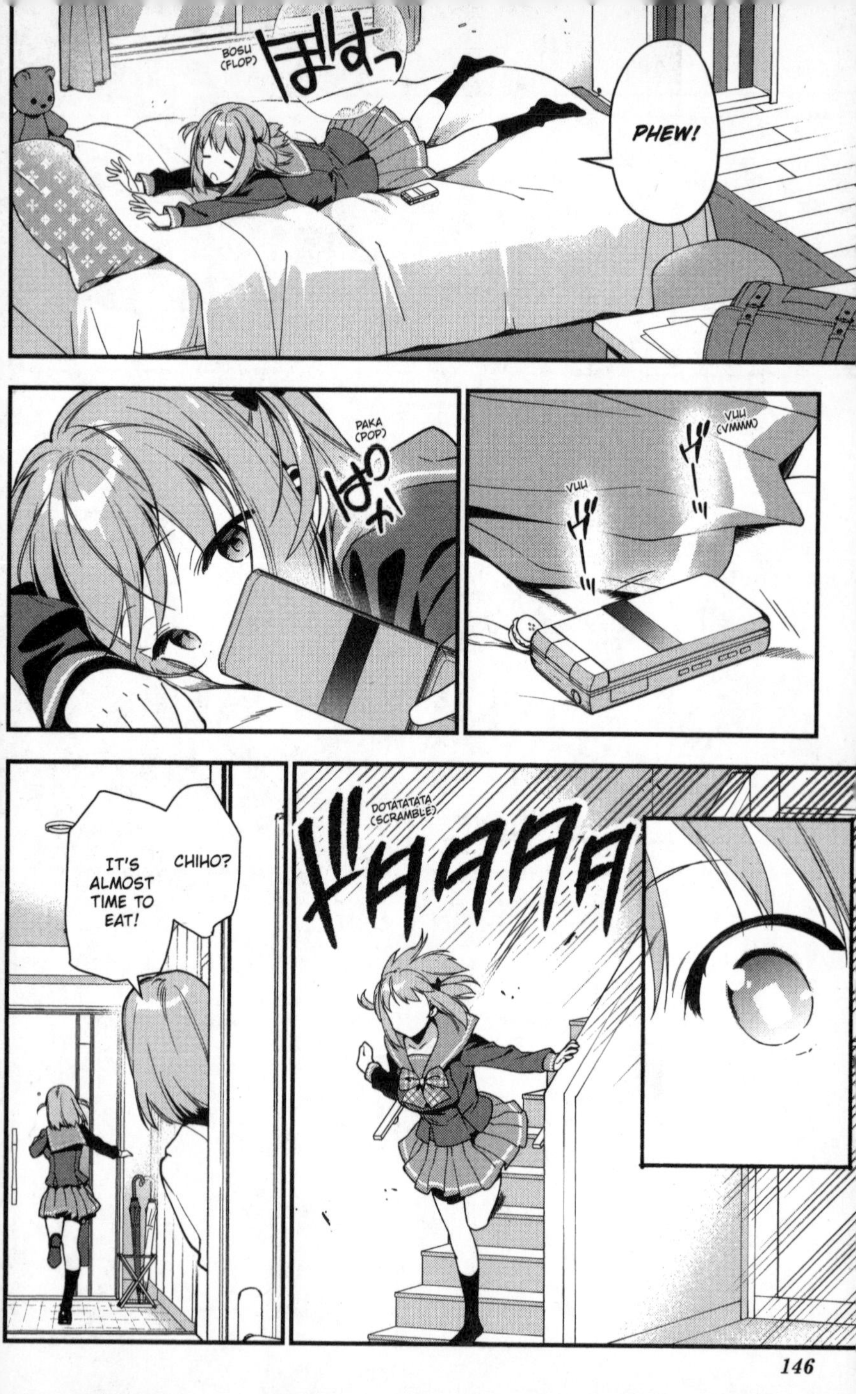
BOSU (FLOP)
ぼすっ
PHEW!
VUU (VMMM)
ヴーッ
VUU
ヴーッ
PAKA (POP)
ぱかっ
DOTATATATA (SCRAMBLE)
ドタタタタ
CHIHO?
IT'S ALMOST TIME TO EAT!

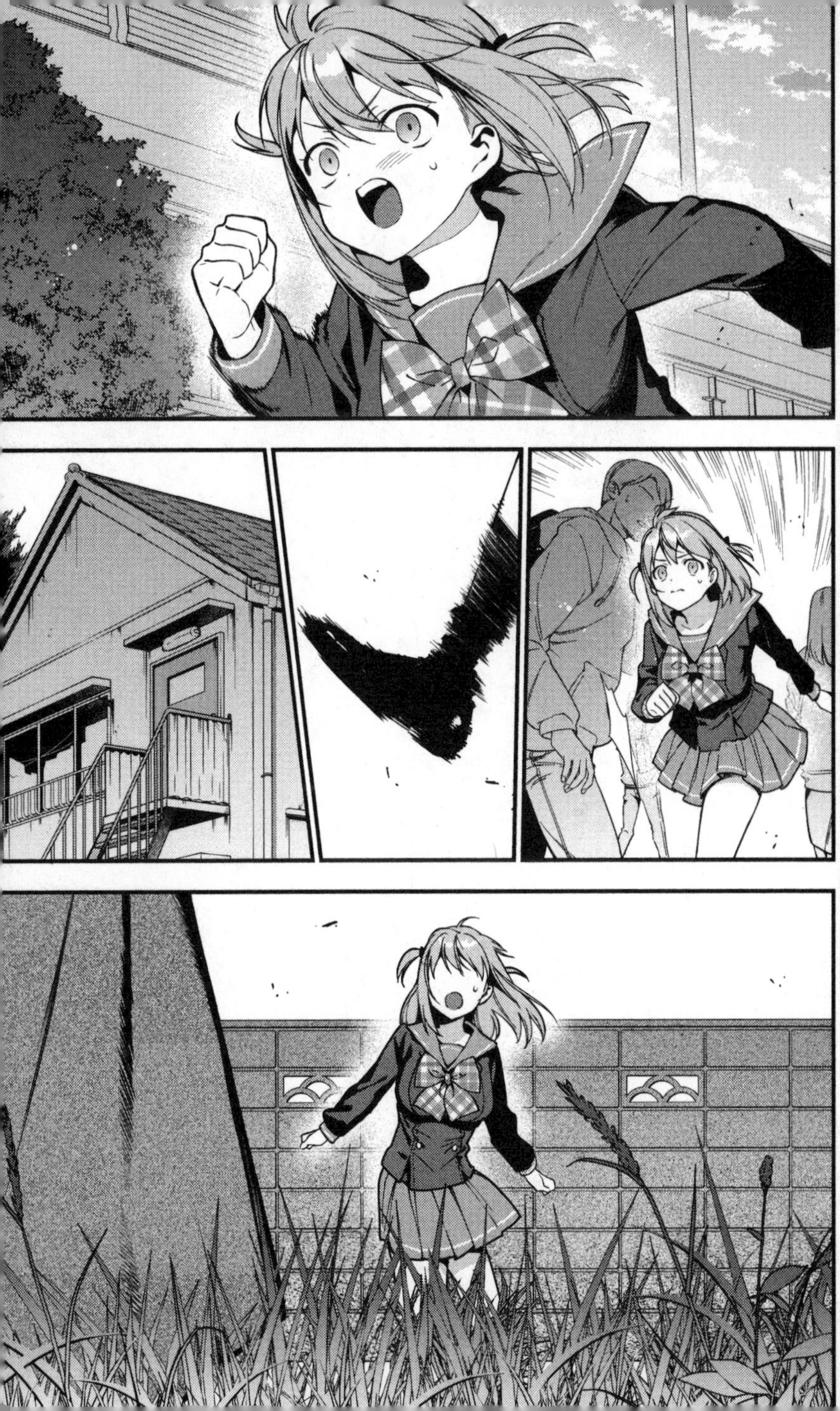

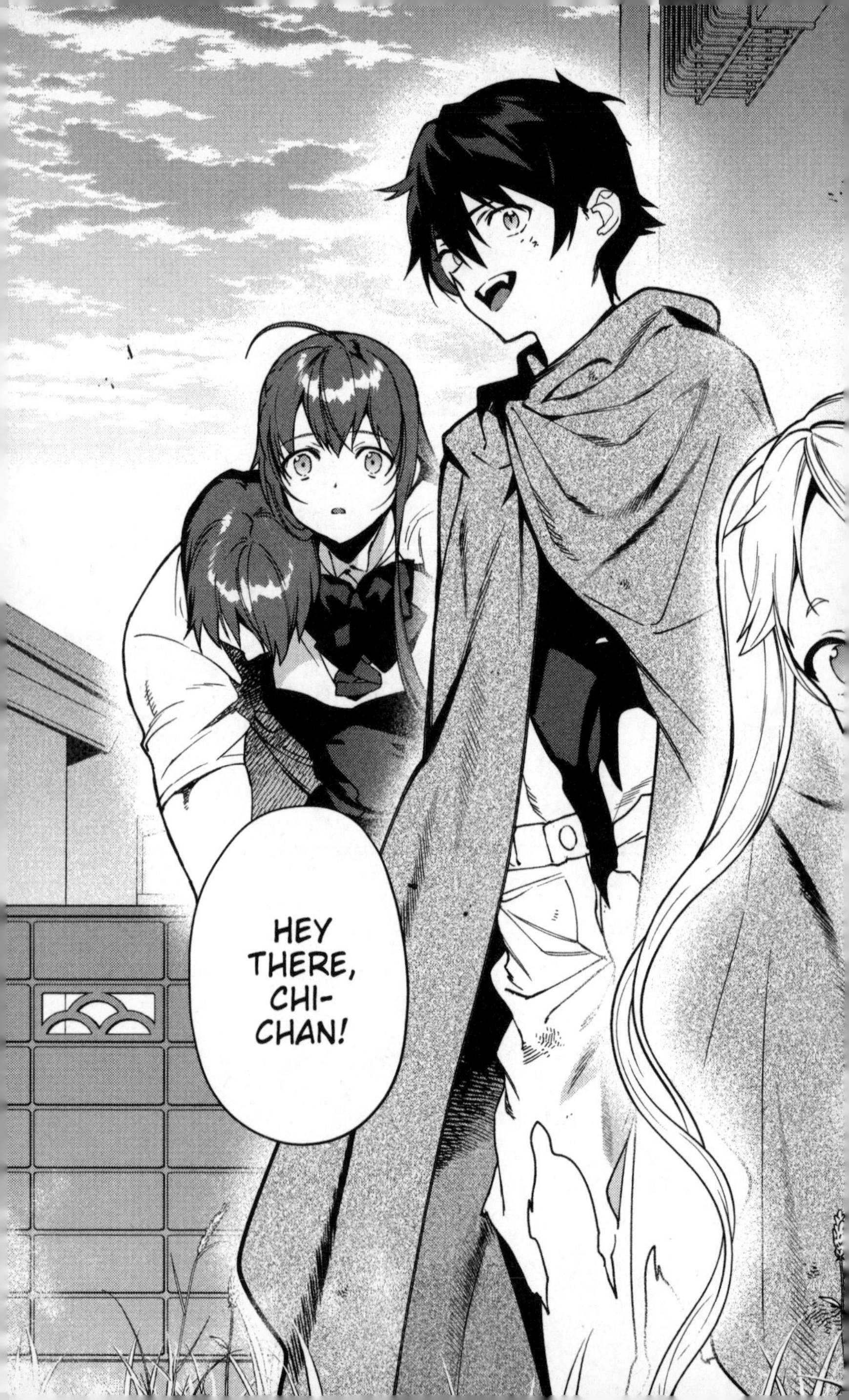
HEY THERE, CHI-CHAN!

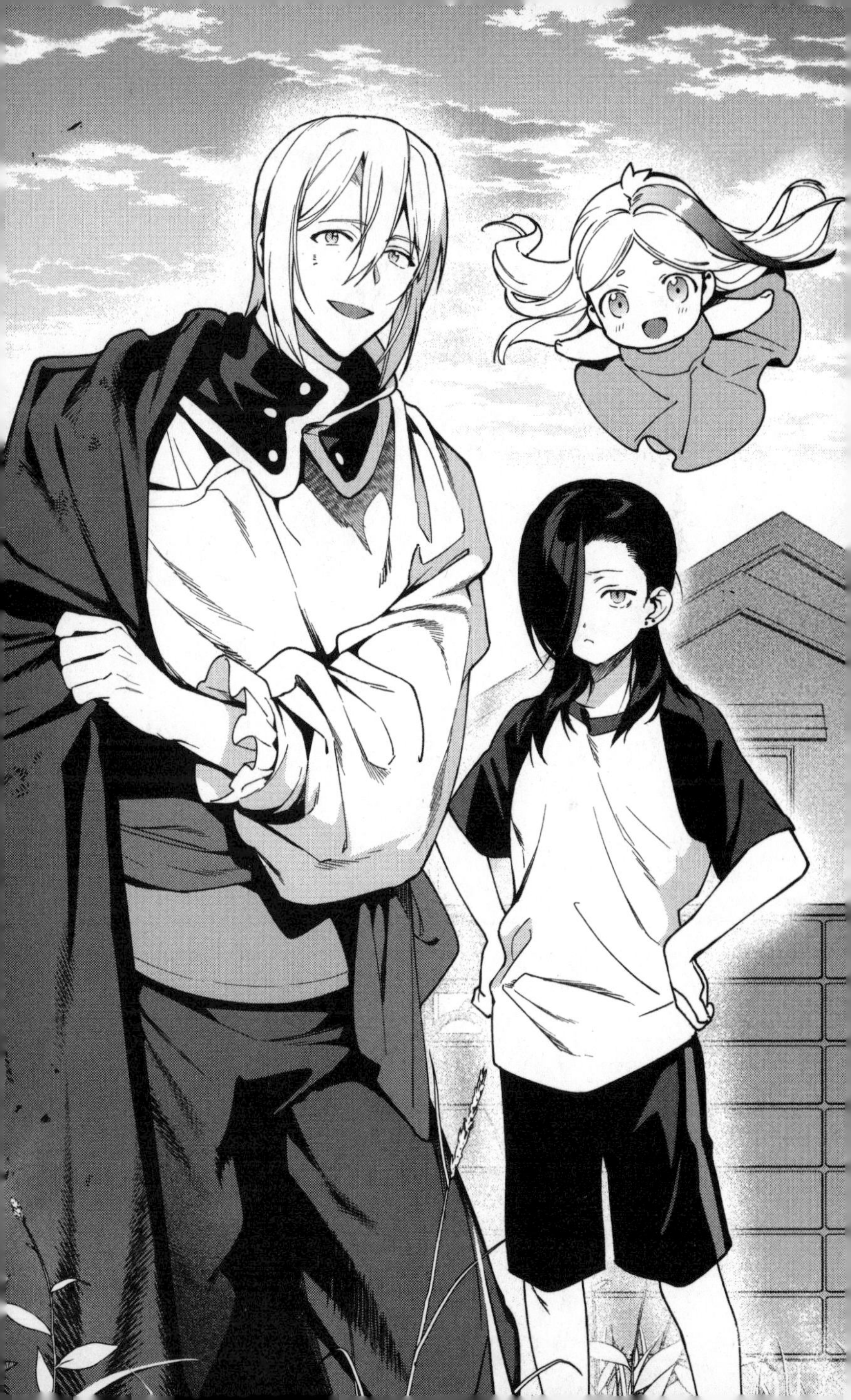

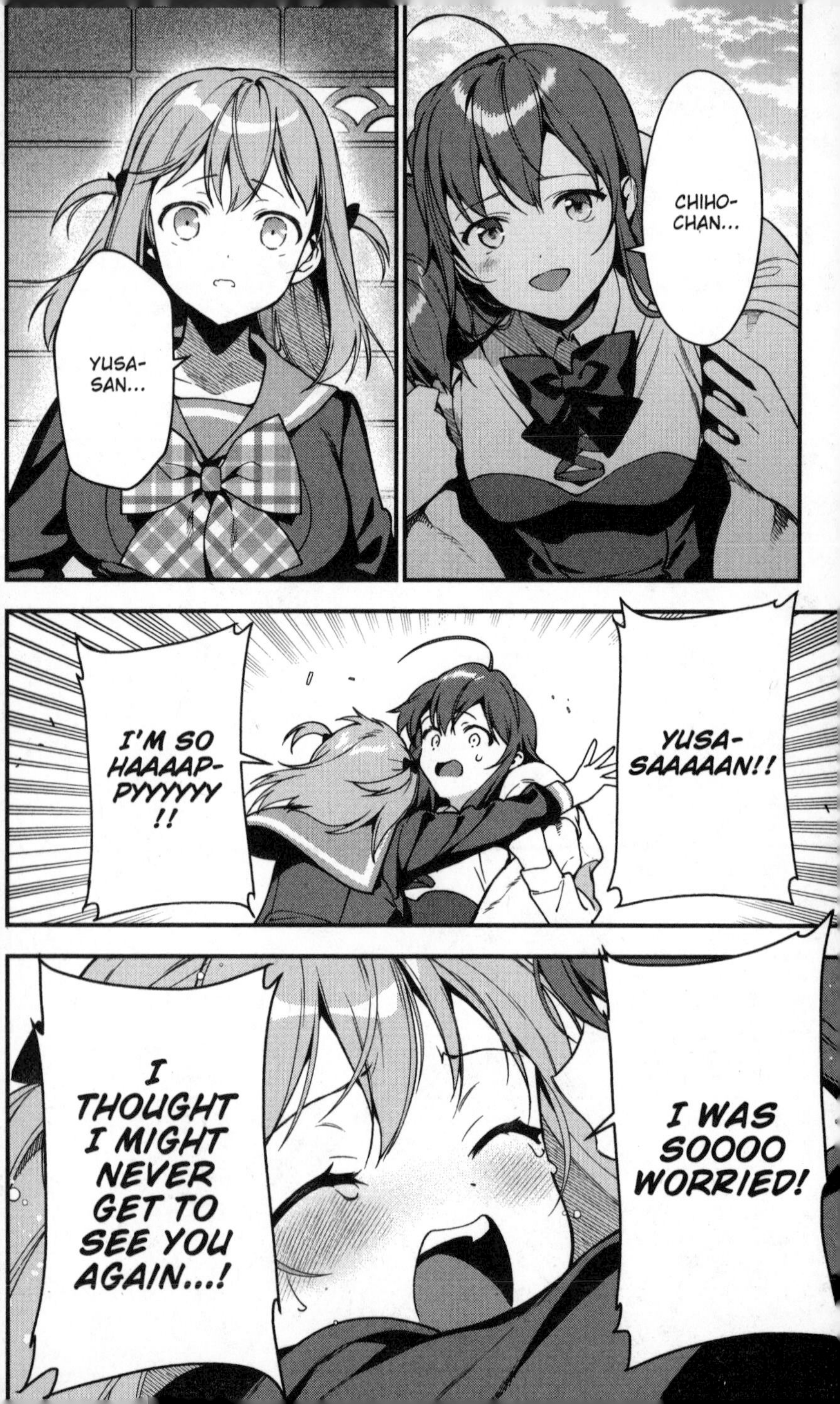
CHIHO-CHAN...
YUSA-SAN...
YUSA-SAAAAAN!!
I'M SO HAAAAP-PYYYYYY!!
I WAS SOOOO WORRIED!
I THOUGHT I MIGHT NEVER GET TO SEE YOU AGAIN...!

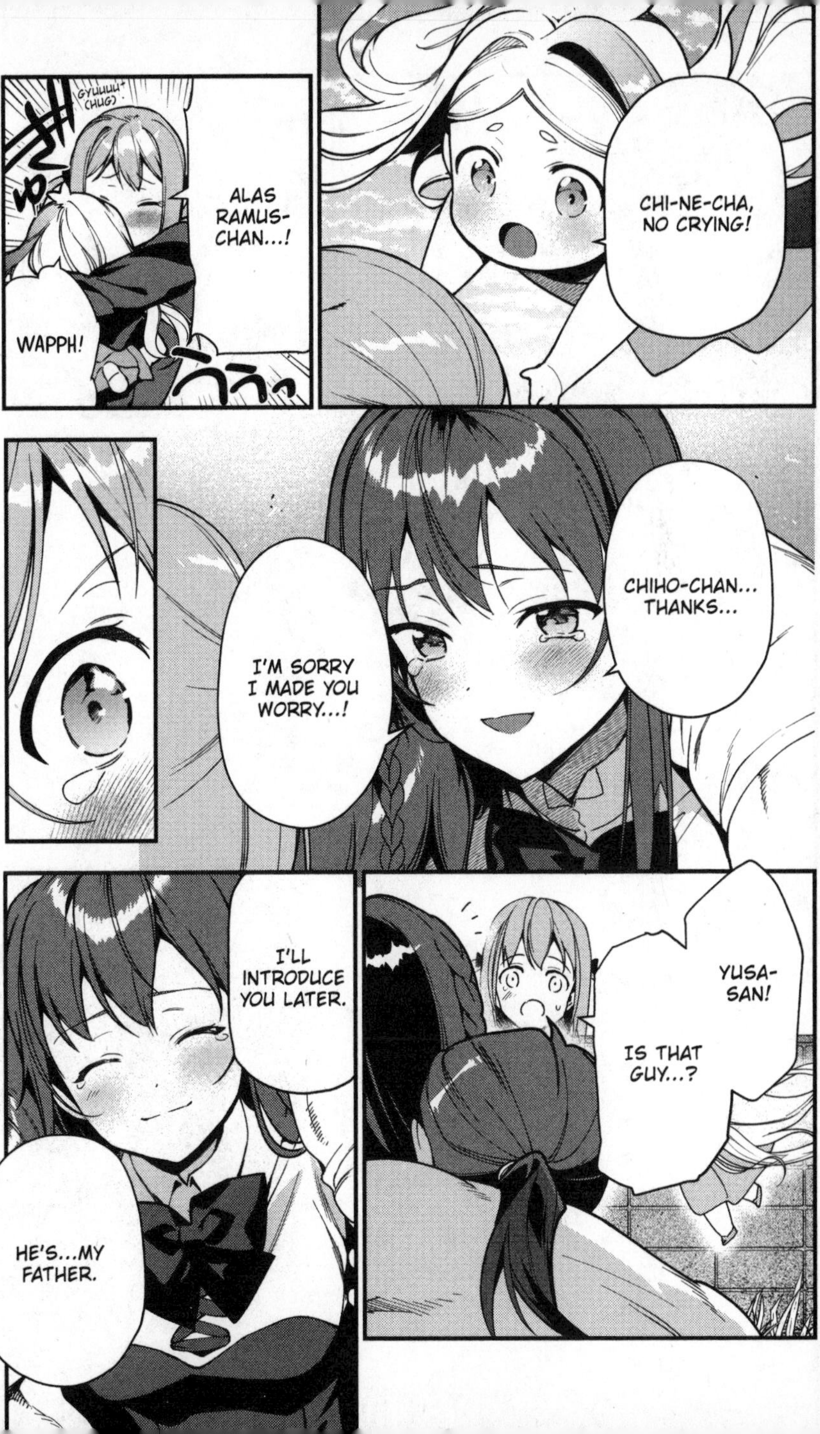
CHI-NE-CHA, NO CRYING!
GYUUUUU (HUG)
ALAS RAMUS-CHAN...!
WAPPH!
CHIHO-CHAN... THANKS...
I'M SORRY I MADE YOU WORRY...!
YUSA-SAN!
IS THAT GUY...?
I'LL INTRODUCE YOU LATER.
HE'S...MY FATHER.

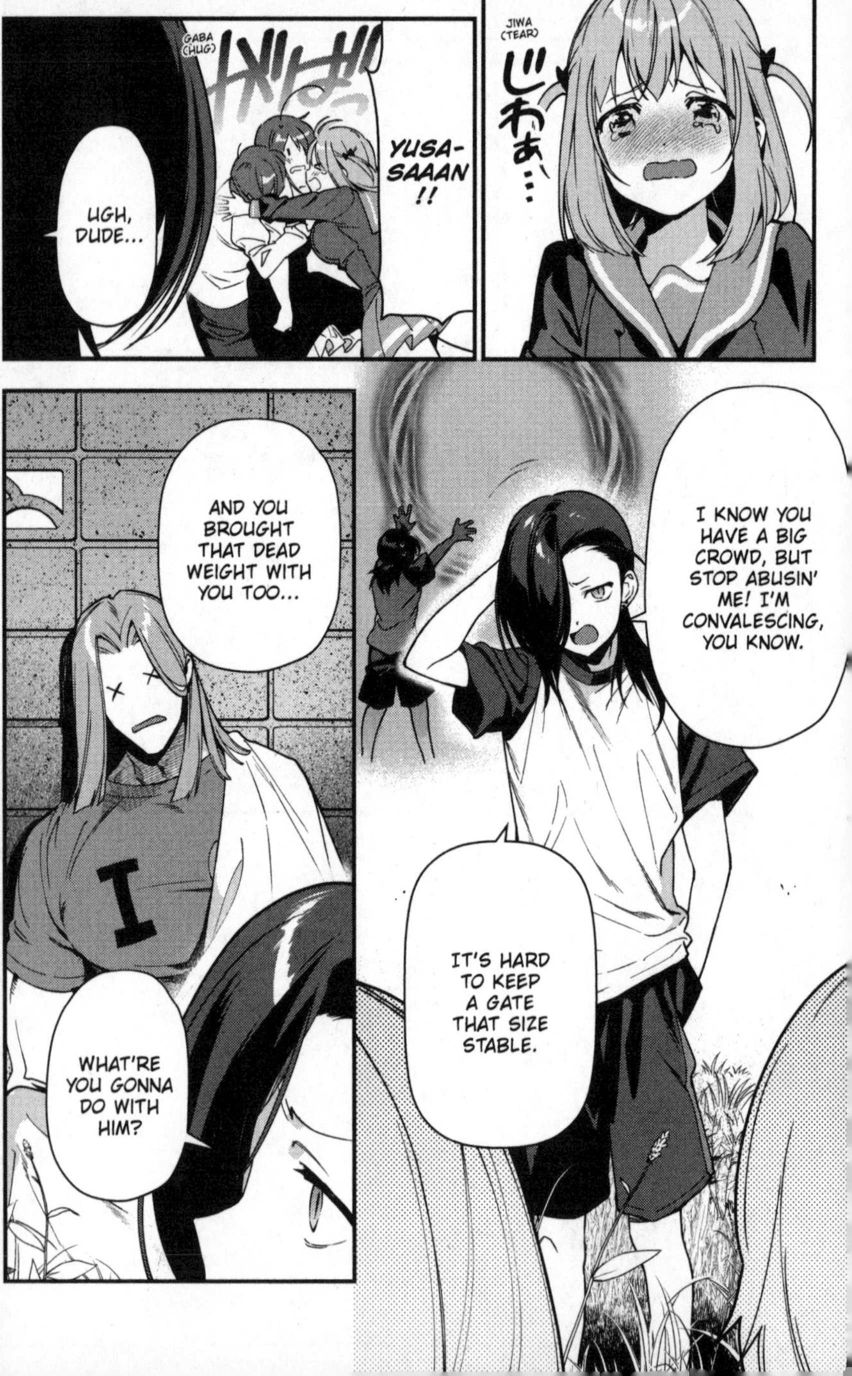
JIWA (TEAR)
じわぁ…
GABA (HUG)
がばっ
YUSA-SAAAN !!
UGH, DUDE...
I KNOW YOU HAVE A BIG CROWD, BUT STOP ABUSIN' ME! I'M CONVALESCING, YOU KNOW.
IT'S HARD TO KEEP A GATE THAT SIZE STABLE.
AND YOU BROUGHT THAT DEAD WEIGHT WITH YOU TOO...
WHAT'RE YOU GONNA DO WITH HIM?

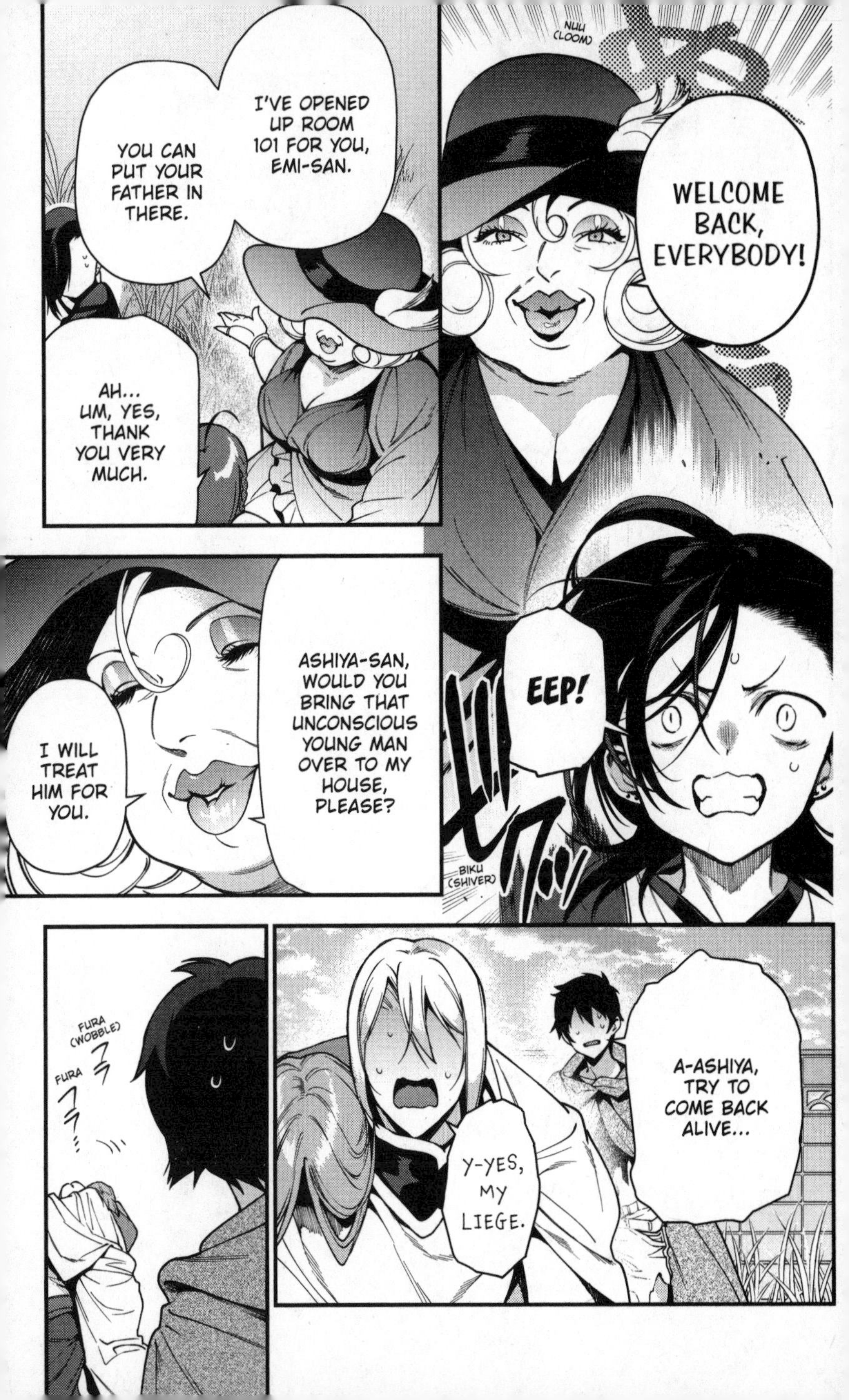
NUU (LOOM)
WELCOME BACK, EVERYBODY!
EEP!
BIKU (SHIVER)
I'VE OPENED UP ROOM 101 FOR YOU, EMI-SAN.
YOU CAN PUT YOUR FATHER IN THERE.
AH... UM, YES, THANK YOU VERY MUCH.
ASHIYA-SAN, WOULD YOU BRING THAT UNCONSCIOUS YOUNG MAN OVER TO MY HOUSE, PLEASE?
I WILL TREAT HIM FOR YOU.
A-ASHIYA, TRY TO COME BACK ALIVE...
Y-YES, MY LIEGE.
FURA (WOBBLE)
FURA

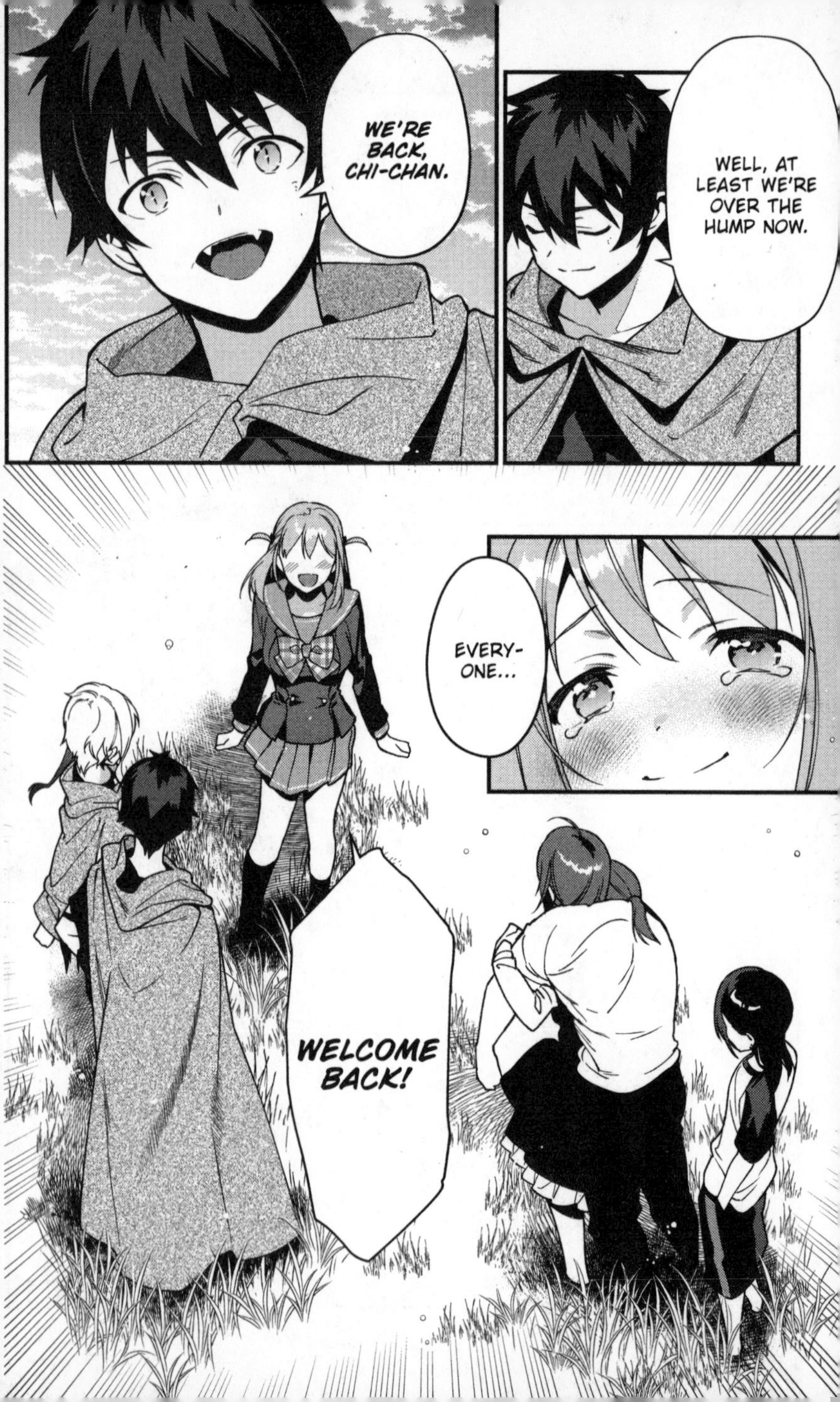
WELL, AT LEAST WE'RE OVER THE HUMP NOW.
WE'RE BACK, CHI-CHAN.
EVERY-ONE...
WELCOME BACK!

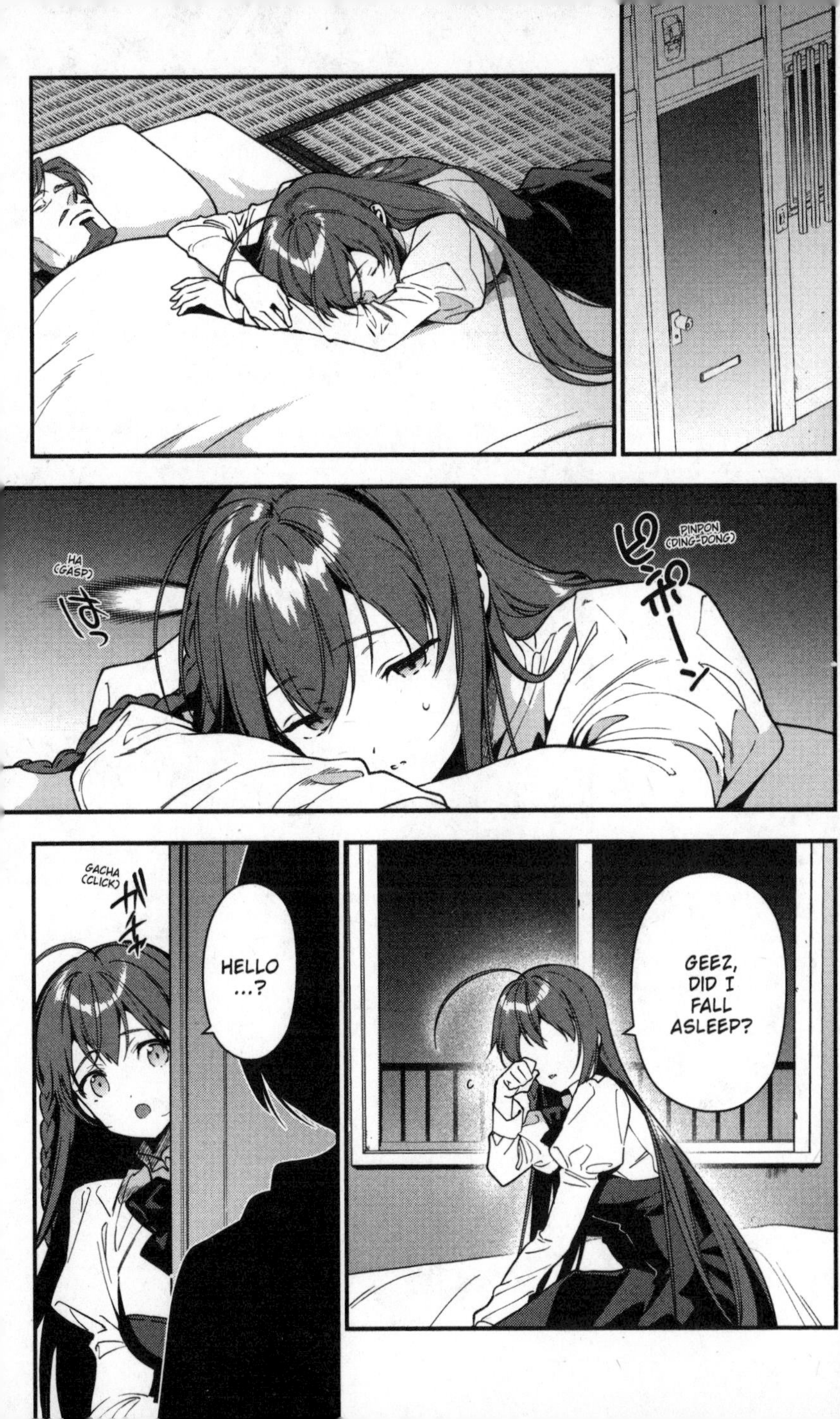
PINPON (DING-DONG)
HA (GASP)
GEEZ, DID I FALL ASLEEP?
GACHA (CLICK)
HELLO ...?

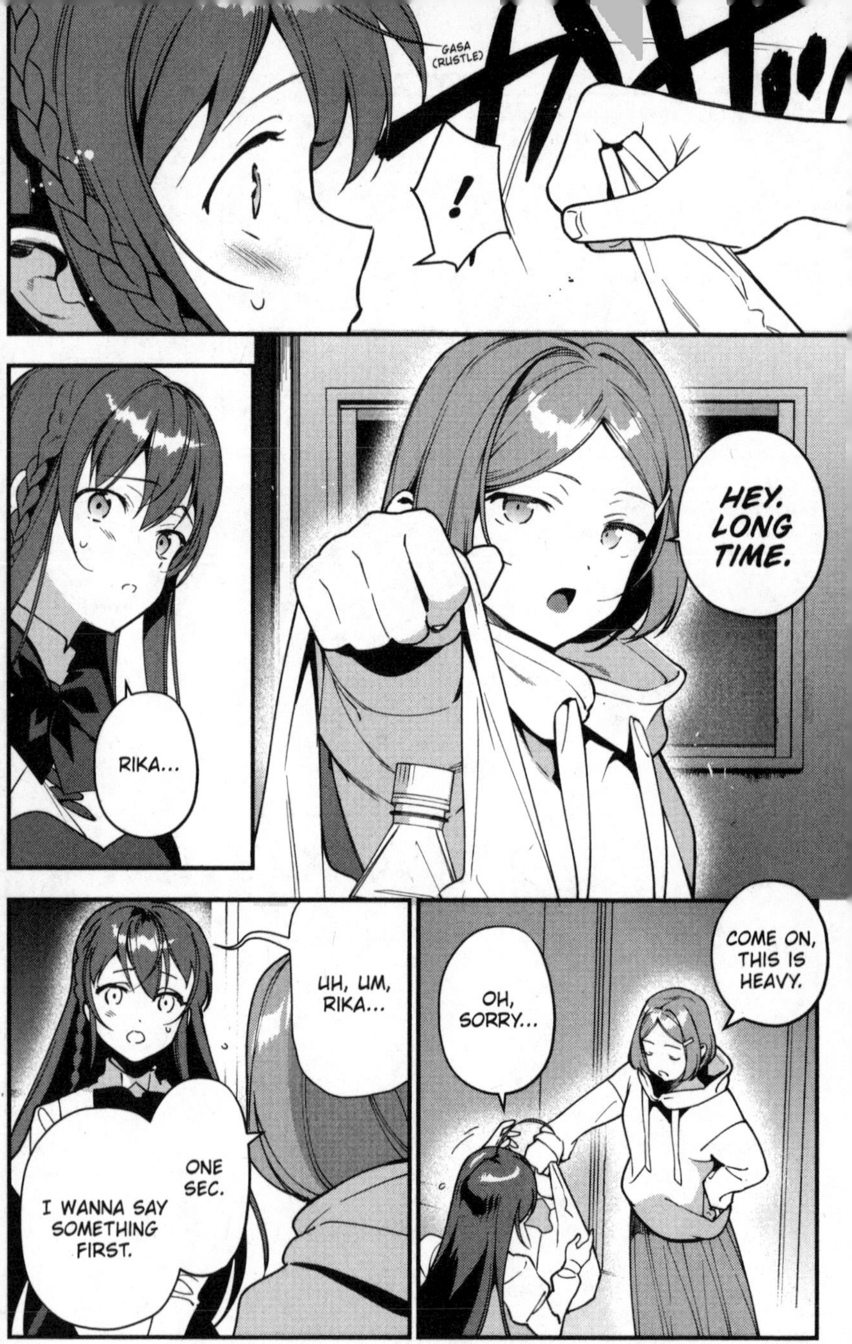
GASA (RUSTLE)
!
HEY. LONG TIME.
RIKA...
COME ON, THIS IS HEAVY.
OH, SORRY...
UH, UM, RIKA...
ONE SEC.
I WANNA SAY SOMETHING FIRST.

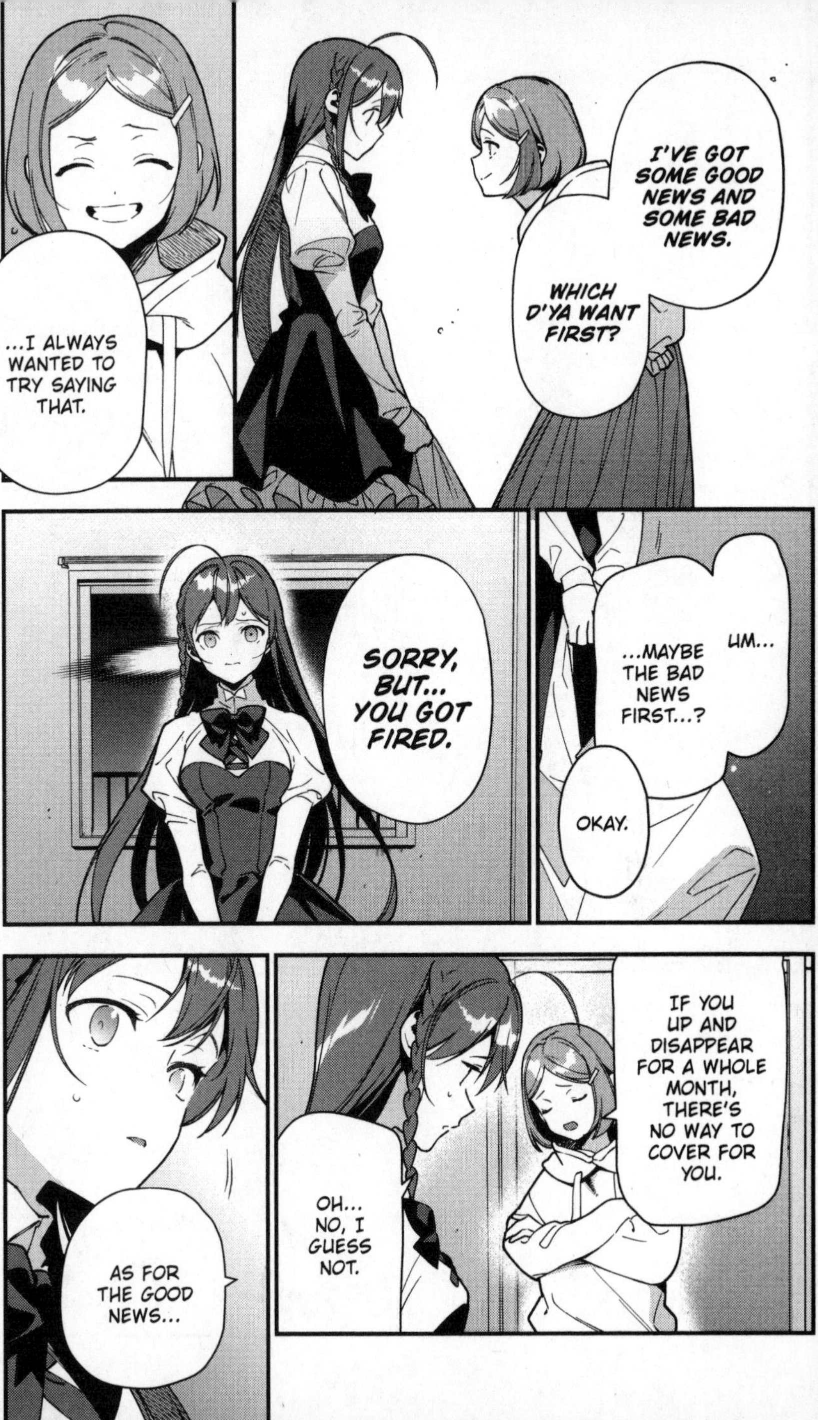
I'VE GOT SOME GOOD NEWS AND SOME BAD NEWS.
WHICH D'YA WANT FIRST?
...I ALWAYS WANTED TO TRY SAYING THAT.
UM...
...MAYBE THE BAD NEWS FIRST...?
OKAY.
SORRY, BUT... YOU GOT FIRED.
IF YOU UP AND DISAPPEAR FOR A WHOLE MONTH, THERE'S NO WAY TO COVER FOR YOU.
OH... NO, I GUESS NOT.
AS FOR THE GOOD NEWS...

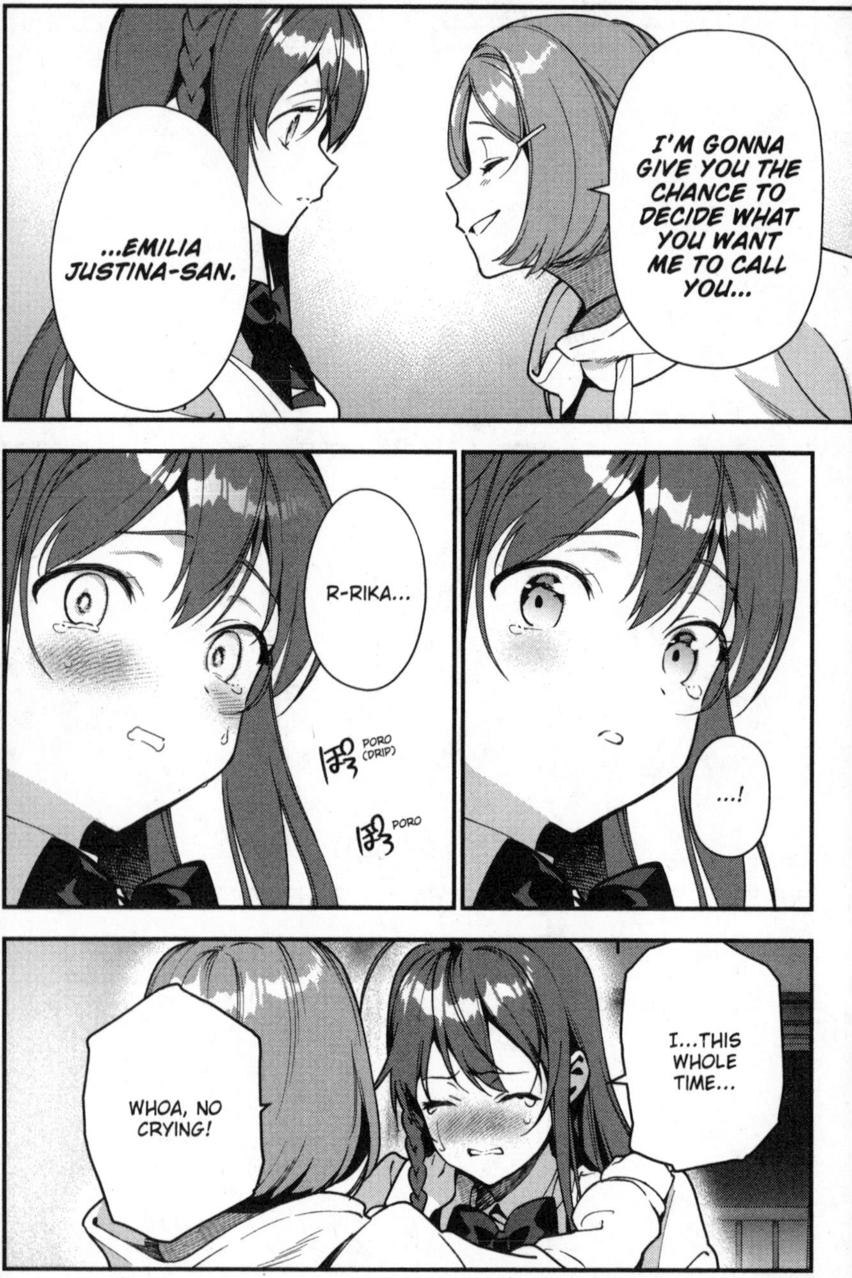
I'M GONNA GIVE YOU THE CHANCE TO DECIDE WHAT YOU WANT ME TO CALL YOU...
...EMILIA JUSTINA-SAN.
...!
R-RIKA...
ぽろ PORO (DRIP)
ぽろ PORO
I...THIS WHOLE TIME...
WHOA, NO CRYING!

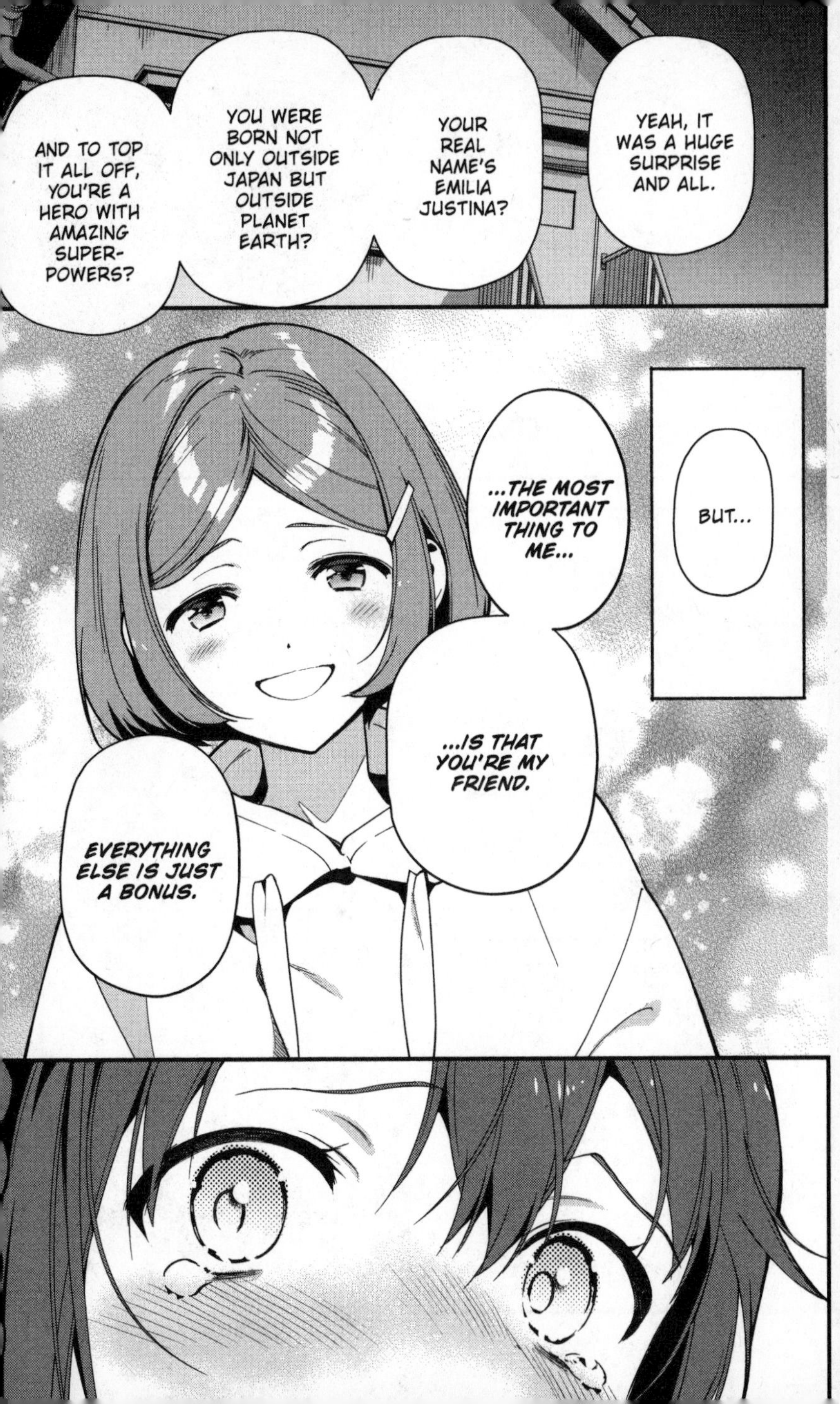
YEAH, IT WAS A HUGE SURPRISE AND ALL.
YOUR REAL NAME'S EMILIA JUSTINA?
YOU WERE BORN NOT ONLY OUTSIDE JAPAN BUT OUTSIDE PLANET EARTH?
AND TO TOP IT ALL OFF, YOU'RE A HERO WITH AMAZING SUPER-POWERS?
BUT...
...THE MOST IMPORTANT THING TO ME...
...IS THAT YOU'RE MY FRIEND.
EVERYTHING ELSE IS JUST A BONUS.

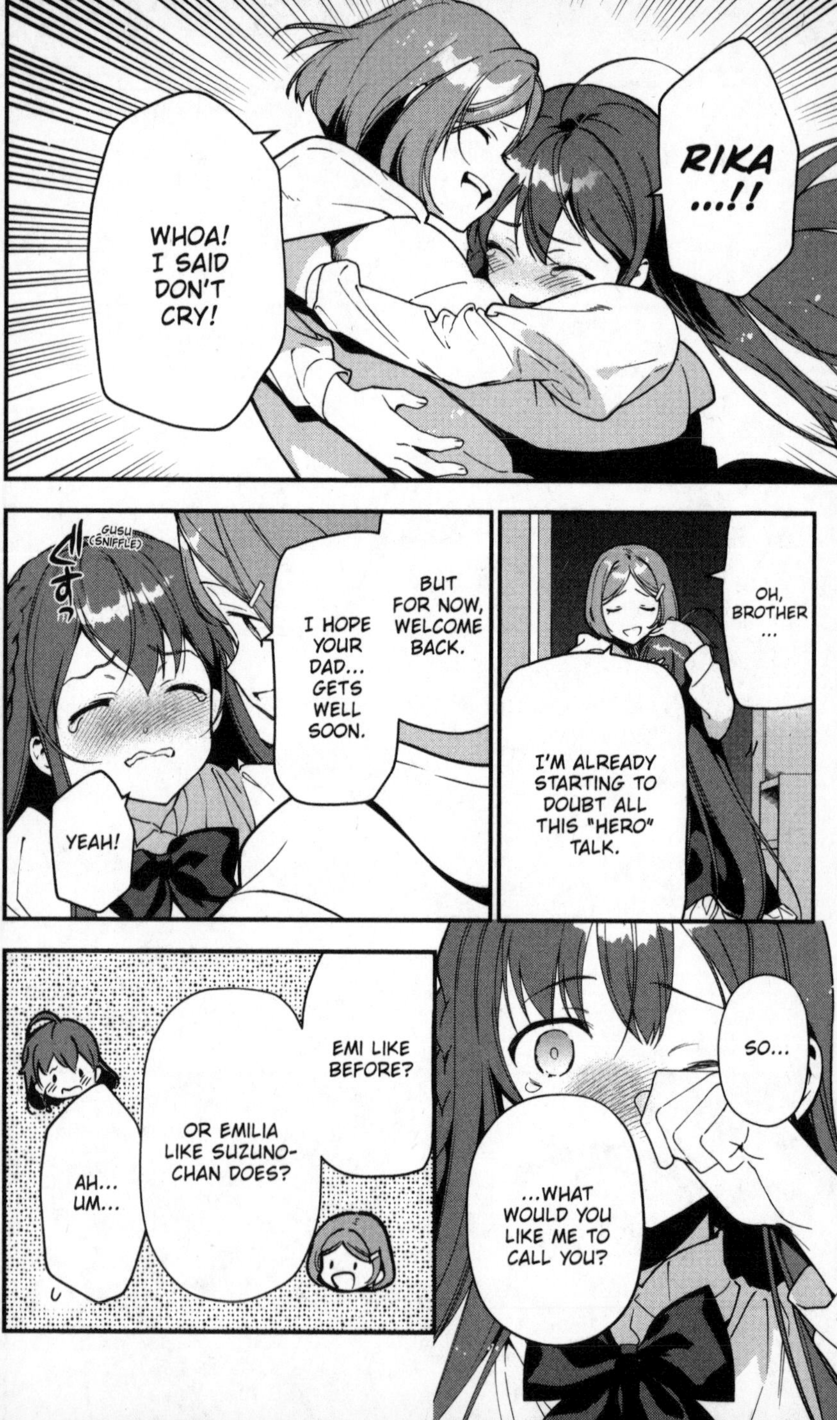
RIKA...!!
WHOA! I SAID DON'T CRY!
OH, BROTHER...
I'M ALREADY STARTING TO DOUBT ALL THIS "HERO" TALK.
BUT FOR NOW, WELCOME BACK.
I HOPE YOUR DAD... GETS WELL SOON.
GUSU (SNIFFLE)
YEAH!
SO...
...WHAT WOULD YOU LIKE ME TO CALL YOU?
EMI LIKE BEFORE?
OR EMILIA LIKE SUZUNO-CHAN DOES?
AH... UM...

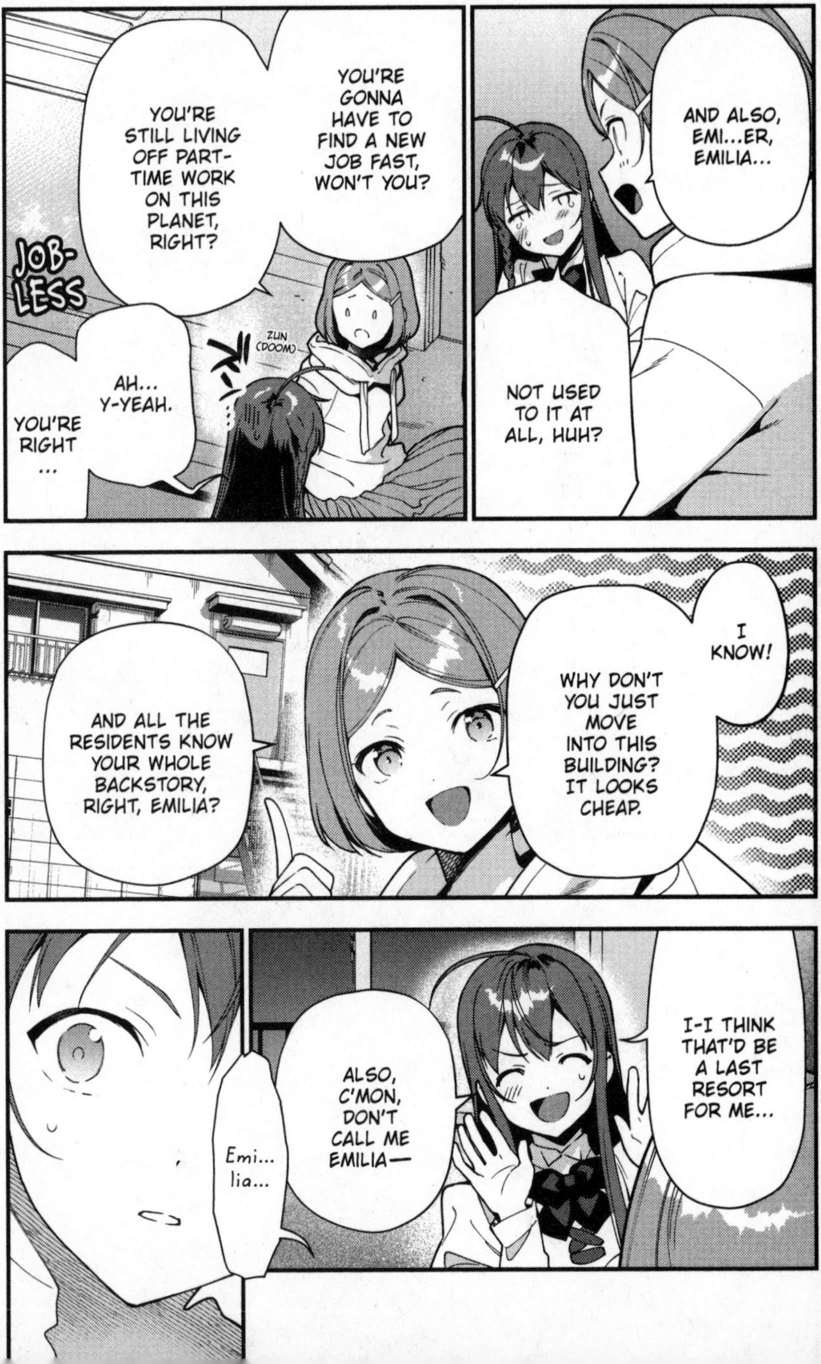
AND ALSO, EMI...ER, EMILIA...
NOT USED TO IT AT ALL, HUH?
YOU'RE GONNA HAVE TO FIND A NEW JOB FAST, WON'T YOU?
YOU'RE STILL LIVING OFF PART-TIME WORK ON THIS PLANET, RIGHT?
JOB-LESS
ZUN (DOOM)
AH... Y-YEAH.
YOU'RE RIGHT...
I KNOW!
WHY DON'T YOU JUST MOVE INTO THIS BUILDING? IT LOOKS CHEAP.
AND ALL THE RESIDENTS KNOW YOUR WHOLE BACKSTORY, RIGHT, EMILIA?
I-I THINK THAT'D BE A LAST RESORT FOR ME...
ALSO, C'MON, DON'T CALL ME EMILIA—
Emi... lia...

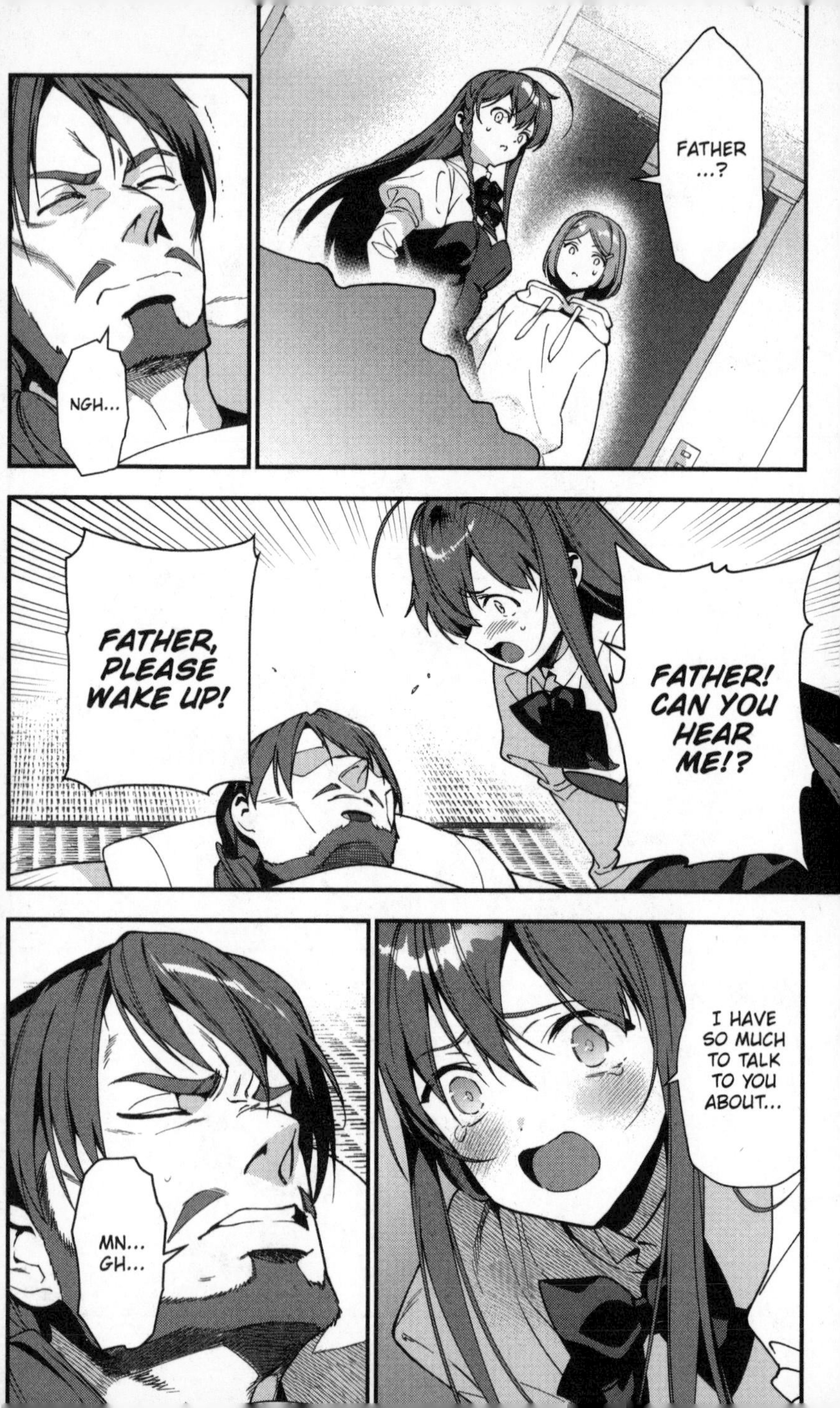
FATHER ...?
NGH...
FATHER! CAN YOU HEAR ME!?
FATHER, PLEASE WAKE UP!
I HAVE SO MUCH TO TALK TO YOU ABOUT...
MN... GH...

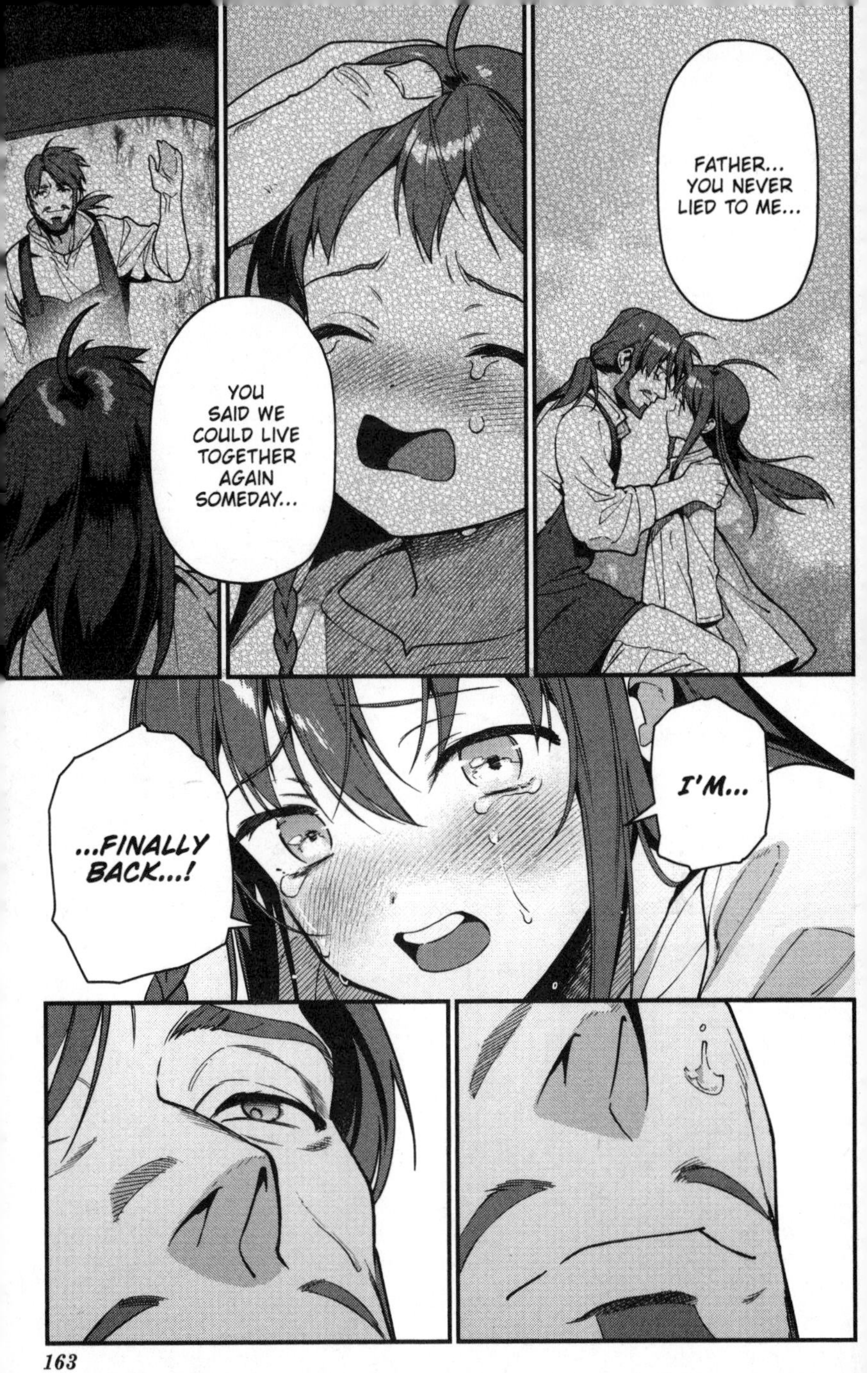
FATHER... YOU NEVER LIED TO ME...
YOU SAID WE COULD LIVE TOGETHER AGAIN SOMEDAY...
I'M...
...FINALLY BACK...!

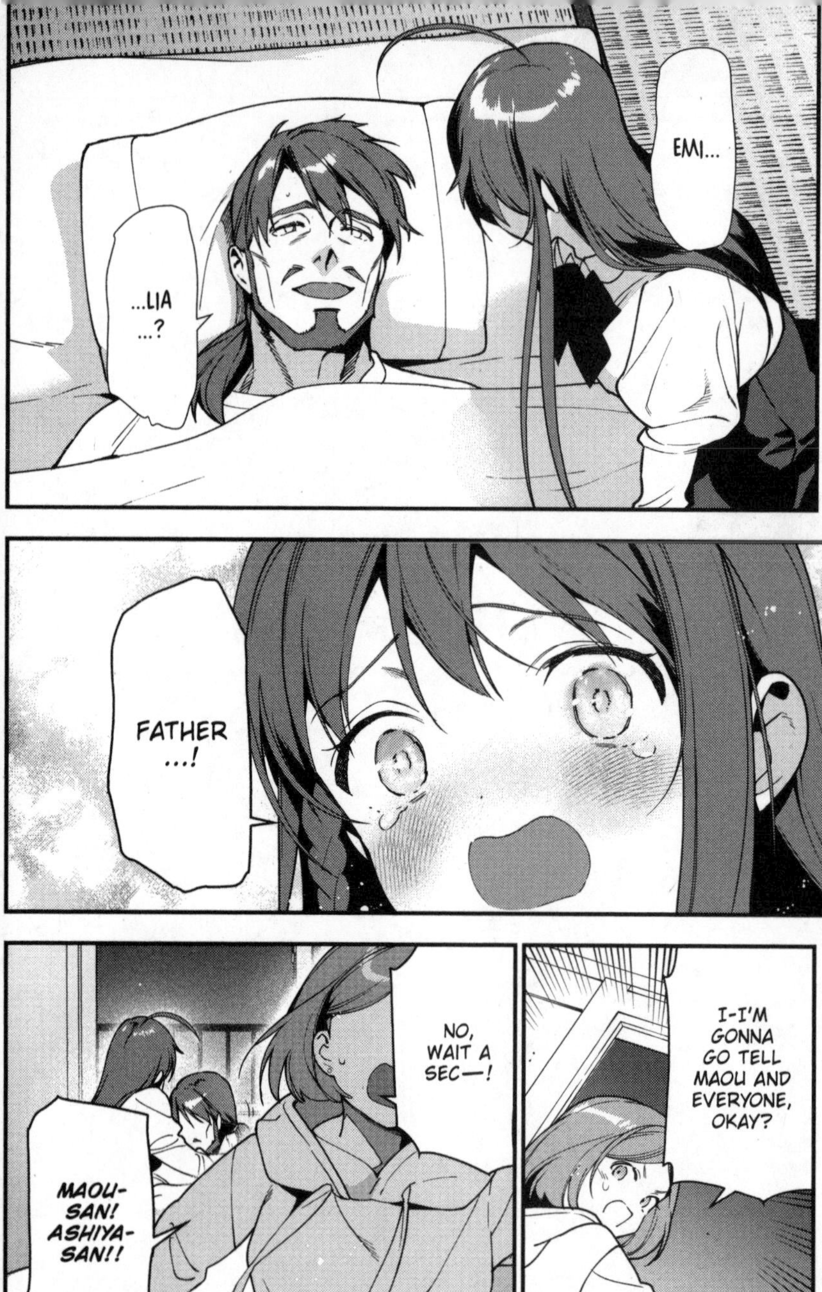
EMI...
...LIA ...?
FATHER ...!
I-I'M GONNA GO TELL MAOU AND EVERYONE, OKAY?
NO, WAIT A SEC—!
MAOU-SAN! ASHIYA-SAN!!

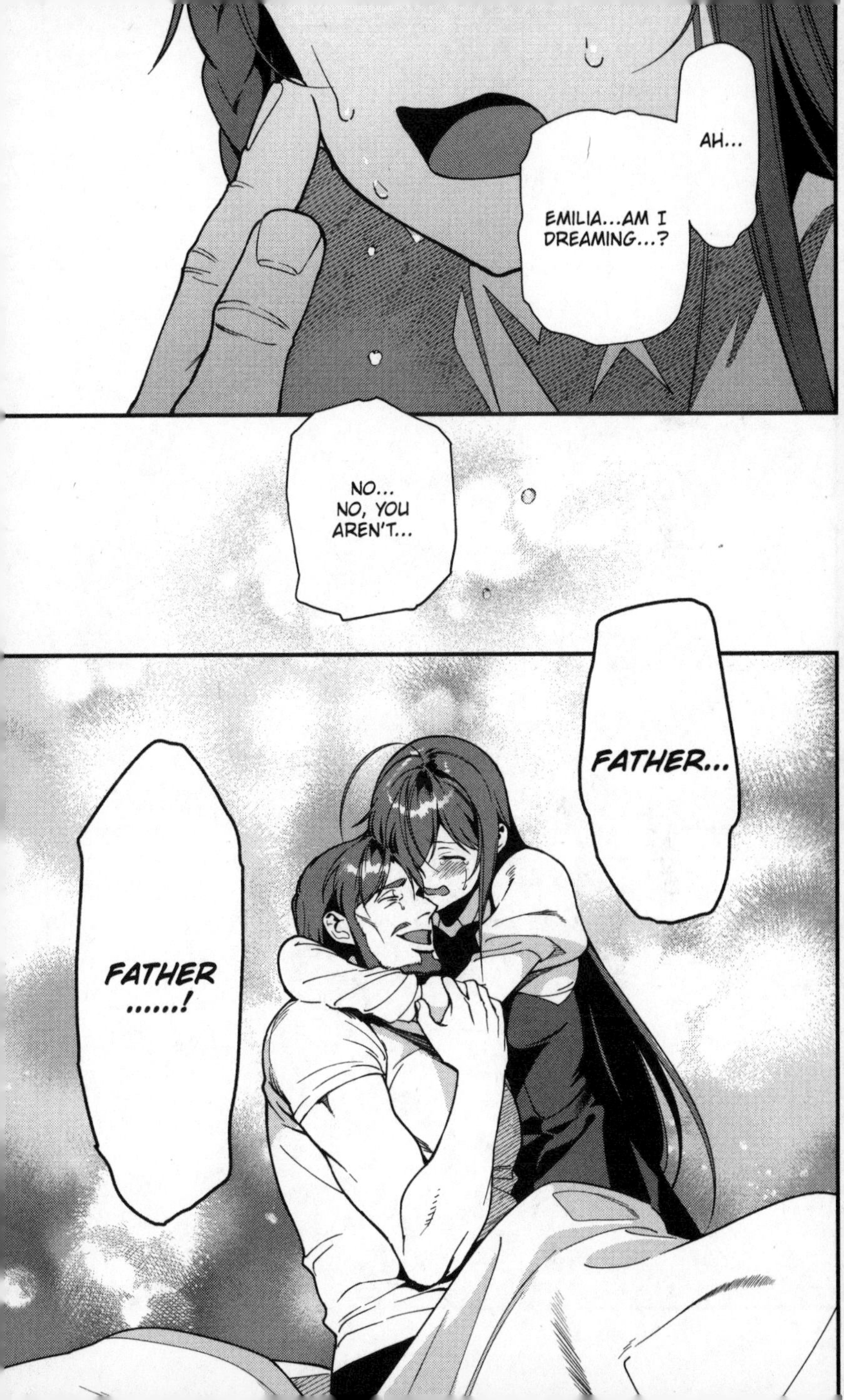
AH...
EMILIA...AM I DREAMING...?
NO... NO, YOU AREN'T...
FATHER...
FATHER ......!

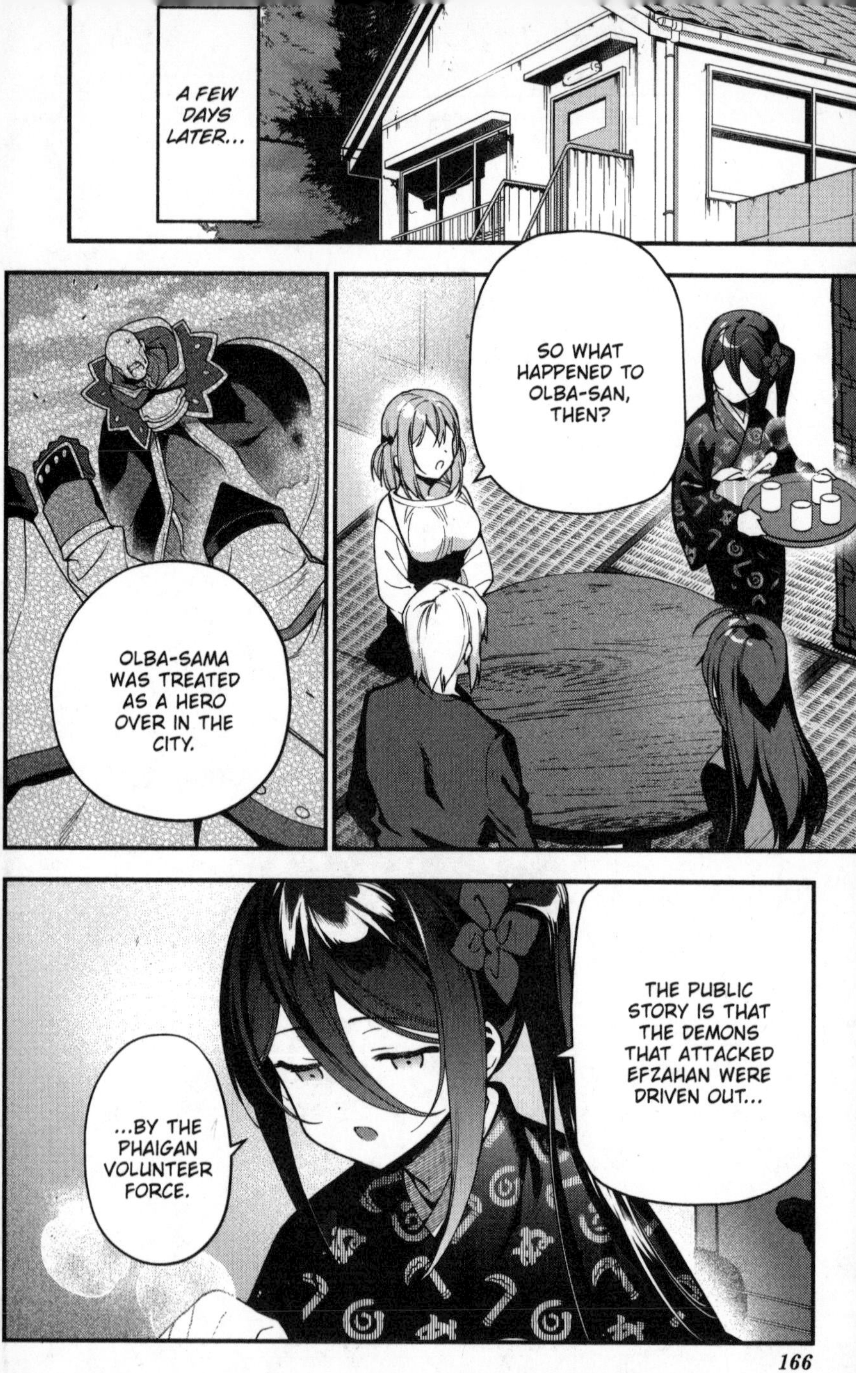
A FEW DAYS LATER...
SO WHAT HAPPENED TO OLBA-SAN, THEN?
OLBA-SAMA WAS TREATED AS A HERO OVER IN THE CITY.
THE PUBLIC STORY IS THAT THE DEMONS THAT ATTACKED EFZAHAN WERE DRIVEN OUT...
...BY THE PHAIGAN VOLUNTEER FORCE.

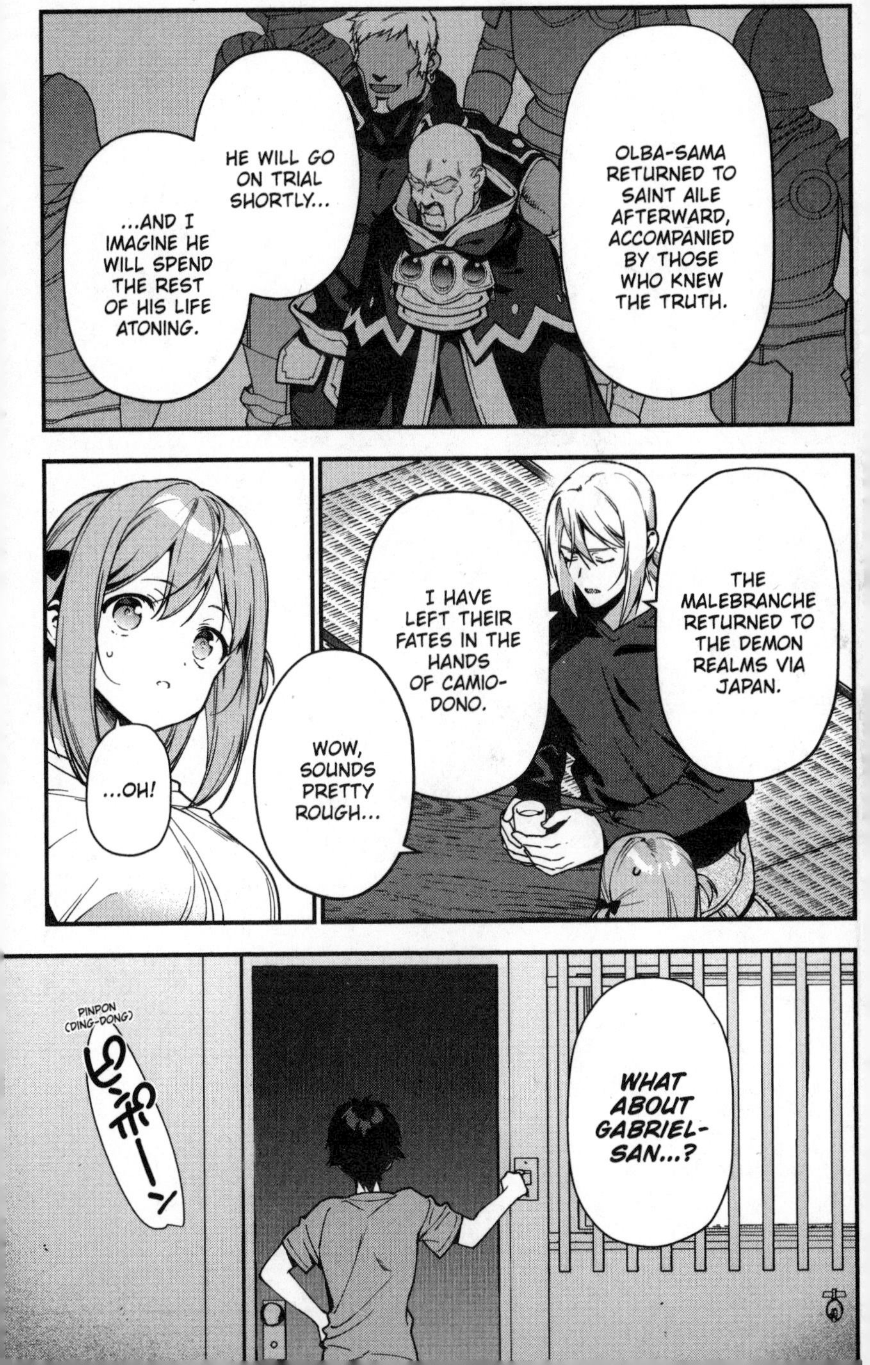
OLBA-SAMA RETURNED TO SAINT AILE AFTERWARD, ACCOMPANIED BY THOSE WHO KNEW THE TRUTH.
HE WILL GO ON TRIAL SHORTLY...
...AND I IMAGINE HE WILL SPEND THE REST OF HIS LIFE ATONING.
THE MALEBRANCHE RETURNED TO THE DEMON REALMS VIA JAPAN.
I HAVE LEFT THEIR FATES IN THE HANDS OF CAMIO-DONO.
WOW, SOUNDS PRETTY ROUGH...
...OH!
WHAT ABOUT GABRIEL-SAN...?
PINPON (DING-DONG)
ピンポーン

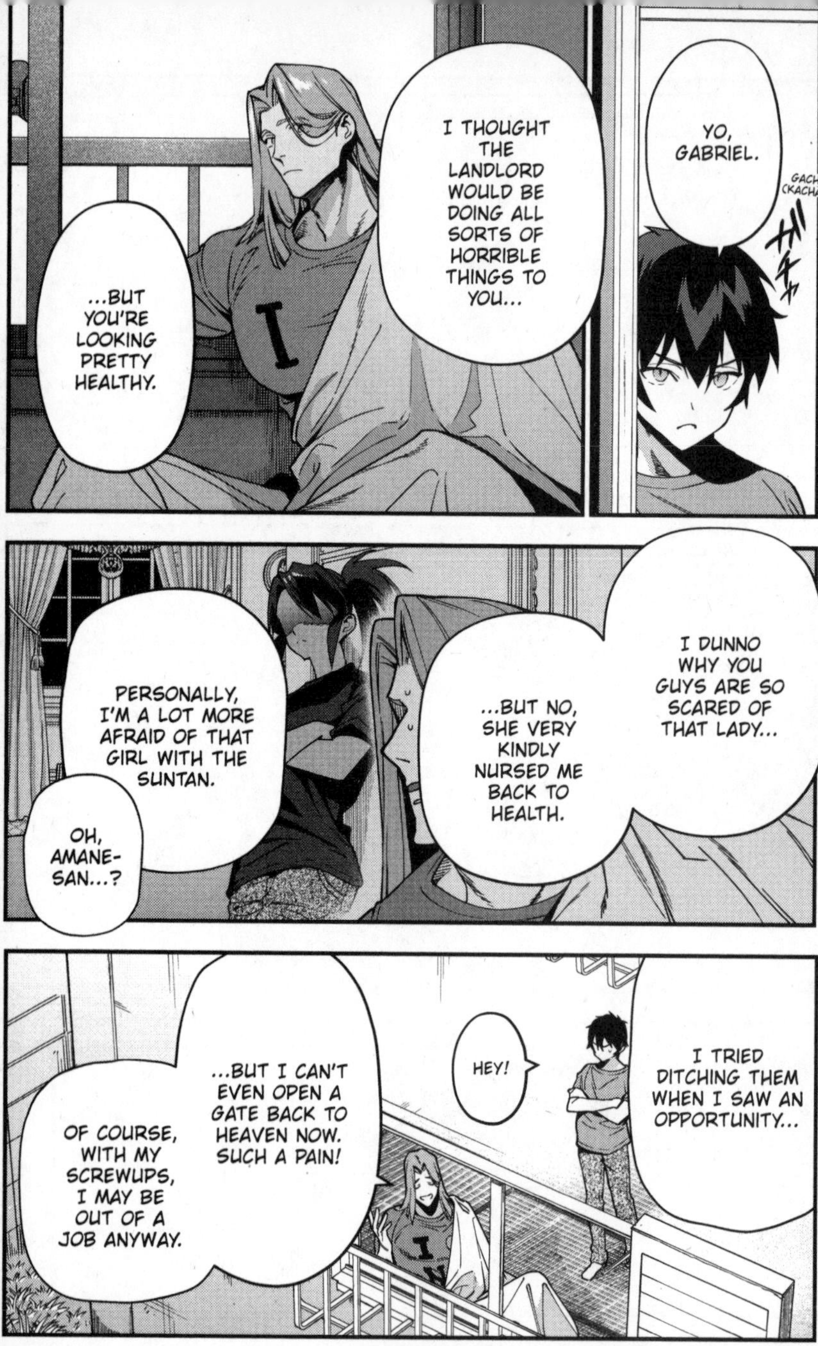
YO, GABRIEL.
GACHA (KACHAK)
I THOUGHT THE LANDLORD WOULD BE DOING ALL SORTS OF HORRIBLE THINGS TO YOU...
...BUT YOU'RE LOOKING PRETTY HEALTHY.
I DUNNO WHY YOU GUYS ARE SO SCARED OF THAT LADY...
...BUT NO, SHE VERY KINDLY NURSED ME BACK TO HEALTH.
PERSONALLY, I'M A LOT MORE AFRAID OF THAT GIRL WITH THE SUNTAN.
OH, AMANE-SAN...?
I TRIED DITCHING THEM WHEN I SAW AN OPPORTUNITY...
HEY!
...BUT I CAN'T EVEN OPEN A GATE BACK TO HEAVEN NOW. SUCH A PAIN!
OF COURSE, WITH MY SCREWUPS, I MAY BE OUT OF A JOB ANYWAY.

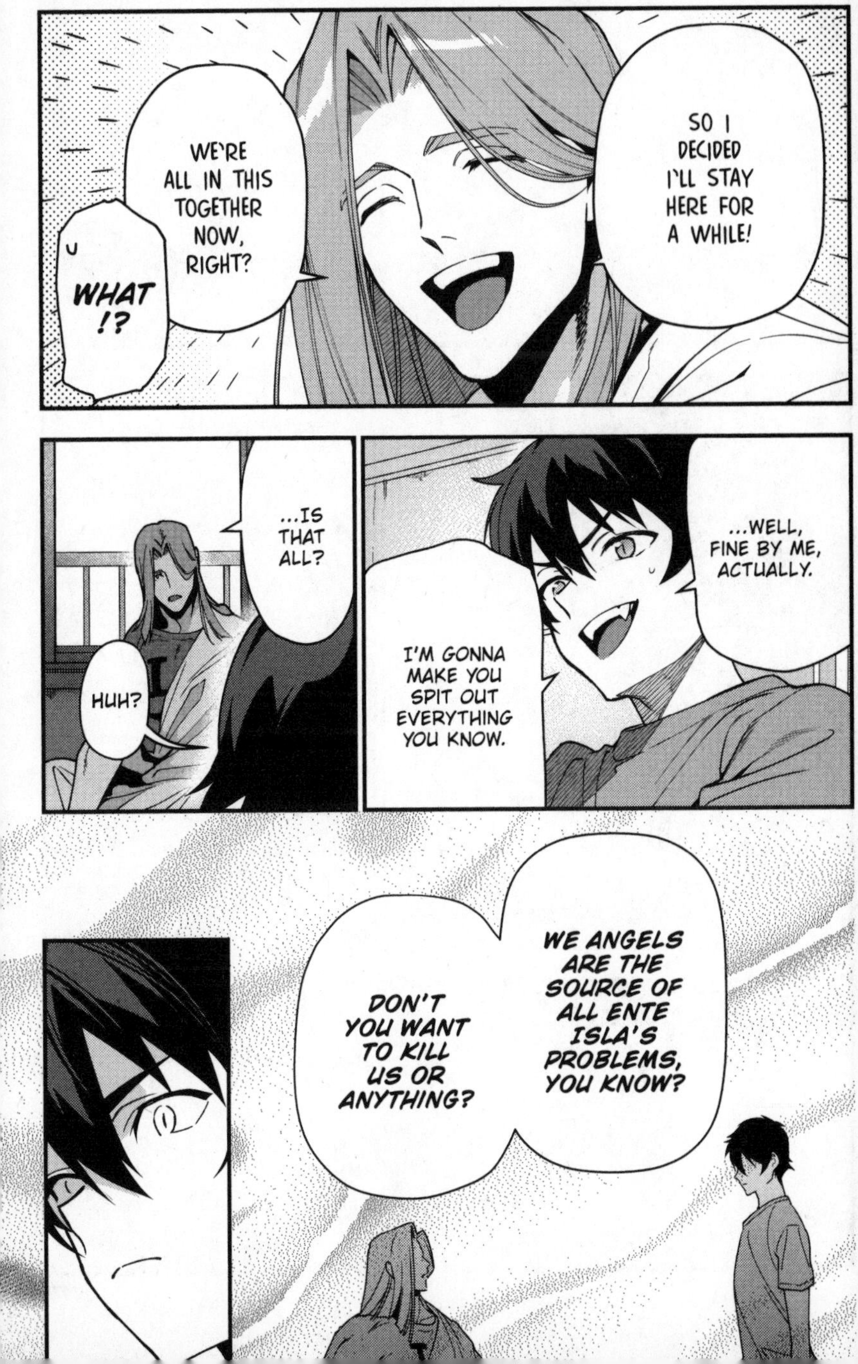
SO I DECIDED I'LL STAY HERE FOR A WHILE!
WE'RE ALL IN THIS TOGETHER NOW, RIGHT?
U
WHAT!?
...WELL, FINE BY ME, ACTUALLY.
I'M GONNA MAKE YOU SPIT OUT EVERYTHING YOU KNOW.
...IS THAT ALL?
HUH?
WE ANGELS ARE THE SOURCE OF ALL ENTE ISLA'S PROBLEMS, YOU KNOW?
DON'T YOU WANT TO KILL US OR ANYTHING?

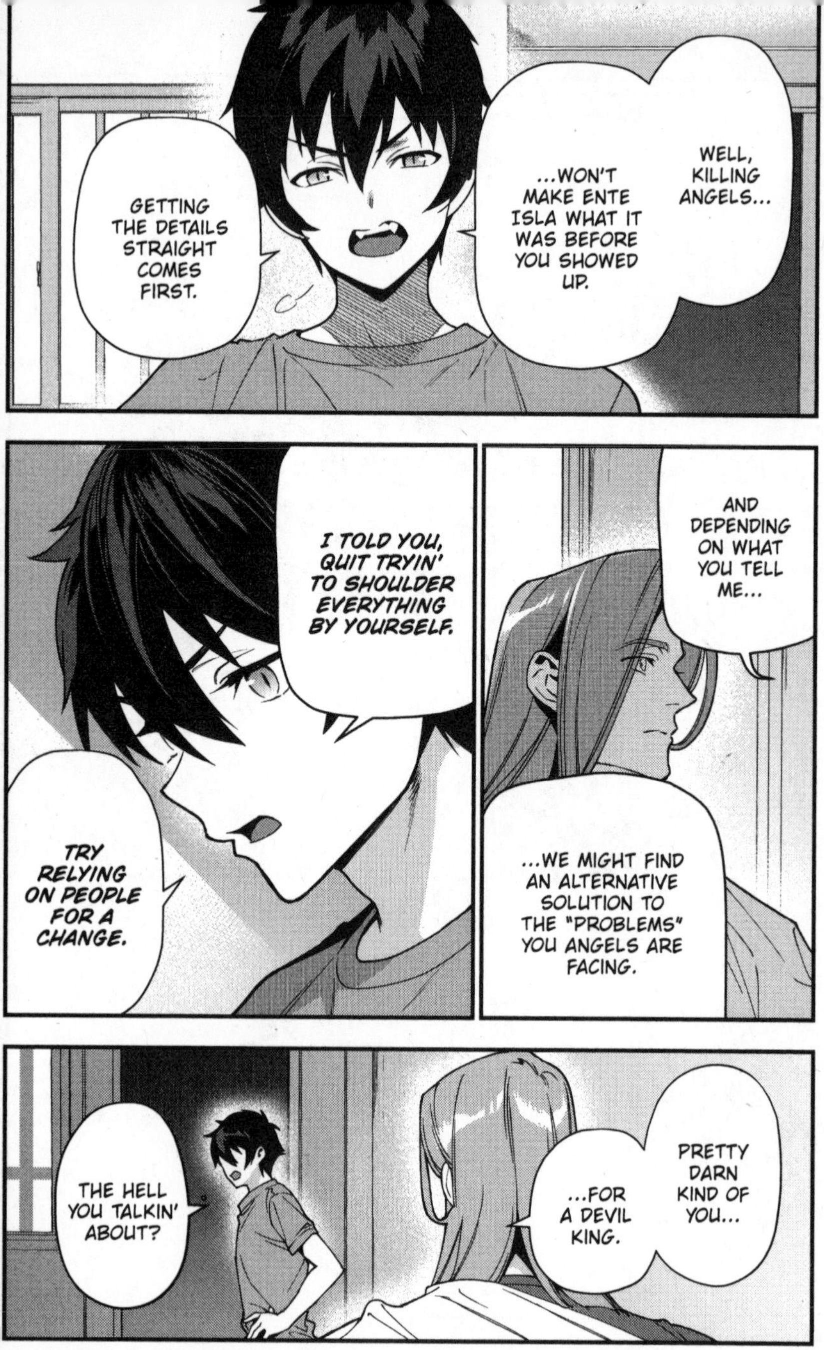
WELL, KILLING ANGELS...
...WON'T MAKE ENTE ISLA WHAT IT WAS BEFORE YOU SHOWED UP.
GETTING THE DETAILS STRAIGHT COMES FIRST.
AND DEPENDING ON WHAT YOU TELL ME...
...WE MIGHT FIND AN ALTERNATIVE SOLUTION TO THE "PROBLEMS" YOU ANGELS ARE FACING.
I TOLD YOU, QUIT TRYIN' TO SHOULDER EVERYTHING BY YOURSELF.
TRY RELYING ON PEOPLE FOR A CHANGE.
PRETTY DARN KIND OF YOU...
...FOR A DEVIL KING.
THE HELL YOU TALKIN' ABOUT?

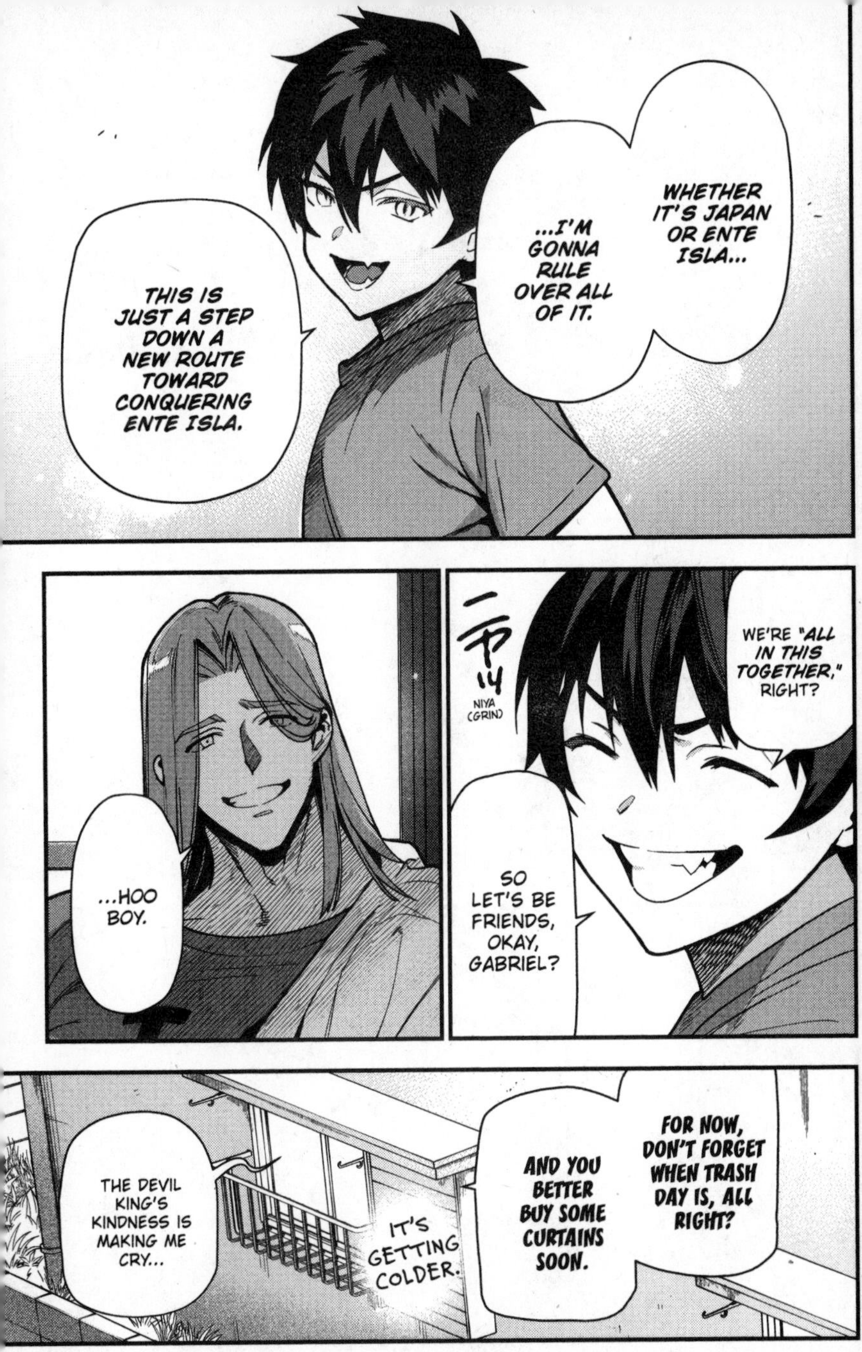
WHETHER IT'S JAPAN OR ENTE ISLA...
...I'M GONNA RULE OVER ALL OF IT.
THIS IS JUST A STEP DOWN A NEW ROUTE TOWARD CONQUERING ENTE ISLA.
WE'RE "ALL IN THIS TOGETHER," RIGHT?
ニヤッ
NIYA (GRIN)
SO LET'S BE FRIENDS, OKAY, GABRIEL?
...HOO BOY.
FOR NOW, DON'T FORGET WHEN TRASH DAY IS, ALL RIGHT?
AND YOU BETTER BUY SOME CURTAINS SOON.
IT'S GETTING COLDER.
THE DEVIL KING'S KINDNESS IS MAKING ME CRY...

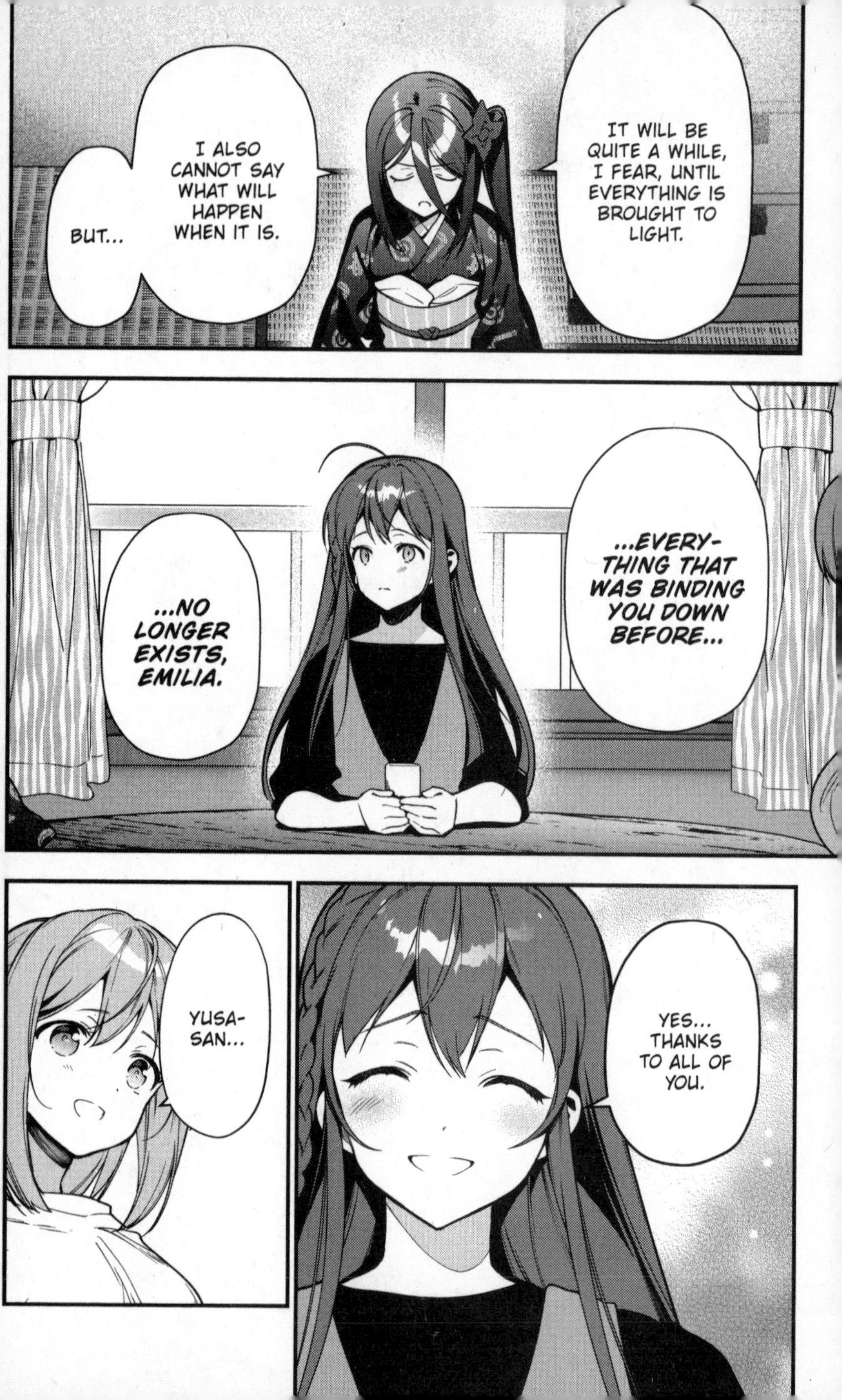
IT WILL BE QUITE A WHILE, I FEAR, UNTIL EVERYTHING IS BROUGHT TO LIGHT.
I ALSO CANNOT SAY WHAT WILL HAPPEN WHEN IT IS.
BUT...
...EVERY-THING THAT WAS BINDING YOU DOWN BEFORE...
...NO LONGER EXISTS, EMILIA.
YES... THANKS TO ALL OF YOU.
YUSA-SAN...

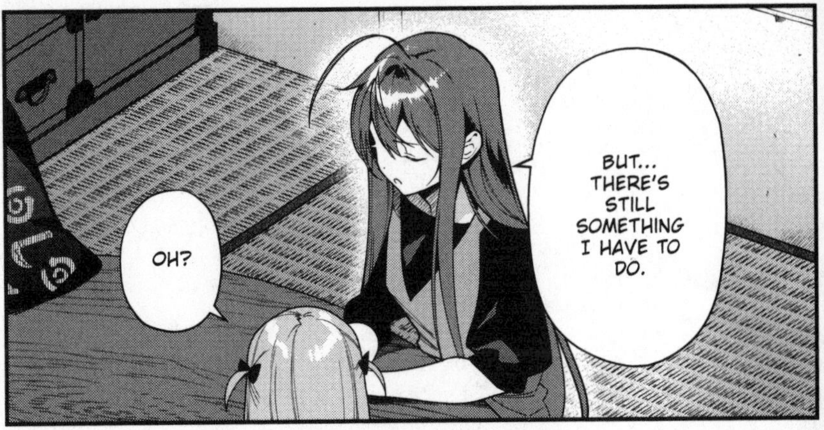
BUT... THERE'S STILL SOMETHING I HAVE TO DO.
OH?

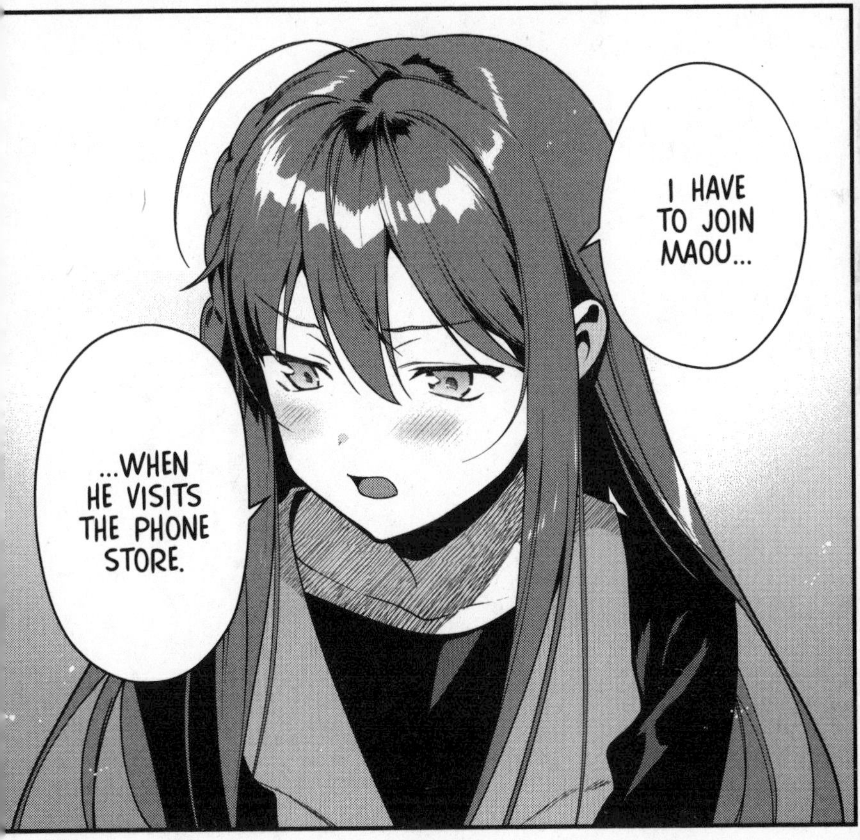
I HAVE TO JOIN MAOU...
...WHEN HE VISITS THE PHONE STORE.

THE DEVIL IS A PART-TIMER!

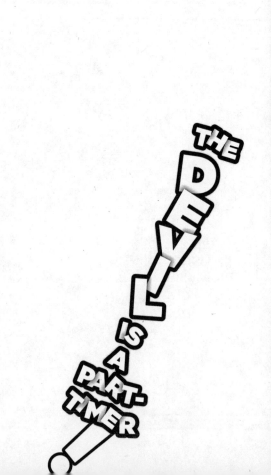

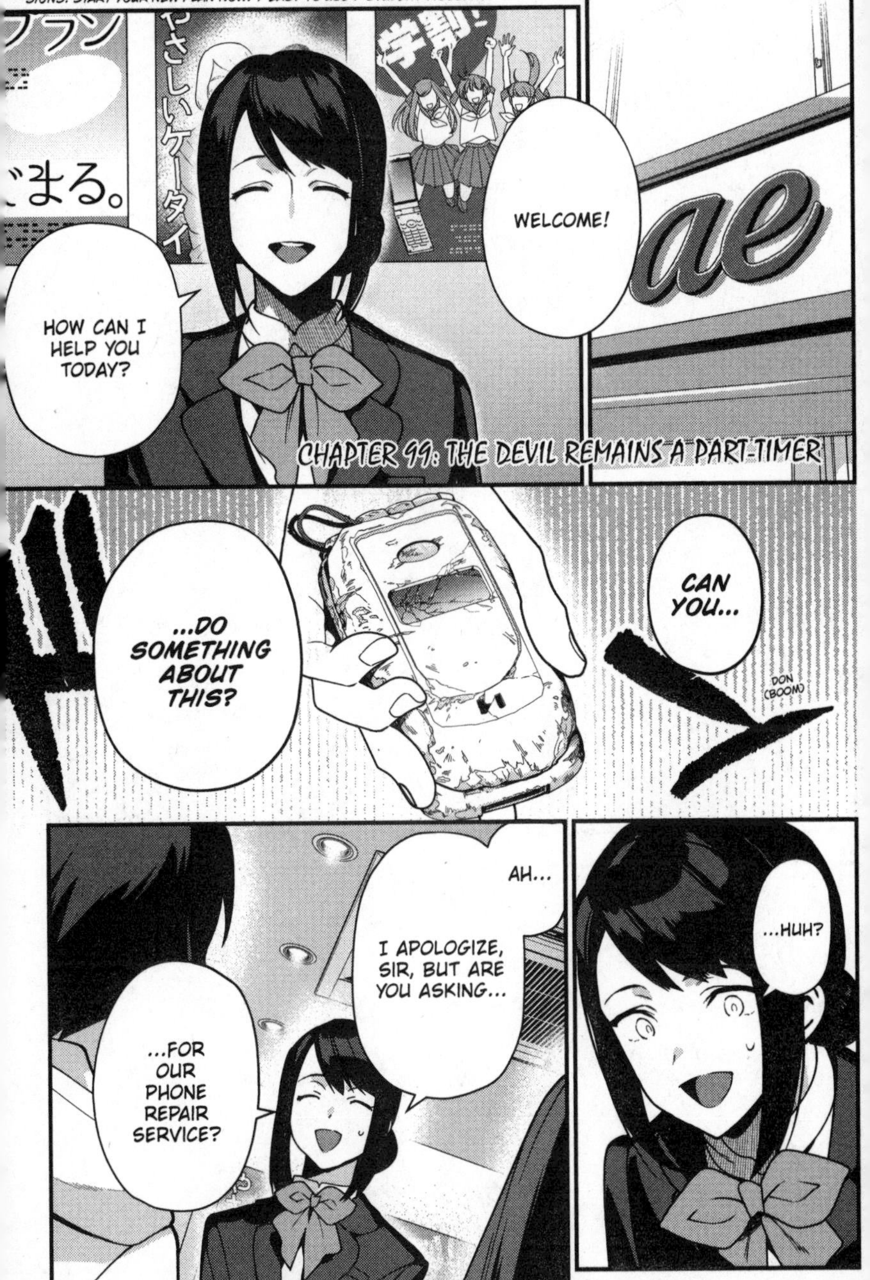
SIGNS: START YOUR NEW PLAN NOW! / EASY TO USE / STUDENT DISCOUNT!
WELCOME!
HOW CAN I HELP YOU TODAY?
CHAPTER 99: THE DEVIL REMAINS A PART-TIMER
CAN YOU...
DON (BOOM)
...DO SOMETHING ABOUT THIS?
...HUH?
AH...
I APOLOGIZE, SIR, BUT ARE YOU ASKING...
...FOR OUR PHONE REPAIR SERVICE?

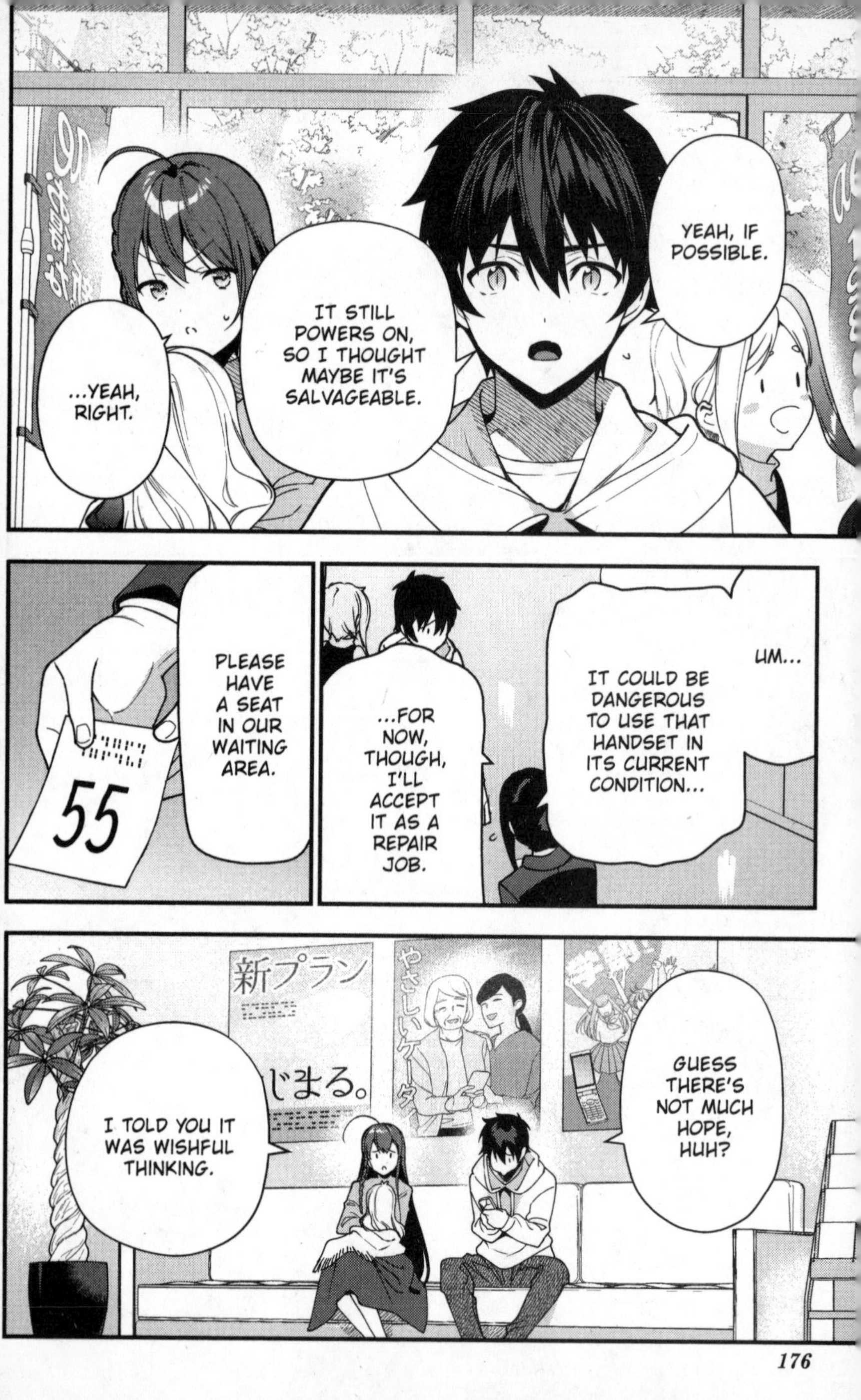
YEAH, IF POSSIBLE.
IT STILL POWERS ON, SO I THOUGHT MAYBE IT'S SALVAGEABLE.
...YEAH, RIGHT.
UM...
IT COULD BE DANGEROUS TO USE THAT HANDSET IN ITS CURRENT CONDITION...
...FOR NOW, THOUGH, I'LL ACCEPT IT AS A REPAIR JOB.
PLEASE HAVE A SEAT IN OUR WAITING AREA.
55
新プラン
やさしいケータ
じまる。
GUESS THERE'S NOT MUCH HOPE, HUH?
I TOLD YOU IT WAS WISHFUL THINKING.

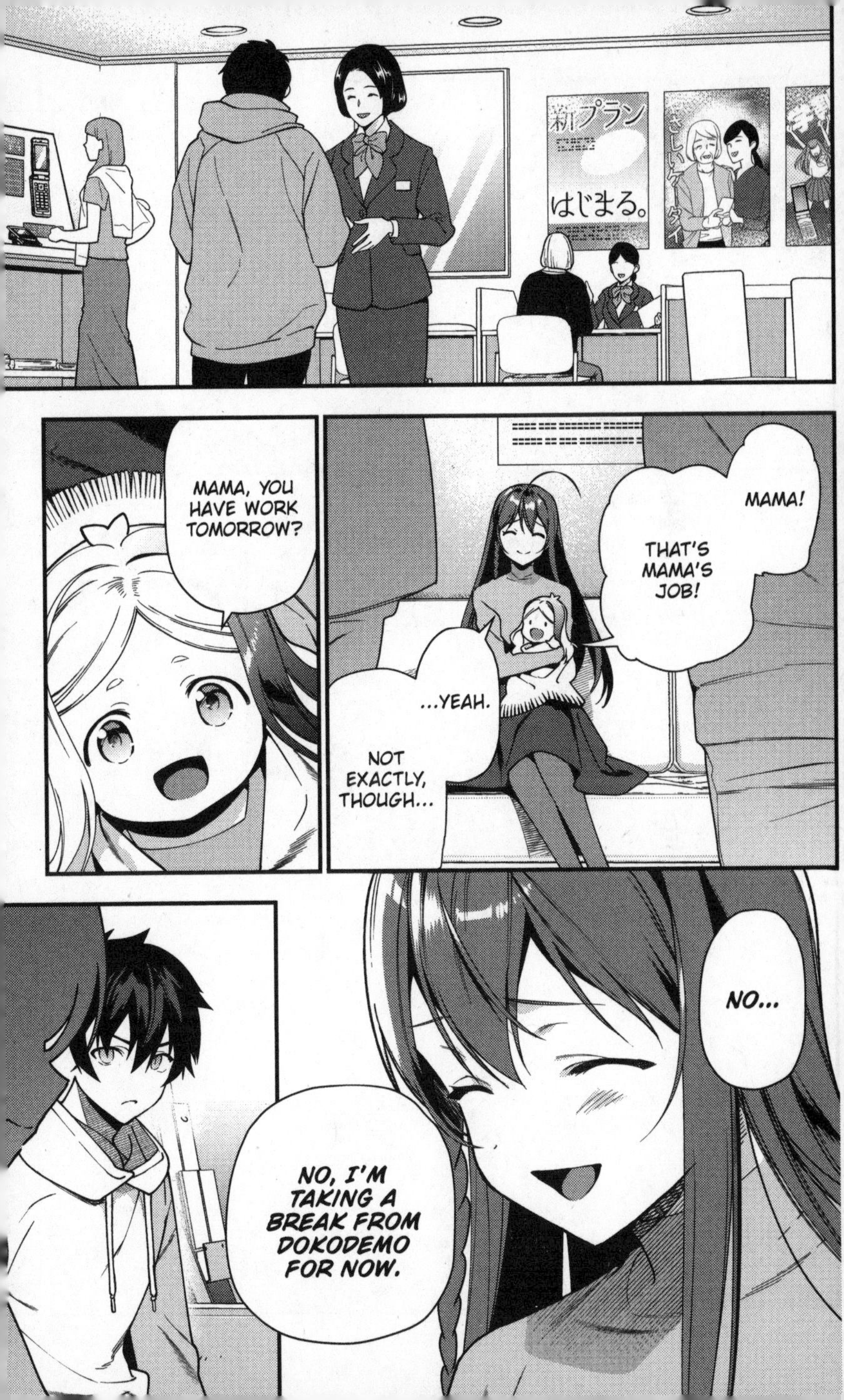
新プラン
はじまる。
さしいケータイ
MAMA!
THAT'S MAMA'S JOB!
...YEAH.
NOT EXACTLY, THOUGH...
MAMA, YOU HAVE WORK TOMORROW?
NO...
NO, I'M TAKING A BREAK FROM DOKODEMO FOR NOW.

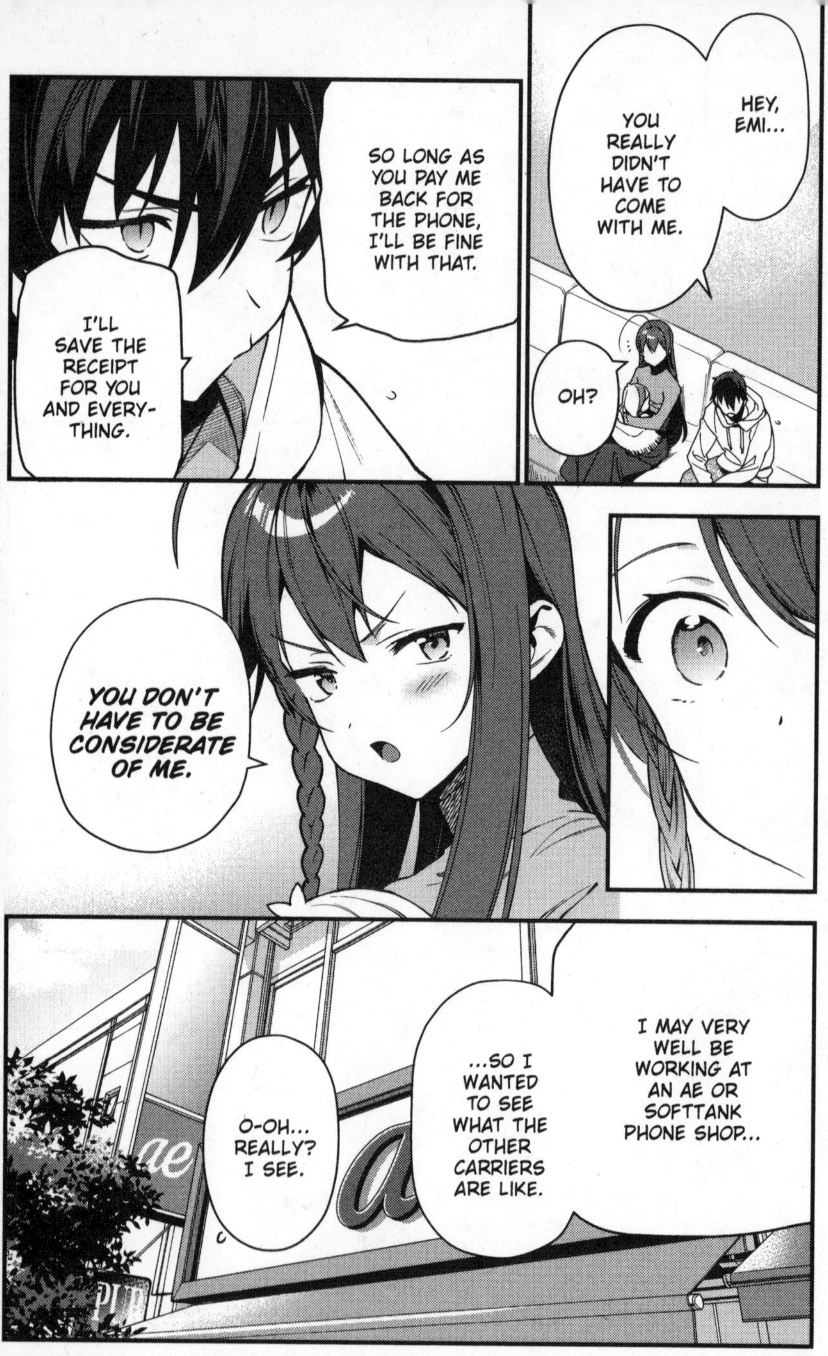
HEY, EMI...
YOU REALLY DIDN'T HAVE TO COME WITH ME.
OH?
SO LONG AS YOU PAY ME BACK FOR THE PHONE, I'LL BE FINE WITH THAT.
I'LL SAVE THE RECEIPT FOR YOU AND EVERY-THING.
YOU DON'T HAVE TO BE CONSIDERATE OF ME.
I MAY VERY WELL BE WORKING AT AN AE OR SOFTTANK PHONE SHOP...
...SO I WANTED TO SEE WHAT THE OTHER CARRIERS ARE LIKE.
O-OH... REALLY? I SEE.

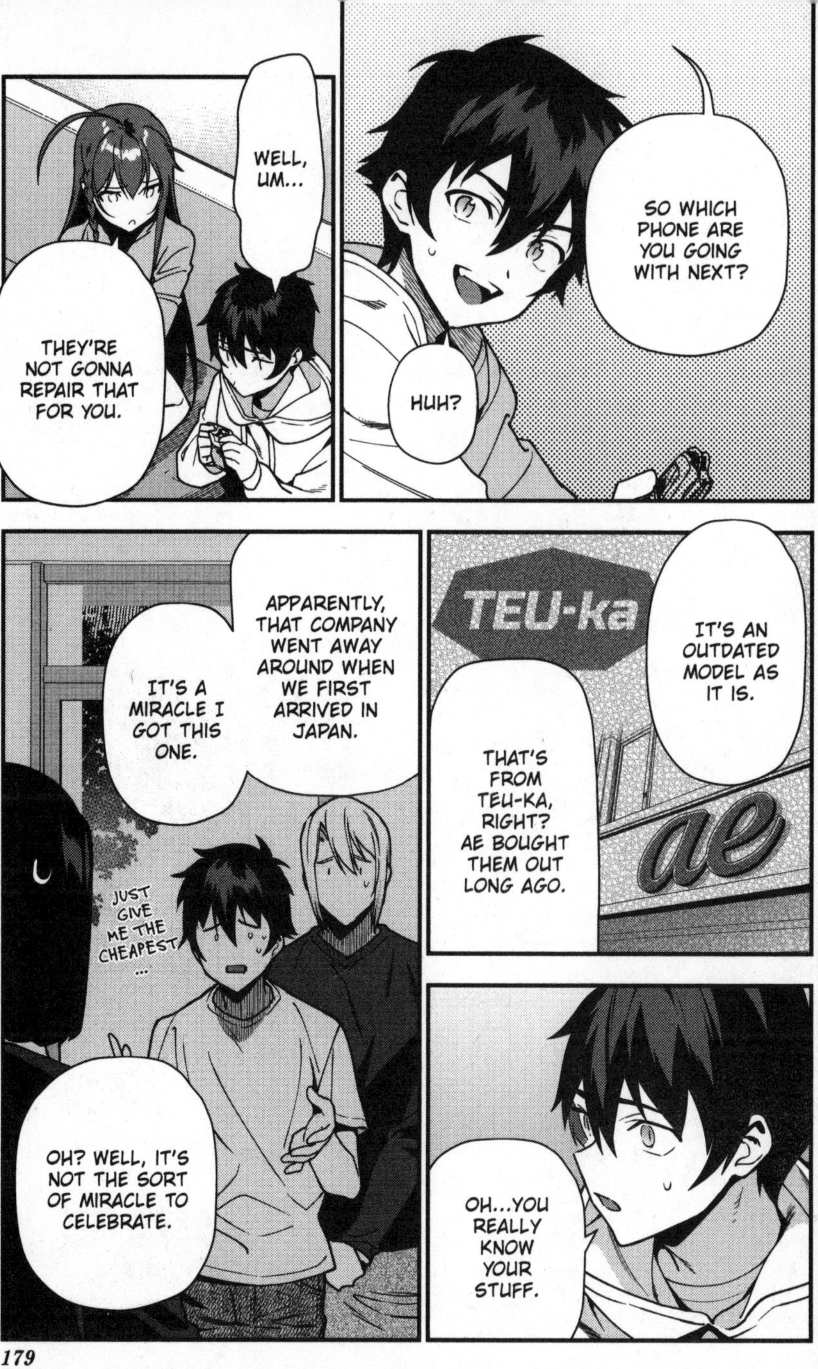
SO WHICH PHONE ARE YOU GOING WITH NEXT?
HUH?
WELL, UM...
THEY'RE NOT GONNA REPAIR THAT FOR YOU.
IT'S AN OUTDATED MODEL AS IT IS.
TEU-ka
THAT'S FROM TEU-KA, RIGHT? AE BOUGHT THEM OUT LONG AGO.
ae
OH...YOU REALLY KNOW YOUR STUFF.
APPARENTLY, THAT COMPANY WENT AWAY AROUND WHEN WE FIRST ARRIVED IN JAPAN.
IT'S A MIRACLE I GOT THIS ONE.
JUST GIVE ME THE CHEAPEST...
OH? WELL, IT'S NOT THE SORT OF MIRACLE TO CELEBRATE.

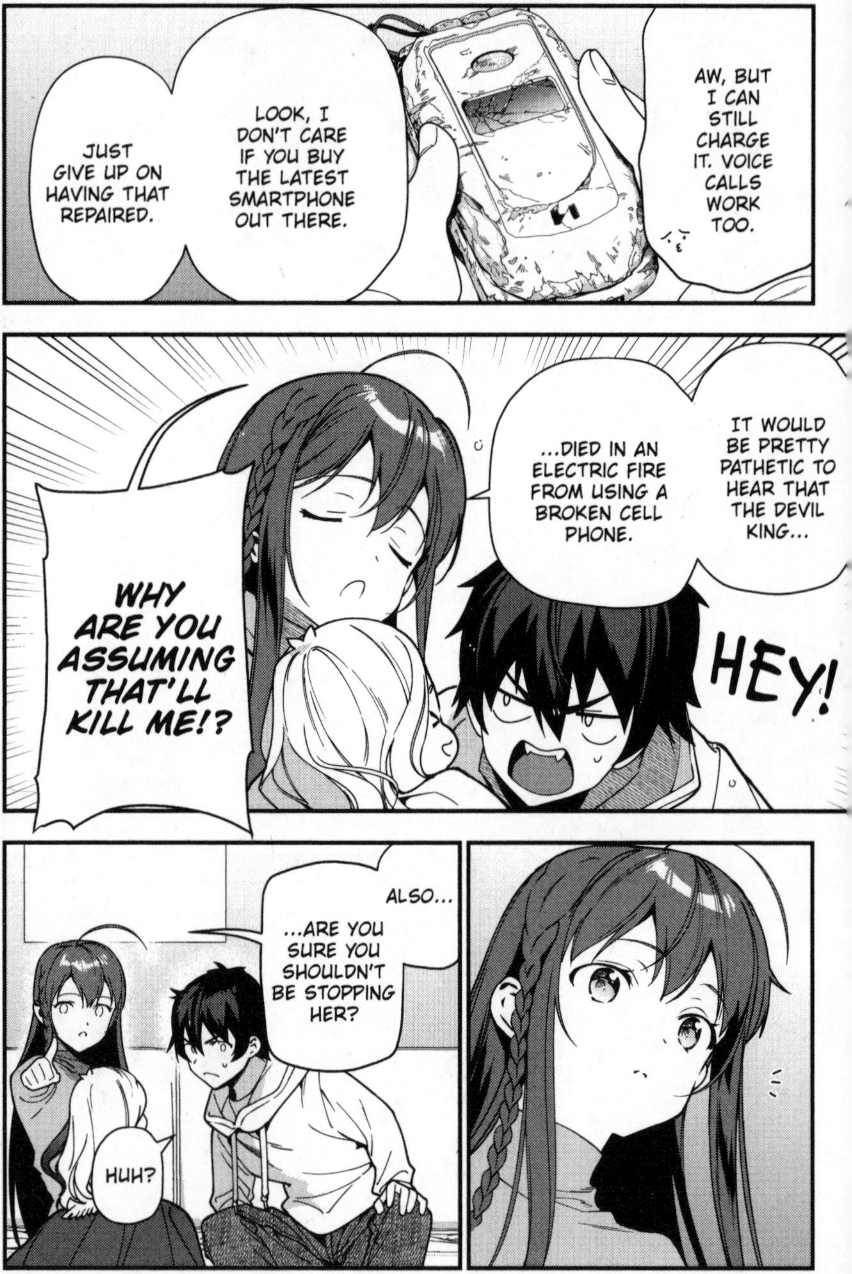
AW, BUT I CAN STILL CHARGE IT. VOICE CALLS WORK TOO.
LOOK, I DON'T CARE IF YOU BUY THE LATEST SMARTPHONE OUT THERE.
JUST GIVE UP ON HAVING THAT REPAIRED.
IT WOULD BE PRETTY PATHETIC TO HEAR THAT THE DEVIL KING...
...DIED IN AN ELECTRIC FIRE FROM USING A BROKEN CELL PHONE.
HEY!
WHY ARE YOU ASSUMING THAT'LL KILL ME!?
ALSO...
...ARE YOU SURE YOU SHOULDN'T BE STOPPING HER?
HUH?

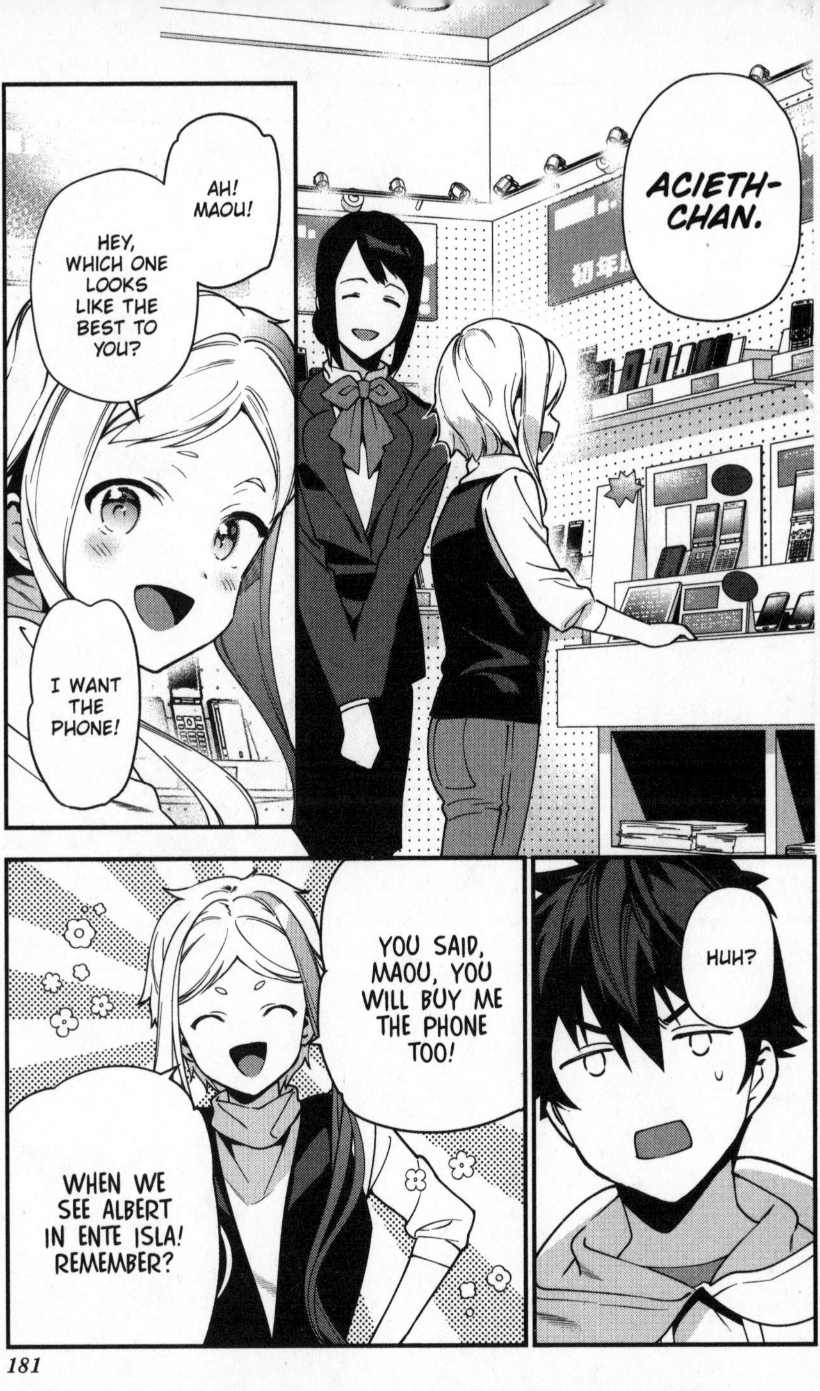
ACIETH-CHAN.
AH! MAOU!
HEY, WHICH ONE LOOKS LIKE THE BEST TO YOU?
I WANT THE PHONE!
HUH?
YOU SAID, MAOU, YOU WILL BUY ME THE PHONE TOO!
WHEN WE SEE ALBERT IN ENTE ISLA! REMEMBER?

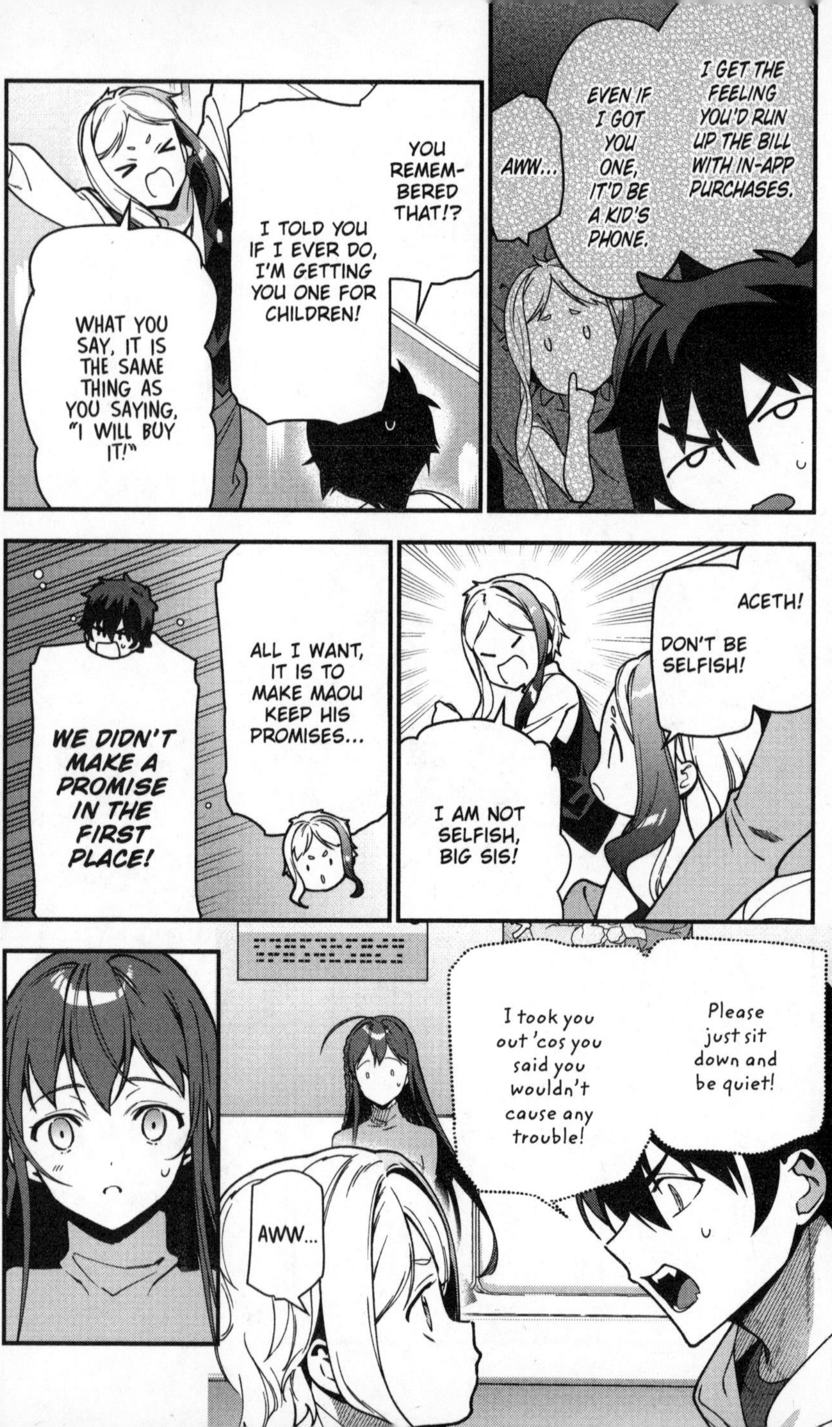
I GET THE FEELING YOU'D RUN UP THE BILL WITH IN-APP PURCHASES.
EVEN IF I GOT YOU ONE, IT'D BE A KID'S PHONE.
AWW...
YOU REMEM-BERED THAT!?
I TOLD YOU IF I EVER DO, I'M GETTING YOU ONE FOR CHILDREN!
WHAT YOU SAY, IT IS THE SAME THING AS YOU SAYING, "I WILL BUY IT!"
ACETH!
DON'T BE SELFISH!
I AM NOT SELFISH, BIG SIS!
ALL I WANT, IT IS TO MAKE MAOU KEEP HIS PROMISES...
WE DIDN'T MAKE A PROMISE IN THE FIRST PLACE!
Please just sit down and be quiet!
I took you out 'cos you said you wouldn't cause any trouble!
AWW...

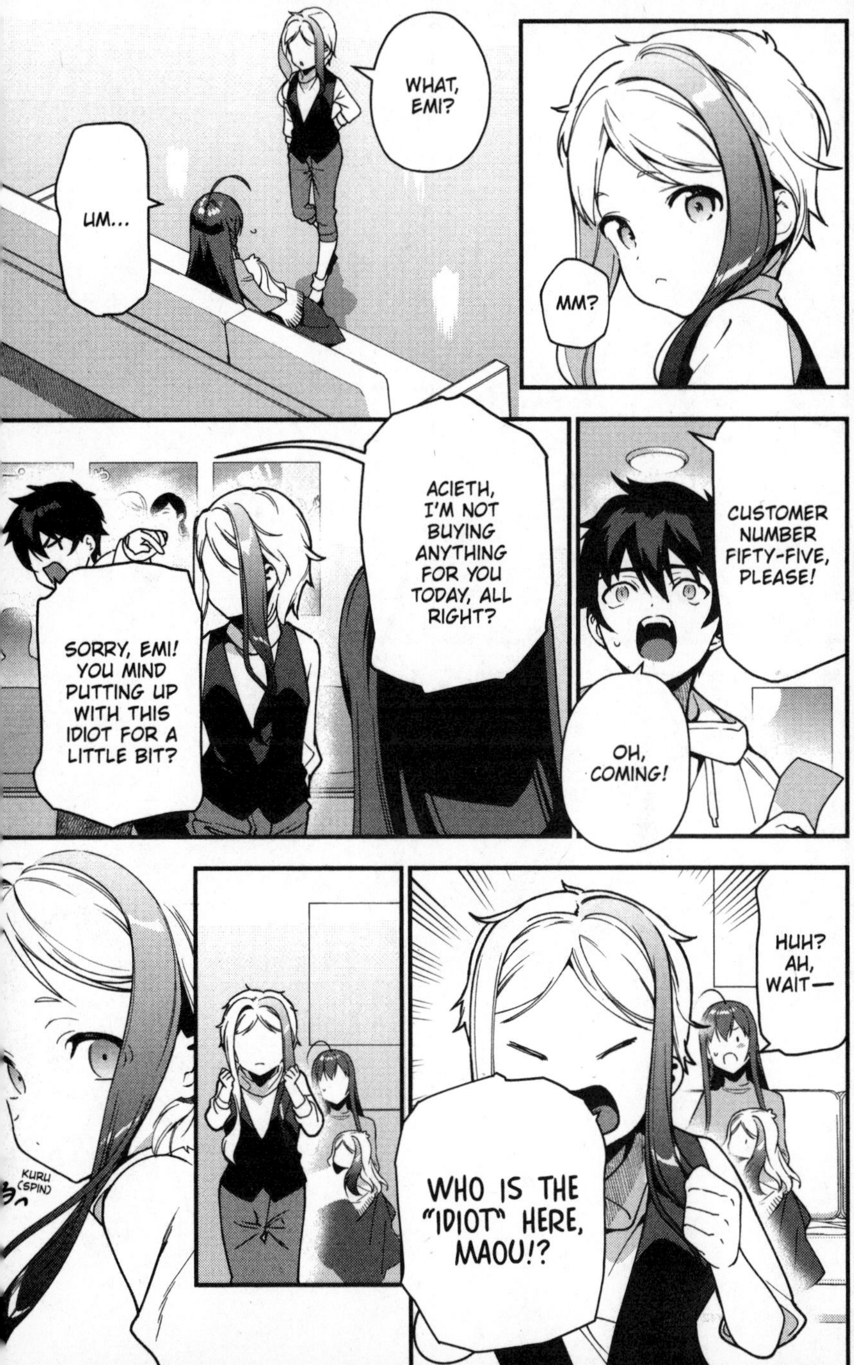
MM?
WHAT, EMI?
UM...
CUSTOMER NUMBER FIFTY-FIVE, PLEASE!
OH, COMING!
ACIETH, I'M NOT BUYING ANYTHING FOR YOU TODAY, ALL RIGHT?
SORRY, EMI! YOU MIND PUTTING UP WITH THIS IDIOT FOR A LITTLE BIT?
HUH? AH, WAIT—
WHO IS THE "IDIOT" HERE, MAOU!?
KURU (SPIN)

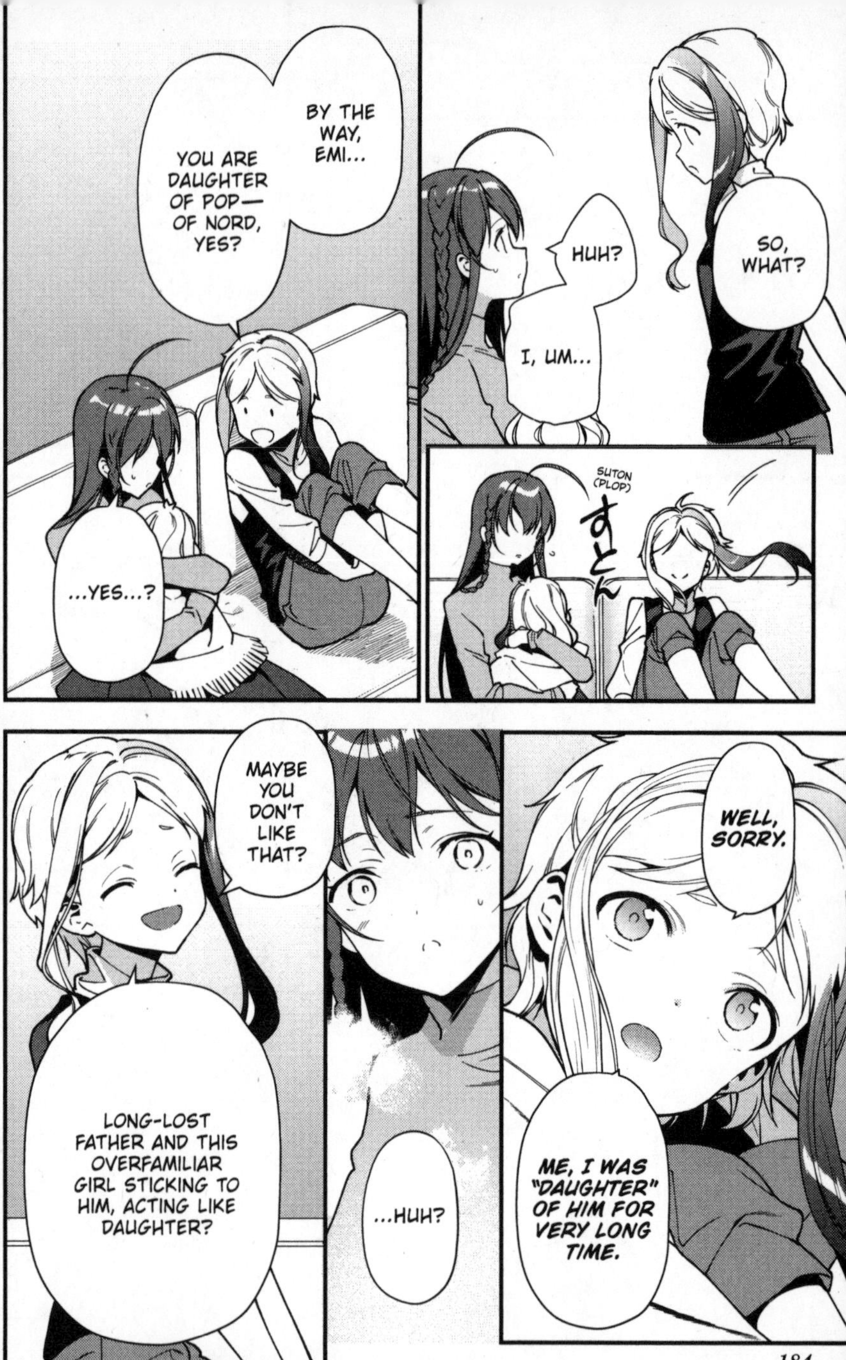
SO, WHAT?
HUH?
I, UM...
SUTON (PLOP)
すとん
BY THE WAY, EMI...
YOU ARE DAUGHTER OF POP— OF NORD, YES?
...YES...?
WELL, SORRY.
ME, I WAS "DAUGHTER" OF HIM FOR VERY LONG TIME.
...HUH?
MAYBE YOU DON'T LIKE THAT?
LONG-LOST FATHER AND THIS OVERFAMILIAR GIRL STICKING TO HIM, ACTING LIKE DAUGHTER?

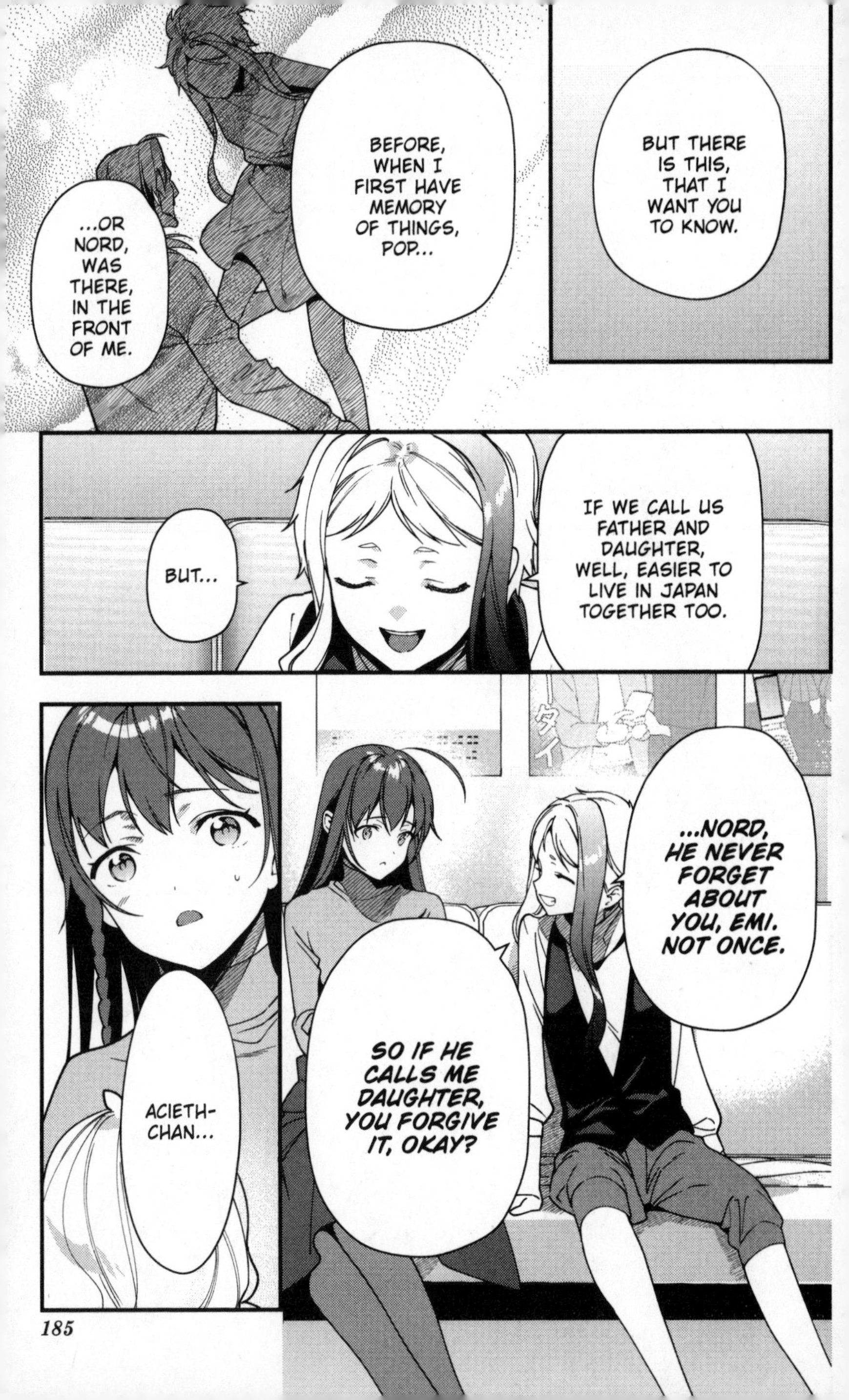
BUT THERE IS THIS, THAT I WANT YOU TO KNOW.
BEFORE, WHEN I FIRST HAVE MEMORY OF THINGS, POP...
...OR NORD, WAS THERE, IN THE FRONT OF ME.
IF WE CALL US FATHER AND DAUGHTER, WELL, EASIER TO LIVE IN JAPAN TOGETHER TOO.
BUT...
...NORD, HE NEVER FORGET ABOUT YOU, EMI. NOT ONCE.
SO IF HE CALLS ME DAUGHTER, YOU FORGIVE IT, OKAY?
ACIETH-CHAN...

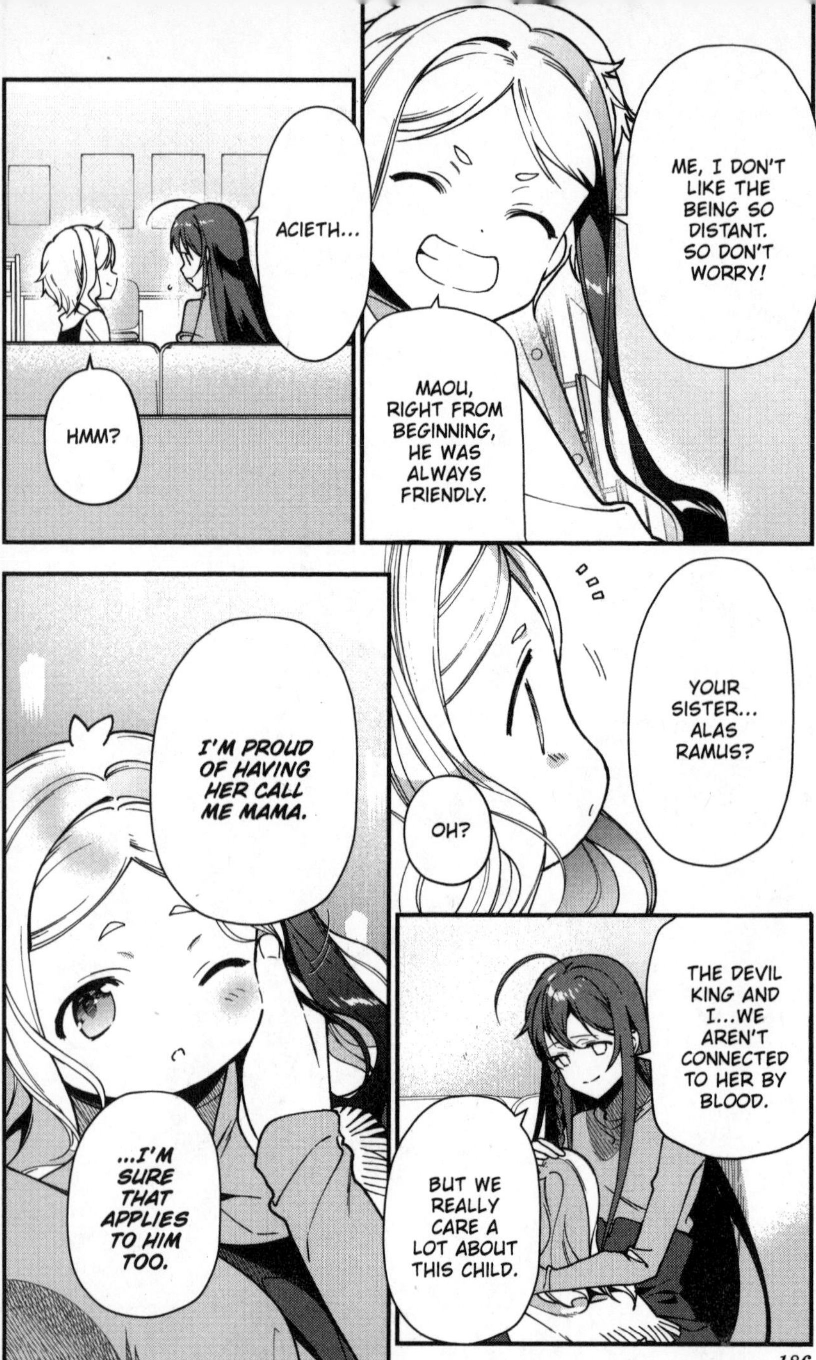
ME, I DON'T LIKE THE BEING SO DISTANT. SO DON'T WORRY!
MAOU, RIGHT FROM BEGINNING, HE WAS ALWAYS FRIENDLY.
ACIETH...
HMM?
YOUR SISTER... ALAS RAMUS?
OH?
THE DEVIL KING AND I...WE AREN'T CONNECTED TO HER BY BLOOD.
BUT WE REALLY CARE A LOT ABOUT THIS CHILD.
I'M PROUD OF HAVING HER CALL ME MAMA.
...I'M SURE THAT APPLIES TO HIM TOO.

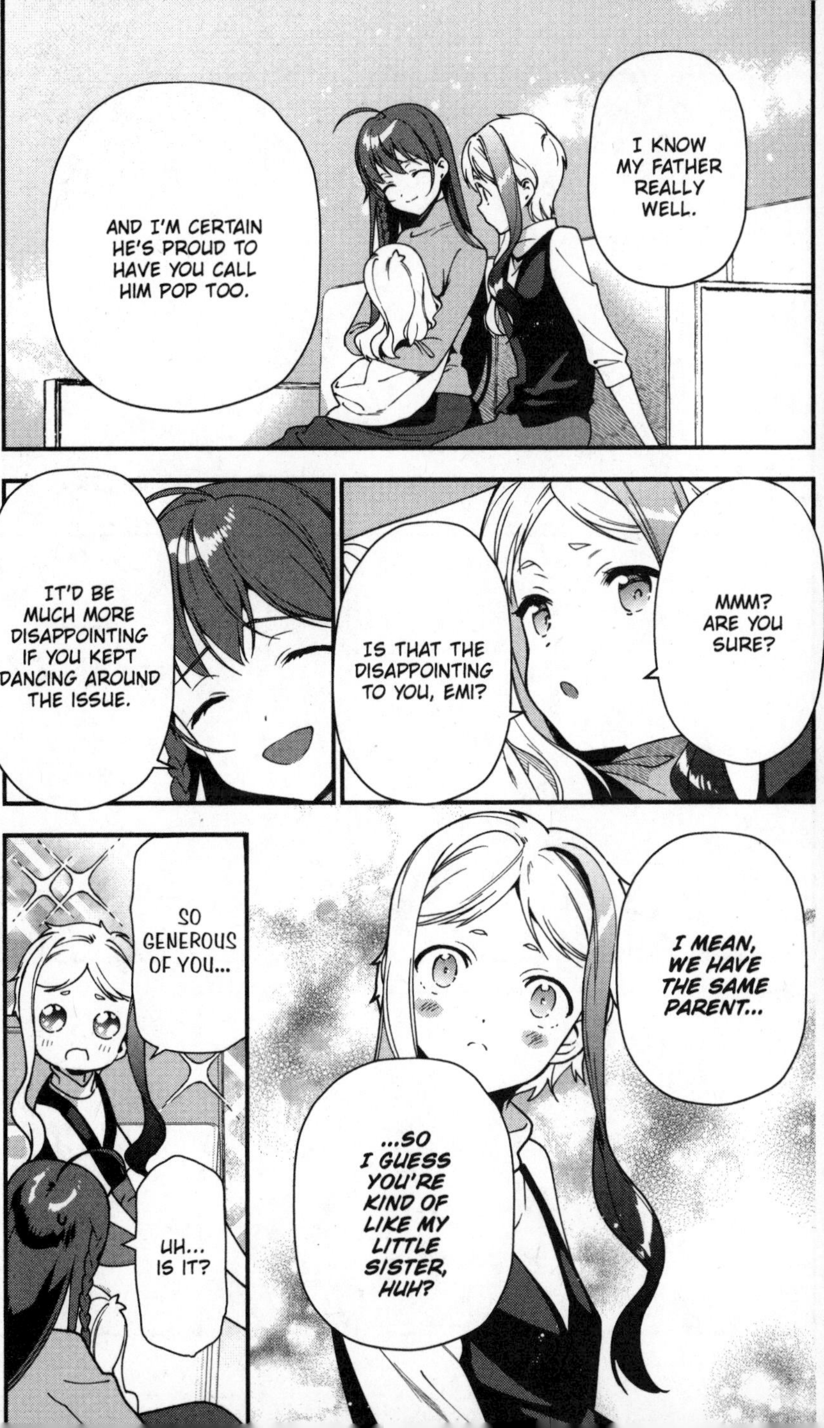
I KNOW MY FATHER REALLY WELL.
AND I'M CERTAIN HE'S PROUD TO HAVE YOU CALL HIM POP TOO.
MMM? ARE YOU SURE?
IS THAT THE DISAPPOINTING TO YOU, EMI?
IT'D BE MUCH MORE DISAPPOINTING IF YOU KEPT DANCING AROUND THE ISSUE.
I MEAN, WE HAVE THE SAME PARENT...
...SO I GUESS YOU'RE KIND OF LIKE MY LITTLE SISTER, HUH?
SO GENEROUS OF YOU...
UH... IS IT?

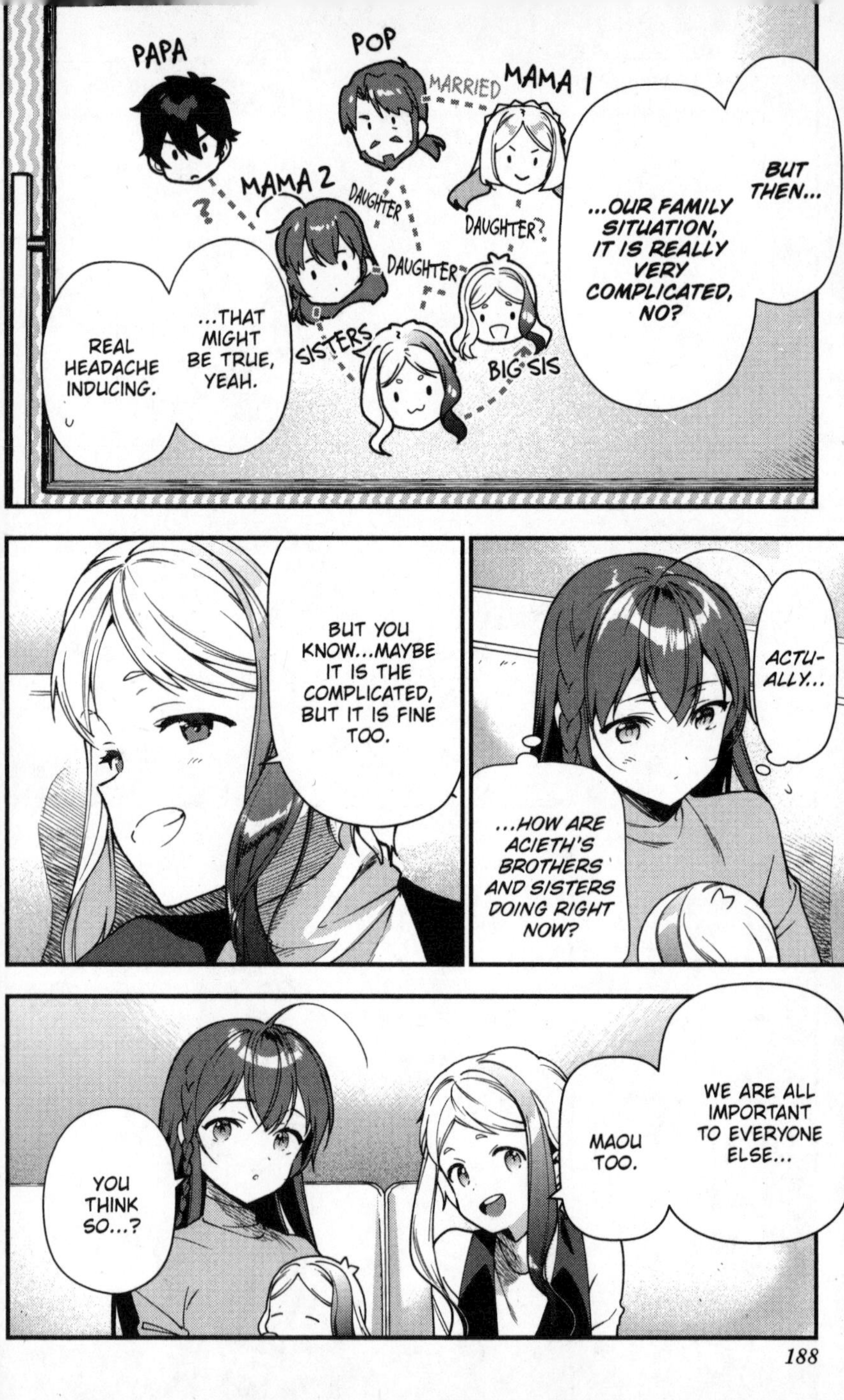
BUT THEN...
...OUR FAMILY SITUATION, IT IS REALLY VERY COMPLICATED, NO?
MAMA 1
MARRIED
POP
PAPA
DAUGHTER?
DAUGHTER
MAMA 2
DAUGHTER
BIG SIS
SISTERS
...THAT MIGHT BE TRUE, YEAH.
REAL HEADACHE INDUCING.
ACTU-ALLY...
...HOW ARE ACIETH'S BROTHERS AND SISTERS DOING RIGHT NOW?
BUT YOU KNOW...MAYBE IT IS THE COMPLICATED, BUT IT IS FINE TOO.
WE ARE ALL IMPORTANT TO EVERYONE ELSE...
MAOU TOO.
YOU THINK SO...?

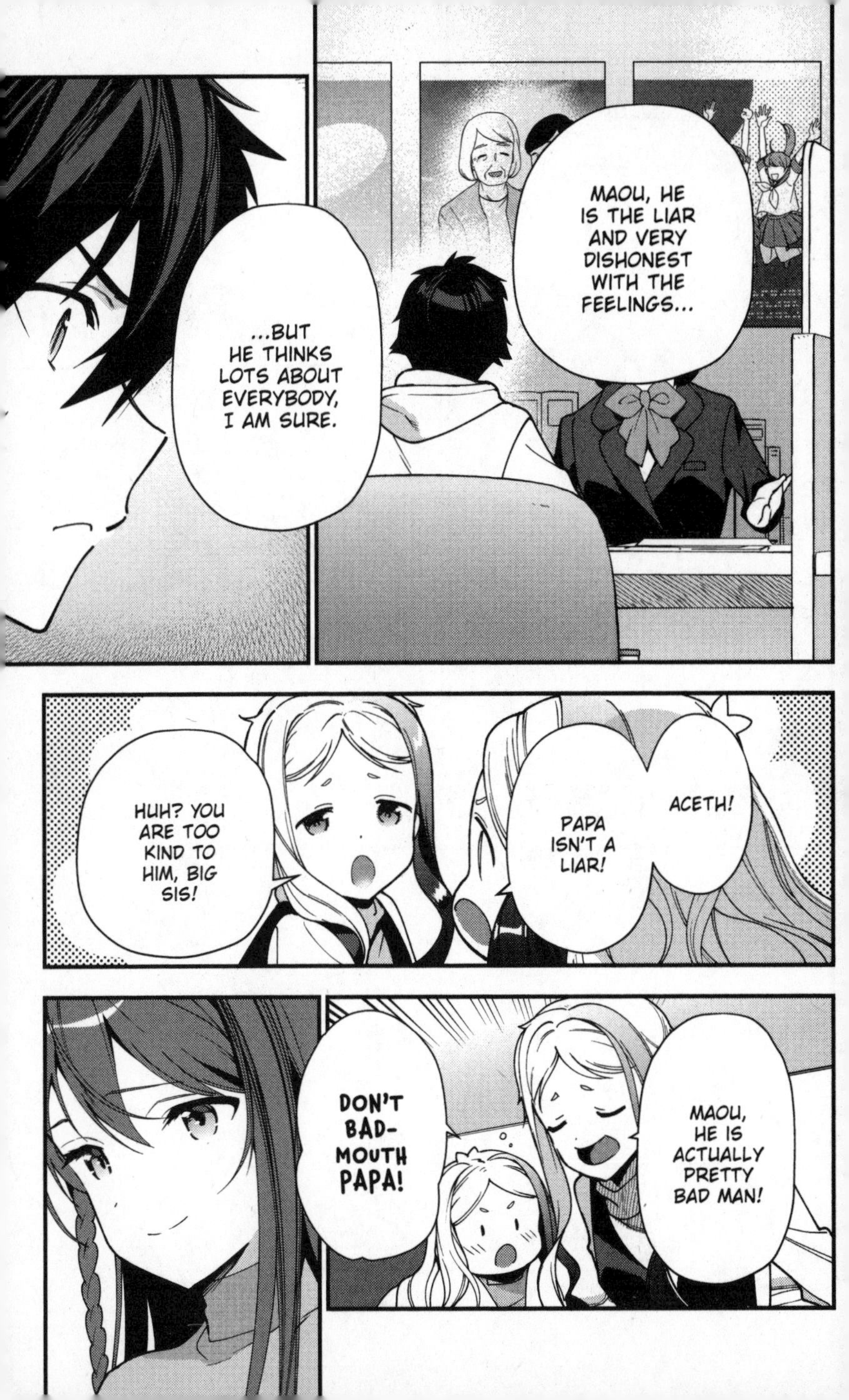
MAOU, HE IS THE LIAR AND VERY DISHONEST WITH THE FEELINGS...
...BUT HE THINKS LOTS ABOUT EVERYBODY, I AM SURE.
ACETH!
PAPA ISN'T A LIAR!
HUH? YOU ARE TOO KIND TO HIM, BIG SIS!
MAOU, HE IS ACTUALLY PRETTY BAD MAN!
DON'T BAD-MOUTH PAPA!

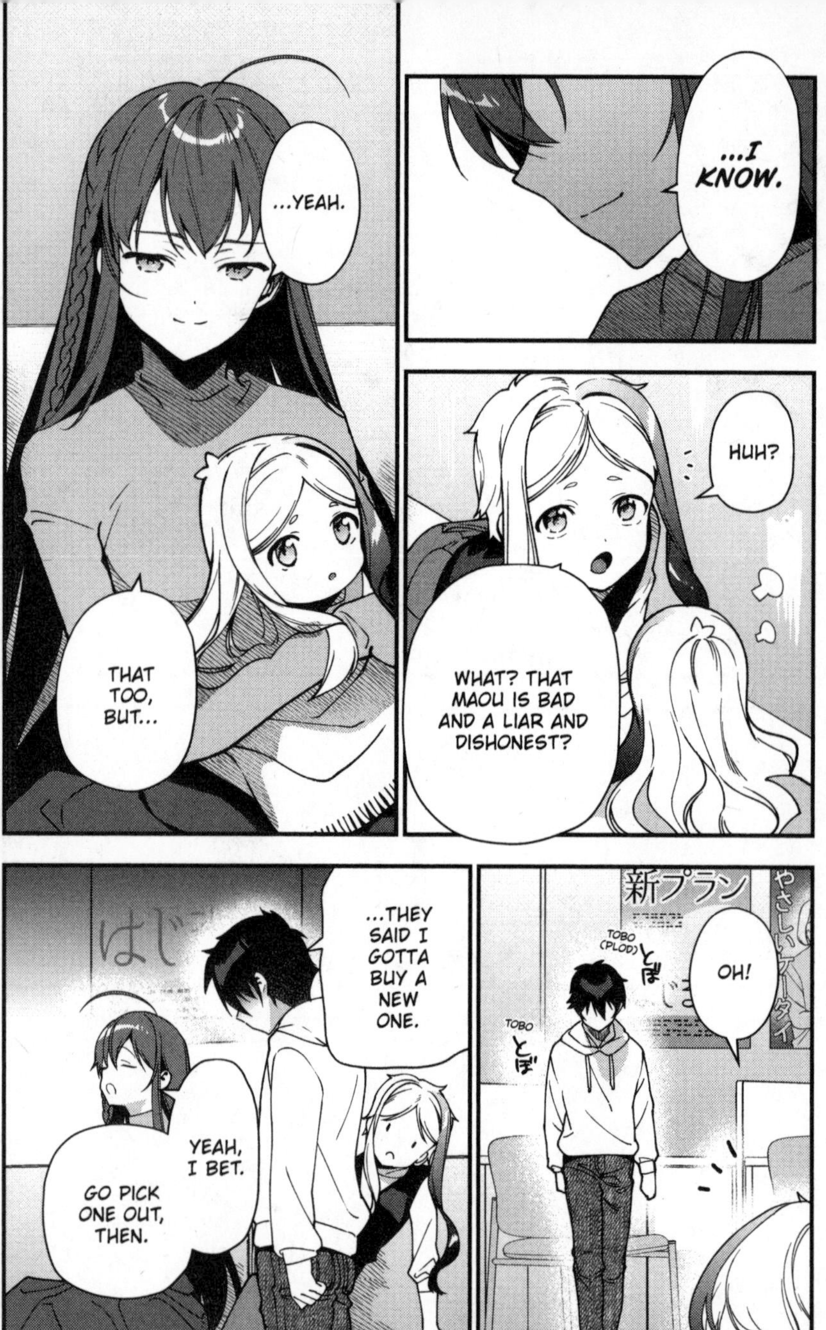
...I KNOW.
HUH?
WHAT? THAT MAOU IS BAD AND A LIAR AND DISHONEST?
...YEAH.
THAT TOO, BUT...
新プラン
TOBO (PLOD) とぼ
TOBO とぼ
OH!
...THEY SAID I GOTTA BUY A NEW ONE.
YEAH, I BET.
GO PICK ONE OUT, THEN.

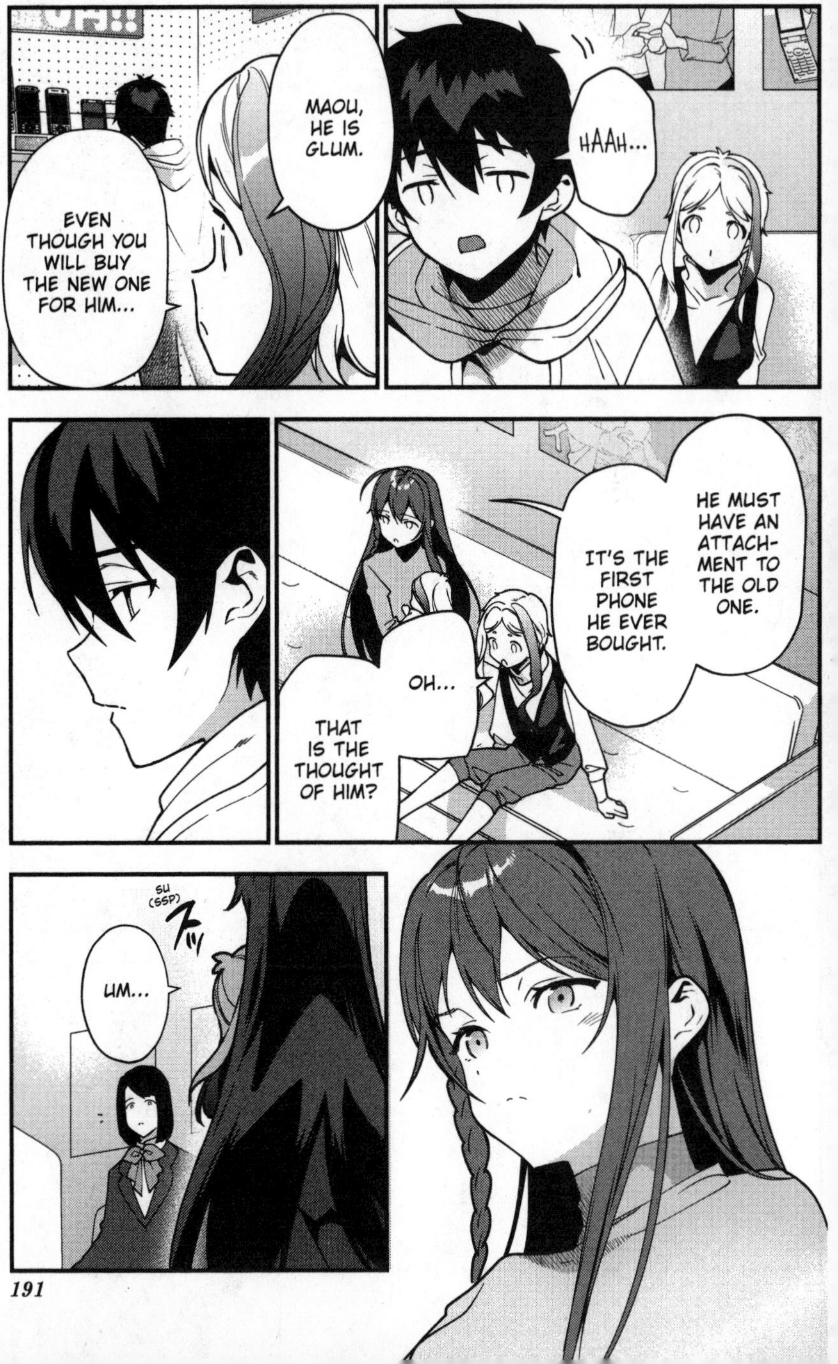
HAAH...
MAOU, HE IS GLUM.
EVEN THOUGH YOU WILL BUY THE NEW ONE FOR HIM...
HE MUST HAVE AN ATTACHMENT TO THE OLD ONE.
IT'S THE FIRST PHONE HE EVER BOUGHT.
OH...
THAT IS THE THOUGHT OF HIM?
SU (SSP)
UM...

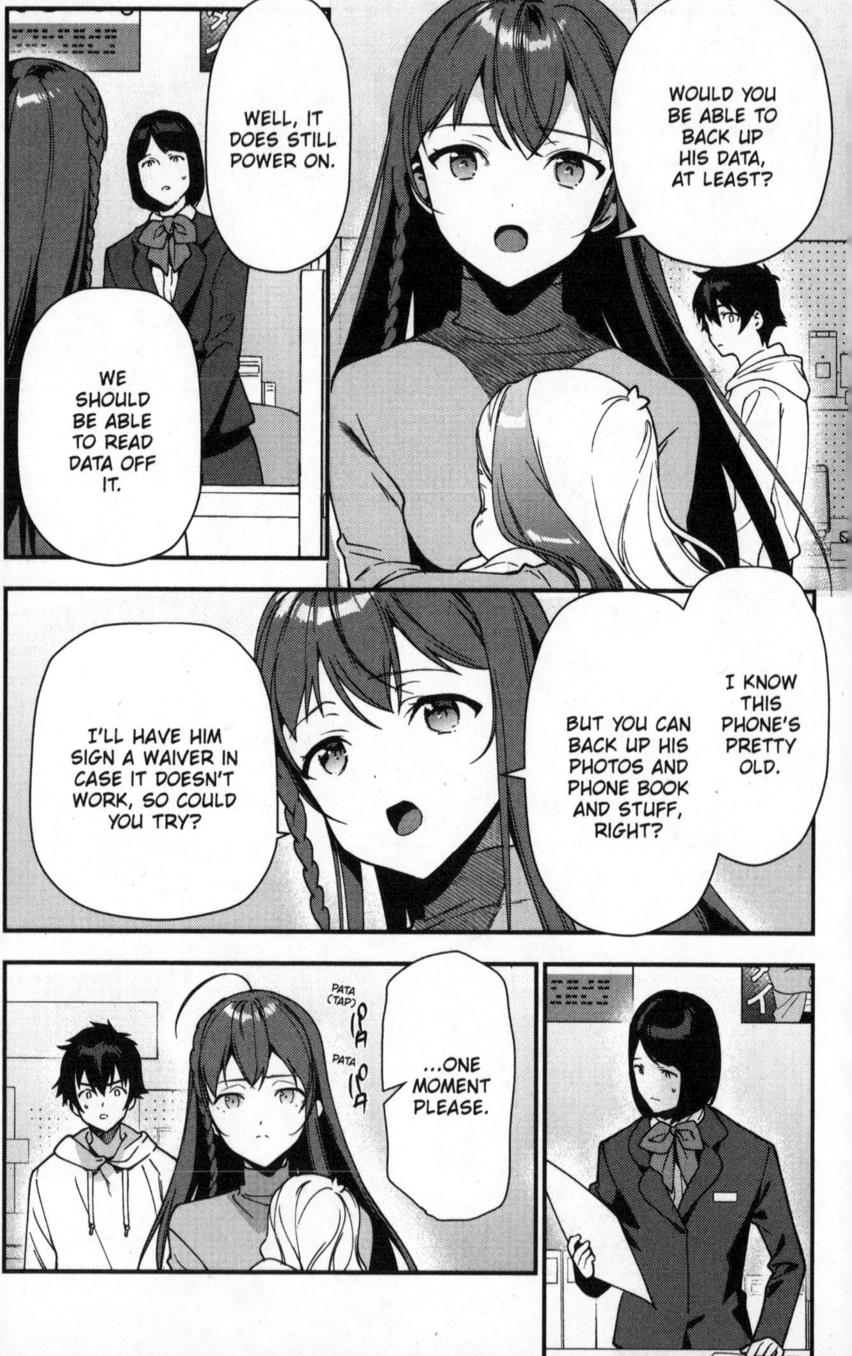
WOULD YOU BE ABLE TO BACK UP HIS DATA, AT LEAST?
WELL, IT DOES STILL POWER ON.
WE SHOULD BE ABLE TO READ DATA OFF IT.
I KNOW THIS PHONE'S PRETTY OLD.
BUT YOU CAN BACK UP HIS PHOTOS AND PHONE BOOK AND STUFF, RIGHT?
I'LL HAVE HIM SIGN A WAIVER IN CASE IT DOESN'T WORK, SO COULD YOU TRY?
...ONE MOMENT PLEASE.
PATA (TAP)
PATA

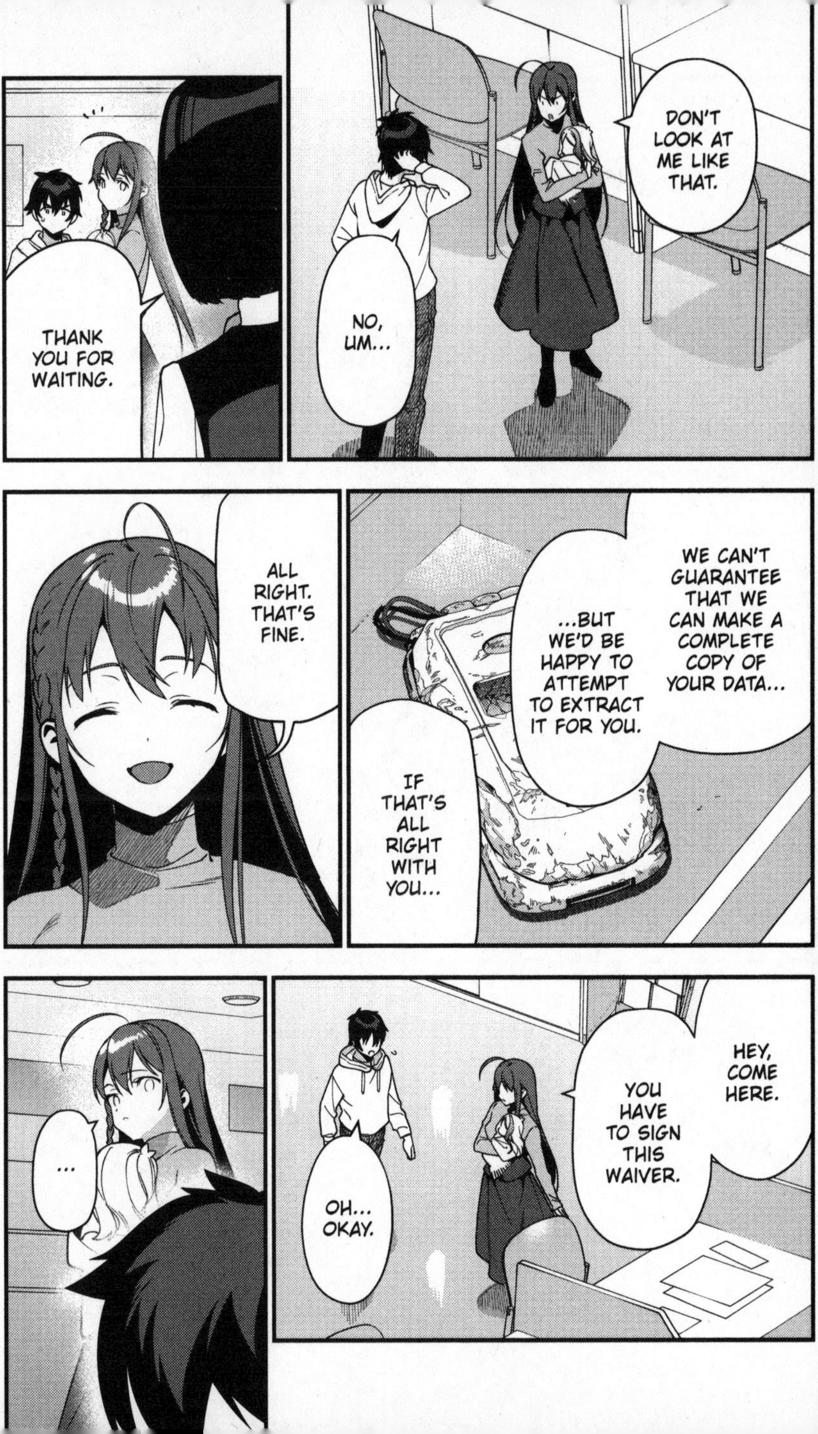
DON'T LOOK AT ME LIKE THAT.
NO, UM...
THANK YOU FOR WAITING.
WE CAN'T GUARANTEE THAT WE CAN MAKE A COMPLETE COPY OF YOUR DATA...
...BUT WE'D BE HAPPY TO ATTEMPT TO EXTRACT IT FOR YOU.
IF THAT'S ALL RIGHT WITH YOU...
ALL RIGHT. THAT'S FINE.
HEY, COME HERE.
YOU HAVE TO SIGN THIS WAIVER.
OH... OKAY.
...

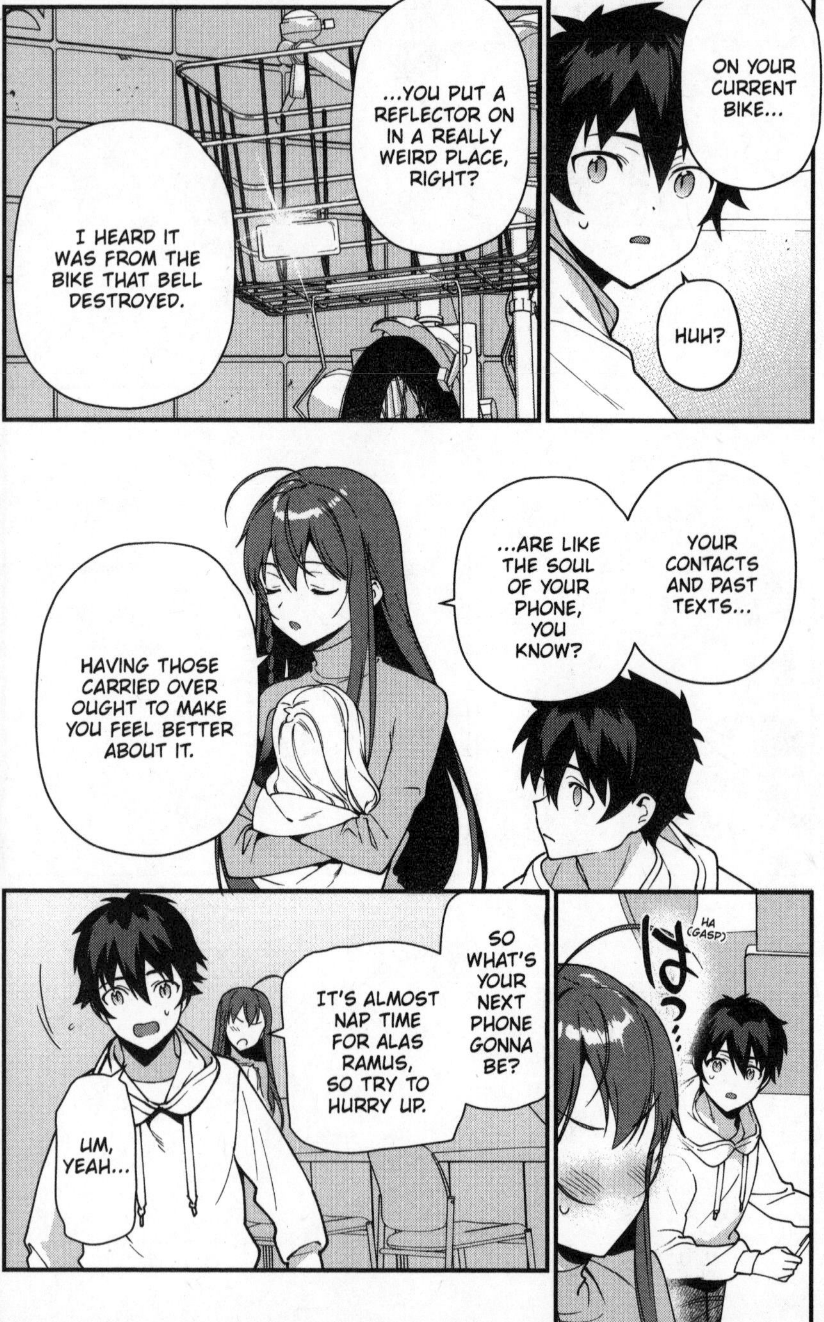
ON YOUR CURRENT BIKE...
HUH?
...YOU PUT A REFLECTOR ON IN A REALLY WEIRD PLACE, RIGHT?
I HEARD IT WAS FROM THE BIKE THAT BELL DESTROYED.
YOUR CONTACTS AND PAST TEXTS...
...ARE LIKE THE SOUL OF YOUR PHONE, YOU KNOW?
HAVING THOSE CARRIED OVER OUGHT TO MAKE YOU FEEL BETTER ABOUT IT.
はっ…
HA (GASP)
SO WHAT'S YOUR NEXT PHONE GONNA BE?
IT'S ALMOST NAP TIME FOR ALAS RAMUS, SO TRY TO HURRY UP.
UM, YEAH...

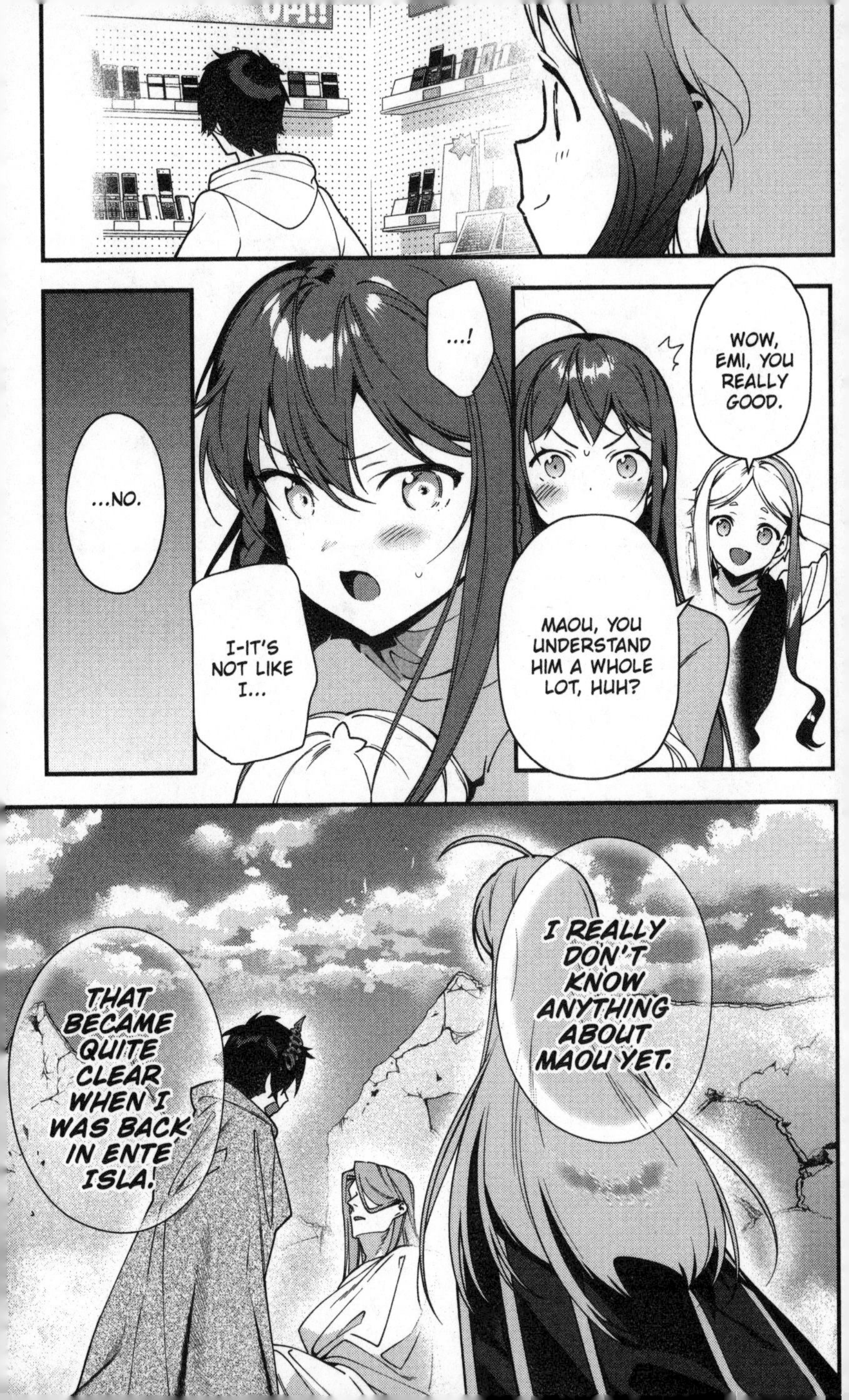
WOW, EMI, YOU REALLY GOOD.
MAOU, YOU UNDERSTAND HIM A WHOLE LOT, HUH?
...!
I-IT'S NOT LIKE I...
...NO.
I REALLY DON'T KNOW ANYTHING ABOUT MAOU YET.
THAT BECAME QUITE CLEAR WHEN I WAS BACK IN ENTE ISLA.

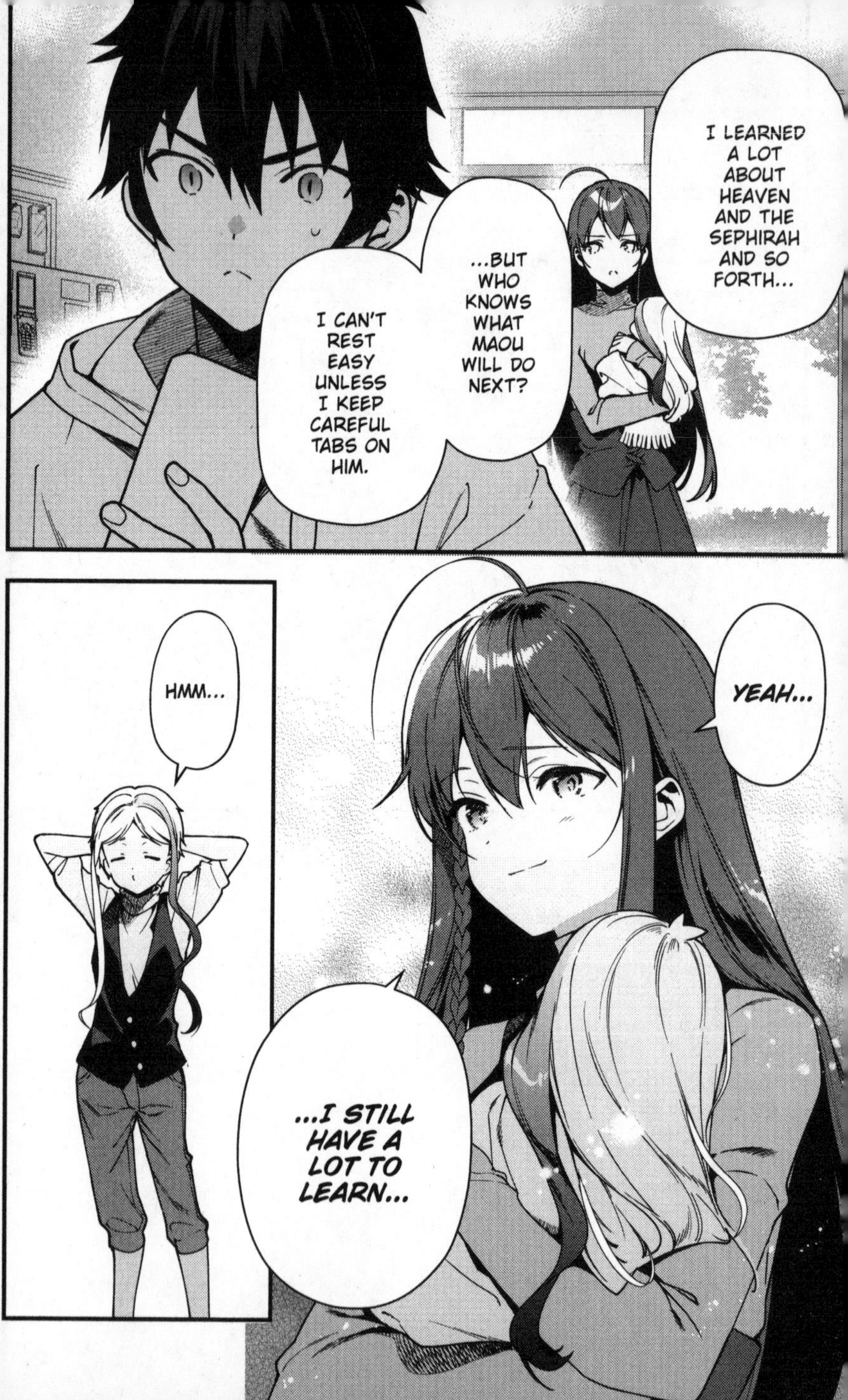
I LEARNED A LOT ABOUT HEAVEN AND THE SEPHIRAH AND SO FORTH...
...BUT WHO KNOWS WHAT MAOU WILL DO NEXT?
I CAN'T REST EASY UNLESS I KEEP CAREFUL TABS ON HIM.
YEAH...
...I STILL HAVE A LOT TO LEARN...
HMM...

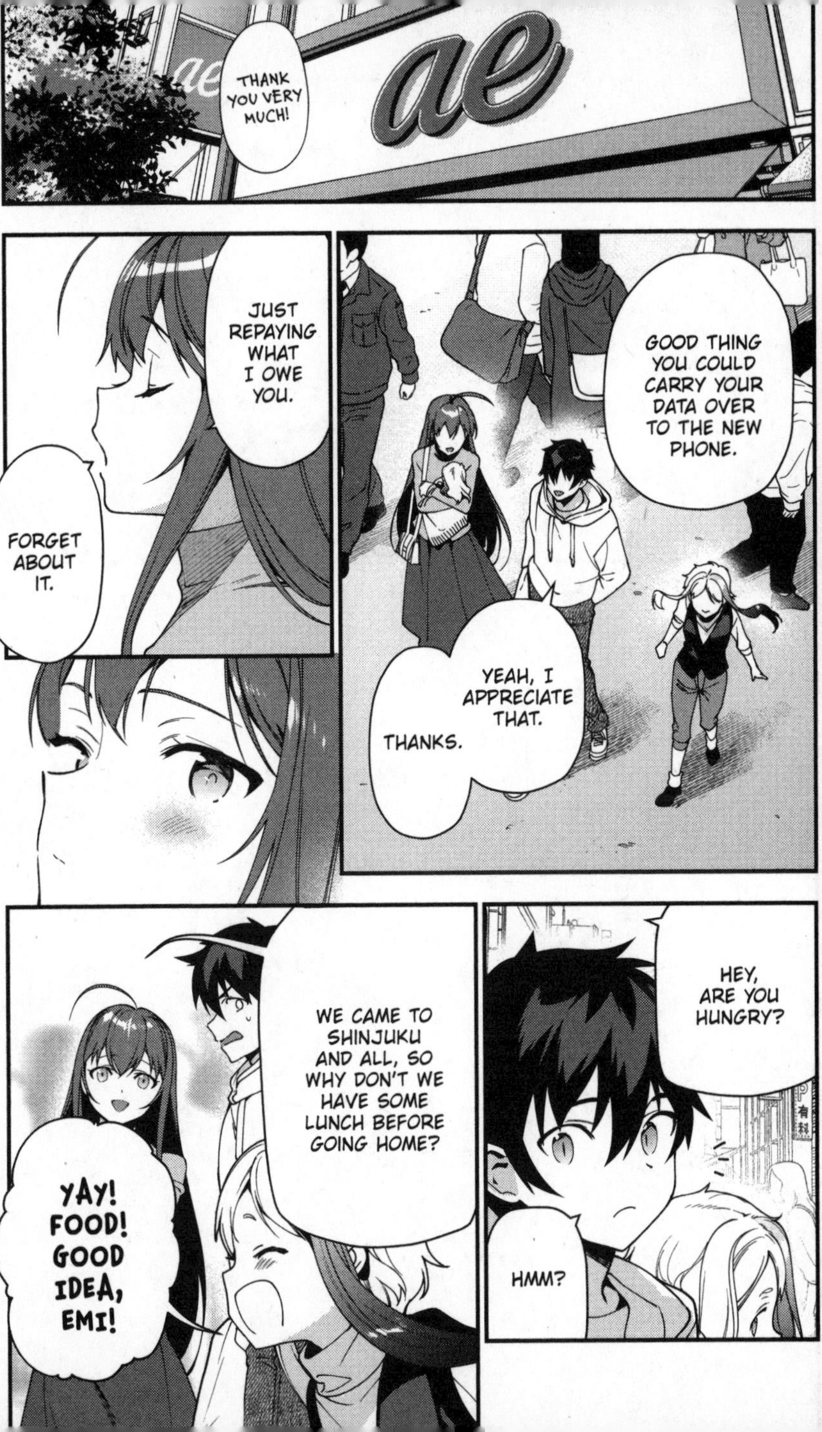
THANK YOU VERY MUCH!
GOOD THING YOU COULD CARRY YOUR DATA OVER TO THE NEW PHONE.
YEAH, I APPRECIATE THAT.
THANKS.
JUST REPAYING WHAT I OWE YOU.
FORGET ABOUT IT.
HEY, ARE YOU HUNGRY?
HMM?
WE CAME TO SHINJUKU AND ALL, SO WHY DON'T WE HAVE SOME LUNCH BEFORE GOING HOME?
YAY! FOOD! GOOD IDEA, EMI!

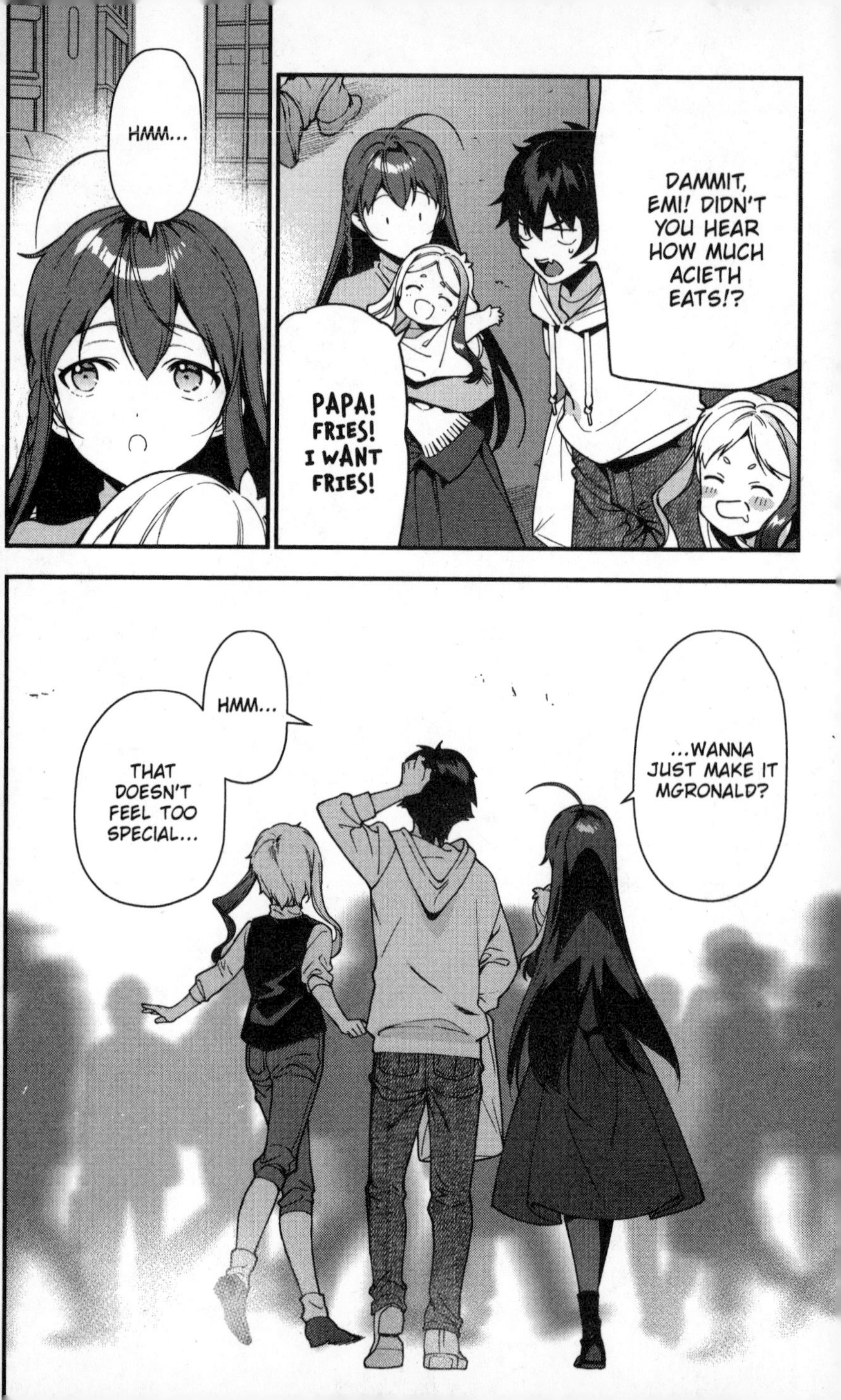
DAMMIT, EMI! DIDN'T YOU HEAR HOW MUCH ACIETH EATS!?
PAPA! FRIES! I WANT FRIES!
HMM...
...WANNA JUST MAKE IT MGRONALD?
HMM...
THAT DOESN'T FEEL TOO SPECIAL...

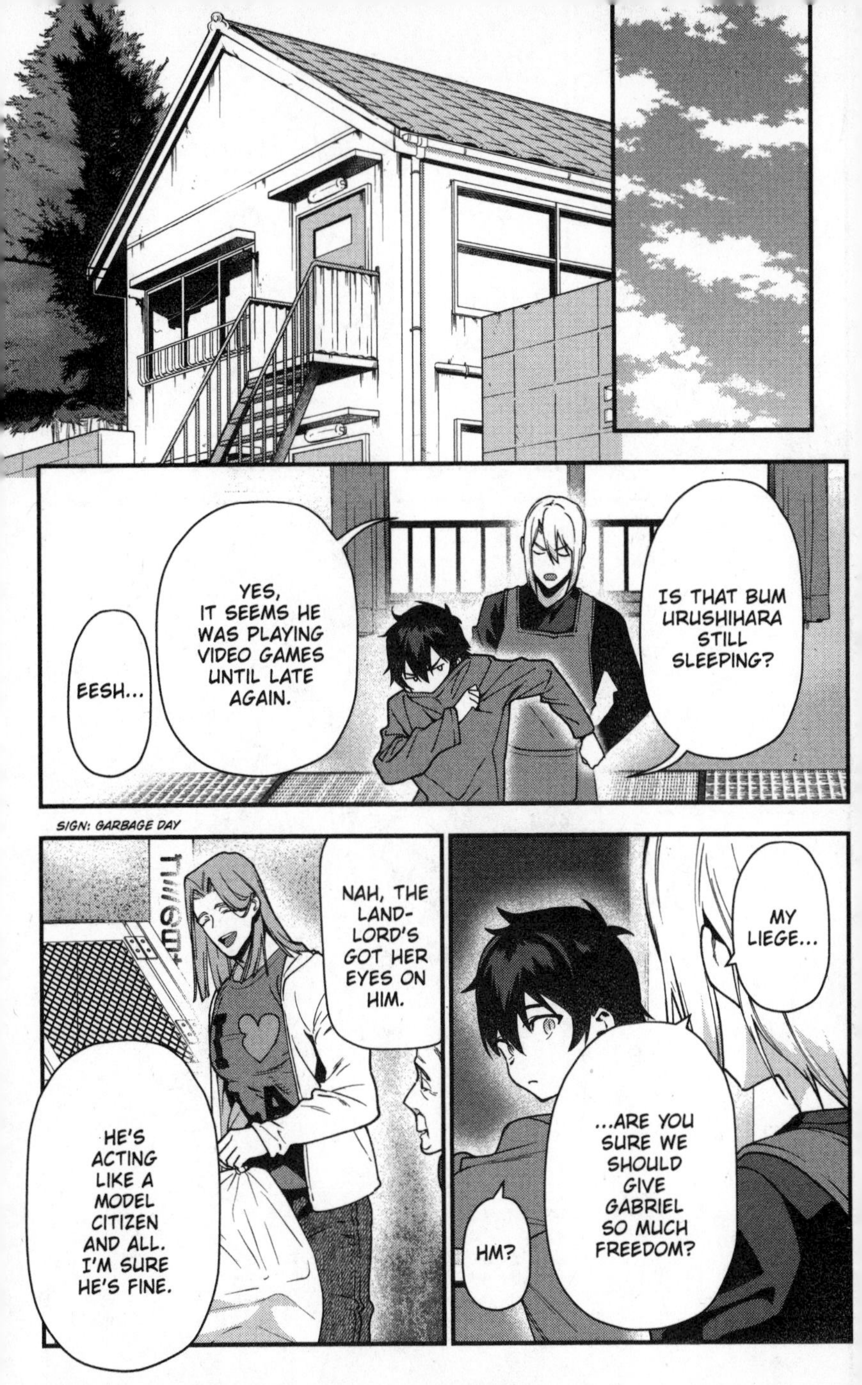
IS THAT BUM URUSHIHARA STILL SLEEPING?
YES, IT SEEMS HE WAS PLAYING VIDEO GAMES UNTIL LATE AGAIN.
EESH...
SIGN: GARBAGE DAY
MY LIEGE...
...ARE YOU SURE WE SHOULD GIVE GABRIEL SO MUCH FREEDOM?
HM?
NAH, THE LAND-LORD'S GOT HER EYES ON HIM.
HE'S ACTING LIKE A MODEL CITIZEN AND ALL. I'M SURE HE'S FINE.

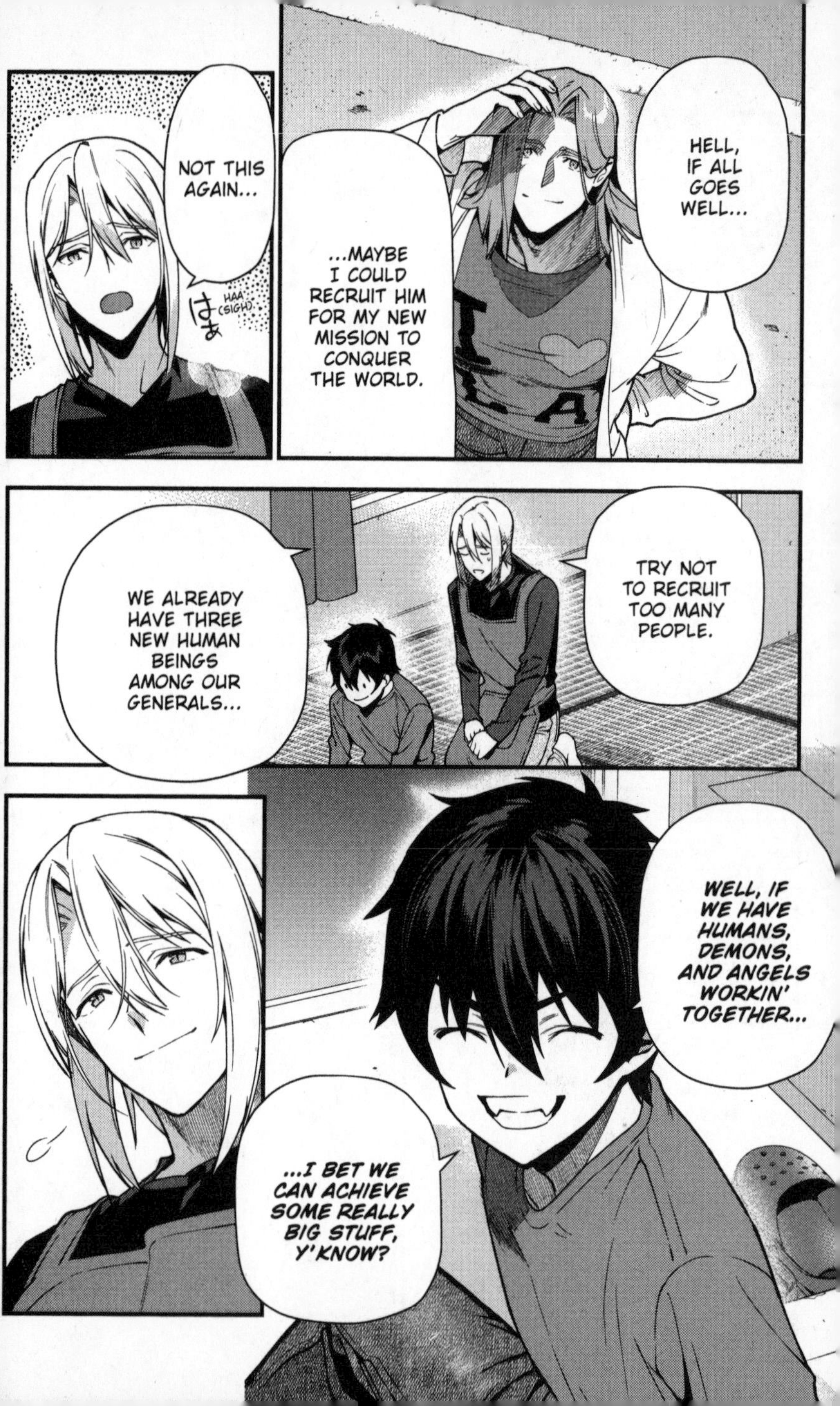
HELL, IF ALL GOES WELL...
...MAYBE I COULD RECRUIT HIM FOR MY NEW MISSION TO CONQUER THE WORLD.
NOT THIS AGAIN...
はぁ HAA (SIGH)
TRY NOT TO RECRUIT TOO MANY PEOPLE.
WE ALREADY HAVE THREE NEW HUMAN BEINGS AMONG OUR GENERALS...
WELL, IF WE HAVE HUMANS, DEMONS, AND ANGELS WORKIN' TOGETHER...
...I BET WE CAN ACHIEVE SOME REALLY BIG STUFF, Y'KNOW?

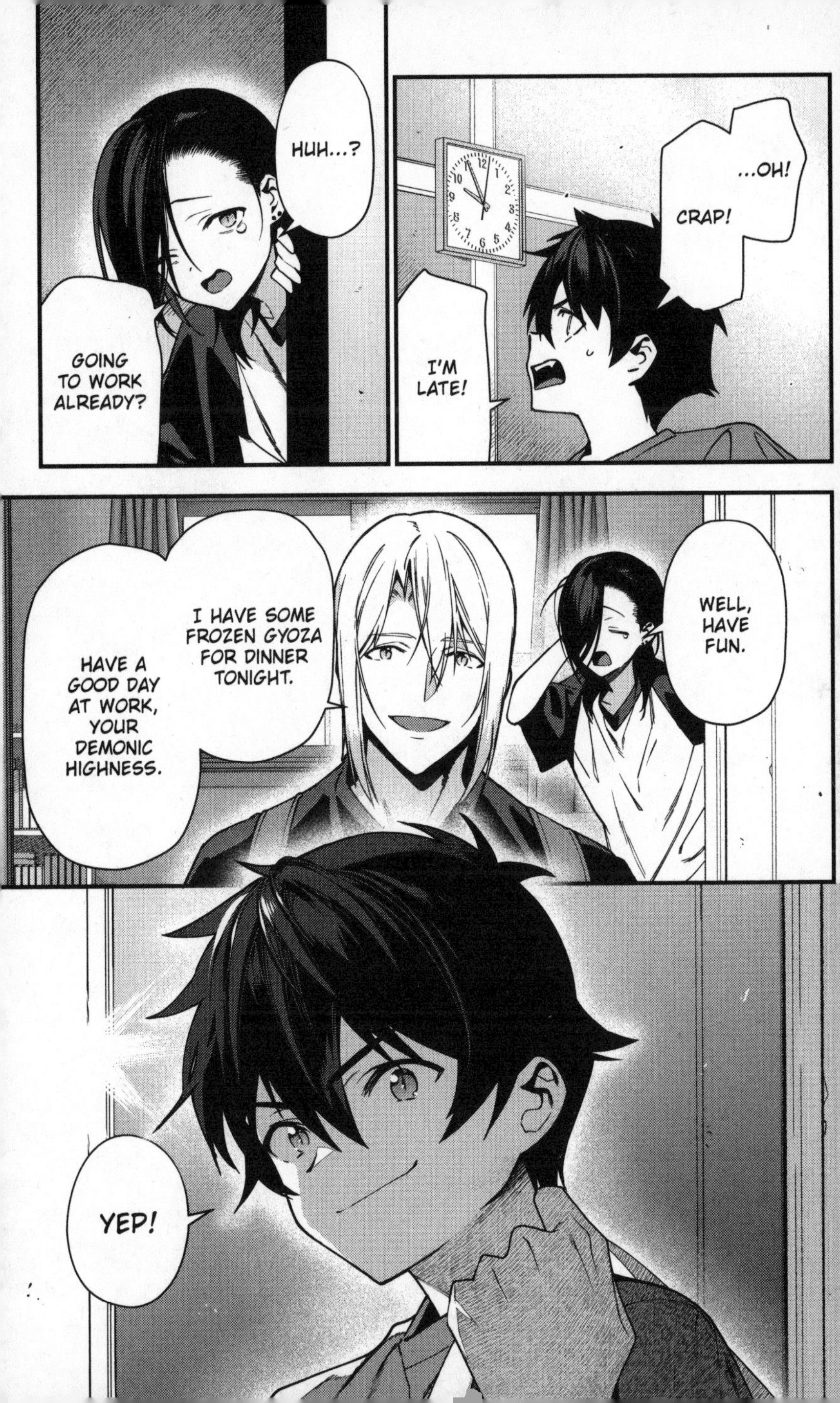
...OH!
CRAP!
I'M LATE!
HUH...?
GOING TO WORK ALREADY?
WELL, HAVE FUN.
I HAVE SOME FROZEN GYOZA FOR DINNER TONIGHT.
HAVE A GOOD DAY AT WORK, YOUR DEMONIC HIGHNESS.
YEP!

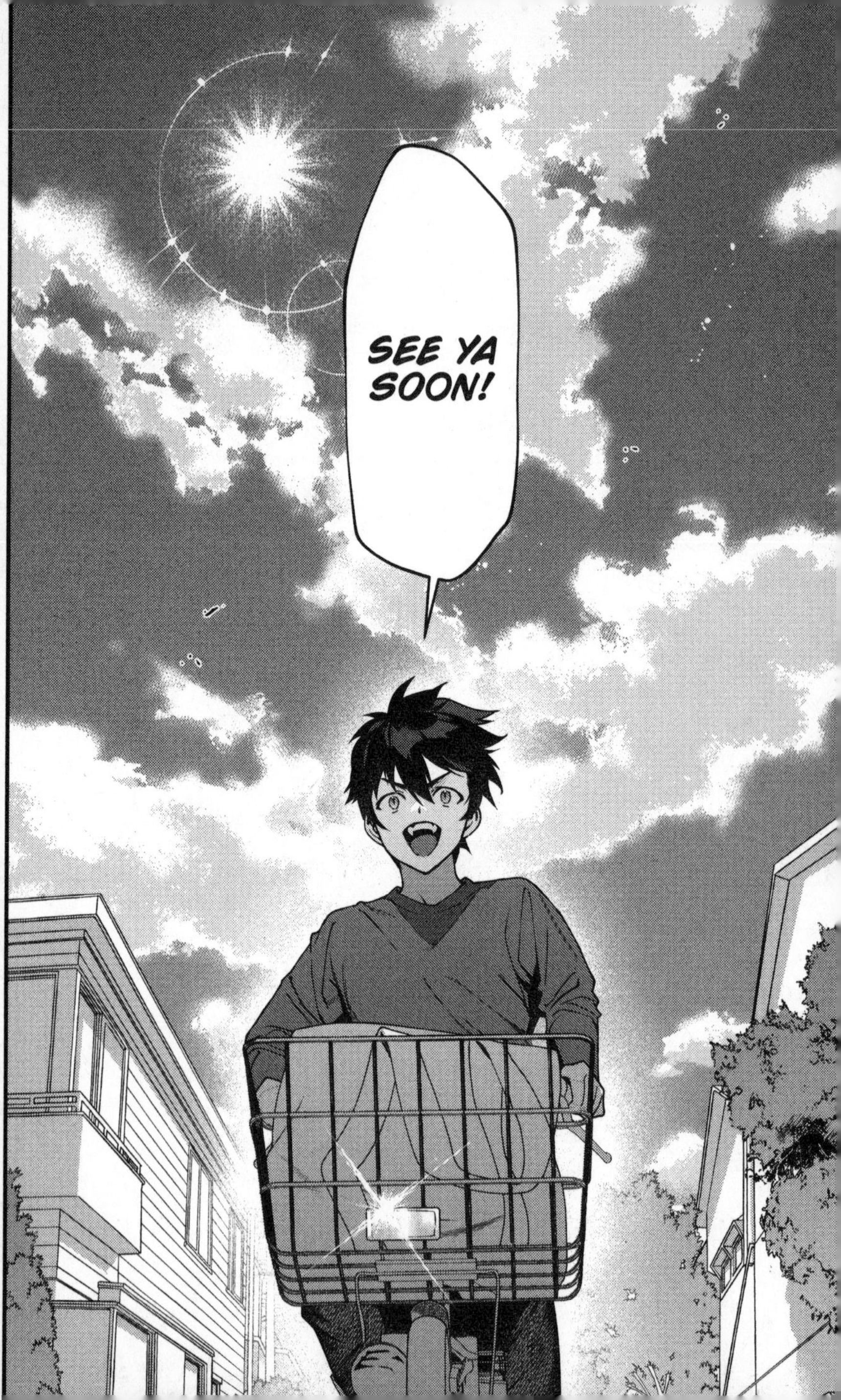
SEE YA SOON!

THE DEVIL IS A PART-TIMER!

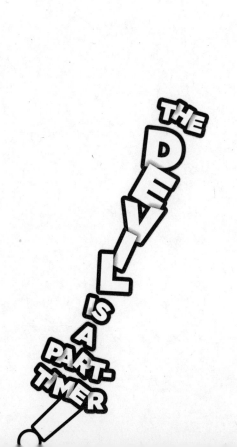

THE ANGELS' PAST

THE ATMOSPHERE OF THE ANGELS' PAST IS DIFFERENT ENOUGH THAT I BET IT SURPRISED A LOT OF READERS. THE FASHION SENSE IS MEANT TO EVOKE 1970s AND '80s SCIENCE FICTION. I PAID ATTENTION TO SILHOUETTES THAT EMPHASIZE BODY SHAPE, AS WELL AS FLOWING LINES AND V-SHAPED ACCENTS.

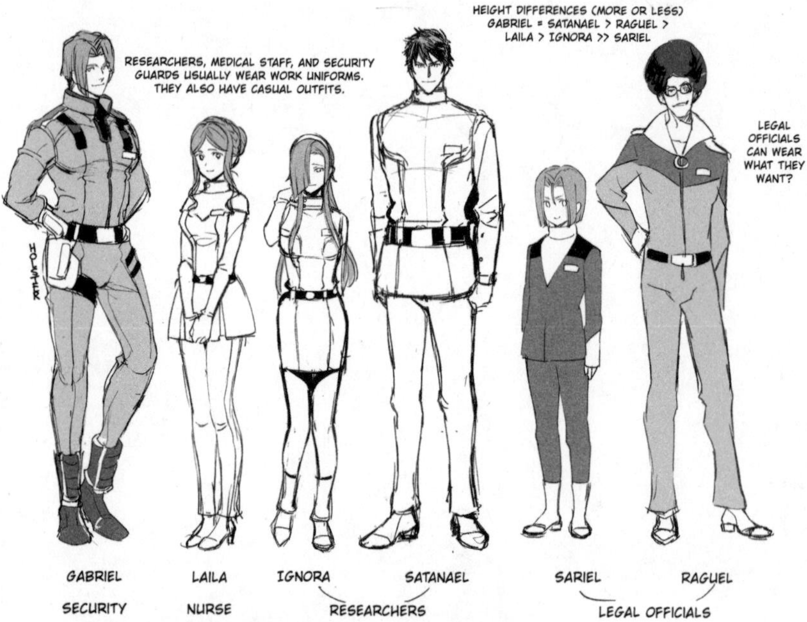

HEIGHT DIFFERENCES (MORE OR LESS)
GABRIEL = SATANAEL > RAGUEL > LAILA > IGNORA >> SARIEL
RESEARCHERS, MEDICAL STAFF, AND SECURITY GUARDS USUALLY WEAR WORK UNIFORMS. THEY ALSO HAVE CASUAL OUTFITS.
LEGAL OFFICIALS CAN WEAR WHAT THEY WANT?
HOLSTER
GABRIEL
SECURITY
LAILA
NURSE
IGNORA
SATANAEL
RESEARCHERS
SARIEL
RAGUEL
LEGAL OFFICIALS

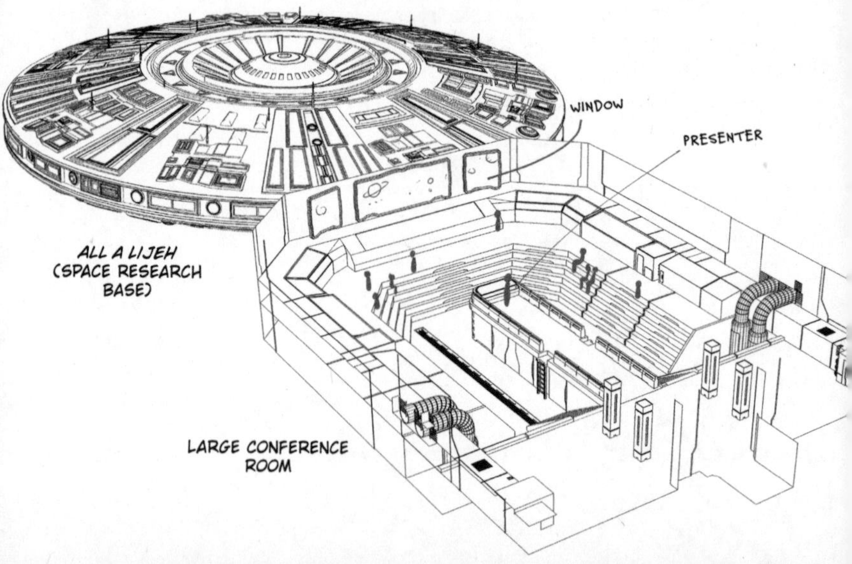

WINDOW
PRESENTER
ALL A LIJEH (SPACE RESEARCH BASE)
LARGE CONFERENCE ROOM

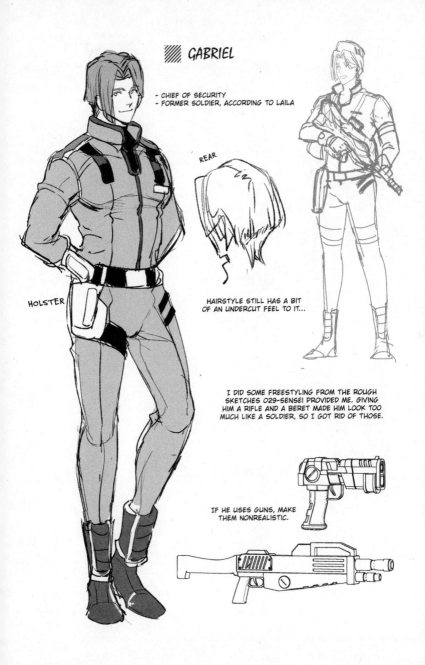

GABRIEL

- CHIEF OF SECURITY
- FORMER SOLDIER, ACCORDING TO LAILA

REAR

HAIRSTYLE STILL HAS A BIT
OF AN UNDERCUT FEEL TO IT...

HOLSTER

I DID SOME FREESTYLING FROM THE ROUGH
SKETCHES 029-SENSEI PROVIDED ME. GIVING
HIM A RIFLE AND A BERET MADE HIM LOOK TOO
MUCH LIKE A SOLDIER, SO I GOT RID OF THOSE.

IF HE USES GUNS, MAKE
THEM NONREALISTIC.

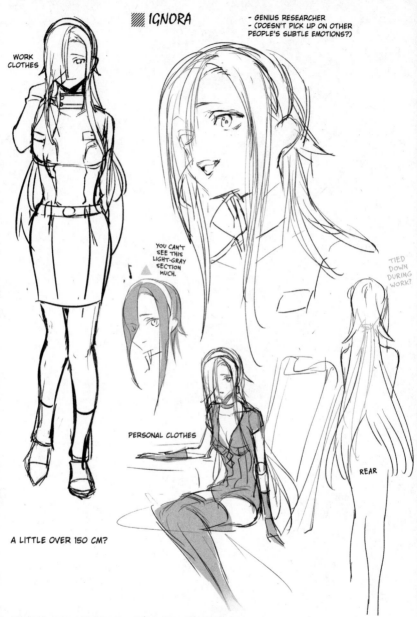

▨IGNORA

- GENIUS RESEARCHER
- (DOESN'T PICK UP ON OTHER PEOPLE'S SUBTLE EMOTIONS?)

WORK CLOTHES

YOU CAN'T SEE THIS LIGHT-GRAY SECTION MUCH.

TIED DOWN DURING WORK?

PERSONAL CLOTHES

REAR

A LITTLE OVER 150 CM?

IGNORA, WHO SHOWED UP IN THE ILLUSTRATIONS FROM THE FINAL NOVEL VOLUME. I SPENT A WHILE THINKING ABOUT WHAT SHE'D BE LIKE BACK WHEN SHE STILL HAD IT TOGETHER (?).

SATANAEL

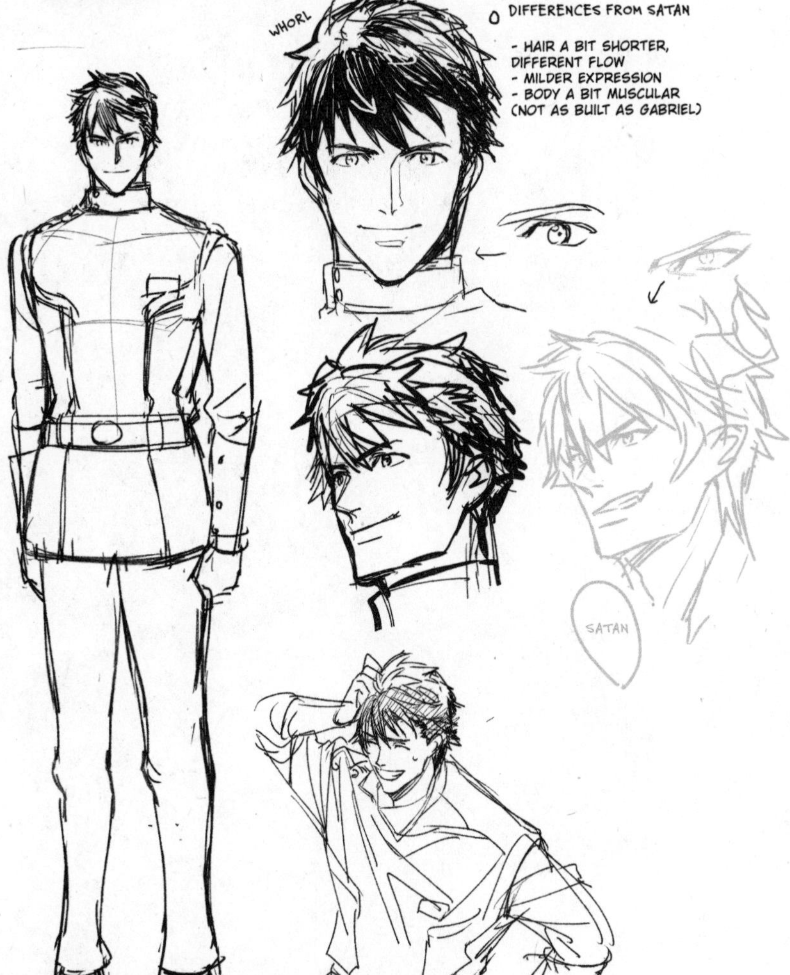
WHORL
DIFFERENCES FROM SATAN
- HAIR A BIT SHORTER, DIFFERENT FLOW
- MILDER EXPRESSION
- BODY A BIT MUSCULAR (NOT AS BUILT AS GABRIEL)
SATAN

MY GUIDANCE FOR SATANAEL WAS "DEVIL KING SATAN WITHOUT THE HORNS," SO I WENT WITH SOMETHING THAT LOOKS SIMILAR BUT WITH SUBTLY DIFFERENT DETAILS.

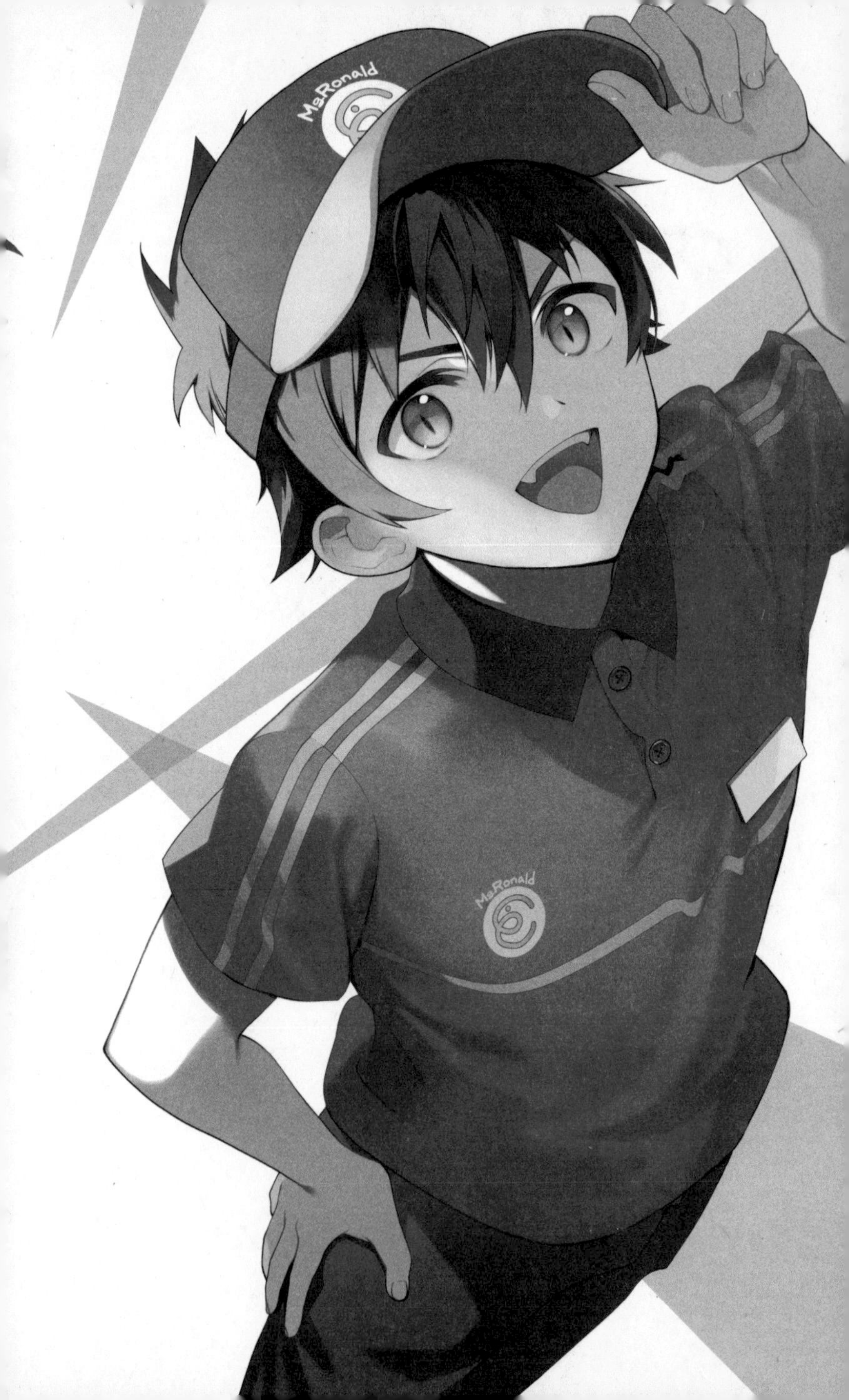
McRonald
McRonald

So the Ente Isla arc comes to a close! Wagahara-sensei agreed to let me stage the final scene my own way in the manga, so those of you familiar with the novels might have been a little surprised. These are some epic story developments I never would've imagined when I first started this (and they sure take a lot of effort to draw), but it was fun the whole way through.

With Volume 19, the manga version of *Devil* has now been running for ten years. I tried to contrast the cover and page-one art with what was used in Volume 1. A lot of things have changed and a lot hasn't, too...

The past ten years have been a lot of fun work for me. I've had the freedom to be totally carefree and draw what I want. Many thanks to Wagahara-sensei, 029-sensei, my editors over the years, everyone else involved, and especially the readers who've supported me this whole time.

The series takes a turning point here, and the next volume will feature a certain side story fans are well familiar with. I've been hoping to draw that for a while, so I'm really looking forward to it. Thanks again for your continued support!

Special thanks:
Akira Hisagi, Takashi Yamano,
and you!

AKIO HIIRAGI

2022.02

THE DEVIL IS A PART-TIMER! ⑲

ART: AKIO HIIRAGI
ORIGINAL STORY: SATOSHI WAGAHARA
CHARACTER DESIGN: 029 (ONIKU)

Translation: Kevin Gifford

Lettering: Brandon Bovia

HATARAKU MAOUSAMA! Vol. 19

First published in Japan in 2022 by KADOKAWA CORPORATION, Tokyo.
English translation rights arranged with KADOKAWA CORPORATION, Tokyo, through Tuttle-Mori Agency, Inc., Tokyo.

Yen Press
150 West 30th Street, 19th Floor
New York, NY 10001

Visit us at yenpress.com
facebook.com/yenpress
twitter.com/yenpress
yenpress.tumblr.com
instagram.com/yenpress

First Yen Press Edition: November 2022
Edited by Yen Press Editorial: Kurt Hassler, Thomas McAlister
Designed by Yen Press Design: Eddy Mingki

Yen Press is an imprint of Yen Press, LLC.
The Yen Press name and logo are trademarks of Yen Press, LLC.

The publisher is not responsible for websites (or their content) that are not owned by the publisher.

Library of Congress Control Number: 2014504637

ISBNs: 978-1-9753-5107-6 (paperback)
978-1-9753-5108-3 (ebook)

10 9 8 7 6 5 4 3 2 1

WOR

Printed in the United States of America